The Fateful Journey

Robert Joost Willink

The Fateful Journey

**The expedition of Alexine Tinne and
Theodor von Heuglin in Sudan (1863-1864)**

**A study of their travel accounts and
ethnographic collections**

AMSTERDAM UNIVERSITY PRESS

This publication was supported by the African Studies Centre, Leiden, Foundation 'De Gijselaar Hintzenfonds' and M.A.O.C. Gravin van Bylandt Foundation

Cover illustration: Photo's of Alexine Tinne, 1860/1861 (T.F.A.) and Theodor von Heuglin, 1862 (State Museum of Natural History, Stuttgart)

Cover design and lay-out: Suzan Beijer, Amersfoort, the Netherlands
Lithography: BFC, Amersfoort, the Netherlands

ISBN   978 90 8964 352 0
e-ISBN   978 90 4851 490 8
NUR   681

In memory of my mother and father

Contents

Prologue

The storerooms all began to look alike to me. Doors were opened, and rack after rack came into sight with plates on which the names of continents and countries were written. While racks were being unrolled, new rows of exotic artefacts continued to loom before my expecting eyes. They seemed to be waiting there silently and secretly for someone or something to come along. On the 'Africa' rack, my brain almost automatically began registering all kinds of features. My eyes rushed from object to object and my internal database made searches of names of regions and people who had once manufactured what was preserved here so neatly.

Many a curator was caught off guard at first by my request to see the Sudan collection that was stored in their museum. Then, after some searching, they conceded that the collection concerned was indeed there and that I was most welcome to come round and have a look. Paying visits to several storerooms in Europe, I was able to have a glance at what Africa travellers had donated some one hundred and fifty years ago.

The heritage of the nineteenth-century expeditions in Sudan lies scattered across Europe in the storerooms of over fifteen museums. Still more could be elsewhere – in private collections or other museums, hiding their history, consisting only of nameless ethnographic items once sold and purchased, without any mention of provenance.

Starting in Italy, I looked at the collections brought to museums by the Italians Carlo Piaggia, Giovanni Miani and Marchese d'Antinori, early explorers of the White Nile in Sudan, just after 1860 (Museo Archeologico in Perugia, Museo di Storia Naturale in both Venice and Florence). Still more from Miani's collection remained in the Museo Pigorini in Rome. Then it was on to England, where substantial parts of the collection of the British first consul John Petherick were preserved at the British Museum in London and the Pitt Rivers Museum in Oxford. In Sibiu, Romania, I found the collection of Transsylvanian tradesman Franz Binder, who returned from Sudan to his birthplace (then named Hermannstadt) in 1863.

Travelling around, I was seized by a longing to map out this entire mid-nineteenth-century Sudanese heritage. The reason was simple: these collections had largely been forgotten and were waiting for someone to gather them up and publish them in a catalogue. However, the scope of such a project made me start to reel. I searched for some kind of delimitation or handy format in which to present the increasing number of interesting items I had found.

My next stop was Vienna's Museum für Völkerkunde, which houses still more of Miani's collections, and the Musée Quai Branly in Paris, where the collections of the French consul Henri Pacifique Delaporte are kept. I had already visited the Kunstkamera in St. Petersburg for Wilhelm Junker's collection. What remained was Berlin, where the collection assembled by Georg Schweinfurth lay. (N.B. *Most of the travellers mentioned above will come up in this book and the catalogue.*)

However, first there was another collection waiting for me. It had come to my attention that the collection of the Dutch explorer Alexine Tinne was in Liverpool. Although the Liverpool Public Museum had been bombarded in 1941, not all of the Tinne collection would have been destroyed.

On 9 April 2008, a fine spring day in Liverpool seemed to be full of promises. On the outskirts of the city, in a storeroom, I eventually perceived some of the relics of a voyage accomplished by Alexine Tinne as two racks are unrolled. Prior to making this trip, I had received a warning by email from Zachary Kingdon, the Africa curator of the Liverpool World Museum: 'I am afraid your request is not an easy one, for a number of reasons.' And he continued by explaining that at first it was not clear how many objects were concerned. Unfortunately, after the bombardment in 1941 quite a lot of the museum's collections still remained unidentified. Especially in the case of the Tinne collections, it was unclear what was exactly left. And, unfortunately again, due to the way in which Alexine's expedition came to an end, the once listed items had never been provided with their proper provenance.

A curator had devoted himself to some attributions sometime around 1880, but since then the collection had been left untouched.

That was hardly surprising.

The accounts of travellers in nineteenth-century Sudan fill a bookshelf of almost two metres in length. Several bookcases full have been written about these accounts. But the books written about the artefacts that were collected – often passionately – by these travellers, if stacked up, would not even reach the height of a fist. At most, four of these fifteen Sudan collections have been identified and catalogued properly.

My research into this one hundred and fifty-year-old Sudanese heritage, which started in 2007, suddenly took on a different outlook. 'Tinne' presented me with the limitation I needed. My initial plan to create a catalogue of all ethnographic items that had ended up in European museums simply had to be altered.

Already during her lifetime, Alexandrine Tinne – or Alexine, as she preferred to be called – was renowned not only as a daring Dutch female Africa traveller but also as the first woman who more than once penetrated the remote regions of Central Africa. In the collections of the World Museum in Liverpool, my research revealed that Alexine Tinne's collection was largely from the expedition she undertook in 1863-4 to the Gazelle-river, a tributary of the White Nile, with her mother, Henriette Tinne-van Capellen, and a man named Theodor von Heuglin. The latter bestowed his own collection from the expedition on the King and Queen of Württemberg, Germany.

At that moment the idea was born to focus my research on both collections preserved in two different cities: Alexine Tinne's at the World Museum in Liverpool and Theodor von Heuglin's at the Linden Museum in Stuttgart. What both of them had assembled separately but simultaneously could then be virtually reunited in a publication, which would also contain a small but relevant part of similar items from other museum collections.

Writing about the ethnographic collections of these individuals demanded that the history of Alexine Tinne and Theodor von Heuglin was to be explored. The account of the Gazelle-river expedition is less well known than other contemporary travel accounts.

Two extensive biographies of Alexine Tinne have been published, one in 1960 in the Nederlands and the other in 1970 in England.[1] The British biography contains a description of the Gazelle-river expedition, with references to sources preserved by members of the Tinne family as well as those, though incomplete, in Dutch archives. On the Dutch side, a somewhat critical biography had appeared ten years earlier by the writer Clara Eggink, who remarks that she was not admitted to the private archives of the Tinne family.[2] For this reason, both biographies were doomed to be inaccurate – not only regarding the full account of the Gazelle-river expedition but also some biographical issues.

Two other biographies – by Kikkert (in Dutch) and Westphal (in German) – are largely based on the above-mentioned publications.[3]

My quest for contemporary sources about this journey led me to appeal to members of the Tinne family. For a while it seemed as though I was to suffer the same fate as Clara Eggink. There was a long silence. However, thanks to the contacts I had made in the meantime with the Liverpool World Museum, I was able to receive the email address of Emily Fabricius, who later was kind enough to introduce me to Alexine Crawford. Both are descendants of the first wife of Alexine's father and her half-brother John, who at that time lived close to Liverpool and took care of her ethnographic collection which was shipped from Cairo to Liverpool. During my visit, I found out that the remembrance of their illustrious forebear was still kept alive.

Besides the numerous letters of Alexine Tinne in The Hague's archives and the published accounts by Heuglin, during my research near London I encountered as yet unpublished correspondence revealing 'new' facts concerning the expedition as well as her life. The valuable rediscovered letters enabled me to capture a fuller picture of the expedition and of Alexine Tinne. They helped to explain more about the motives behind her journeys and the way these enterprises were supported by her personal means.

The full account of the journey deserves to be presented in its completeness, from a historical-scientific point of view, but also because of its drift of events, which is particularly compelling due to Tinne and Heuglin's personal views on the series of dramatic occurrences and their unique impressions of contemporary Sudan.

While writing, I started to compose the catalogue of their surviving ethnographic collections. After almost 150 years, the Tinne collection (which after the necessary searches has turned up again) now rejoins Heuglin's collection. Both are of great historical importance. Like other travellers in nineteenth-century Sudan, Tinne and Heuglin assembled a collection of ethnographic items as part of their travel programme. Besides their value as an irreplaceable document of this journey, both collections represent rare specimens of an early date belonging to the material cultures in regions of Sudan.

This book places the travel accounts and the collections next to each other in two separate parts. The ethnographic component is occasionally mixed with the travel history. As a correspondent of a renowned magazine in Germany, Heuglin was continually occupied with his travel accounts which he sent every two weeks to his editor Petermann. Most of his accounts dealing with the characteristics of ethnic groups (their habits and customs as well as their daily utensils) have been taken up in the separate catalogue attached to this book.

Although the expedition constitutes the main part of this book, the story of the journey itself covers less than 55 pages. The preamble to the journey and its aftermath occupy twice as many pages. This book is not meant to be a complete biography either of Alexine or Heuglin. Telling the story of their expedition means that a few years of their lives have been enlarged or magnified. However, without casting a glance on their lives before and after this enterprise, it would never become clear to what extent the expedition's dramas had been foreshadowed in the previous years and how they would reverberate in the years after the expedition. And the book also offers descriptions of contemporary Sudan, without which the expedition would be placed in a void.

—

Introduction

From the end of January 1863 until mid-December 1864, the Dutch traveller Alexine Tinne and the German zoologist Theodor von Heuglin (hereafter: Heuglin) carried out an expedition to the vast region of the Gazelle-river, a western tributary of the White Nile also known as the Bahr el-Ghazal (the Arabian name). Their private fortune enabled Alexine and her mother, Henriette Tinne-van Capellen, to prepare and maintain an expedition of immense proportions. No expense was spared. A steamboat was engaged together with transport vessels for the accompanying people, beasts of burden, and provisions. Guides, attendants, crew, servants and soldiers were hired, together forming a 'train' of more than 150 people, which after three months had increased to more than 550.

The enterprise initially seemed to offer much promise. However, as a journey it was far from successful. The expedition ended in disillusion after only four months. Its members were almost incessantly struck by fevers and dysentery due to the marshy area, and this gave the journey a most disastrous turn. Heuglin recounted later about their return to Khartoum:

> Scarcely fourteen months had passed since the flotilla set sail from here, with many-colored pendants, and amid song, beating of drums, and firing of muskets, laughing at all dangers, and not foreseeing that the expedition must already carry in itself the germ of its destruction. The pendants have been torn to shreds by the storm; the black mourning flag floats from the stern of the ships; not with music and song, but mute, bowed down, and broken, the diminished little party re-enters Khartoum.[1]

Henriette van Capellen, two European maids, and a companion of Heuglin had fallen victim to the fatal diseases that perpetually hovered over these swampy African regions. And soon after Alexine's arrival back in Khartoum in May 1864, Adriana van Capellen, Henriette's sister, who had not accompanied the expedition, died.

The story of the Bahr el-Ghazal expedition revolves around two more or less contrapositive themes: wealth, which was the main factor enabling the Tinnes to accomplish their enterprise, and death, which ultimately caused the abortion of the expedition. This book will delve into these themes extensively as we follow Alexine Tinne and Theodor von Heuglin through to the aftermath of the expedition. From Khartoum they had to return to Cairo, reaching the city in mid-December 1864. For two thousand miles they had carried the two bodies of Henriette and Flore along, first by ship to Khartoum, then as a camel load, traversing the Nubian desert to Suakin at the coast of the Red Sea and from there by boat to Suez where they stayed for a while near the digging activities at the canal. In February 1865, Heuglin left Cairo to return to Württemberg, Germany.

For almost six months, Alexine Tinne stayed in Cairo; she was not to return to the Netherlands in her lifetime. In her dwelling in the old quarter of Cairo, she lived in solitude and kept her collection of ethnographic specimens in large open rooms. In June 1865, she left the city and started a tour to visit Crete, Greece, Italy, France, Sardinia and Malta. She then went from Marseilles to Algiers, where she stayed from October 1866 until November 1867. After an unsuccessful attempt to venture beyond the southern borders of Algeria, she landed in Tripoli in October 1868, intending to fulfil her long-cherished wish of penetrating deeper into the Sahara to reach the territories of the Touaregs. But while travelling in their area, she was murdered on 1 August 1869.

The expedition and its failure

This book wishes to recover what possessed Alexine Tinne and her mother to enter the marshy regions of Sudan, a part of Africa that was then known to be extremely insecure and dangerous for Westerners. Even for experienced explorers, the White Nile region was tempting for its undiscovered and 'promising' inner lands but haunted by insidious diseases and often hostile 'tribes'. Did the Tinnes both cherish an unspoken ambition to be hailed as Central Africa's first (female) explorers, if they returned safely and successfully?

The expedition's abortion, brought on by the death of Henriette Tinne, made headline news around the world at the time. The decease of the wealthy Henriette and the resulting distress of Alexine, her equally wealthy daughter, set this journey apart from most stories of fatally ending African trips made by Europeans in the nineteenth century. Despite their wealth, which enabled them to launch this huge enterprise, even the daring Tinnes had not been able to fulfill their self-chosen task of entering these far-away regions in Central Africa. Indeed, the expedition's failure was in some ways a result of their wealth. This was the conclusion of John Hanning Speke who after discovering the source of the Nile, was passing close by the region in which the Tinne expedition was dwelling. In his letter, Speke states that this kind of enterprise should be accomplished only by two persons and certainly without a huge 'train'. He warns against this kind of 'exploring journey' particularly because of the terrible effects of the African climate. Both women chose not to take heed of Speke's critical advice. It was May 1863, and they had already been on their way for three months with everything going quite well. By July of that year, however, Henriette was dead. She had found her end amid the almost permanent torrential rainfall and unrelenting diseases while waiting to find a suitable moment for the huge travel caravan to move on to a better place to stay.

The expedition's protagonists

This book describes the protagonists of what has come to be known as the Tinne-Heuglin expedition.[2] Although Henriette acted as treasurer, she had more of a facilitating role in the enterprise, supporting the realisation of her daughter's wishes. Alexine was definitely the life and soul of the enterprise. Her wishes were always taken seriously by Henriette, who complied with most of them. The journey was conceived by both Alexine and her mother as a kind of pleasure trip during which explorations would be made, all with as much comfort as possible. This last aspect had been unconditional for Henriette and made her refuse to follow Heuglin's proposal of continuing the expedition in a smaller group without the luxuries she had been used to, such as being carried in sedans by porters. Although Alexine had actually been in favour of Heuglin's itinerary, she respected the wish of her mother, who at the time was sixty-five-years old.

Like Speke, Heuglin himself was well aware of the expedition's over-organisation, which hampered progress and caused all sorts of problems for the maintenance and nutrition of all the people, the routes to be taken and places to stay. Though Heuglin was equally critical of the ridiculous proportions this expedition was taking, knowing that these would cause complications that would only be enhanced by likely diseases, he joined the 'Tinne train' because he desperately wanted to enter these unknown regions. Despite this desperate urge, after the death of Henriette Tinne, he did not continue the journey on his own. His decision was due to several reasons: his own sickness, the lack of means at his disposal, and his desire to deliver Alexine, who was in a bad condition, safely back to Khartoum.

The break-down of the Tinne expedition meant that Heuglin failed to achieve what he had aimed for: entering the country of the Azande people and the watersheds to the southwest of the Bahr el-Ghazal region. Although the breakthrough he had hoped for in his career as a scientist and discoverer did not occur, the enquiries he made in Khartoum before the expedition and his actions during the journey saved him from a real disaster in his scientific career. He had not visited the southwest, but he had gathered new facts about the people and the geography. This information was worked out in his letters and subsequently published, enabling him to salvage his reputation.

Besides being a well-known Africa traveller, Heuglin was a zoologist who liked to carry out his research on his own. During the preparations of the expedition he kept himself somewhat aloof, expressing his gnawing worries and doubts only in his correspondence to Germany. He was, however, of vital importance to the whole expedition and later became crucial in Alexine's rescue by bringing her safely back to Khartoum and from there to Cairo. The death of Heuglin's friend, Hermann Steudner, who was the first of this expedition to fall victim to a fatal disease, was soon largely overshadowed by that of Henriette Tinne and the drama of Alexine's distress. The almost legendary status allotted to Alexine Tinne, in particular after her death in 1869, does not seem to have extended to Heuglin. He has been known as the somewhat arid – even dull and dry – scientist who stayed in the background and who was 'lucky' to have been given the chance by the

Tinnes to travel in their company.[3] This image needs to be corrected. Accounts by John Tinne and Margaret Tinne-Sandbach and some notes of Alexine throw a new light on his character and show him to be a different man than he has been described until now. He was a scientist with a mission and a great sense of duty, a fairly pleasant companion who did not receive a penny from the Tinnes but had to pay for every expense himself.

Heuglin's feat was his contribution to the map of 1865 (included in this publication), exquisitely and meticuously drawn by his publisher Petermann, which showed the basin of the eastern and western affluents of the White Nile with the Gazelle-river, until that date internationally largely considered *terra incognita*. By making use of the information he received from his Khartoum sources, Heuglin was able to map out the regions that European and Arabian traders had visited before. The confused water courses to the west of the White Nile were finally made intelligible. This map only needed to be worked out for the entire Azande area, which stretched out in a southeast direction. This was achieved by Georg Schweinfurth, who added a vast amount of new information some nine years later.[4] Heuglin's accounts concerning the watersheds in southwestern Sudan proved to be correct. His remarks concerning the Azande, all collected secondhand, were taken note of by Schweinfurth before his descent into these parts of Central Africa. Although the Tinne expedition had not visited a large part of these mapped-out regions, Heuglin's contribution to the entire map of the Bahr el-Ghazal basin was considered by him and by Petermann to be the expedition's major scientific result. Heuglin's other achievements include his full accounts regarding the botany and zoology of the regions he traversed.

The expedition's aftermath became a joint venture between Alexine Tinne and Theodor von Heuglin. The dramatic events that forced them to interrupt and end the expedition were experienced by Alexine as heavy blows struck by 'Fate'. Driven by the passion of being on the move, she had up to then been able to maintain her way of travelling as an adventuress-explorer, even during the unfortunate period in which disease struck continuously and she herself was often too ill to move on. The turning point in her life came with the deaths of her mother and two of her beloved maids, who were much more to her than just her Dutch servants. She was to receive another blow after her return to Khartoum when her aunt, the last relative left in Africa, unexpectedly passed away.

In letters written once she had returned to Cairo, she complains about having been ill-treated by 'Fate'. Even though it had been mainly her idea to travel through areas hitherto untrodden by Westerners, in her letters the tone is more one of self-pity than of guilt.

All of a sudden Alexine was confronted with the fragility of life and, falling into a state of distress after returning to Cairo, she was forced to make a thorough evaluation of her past and future. She renounced the European lifestyle. An account of Margaret Tinne-Sandbach, her sister-in-law, describes her as being in a depressed state of mind, but her 'stubbornness' is mentioned as well, and her Arabian dresses and non-European habits, like riding on a donkey through the streets of Cairo. Her return to Cairo after the expedition's abortion demanded a difficult journey of over 12 months during which she and Heuglin became largely dependent on each other. But ultimately she preferred to live in a kind of solitude, assailed by all her experiences. Though she appreciated Heuglin and considered him indispensable and helpful, Margaret's account provides us with another poignant detail in the expedition's history. She is frightfully clear about the way in which Alexine dismissed Heuglin when she did not need him anymore.

From a gender perspective, Alexine Tinne's narrative of the expedition can be conceived as a feminine response to the African itinerary, retrospectively producing divergent ways of interpretation. Her epistolary account of her travels could be presented as mediated by diversity, by a network or a complex of diasporic conjunctures, conflicting histories (male versus female antagonists) and by conditions of displacement.[5] From the beginning, however, it will become clear to the reader that it was not the author's intention to consider 'travel' as 'travel theory' and to create a discourse about Alexine Tinne's significance in the light of the recent (post-)modern literature on travel accounts. It is questionable whether any of these theories would yield an additional enrichment or deepening of her narrative and her presence in this book. In assessing, for instance, the theory that the mapping out of parts of the planet can be seen as a fundamentally 'patriarchal' concept and therefore perceived as an inherently male act – since the intention is to circumscribe, define, and hence control the world[6] – one can only accept this as a possible theory which, in this context, would merely refer to the fact that Alexine Tinne was accompanied by a man, Theodor von Heuglin, an expert in map-making. This situation as a matter of fact did not result in any conflict; on the contrary, she was enchanted by his map of the region they both roamed in the autumn of 1863.

If these types of discourse were the point of departure or the frame of reference, Alexine's narrative would – to my mind – be contained too much in a construction based upon a modern, contemporary conception in order to prove or illustrate some kind of theoretical point of view.

In their impressions and emotional outpourings, Alexine's letters do indeed represent significant ego documents of Victorian women's travel writing, reflecting her often very personal, subjective responses to all kinds of events. As regards their content, many of her letters are often self-evident and do not need additional comments. Where necessary, text links and analyses have been provided. The quotations from her letters will follow the itinerary, which is reported chronologically, and accompanied by Heuglin's accounts they create a substantial and crucial seam within the expedition's entire course.

The woman who emerges from the pages of her thin correspondence papers – often written all over in haste – did not take up travelling for the purpose of trying to free herself of the constraints of contemporary society. Only gradually did she become aware that travelling was in fact a search for identity and that 'adventure' made it possible for her to realise her potential, which was situated outside the boundaries of a restrictive social order.

Whether emanating from a theory or not, the interpretations or explanations of what she recorded during her 'quest for adventure' will leave less room for the romantic myth of an exceptional woman that was different from other women and therefore empowered – an intrepid traveller that could endure hardships and perform feats no normal woman was capable of carrying out. Drifting along on the tide of daily occurrences, Alexine seemed to be propelled by events that were beyond her control. The path to 'adventure' turned out to be paved with personal dramas and reversals. People on whom she was dependent were far less manageable or pliable than she had initially expected. The exciting and gripping 'adventure' gradually altered into a very personal struggle with her environment. Thrown back on herself, her willpower and perseverance would drag her towards an overpowering and irresistible 'adventure' that swept her along to her end, as she herself had more or less predicted. Just before her final journey she made a personal evaluation of herself that presents a perplexing view of her past and the subsequent (last) year of her life.

The Bahr el-Ghazal expedition turned out to be a fateful journey not merely for the loss of four of Alexine's nearest relations. 'Fate' also struck in a more peculiar way. The traumatic impact of the journey would bring a radical change in her experience of travel. The former lust to travel was lost. The fatalistic way in which she re-assumed her journeys will be dealt with in the section on the aftermath of the expedition.

From a modern point of view, Heuglin's presence in Sudan could be interpreted as that of a 'precolonialist' explorer with a scientific mission. His task was to him an obvious one: to gather and assemble information on the geography, flora, fauna and people of the area. Although there was international competition in acquiring new geographical data, in the accounts Heuglin provided to Petermann no possible future annexation policy or the like was revealed or alluded to as the primary reason for his expedition into the Bahr el-Ghazal area. Moreover, in 1865 the 'Deutsche Bund' was in a weakened condition, consisting of a range of small states which individually (including Württemberg) were not at all capable of any territorial expansion. As a result, it would be a profound mistake to establish Heuglin as a 'precursor of imperialism', the political-cultural form of expansion and control that was to flood the African continent one to two decades later, even though the accurate descriptions in his geographical and ethnological accounts could be regarded as prerequisites to a colonial programme. But as a representative of nineteenth-century German scholarship, Heuglin was in fact guided by a broadly humanistic agenda.[7]

From a different point of view on 'gender' relations, there is a small but conspicuous detail in Tinne and Heuglin's relationship during their lengthy journey. They were able to establish a cooperation that can be assumed to have been limited to good companionship as participants in a perilous journey. Not the slightest indication has been found of any deep or genuine friendship, let alone a love relationship. The fact that their contacts were maintained at a polite distance is illustrated by the small notes of Alexine addressed to her companion, which always opened with 'My dear Mr. Heuglin…'.

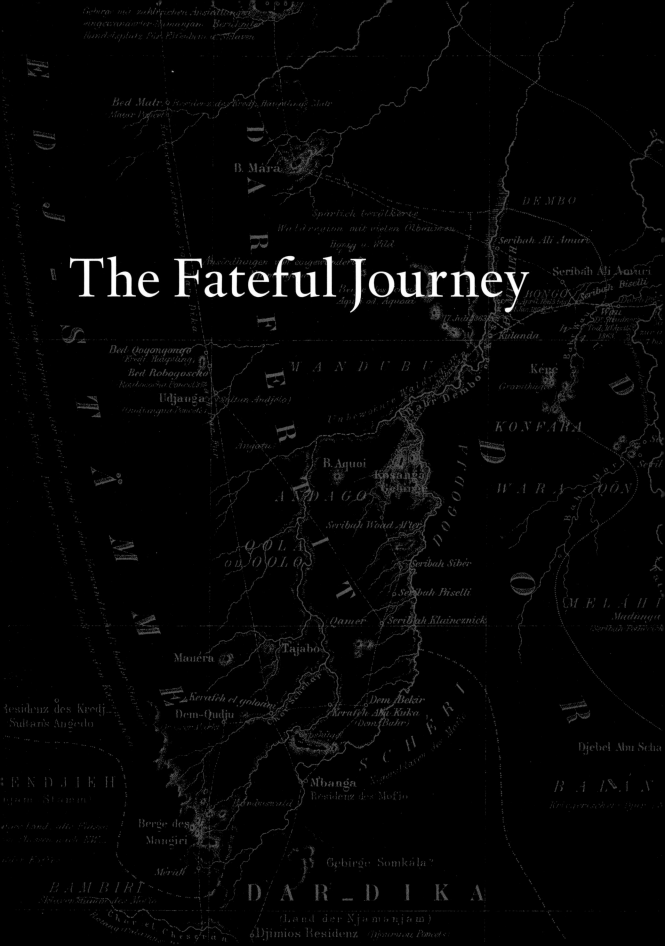

The Fateful Journey

CHAPTER 1

Sudan: the place for adventure, trade and science

Destination: Sudan

On paper, Africa in the middle of the nineteenth century represented a mishmash of ancient kingdoms in decay (in the Congo regions so far known, Nubia and Darfour), some colonies (South Africa, Sao Tomé, the coastal areas of Angola and Mozambique), a huge blank spot in the centre as well as alongside the coasts.

On the west coast, some European countries had created establishments running along the entire coastal area from Gabon to Benguella (nearly 2000 miles) that carried on trade with the inlanders. Until 1869 explorers, traders and missionaries only incidentally rounded the Cape of Good Hope. North Africa could always easily be reached from Europe; East Africa was to become accessible after the completion of the Suez Canal in 1869. For explorers, Egypt with its Nile and Sudan with its White Nile and its unknown sources was far more interesting and intriguing than attempting to reach the innerlands of Congo from the western side. Compared with other parts of the continent – for example, Africa's southwestern coast with its Portuguese properties but largely unknown hinterlands – Sudan was an extensive region where one could travel around seemingly freely. However, the Nile and its extension, the White Nile, were not as easily navigable as they seemed. Already far above Khartoum, cataracts forced the traveller to make a detour of some 300 miles through the Nubian desert. In 1769, it was here that James Bruce branched off to march on to Abyssinia, where he arrived a year later as the first European to behold the source of the Blue Nile. Frédéric Cailliaud was in the neighbourhood of Khartoum in 1821 (which then still had to be built) and described the ruins of Méroé in the kingdom of Sennār. Other Europeans (Werne and d'Arnaud, who will be introduced below) traversed two decennia later the same desert in order to be able to continue their journey on the Nile just above the town of Berber, until new and larger rapids above the 4° latitude finally forced them to run ashore.

In this story of the Bahr el-Ghazal expedition, we will be coming across several names of lesser known explorers and traders. Well-known names such as Livingstone and Stanley do not figure in our story. Livingstone, however, will enter the stage just for one moment at the end, when he expresses his idea of the historical significance of Alexine Tinne and her mother. At the time of the expedition itself, he was busy collecting funds for his third great journey which was to prove that the *Caput Nili* was to be found in Lake Mweru. Actually, this was nearly 500 miles south of Lake Victoria, which in 1862 correctly had been indicated by John Hanning Speke as the primary source. At that time, Stanley still had to make his career as a reporter for the *New York Herald* and had yet to set foot in Africa. It was only in 1869 that he received the assignment to find Livingstone, in which he would succeed in 1871.

In the voluminous accounts of the sessions of the British geographical societies, it is explained in great detail why Sudan would suddenly play such a prominent role on the international geographical scene. The minutes of some of these sessions in 1863 and 1864 provide a good indication of the importance Sudan represented and the interest with which the Tinne-Heuglin expedition to the Bahr el-Ghazal region was followed.

In England in the beginning of the 1860s, many were not interested in the blank areas that could be reached via the river Congo in Africa's innerlands but were instead eager to enter Sudan with its White Nile and its sources, hidden somewhere deep in Central Africa. As a matter of fact, Austria cherished identical ambitions, having Venice as its harbour where its explorers left for North Africa.

John Tinne's lecture

On 12 May 1864, John Abraham Tinne – the stepson of Henriette Tinne-van Capellen and half-brother of Alexine Tinne – read a paper before the members of the Historic Society of Lancashire and Cheshire, established in Liverpool. The lecture was titled *Geographical Notes of Expeditions in Central Africa, by three Dutch Ladies*. Tinne related how these 'three Dutch ladies' left their home in The Hague in July 1861 and went to Egypt. Once in Alexandria in August, they started their third journey there, having previously visited it in 1856 and 1858, and proceeded through Egypt to other countries adjacent to the Nile to end up in Sudan. He made a clear statement about the reason why they made these travels: it was 'adventure' they sought.

In Tinne's story of the expedition, the three women were left anonymous. His paper just concerned 'three Dutch ladies' who were 'his relations', travelling in Sudan. Although John Tinne did not provide their full surname, on that evening in Liverpool every listener must have known of whom John Tinne, their fellow citizen, was talking. He might have preferred to avoid any publicity around his three relatives. Since 1 July 1863, the outside world had received no more letters from two of the Dutch women on their Bahr el-Ghazal expedition in Sudan. It was only after Alexine had returned to Khartoum on 30 March 1864 that the news of Henriette Tinne-van Capellen's death and the expedition's abortion was sent to Europe, along with the message of the deaths of Flore and Anna, their Dutch maids, and of Adriana van Capellen, Henriette's sister, who had not accompanied them on this journey and had been waiting in Khartoum for their return.

Just after his lecture, John Tinne received word of Henriette's death and added an appendix to the publication of his paper while it was still in print. In this appendix, the Tinne name has been abbreviated to 'T': 'Most disastrous and melancholy intelligence was received communicating the death of Madame T.', he writes. This 'T' however is later explained in a footnote of the text by the names of 'Madame Tinne' and 'Mademoiselle Tinne', which appear together with that of Adriana van Capellen.

By 1863, geographic circles in England had already taken notice of the expedition of 'the Dutch ladies' and thereby as well of the name of Tinne. On 23 November 1863, the expedition was referred to during a session of the Royal Geographical Society in London. One member had remarked that there was a need for exploration of the Gazelle-river in Sudan, which was still considered a possible main source of the Nile. He was reminded by the president of the society, Sir Roderick Murchison, that this was being carried out by 'the Dutch expedition'.[1] This answer must have raised the curiosity of the society's members and begged an explanation. There now appeared to be a 'group of ladies' from The Hague who were dwelling in Sudan, more particularly in the area of the Gazelle-river, to which international geographical attention was drawn. The Dutch 'ladies' Henriette Tinne-van Capellen and Alexine Tinne were known to be directly connected with the British Tinnes, which brought forward the necessity of asking John Tinne to attend the meeting and answer questions about the intentions of the Dutch Tinnes, providing facts that could throw light on their expedition and his relationship with the women who were involved.

Quoting from some letters sent to him by Henriette, he made it clear that there was no such thing as a discovery expedition. The 'ladies' were only there for adventure. This answer must have been surprising for its simplicity. So it was just for pleasure that the women were there in this remote and inhospitable part of Africa! The name of 'Von Heuglin' was also mentioned by Murchison and Tinne as a co-traveller on this adventurous trip, indicating that a scientist had been asked by the Dutch women to join them on their tour.

By adding this information of a scientist accompanying both women, John Tinne (see illustration 1) correctly reported what Henriette and Alexine had told him in their letters. From its start, the expedition to the Bahr el-Ghazal had been conceived as a combination of adventure and science, or rather as an adventurous enterprise. The addition of expertise was to give it more credit and status, drawing more serious attention from the outside world.

In his lecture, John Tinne had included this message of the participation of 'scientists' in the expedition, as it apparently furnished an additional value to this Dutch initiative. The title he gave to this lecture – *Geographical Notes…* – endowed this trip with a more scientific significance. In the printed version of his lecture, an excellently drawn map was included. It was based on the sketched map by Heuglin, which was sent by Alexine Tinne to John Tinne after the abortion of the expedition and her return to Khartoum. She had been keen to put her initials A.T. somewhere on the map, indicating the place the expedition stayed from June that year.

The fact that Heuglin was accompanying the Tinnes as a scientist may have already been known to some members of the Royal Geographical Society in November 1863. In the summer of 1863, the proceedings of this expedition had been published as part of *Inner-Afrika*, a separate edition of the magazine *Petermann's Mittheilungen*. In his reference to the Dutch initiative, Murchison made clear that he also was well informed about the existence of this expedition. He must have read the pages in *Inner-Afrika* that contained Heuglin's accounts.

The questions posed to Tinne during the London-session indicated the interest in the subject of Sudan's geography that had been raised in official geographical circles in England. In the autumn of 1863, the issue of the sources of the Nile had not yet entirely been solved, despite Speke and Grant's claim of the discovery of the White Nile source in December 1862. Why an expedition was being undertaken on the Gazelle-river was therefore the subject of much deliberation. Some geographers believed this river might be a possible main source of the Nile. Noting the remark of one member at the meeting in November 1863, it appeared that there was a very large drainage running into the White Nile from the Bahr el-Ghazal which therefore could be a considerable, possibly larger, confluent of the Nile. The results of the 'Tinne' expedition could therefore deliver a most important geographical finding. On that evening, however, no further questions were posed. Having organised Speke's journey to Lake Victoria, most members of the Royal Geographical Society were clearly convinced of Speke's claim of having discovered the largest and genuine source of the Nile.[2]

Sudan and its visitors

These discussions regarding the expedition were taking place quite some time after the enterprise had gotten underway. In London, the expedition was discussed when it had already been on its way for ten months, and in Liverpool, Tinne gave his lecture when the expedition had already been aborted, although nobody in England had yet been informed about this.

A closer look at what occurred at these meetings in London and Liverpool reveals a focus on two words that touch on the presence of these 'lady travellers' in Sudan and more generally on the phenomenon of Western travellers there: 'adventure' and 'science'. Adventure was considered to be the crucial reason 'the three Dutch ladies' went to this region so closely followed within international geographical circles. Science refers in particular to Heuglin's role in this enterprise as an expert in geography and zoology.

In addition to 'adventure' and 'science', there was yet another important reason for being in Sudan. After having arrived in Alexandria and Cairo, many Europeans went straight up to Khartoum in Upper Nubia at the entrance of Central Africa looking for the trade in ivory. Already long before 1860, this trade had become a significant reason for entering Sudan. During her Africa travels, Alexine Tinne was also to be confronted with the ivory trade as it became gradually intermingled with the slave trade and evolved into a source of irritation in the relationship between Europeans and the Turkish-Egyptian authorities.

Other Europeans were in Sudan for diplomatic postings. In Khartoum, the capital of Sudan, this kind of appointment had only just been introduced. Consularships in Sudan were honourary and generally did not provide salaries. Except for the Austrian Empire, European governments limited themselves to the services of European persons who were already involved in the Sudan trade.[3] In this history of the Tinne-Heuglin expedition, we will encounter some representatives of European countries who can be held up as examples of the interdependency of diplomacy and the ivory trade.

These three principal reasons for being in Sudan were more or less inter-related. Carrying out trade in these regions was virtually impossible without plunging oneself into all kinds of adventure. Being there for the purpose of adventure was virtually impossible without being confronted with the trade in ivory and slaves and the resulting war-like situations. Besides, to perform this journey the traveller had to perform a kind of trade, as s/he was forced to do business with local inhabitants to obtain food and housing. And if one was in Sudan for scientific purposes – geography or zoology, for example – then it was almost inevitable that travel was involved.

Travelling beyond Upper Egypt

To enter Sudan, European travellers had to start in Egypt. Lower and Upper Egypt together represented a vast area with a length of 1500 miles. In the 1850s, Egypt had become an established stop on European tourists' journeys. Travels on the Nile were offered that allowed sightseeing of Egyptian antiquities that lay scattered along the Nile's embankments. Some visitors proceeded southwards to have a look at the Nubian antiquities. But any further than that was beyond the usual tourist's tour. Khartoum in Upper Nubia was 2000 miles south of Cairo and located in Sudan, a vast country that in Egypt was called Bilad al-Sudan – 'country of the Blacks'. Sudan had been

1 Photo of John A. Tinne
Courtesy: Tinne Family Archive
Date: ca. 1860.
Dimensions: 14 x 8 cm. Albumen print

part of Turkish-Egyptian territory since 1821. No antiquities were to be found there. And if there had been any, visiting Sudan was virtually out of the question due to the unbearable climate and the numerous risks and dangers.

Ascending the river towards Khartoum, only Westerners with a specific purpose were to be found. Tourist-like curiosity had to make way for adventure-like eagerness to travel to places that were increasingly inhospitable. This desire for adventure could very well be awakened by reading travel accounts, as was the case with 'the Dutch ladies'. Before 1860, some books on travel experiences in contemporary Sudan had been published. Ferdinand Werne's *African Wanderings* and *Entdeckung der Quellen des Weissen Nil* of 1848 recounts his stay in Khartoum and expedition in 1840-'41, while Brehm's *Reiseskizzen aus Nord-Ost-Afrika*, published in 1855, tells the story of his five-year sojourn in Sudan. Bayard Taylor's *Journey to Central Africa* of 1854 provided a more recent account of an ascent to Khartoum, and then there was Charles Didier's 1858 book, *500 Lieues sur Le Nil*, which described places to be visited when navigating on the Nile. Already in its year of publication, Taylor's account of his travels from Cairo to Khartoum had ten editions in New York (he was an American citizen). Didier was successful in France, and Brehm's book had two editions. The success of these books did not, however, result in a new era of travels. While describing all the interesting travel events and peculiarities they encountered on their way, Werne and Bayard Taylor, and to some extent Didier as well, described the myriad dangers that were to be expected. Their success demonstrated that the public liked to read about the risks and hazards that were involved in visiting places in Sudan. For certain persons, however, these perils must have raised their appetite for a journey to Sudan. From one short remark by Henriette Tinne it can be concluded that 'Didier' had been an influential book for her and Alexine, inducing them to make the journey to Cairo and from there to Khartoum. In a letter to Sara, her younger sister, written just after their arrival in the town, she notes: 'Nous sommes arrivées à Khartoum *500 Lieux sur le Nil* …'.[4]

While crossing the regions up river from Upper Egypt, Western visitors indeed had to fight for their survival. The threat of death by disease was always present, as was the risk of encountering dangerous situations. The *L'Afrique nécrologique*, a list drawn up by the French explorer Henri Duveyrier in 1874, registers all casualties of Europeans that occurred between around 1800 and 1874, including 'Madame Tinne' and 'baronne A. van Capellen'. These casualties, the result of murder, fatal diseases or simply recorded as 'lost forever' are set out in an adjoining map.[5]

Travelling up the Nile beyond Khartoum was outright dangerous because of the hostilities between Turkish-Egyptian authorities, Arab traders and the non-Arab native population. Even to an experienced Africa traveller like Heuglin, it was difficult to prepare oneself for the dangers that could be encountered, as it was unclear from which side and to what extent hostilities might break out. As will be explained later in this book, Heuglin and the Tinnes experienced more obstruction and annoyance from the traders than from the native population, which had been expected to be hostile towards the expedition.

For Europeans wishing to travel in Sudan, it was far from evident what preparations should be made. The measures to be taken during the preparations of the Tinne-Heuglin expedition were certainly not explicit. Obviously it was well known what kind of lethal consequences a European could expect on his journey, but what could be done to prevent oneself besides hiring soldiers, purchasing goods to be bartered en route for nourishment and necessary equipment, and bringing along sufficient quantities of provisions and sufficient doses of quinine? The Tinnes spent at least £10,000 to have the Bahr el-Ghazal expedition fitted out as best as possible, but even then the enterprise ended in failure precisely for the reason that it had been too massively equipped. Diseases were a direct threat and will therefore be a prevailing topic in this book. Several diseases had to be faced, but no adequate preventative treatment was really known. There was quinine, which was known to be both a preventive and curing medicine, but only to some extent given the complications that arose from its side effects. One could only hope that one was not afflicted too severely by fevers and diarrhoea. On Duveyrier's list are names of men who remained in good health for years and were suddenly taken away. Even an experienced Africa traveller like Heuglin, who had dwelled in Sudan many years without serious diseases, survived the expedition by the narrowest of margins.

Given the considerable risks involved in travelling in Sudan, 'adventure' and 'science' could not have been the only motivations of 'the Dutch ladies' and Heuglin, respectively, for undertaking this expedition. Additional information is needed for a clearer understanding of what was going on in the minds of our protagonists to perform this kind of utterly risky enterprise. The story of the Bahr el-Ghazal expedition also brings us therefore to their state of mind, revealing their more personal reasons for cherishing these aspirations. Some characteristic facts of their lives preceding their encounter in Khartoum are useful in trying to understand their urge to be 'adventurous' and 'scientific'.

The Tinne family: a Dutch-British connection

The Tinnes were Dutch sugar merchants and shipowners. Philip Frederik Tinne, Henriette's husband, was born in the Netherlands in 1772. He made a good income with his sugar and coffee plantations in Demarara in Guiana in the West Indies, where the Netherlands and England had their alternate range of interests. After a fortunate partnership with Samuel Sandbach, who was an acquaintance of his first wife Anna Rose (of Scottish origin), he became the co-founder of a successful mercantile business by which his capital increased considerably. In 1812, the Sandbach, Tinne & Company was founded in Liverpool, a city that enhanced Tinne's British trade interests and allowed him to distance himself from the turmoil of the Napoleonic wars on the continent. His partner urged Tinne in 1823 to take on British nationality. Besides growing coffee, Sandbach, Tinne & Co. acquired several sugar plantations and prospered. The Sandbach-Tinne capital was to become immense after the huge profits in cane sugar from the West Indies during the 1830s. In addition, the company received an extra financial boost of about £100,000 in 1835 as compensation from the British government for companies who had given up their slaves on the plantations (consequent to the 1834 Act of Abolition).

After his first wife died in 1827, Tinne returned to Holland, leaving his eldest son John Abraham Tinne in Liverpool. Three years later, he married Lady Henriette Maria Louise van Capellen. This event illustrates how Philip still maintained his Dutch connections. Henriette was a daughter of the esteemed vice-admiral Theodoor Frederik van Capellen and was appointed as lady-in-waiting to Queen Sophie von Württemberg (who later married the future King William III), just as her sister Adriana had been to Queen Anna Paulowna at the court of King William II. The married couple chose to reside in the Netherlands and in 1832 moved into a house on the Heerengracht in The Hague. Four years later, they moved to the Lange Voorhout

2 Photo, representing the
Lange Voorhout,
The Hague.
Directly to the left
the numbers 34/36.

Courtesy: Tinne Family Archive
The photo belongs to the series made by Alexine Tinne in
the winter of 1860/61 of locations around her house (nr. 32
Lange Voorhout) including several views of The Hague.
Dimensions: 36 x 45 cm. Collotype

32. Henriette maintained close connections with the court, in particular with Princess Sophie. Alexandrine Petronella Francisca Tinne was born on 17 October 1835 as an only child. Tinne's elder son, John, had by this time already been admitted as a partner into his father's firm in Liverpool. On the occasion of his second marriage, Philip passed on a part of his fortune to his sons and Henriette. When he died in 1844, the family had just returned from an extensive tour to Rome, Florence and Naples. Philip left between £80,000 and £100,000 to his survivors, of which £33,000 was bequeathed to Alexandrine to receive when she was twenty-one.[6] The rest of this inheritance was divided between his sons – John Abraham and William Thomas – and Henriette, who used her inheritance and the interest on this money for her personal needs and the long journeys she later made with

Alexine. When in 1856 Alexine reached the age of twenty-one, her bequest had increased to £69,000 thanks to the good business of the company run by John Tinne. She made use of this money for her later journeys. The inheritance she left John Tinne after her death in August 1869 amounted to more than 1,000,000 Dutch guilders, which was at that time the equivalent of around 100,000 English pounds.[7] This inheritance included what her mother had left her after her death at the end of July 1863.[8]

Alexine Tinne's lust for travel

After Philip Frederik's death, mother and daughter Tinne stayed in The Hague as their temporary Dutch home base. The Tinne family was regarded as a very wealthy family that frequently took part in The Hague's social life. Having always had plenty of means at their disposal, Henriette (see illustration 11) and Alexine developed a particular attitude and behaviour that reflected a carefree life.

Dutch was a language that Alexine had learned when she was young but almost never used in letters or conversations. When her father was still alive, the family had spoken English together, which Henriette continued to speak with Alexine. For the better-situated circles in The Hague (the 'Haguois'), French was still the common language for conversation in the 1840s and 1850s, having received a new impulse during the French occupation of the Netherlands in 1806-1812. A French governess had been engaged for Alexine. Reading her letters, however, one might conclude that she never fully mastered these languages. Her French remained the Haguois of The Hague. Her frequent absence from The Hague must have been the reason why she received lessons from several tutors for different subjects. Alexine herself had been responsible for her own education to a large extent, which may have encouraged her to conduct her own research into all kinds of matters. She developed a keen interest in geography, painting and photography; the last subject she managed to master extraordinarily well, making fine and large pictures of locations in The Hague, including the interior of her house on the Lange Voorhout when she was around 25 years old (see illustrations 2 and 3).

Photography would occupy her for the rest of her life (see illustrations 2-3, 6, 9, 19-22). She continued this activity during her Third White Nile trip in

3 Photo, representing the room, ground level, at the garden side, Lange Voorhout 32, The Hague.

Courtesy: Tinne Family Archive
The photo is supposed to have been made by Alexine Tinne in the winter of 1860/61.
Dimensions: 36 x 45 cm. Collotype

4 Photo of Alexine Tinne,
The Hague

Courtesy: Tinne Family Archive
The photo is an excision of the one (see illustration 5) which was
taken in the garden of the house Lange Voorhout 32, The Hague.
Date: 1860/61
Dimensions: 10, 5 x 6,5 cm. Albumen print

5 Photo, representing Alexine
Tinne, sitting for her portrait in
the garden of the house Lange
Voorhout 32, The Hague.

Courtesy: National Archives, The Hague
The photo was presumably made in 1860/61.
Dimensions: 21 x 29 cm.
Albumen print

1862 and presumably during the one to the Bahr el-Ghazal as well, and from
1864 and 1865 in Cairo up to 1869 in Tripoli. Geography was one of her favourite subjects in her early youth and remained so later, though more in the
practical sense of travelling. The story went that she was always happy reading and learning with an aptitude to grasp facts herself. Uncle Hora Siccama, who had married Henriette's younger sister Petronella, recalled discovering Alexine sprawled on the floor over a book borrowed from the Royal
Library in The Hague. She was about ten years old at the time, and he noted
that the large book contained a subject on geography.[9]

A couple of letters she wrote to her niece Jetty Hora Siccama indicate that
Alexine definitely felt a certain 'call of the East', then a fashionable phenomenon in circles of the European gentry and *haute bourgeoisie*. Jetty, nine

6 Photo of Alexine Tinne,
The Hague
Courtesy: Tinne Family Archive
Date: 1860/61
Dimensions: 10, 5 x 6,5 cm.
Albumen print

years younger, would be her beloved friend with whom she corresponded
during a considerable part of her travels from 1860 to 1869. In these letters
to Jetty, whom she called 'Smous' (in Dutch, the verb 'smoezen' means 'exchanging confidences'), she writes about being in a wild mood and putting
on a broad Arabian belt which made her feel like a child of the desert. Her
action was prompted by her reading of Lady Hester Stanhope's *La reine de
Palmyre*, the name that Alexine called herself in her early letters to Smous.[10]
In addition to literature on the East, she owned books about Africa. She
stated in a letter that she had read the accounts by James Bruce (*Travels to
Discover the Source of the Nile in the Years 1768-73*) and presumably also Livingstone's *Missionary Travels* (1857) and Burton's first accounts of his search
for the sources of the Nile (1857). Keeping up with international geographical magazines, also those concerning Sudan, would have been easy for Al-

7 Photo of Alexine Tinne and her
   dog Matushka[?] in the house
   Lange Voorhout 32, The Hague.
   Courtesy: Tinne Family Archive
   Date: c.1860
   Dimensions: 10, 5 x 6,5 cm.
   Albumen print

exine, with the Royal Library next-door to her house on the Lange Voorhout.

Alexine's desires and interests in travelling were developed early. As a
young girl, she accompanied her father on his travels through France, Swit-
zerland and Italy, and after his death in 1845 she travelled with her mother
to the south of France and to Spain, then to Sweden and Norway, up to the
North Cape. After staying in Pau near the Pyrenees from 1847-1848, she and
her mother subsequently moved back to The Hague where they lived almost
permanently from 1849 to 1854 in their monumental house on the Lange
Voorhout. Alexine occupied herself with the study of literature, history and
geography. These six years of study were a preparation for her more substantial travels. In 1849, Henriette's royal connections became stronger,

causing Queen Sophie's attention to be drawn to Alexine. Sophie developed a great interest in her, and this protection was to be of great value to her on her visits to foreign courts. During the Africa travels that mother and daughter made together, Queen Sophie sent letters expressing her concern about the dangers they were risking, and in June 1864 she sent her deeply felt condolences after having received the news of Henriette's death.

Bit by bit, Alexine developed an appetite for travelling. The journeys she made to England, France, Spain and Scandinavia had been exciting for both her and Henriette, encouraging their lust for more. In her correspondence, Henriette would give evidence of her great love towards her daughter, expressing her willingness to fulfil practically her every wish. On these journeys, Alexine depended on Henriette's role of intermediary between her and the outside world and of being the provider of her solutions. No expense was spared on these journeys; they renounced as little luxury as possible. Every region they travelled through represented a different world, giving them a strong incentive for continuing what they were already practising. Henriette was essential for smoothing and paving the roads of Alexine's increasing passion for travelling.

Due to their choice to stay abroad frequently, their relationships with the family and with court life inevitably became distant. In October 1855, they left The Hague after saying goodbye to Adriana ('Addy') van Capellen and Queen Sophie. Via Düsseldorf, Kassel, Weimar, Dresden and Leipzig they reached Stuttgart in Württemberg where they visited the parents of Queen Sophie. The journey subsequently went across the Alps to Verona, Milan and finally Venice. Although Alexine had fallen ill, and despite the fact that Henriette strongly disliked sailing, they decided to cross over to Trieste because from there a boat was on the verge of leaving for Alexandria, a journey that would take an estimated 120 hours. Their first step on African soil when they they disembarked in Alexandria at the end of December 1855 set the course of their subsequent travels.

Their destiny was also settled the moment Alexine decided to teach herself to speak and write Arabic [11] and became eager to go to Cairo, which they reached in January 1856. Staying in the Shepheard's Hotel, they were welcomed into a new social life amid renowned people like Linant de Bellefonds and Ferdinand de Lesseps. Women were seldom seen there, which meant that they enjoyed much attention. She became enchanted by the Ara-

bian lifestyle which, as she said, 'connected the picturesque with the attractive, freedom with modernity'.

Step by step, she had introduced herself and her mother to travelling in Egypt, following the route that European tourists were prone to take when visiting these regions for the first time and according to what could be read in *500 Lieues sur le Nil*. This involved visits to Cairo and Alexandria and from there going southwards to places like Luxor, Philae, Edfou and Karnac.

The ancient cities of Luxor and Thebe were visited in the company of C.W.M. van de Velde, a Dutch lieutenant of the Royal Navy. The group subsequently crossed the desert area to Quseir at the Red Sea, which they reached in the beginning of March 1856. After returning to Cairo on 16

March, Van de Velde invited them to join him on a journey to Syria, visiting Jerusalem, Jaffa and Jericho near the Dead Sea. As the renowned author of *Narrative of a Journey through Syria and Palestine in 1851 and 1852*, Van de Velde could demonstrate his vast knowledge by retelling his travel experiences. They stopped in Damascus at the end of May and from there proceeded across the Lebanon to Beirut, where they embarked for Alexandria after a stay of several months. Once back in Cairo, Henriette announced in a letter: 'I finally complied to Alexine's wish to sail up the Nile'.[12] For Alexine this must have been a moment of intense satisfaction.

The journeys they made to Egypt, Syria and Palestina in 1856 were to be their tryout trips for new ones to Egypt and up the Nile. Impatient to return to Cairo, Alexine had planned their return, desperately yearning for a second Nile voyage. At Christmas they stayed again in the Shepheard's Hotel in Cairo. Alexine suffered frequently from fevers which required her to stay in bed, but only for one day. The next day she was making trips on a donkey across the nearby desert and did not return until dark. Leaving for the Netherlands before the summer of 1857, Henriette notes in her diary: 'Alexine's beau rêve is now to go to Khartoum'. Already during their first stay in Egypt they had established contact with S.W. Ruyssenaers, the Dutch consul general in Alexandria. Even for Ruyssenaers, it appeared impossible to fulfill Alexine's wish of hiring a steamer to go up the Nile. They were, however, able to reach Wadi Halfa, the third cataract of the Nile, by *dhahabiyya* [a luxury sailing boat with cabin hut] in seven and a half weeks, after having visited the temple of Abu Simbel. Thereafter they sailed back to Cairo to return to Europe via Beirut, where they stayed for seven months. Next they sailed to Turkey and then via the Adriatic Sea to Italy, reaching The Hague in November 1857 after a detour to Vienna, Prague and Dresden.[13] In her diary Henriette wrote: 'I never saw my nice house with so much pleasure. Alexine and I enjoyed everything, so comfortable, so clean, so our own.'[14]

The pleasure of coming home after having travelled for more than one and a half years was again of short duration. Instead of settling down and reminiscing fondly about their travel experiences which by then were already impressive, mother and daughter Tinne were overcome by a tenacious sort of restlessness. They only stayed at their house on the Lange Voorhout between November 1857 and the summer of 1860. During that period (see illustrations: 4-7, 8), Alexine started to become more professional in photography and also frequented the nearby manège in the Kazernestraat (see illustration 9). Meanwhile, she and her mother made journeys to Moscow and England. From there they crossed the Channel in November to Calais and went to Paris, where Bingham took a photo of them together with Jetty Hora Siccama, who apparently had been invited to join them on this trip (see illustration 10). These European tours made way for their definitive leap to Africa.

Preparations for their third journey to Cairo in 1861 were already made in July 1860 and subsequently worked out during the winter and the following spring. Henriette had invited her sister Adriana van Capellen (see illustration 12) to join her and Alexine. It was Alexine who had decided to go ahead of her mother and aunt, leaving by ship on 20 July 1861 from Amsterdam to Marseille. There she would wait for Henriette and Adriana who were to travel by train to Paris and from there to Marseille. From Marseille, they proceeded to Alexandria via Livorno, leaving the boat to visit Pisa. After a sailing tour to Crete, they arrived in Alexandria in September 1861. They met Ruyssenaers again, who resided in this city and who was going to play a significant role in the aftermath of the Bahr el-Ghazal expedition.

The Hague circles

It is questionable whether Alexine and her mother were trying to escape the circles of the gentry and the *bourgeoisie* in The Hague. No clear signs exist that they considered these circles to be particularly oppressing or boring. There may have been tedious days in The Hague, urging in particular Alexine to find some compensation, which she most likely must have found in her photography or books. Alexine's desire for travelling must have been the main source for this unceasing search for adventurous trips in more and more distant regions, resulting in an itch to attain North Africa. This itch was reinforced by some of her intrinsic traits of character such as an enormous willpower that enhanced her desire to have it all her way and an apparent wish to be different from 'the rest'.

The desire to dwell in foreign parts touched a responsive chord in her mother. Henriette not only presented herself as fertile soil for Alexine's craving for adventure, she even cultivated this by acting as an eager participant. Travelling brought Henriette the necessary distraction from her husband's death and court life's tight protocols. When Alexine revealed herself as an

9 Photo of A. Tinne in The Hague   Courtesy: Tinne Family Archive
   Manège, Kazernestraat 50,   Date: 1860/61
   The Hague.   Dimensions: 14 x 8 cm. Albumen print

10 Photo of A. Tinne, H. Tinne-
van Capellen and H. Hora
Siccama at Paris

Courtesy: Tinne Family Archive
Date: 1860
Photo: Studio Bingham, Paris
Dimensions: 10, 5 x 6,5 cm. Albumen print

11 Photo of Henriette Tinne-van Capellen.
Courtesy: Tinne Family Archive
Date: 1860/61
Photo, taken (presumably by A. Tinne) in the garden of the house Lange Voorhout 32, The Hague.
Dimensions: 10, 5 x 6,5 cm.
Albumen print

even more passionate lover of excursions, she brought her mother along all the way to the Near East and ultimately wound up in Egypt up the Nile. Some lines in their letters indicate that they only gradually came to prefer the freedom tasted during their voyages to life in The Hague society and around the court. Travelling abroad meant satisfying their cravings, which were enhanced by extremely favourable financial conditions: their inheritances provided them each with interest that resulted in yearly allowances of up to £5000. The unique partnership of mother and daughter, proven to be solid during their previous travels, provided a second indispensable condition for establishing their future African journeys.

12 Photo of Adriana van Capellen.
Courtesy: Tinne Family Archive
Date: c.1860
Dimensions: 10, 5 x 6,5 cm.
Albumen print

The firmness of their choice of leaving for Africa stood severe tests. In her position as lady in waiting, Henriette was severely criticised by Queen Sophie who attempted to dissuade her from travelling to Africa. Her judgment is stated in several letters to Henriette, even when the latter was already in Khartoum.

In Alexine's letters to her niece Jetty and in those from Henriette to John as well, what can be detected is a certain pride regarding their stay in the North of Africa, far away from The Hague. Alexine certainly loved to demonstrate how she was able to perform these deeds, which no 'lady' in her circles in

The Hague ever could or would accomplish. The somewhat boastful tone in Alexine's letters was to change after the deaths of her mother, aunt and two trustful maids. The proud sort of enthusiasm that had been omnipresent during her travels on the White Nile voyage makes way for bitterness and sometimes utter distress. Added to this new tone of grief are anger and indignation towards people and towards the fate that had befallen her. These last traits seemed to have sprung from the same root as her tenacity and quick temper, which were frequently noticed by her mother and also by Heuglin.

From the Netherlands to Sudan

Did their Dutch background somehow induce the Tinnes to proceed to the Near East, North Africa and further to Sudan? At that time, professional Dutch explorers visited mostly the Dutch East Indies or Suriname. Around 1860, Dutchmen were present in the west and central part of Africa, where they settled as tradesmen along the coast from North Angola to the Loango region.[15] There are no accounts available of Dutch traders who entered North Africa and Egypt in the nineteenth century going up the Nile in order to arrange their affairs in Sudan. In the Near East, as mentioned before, only Van de Velde had been a traveller, and a renowned one at that. Alexine's primary travel mania took place within the constellation of the 'call of the East', which encouraged the Tinnes to visit Palestine, Syria and Egypt. At that moment, her lust for travel was kindled. She wished to undertake a more adventurous kind of journey with discovery as a component, which arguably was decisive for their choice of Central Africa. Enabled by their wealth, they could extend their destination from North to Central Africa. After having ascended the Nile, attaining Sudan became a logical continuation of their previously accomplished voyages.

In her exceptional decision to travel to Sudan, a remarkable resemblance exists between Alexine Tinne and another Dutchman who was in Sudan for some years two decades later. After having been a war reporter in Spain and the Balkans, Joannes ('Juan') Maria Schuver went to Egypt in 1880 and traversed the yet uncharted area between the Blue and White Nile and the regions bordering Ethiopia.[16] A comparison between the Tinnes and Schuver reveals another strange similarity. Schuver also wrote in several different languages, but mainly English and French (it was Petermann who translated these accounts into a stiff German). Like the Tinnes, Schuver was a wealthy scion of a Dutch trading house who used his money to find adventure – an amateur explorer, like Alexine, rather than a true one. And furthermore, both were murdered in North Africa: Alexine in the Libyan desert at 33 years of age, and Schuver in Sudan near Meshra el-Rek at 31 years of age.

Heuglin in Africa: vice consul, traveller and scientist

At the beginning of July 1862, Theodor von Heuglin arrived in Khartoum as the leader of an expedition that was to have a rather unsuccessful outcome. Organised by August Petermann, director and editor in chief of the internationally highly rated geographical magazine *Petermann's Mitthei-lungen*, the expedition was supposed to clarify the destiny of the explorer Eduard Vogel, who had entered in 1856 the empire of the Sultan of Wadai – an area strictly closed off to Westerners – after which nothing was ever heard from him again. Heuglin had already visited Sudan in 1851, the year in which he settled down in Cairo at the age of 27, making trips from there to the coast of the Red Sea and Upper Egypt. Not so much an adventurer as a discoverer – an *Afrikareisender* – Heuglin wanted to develop the techniques of Africa travel and follow in the footsteps of his illustrious contemporary Heinrich Barth who traversed the western regions of Sudan.

Born in 1824 as son of a clergyman at Hirschlanden in Schwaben, Germany, Heuglin soon appeared to be attracted to the field of natural sciences. After becoming a mining engineer in the Polytechnical School at Stuttgart, his special interest in Africa was aroused by Baron J.W. von Müller, himself then a famous Africa traveller. In a collection of biographies of Schwabian historical personalities, Heuglin has been described as someone with a strong will, in particular when carrying out his self-imposed tasks regarding foremost his work as a scientist specialised in ornithology, but also in studying topics of cartography or geography, zoology and ethnography. In his drawings and watercolours, he demonstrated a remarkable talent as an artist.[17] His ability to be persistent was badly needed during the last part of the expedition, when Alexine Tinne was ill, in low spirits due to the desperate conditions and in great need of support by her travel companion on her way back to Cairo.

Though an engineer by profession, Heuglin's broad scientific interests prevailed and were directed towards geography and zoology, with birds as his specialty. At the end of 1851, he travelled to the Sinai with Alfred Brehm, who shared with him a passion for zoology, and in the next year he was in Nubia in the southern part of Upper Egypt. Teaching himself spoken and written Arabic, he ascended to Khartoum to become a secretary of the Austrian consulate in October 1852. Before he left for Egypt, Heuglin had made valuable contacts in the local scientific world which resulted in his corresponding membership of the *K.K. Akademie der Wissenschaften* (the Imperial and Royal Academy of Science). Both his post at the Austrian consulate in Khartoum and his membership in the Academy were to prove to be useful in particular in combination with his next travels. The consulate of the Austrian Empire in Khartoum was linked to its mission in the city in order to protect the interests of the Catholic Church in Sudan, also located in two other missions up the White Nile (Heiligenkreuz and Gondokoro).

In Khartoum during the mid-1850s, Heuglin proved that he was not only a scholar but also someone capable of fulfilling the job of vice consul in Khartoum, which mainly consisted of practical consular activities on behalf of Austrians in Sudan. Shortly after having been appointed secretary in December 1852, he joined the Austrian consul Constantin Reitz on an expedition to Abyssinia, the vast region just to the east of Khartoum. Reitz had planned this trip in order to establish good relationships with local rulers in the province of Galabat. The journey led to the city of Gondar and Lake Tana, the source of the Blue Nile, and from there to the province of Tigre. Heuglin then made his own way back to the province of Galabat as a kind of training on the job, improving his travel and drawing techniques. After meeting up again, both Reitz and Heuglin fell seriously ill with dysentery to which the consul himself succumbed. In June 1853, Heuglin reached Khartoum and was appointed Reitz's successor in the consulate.

From Khartoum, the new vice consul immediately set out on a trip following the White Nile upstream, bringing back an important collection of animals both dead and alive. From this period dates an account by Didier, the French voyager, describing his encounter with Heuglin and visit to his house, which was indeed full of samples of animal species destined for the Viennese zoo.[18] The dead animals were donated to the cabinets of natural history in Vienna, and Stuttgart in Württemberg; while the living animals ended up in the zoo of Schönbrunn Palace near Vienna. The notations concerning geography and zoology he made during this journey were worked out in 1857 in his first extensive publication.[19] Gradually, Heuglin began to establish his name as an experienced and qualified traveller and scientist. A token of this esteem was his raising to the peerage by the king of Württemberg in 1855, which gave him the privilege of placing the predicate 'von' before his surname 'Heuglin'. His second expedition in 1857-1858 headed towards the submarine vegetation and fauna down the west coast of the Red Sea. In order to recover fully from the thrust of a spear inflicted by a native, Heuglin was forced to return to Austria and Germany where he made a second donation of animal species and ethnographic objects to the Royal Cabinet in Stuttgart.

His appointment in 1861 as leader of *'Die deutsche Expedition in Ost-Afrika 1861 und 1862'* marked the peak in Heuglin's career as an African traveller. The two previous expeditions to clarify the whereabouts or destiny of the traveller Eduard Vogel had had a disastrous end for the expedition's leaders, who were killed in the same way as Vogel himself was, as was later revealed. The invitation by August Petermann gave Heuglin the chance of building up this expedition with the best possible staff and equipment. Choosing his companions, he insisted on the linguistic and ethnographic support of the Swiss scientist Werner Munzinger, who had stayed for several years in South Ethiopia (then Abyssinia) and also was a renowned Africa traveller. Other members were the Austrian Martin Ludwig Hansal and the botanist Hermann Steudner, together with Theodor Kinzelbach, astronomer and physicist, and Hermann Schubert, also an expert in botanics. The expedition had a two-folded purpose. Besides its main goal – the finding of Eduard Vogel – various scientific tasks had to be accomplished: for instance, the research of the landscape between the Nile and Lake Chad. While some members of the expedition wanted only to focus upon the 'Vogel' case, Heuglin preferred to prioritise its scientific tasks.

On 21 March 1862, the five members arrived in Cairo (see illustration 13: a photo of the expedition group; illustrations 14, 15: Heuglin and Steudner; illustration 16: Heuglin, decorated on 23 March by the Viceroy of Egypt). After their voyage from Suez on the Red Sea to Massaua and their arrival in the countries of the Bogos in Abyssinia with its principal town named Keren, mounting differences of opinion arose. Instead of going straight from Massaua to Khartoum in order to enter Wadai, Heuglin wanted to seize the opportunity to pass by Kaffa and other regions which were then

13 Photo, representing the Abyssinian Expedition at
Cairo, March 1862. From left to right: Werner
Munzinger, Martin Hansal [?] (standing), Hermann
Steudner, Theodor von Heuglin (sitting).
Courtesy: Archive of the State Museum of
Natural History Stuttgart, Convolute Heuglin.
Date: March 1862
Dimensions: 38 x 48 cm. Albumen print

14 Photo of Von Heuglin, March 1862.
Courtesy of Museum für Naturkunde, Stuttgart
Date: March 1862
Dimensions: excision from photo (illustration 13).
Albumen print

15 Photo of Von Heuglin and Steudner,
March 1862.
Courtesy of Museum für Naturkunde, Stuttgart
Date: March 1862
Dimensions: excision from photo (illustration 13).
Albumen print

16 Photo of Von Heuglin,
March 1862.
Courtesy of Museum für
Naturkunde, Stuttgart
Date: March 1862
Dimensions: 16 x 22 cm.
Albumen print

hardly known and a subject for research. It soon became clear that the expedition could not be continued on a united front. Heuglin went on by himself with Steudner and Schubert at his side. While Heuglin and Steudner
marched from Mai Sheka to Southern Abyssinia, Munzinger and his companion Kinzelbach went into a westerly direction. After having traversed
the country of Nunma and Barea, both men reached Khartoum via Kassala
and then pushed on to el-Obeid with the intention of entering Wadai via
Kordofan. This last destination, however, was never reached. Nonetheless,
they were able to acquire the genuine information that Vogel had been murdered some five years before.

Although the expedition had split up, it had not been called off but rather continued in a different form. Heuglin was discharged by the committee in Berlin from his leadership, which was handed over to Munzinger. By boat on the Blue Nile, Heuglin and his companions arrived in Khartoum in July 1862, which Munzinger and Kinzelbach had already reached three months before, just in time to be able to witness the sojourn of the Tinnes from 11 April to 11 May. However, no documentation exists about contacts made between these representatives of scientific discovery and the aficionados of more adventurous kinds of journey.

In the meantime, a vehement discussion had broken out among some news-papers in Berlin about the events during the expedition and Heuglin's role in it. After Heuglin had been attacked heavily, the initiating committee decided to discharge him of his leadership. In his correspondence with Peter-mann from Africa he defended himself, pointing out that the scientific results of a part of their travels had been fruitful. However, the main purpose of the expedition – investigating the fate of Vogel – was fulfilled not by Heu-glin but by Munzinger and Kinzelbach, who informed the world about Vogel's unfortunate death. Heuglin did find support in the form of Alfred Brehm and also August Petermann, men of stature in the world of Africa travels and themselves considered eminent scientists. When almost two years later the account of the Abyssinia expedition was finally published in 1864 in a special edition of *Petermann's Mittheilungen*, the emphasis was laid upon the positive geographical results and no mention was made of the in-ternal differences that had caused it to split up.[20] Both Brehm and in par-ticular Petermann were to play a supporting role in Heuglin's other publica-tions as well as in his activities in the coming years up to his death in 1876. Thanks to both Brehm and Petermann, Heuglin's publication on the Tinne expedition to the Bahr el-Ghazal was already partly published before 1865. In 1869, Heuglin's own definitive version of the story appeared with a fore-word by Petermann and Brehm. Nevertheless, his fame as an Africa travel-ler had somewhat paled by the events during the Abyssinian mission.

It had no doubt crossed his mind while being blamed for his failures during the Abyssinia expedition that returning to his homeland was not the best option of dealing with his future as a scientist. After the criticism that was passed on him in Germany, Heuglin decided to stay in Sudan hoping for an opportunity to start, or participate in, a new expedition.

CHAPTER 2

The White Nile and Khartoum

The White Nile excursion of the Tinne party

As soon as Henriette Tinne-van Capellen, Alexine Tinne and Adriana van Capellen arrived in Egypt for the third time on 22 August 1861, they began looking around for a fitting goal for a new journey southwards. They moved around in the diplomatic circles of Alexandria and Cairo and made the acquaintance of Ludwig Krapf, who had been a German missionary to the King of Shoa in Abyssinia, and had endeavoured to introduce Christianity into the distant region, recording with his companion Rebmann in 1848 the existence of the snow-crowned peaks of the Kilima Ndjaro under the very equator.[1] Krapf may have been approached by the Tinnes because he was an expert on Central Africa. As the next object of their travels, they must have discussed Khartoum and their proceeding up the White Nile in his presence. There were also vague plans of procuring a residence in Cairo. 'Dr. Krapf talked a deal with Alexine about a place to remain for the summer. He spoke of Gondar, the capital of Abyssinia, as a healthy place, the King Theódoros as a friend of his to whom he would give us introductions, and afterwards we had quite arranged in our minds to go to Khartoum according to the journal he gave us', as Henriette relates in her diary.[2] If they had left at that time, however, they would have encountered the rainy season in Gondar and moreover would have found themselves in the midst of a new war in which emperor Theódoros was then engaged.

In Cairo they lived, after a short stay in the Shepheard's Hotel, in a 'petit palais' named Gazr el-Minieh (the castle el-Minieh) and wintered there in the outskirts of the city. Finally the decision was made to leave for Khartoum first and reside there for a short time before making further plans. Thus Alexine's wish to go up the Nile for the third time and head for Khartoum had been fulfilled. It was at this moment that Henriette wrote to John for another transfer of £1000. In her diary Henriette notes the financial arrangements that had to be made for the coming journey up the Nile and their possible stay in Sudan:

> They have given me £200 in gold, £90 in silver dollars [Theresia Thaler], a banker's note for £200 for a house in Khartoum, and a credit of £500 more. These two last sums at 10%. I have written for a second £1000 from Glyns and have besides transferred Fl. 10.000 [equivalent of £1000] to the Bank of Egypt from the bank in The Hague. I hope this will take me as far as Khartoum, but really money flies so fast there is no keeping account [sic]. Halib [her assistant] has spent between provisions for the boat and for the desert, tents, camels, saddles, and a hundred nameless articles more than £400.[3]

In a letter to her niece Jetty on 7 January, Alexine writes about having met d'Ablaing in Cairo by coincidence. 'We have here a Dutchman, baron d'Ablaing, a nice boy. I have showed him Cairo, as far as I could… He has departed for Abyssinia and I for the Sudan (…). I just bought a superb carabine for the hunt on big game, for it would be a pity when while staying in the Sudan, not to be able to shoot a hippopotamus or rhinoceros every now and then.'[4] In January the next year the Tinnes and d'Ablaing would meet each other again in Khartoum. At that time d'Ablaing had intended to go up the White Nile. He changed his mind, however, when he was asked by the Tinnes to join them on their next expedition to the Gazelle-river.

In a letter on 8 January from Gazr el-Minieh, Henriette refers to the immense amount of luggage they had to carry with them on the Nile and across the Nubian desert. They left the Nile at Korosko in order to cut off a detour with cataracts, leaving behind in their words 'the Nile, Tourists and Civilisation' and arriving at Abu Hamad, some 700 miles southwards, after the fourth cataract of the Nile.[5]

> On the moment of our departure which cannot be compared to anything, except the exodus of the children Israels, I would like to write you a small bid of farewell before one takes our last table away. For the size of this house we actually were scantily furnished, but now we are moving out it seems we have gathered a huge mass of furniture. Fl.1600 provisions! Because Halib says

over there we cannot get anything. Amongst other things there is no money. One has to take along everything, so I was urged to carry 800 pounds in copper money: a load for ten camels, 40 water vessels, six tents, iron bedsteads, mattresses, weapons, shortly all we need to spend eighteen days in the desert without any water. In the third boat there is everything we took with us from The Hague: 32 cases of furniture, gravings, books, mirrors, totally unknown things in these surroundings. You can imagine everybody's astonishment about our preparations: one accuses us of spending a thirty million pounds sterling yearly. One speaks about kidnapping and thiefs [sic]. Poor Addy looks green of fear. She sees herself being locked up in a harem (…). She trembles with fear when Alexine arranges her pistols, her revolvers (she has five of them) and her carabines…[6]

The three of them embarked in three hired boats on 14 January 1862, reaching Korosko in eight days. Here they had to disembark in order to traverse the Nubian desert by a caravan which stood at their disposal. In charge of the entire caravan of 102 camels was Sheikh Ahmad who over the years had escorted many Europeans through the desert from Korosko to Abu Hamad and was given letters of introduction which the Tinnes had received from Ferdinand de Lesseps and Linant de Bellefonds in Cairo. 'He is black as coals, not the blue Negro black but a rich, glowing black with the most intelligent face possible, a fine nose, and a pretty mouth with a well-trimmed beard and moustache. He talked with all like a gentleman and his manners were above par.' Alexine's five dogs were carried in special panniers. The Tinnes were packed with all their equipment on camels, their bedding came in useful during the night as well as day. The huge caravan departed on 25 January. After three days and nights on camel back (they made use of special saddles) 'everybody was tired except Alexine', who developed a 'close friendship' with the sheikh, Henriette wrote after they had reached Abu Hamad.[7] On 23 March the caravan arrived at Berber where Henriette celebrated her sixty-fourth birthday on 1 April. After their arrival she remarked: 'The road from Abu Hamed to Berber leads alongside the river which often one cannot see because it is hidden behind a curtain of trees (…). You have no idea how prosperous farmers are here. Our journey really had something of a triumphal procession. Everywhere one turned out to us shouting of joy.'[8] After a stay of over a week, the party installed themselves in several boats and set sail for Khartoum.

When on 11 April the Tinne party approached Khartoum at the confluence of the White and Blue Nile, Henriette described the river 'as being neither interesting nor pretty'. Renting a house in the town was at first not successful. They had to camp on the embankment alongside their four boats which were sailing under the Dutch flag. Eventually lodgings were provided for by Georges Thibaut, the French consul in Khartoum. They could stay on the southern bank, encamped in tents in a pleasant garden. When they found out that this would be a very disagreeable residence once the rains would set in, they searched for transport facilities that would bring them further upwards.

Directly after their arrival the three of them became drawn into the main talking point in Khartoum at that moment: the discovery of the source of the White Nile, by Speke and Grant who had been sent out to East Africa by the Geographical Society a year ago. In her decision to ascend the White Nile to distant regions southwards, Alexine did not hesitate too long. On 7 May 1862 she writes from Khartoum to her 'Dear Smous', announcing their departure for the White Nile. '(…) Don't get frightened, we are going to build – a house (…) on the 13th Degree, which should be the nicest place of the river, as one says here, because one can't stay in the bark because of the rains, this is the only thing to do.' One more house was also meant for their soldiers. 'Not that this is a dangerous country, but the Shilluks are rapacious and likely to give us trouble'. Perhaps they would proceed to Lake Victoria, 'but we have to decide for that'. In a postscript to uncle Hora Siccama she writes: '(…) a Frenchman invites us to try and penetrate with him to Lac Victoria, alias Ukararé, situated under the Equator, nobody did it before – we will decide later (…).'[9]

In one month's time, just before the wet season started, they had to make preparations for their White Nile trip which was to take them from Khartoum to Gondokoro, some seven hundred miles southwards. Again Thibaut must have played a role in the preparations for their journey, also at the diplomatic level, knowing the right channels for the best equipment.

Meanwhile all three of them wrote to their relations in The Hague and Liverpool. Henriette also attended to Queen Sophie with some news, upon which an answer came which left no doubt about the reservations the Queen felt about their staying in Central Africa:

'T Loo, June 12th 1862, I received your kind letter from <u>Chartoum</u>. Yes indeed (…) written from another world, & I deeply regret your not returning, as you had promised, after a year, a long year of absence. I understand curiosity, but when once the vague feeling is satisfied, I can not conceive the pleasure of living with uncivilised people, whose language (…), whose religions, whose customs are strange and imperturbable [sic]… Many kind affectionate messages to Alexine. Tell her to come back. Tell her Europe is much better than savage Africa. Six months before, Sophie had told Henriette she would 'expect them home' by August 1862.[10]

On her trip on the White Nile, 'savage Africa' to Alexine still meant a region for sightseeing which could be visited in a relatively comfortable and safe way.

On 11 May they left Khartoum after having obtained, with the help of Thibaut, a steamer belonging to Prince Muhammad 'Abd al-Halim, one of the relatives of Saïd Pasha, formerly governor general of Sudan. Louis de Tannyon, employed as an engineer on Prince Halim's steamer and also as his French huntsman-in-chief, acted as captain of the steamer. The price of this rent was 25,000 French francs, the equivalent of £1000. The large *dhahabiyya* they were able to hire with it had once belonged to Alfred Peney, a French doctor in Khartoum who had died the previous year on an expedition with Andrea Debono at a point above 4° latitude up the Nile. In this boat a large quantity of clothes, books, Alexine's drawing materials, some examples of her photography, and presumably her photography equipment (her camera and all that was required to process photographs) was packed. With the four boats being dragged by the steamer, they would search up the river for a suitable residence during the wet season. Having left Khartoum, they were at first delighted with this part of the river, being different from that above the town, comparing it with 'Virginia Water, near Windsor'.

During their ascent up the White Nile, two problems arose which were to present themselves to Alexine far more intensely the next year and would become decisive for the results of her stay in Sudan. While talking about their journey up the Nile, the Tinnes in Cairo were well informed about the chance of becoming seriously ill in and beyond Khartoum. To travel around either of the Niles also meant that one had to face the increasing hostility of the native people who were trying to defend themselves against the raids of private armies maintained by Arabian and Western traders. From Khartoum, travelling upwards meant that the phenomenon of slavery would occur more frequently. Because a new law was to be introduced in July 1862 obstructing the import of slaves to Khartoum via the Nile, already before the summer the slave trade had been shifting to areas of the Upper White Nile where it took place on an unhampered scale that was hitherto unknown.

Having followed the course of the river to the 13th latitude, Alexine sent a letter to her niece Jetty from the place called 'Montagnes des Dinkas' (Jebel Dinka), where she witnessed a slave raid. After an uproar during the night in which slaves escaped but some were captured again, she went to see the next morning if she could purchase some of them to set free. She returned after having achieved nothing. The next morning, two women of age came to her saying they were left by their master because they were in too weak a condition to be sold. Traders were allowed to enslave them without purchasing them. Alexine had already purchased four slaves. After having bought these two as well, one died soon after, and the other was stolen from her. On 17 June in a long letter to 'Smous', Alexine speaks about her dismay. She is profoundly shocked by the scenes of people being dragged away, slain and chained for transportation (see appendix 1: The White Nile journey of the Tinne party, Letter A. Tinne to H. Hora Siccama, 17 June 1862). She tells Jetty about her purchase of a 'petite négresse', 'a small Abbysienne, of 10 to 12 years, whose name is Goulba and promises to become a fine beauty…'.[11]

There is an element of irony in Alexine's efforts to redeem several slaves in Sudan. The provenance of the enormous capital behind the Tinne name – the flourishing sugar trade established by her father by means of slave traffic in the Dutch and British West Indies – must have been well known to Alexine. This capital had increased substantially with the huge profits in cane sugar in the West Indies during the 1830s, which received a further boost in 1835 from the British government when companies were compensated for giving up their slaves on the plantations, who had been mostly imported out of West Africa. In using a substantial sum of money to purchase a number of slaves in Jebel Dinka[12], Alexine was spending capital that had once been earned at the cost of slavery. In her letters, Alexine never referred to the provenance of the capital she was entitled to use, but one could argue that, in addition to compassion, some feelings of guilt forced Alexine to buy out some of these people once she had witnessed the miserable conditions these 'slaves' were kept in.

After Kaka and Heiligenkreuz, they reached Gondokoro on the 4° latitude on 30 September. Here the Tinnes as well as most members of their group were attacked by fevers. After being sick in bed for one week, Alexine struggled to her feet. With the steamer leading the way, the flotilla sailed out of Gondokoro on 22 October back to Khartoum, where the group arrived on 20 November (see appendix 1: The White Nile-excursion of the Tinnes).

Khartoum in the summer of 1862

One and a half months after the Tinne-van Capellen convoy had left town to work its way up the White Nile, Heuglin settled himself in Khartoum with Hermann Steudner and Hermann Schubert (see also: appendix 2, Letter Guillaume Lejean). Khartoum had undergone important changes since 1860 when he had visited the town for the last time, Heuglin tells Petermann in a letter. He felt the loss of the town physician Alfred Peney terribly, the Frenchman having been renowned for his friendly social character. Later he relates how John Petherick, the British vice consul, had gone southwards up the White Nile to pay his respects to Speke and Grant, who were travelling north down the Nile as the men claiming to be the discoverers of the sources of the Nile. Samuel Baker now lived together with his wife in Heuglin's former house, which still housed the latter's collection of maps and zoological specimens shot by. Heuglin's immediate neighbour was Eugène de Pruyssenaere who would accompany him on his trip to Mount Arash Kol in September.[13]

As a colleague from Heuglin's past consularship, Georges Thibaut had made room for them in a house with stables for their horses, located on the same square as the government buildings in the centre of town. Due to the wet season which had started in June, they were unable to make another trip until the end of September. What Heuglin hoped for was to receive the means to proceed with his voyage to the region to the west of the White Nile. As it turned out, however, there was no budget left, particularly on account of their expenses due to their longer stay in Abyssinia.[14]

Settling down for a longer time offered Heuglin, Steudner and Schubert the opportunity to sort out their scientific collections, the observations they made for the mapping out of Abyssinian territories they had traversed, and all the notations in their diaries and notebooks. And there was the somewhat nasty business of clearing out the problems that had occurred between Heuglin and the committee supervising the expedition from Germany. Geographical societies insisted on an evaluation drawn up by Heuglin, Munzinger, Steudner, Schubert and Hansal. They had to trace the exact events that had occurred.

Heuglin tells Petermann he was able to make some new acquaintances. Khartoum was the pre-eminent spot for members of the European and Arab communities to gather the necessary enquiries for possible routes. He makes clear that the Bahr el-Ghazal stood firmly as his new destination, meticulously conducting research on the various possible routes.

Heuglin's view on Sudan's state of affairs

In July, Heuglin began to write letters from Khartoum to Petermann in Gotha, Germany. The letters cover the period from his arrival in July 1862, his departure on 25 January 1863 up to 10 May, when the expedition navigated through the basin of the river el-Ghazal and further to the Jur. Together with his personal observations on the situation in Sudan, partly based on information he received from various travellers, they were taken up as a contribution for the book *Inner-Afrika*, which was to be published by Petermann in the summer of 1863.[15] He continued these accounts of the expedition during the march to the Kosanga mountains, and, after its abortion at the end of that year, back to Khartoum and all the way to Suez and Cairo, where he and Alexine Tinne finally came to rest in December 1864. The last part was published by Petermann in 1865 as a separate issue with the title *The Tinne'sche Expedition*.

During this period he also sent in his accounts for Petermann's monthly report *Mittheilungen aus Justus Perthes' Geographischer Anstalt über wichtige neue Erforschungen auf dem Gesammtgebiete der Geographie* (or *Petermann's Mittheilungen* for short), an authoritative geographical magazine of the second half of the nineteenth century. Heuglin was prodigious in his production of letters and had in the past already been one of Petermann's correspondents from northeast Africa (while on his expedition with Munzinger in 1861-1862).

In the letters he dispatched to Petermann, Heuglin looks back on the previous events during his stay in Khartoum. All letters deal with several issues expected to have value as current news from the Egyptian Sudan and the White Nile, including recent political developments, the geography, itineraries from Khartoum to nearby regions, and the ethnography of peoples on the White Nile and its affluents, generally concluding with an appendix on his zoological studies.[16]

What he writes about the possible routes to the southwest of Sudan and about the ethnography of the region can actually be regarded as an extensive preparatory study, conducted between July 1862 and January 1863, on behalf of the expedition to the Gazelle-river, in which Heuglin desperately hoped to fulfill a new role.

After having provided Petermann with facts about the trip he made to the Jebel Arash Kol, the level of the Nile and some meteorological matters, he proceeds to analyse the situation in the Egyptian Sudan and on the White Nile. From a historical point of view, this is a most important account of the latest state of affairs in the Sudanese slave trade, which occurred on an extensive scale and was to persevere despite national and in particular international policies of discouragement.

Heuglin wanted to provide Petermann with more than just enquiries regarding the state of affairs in Sudan. His contribution to *Inner-Afrika* contains a personal statement. Besides an overview of persons who had made several geographical discoveries, he mentions names of men who were involved in destructive actions concerning large quantities of native people. His story of the situation contains a direct accusation against traders who committed 'all kinds of atrocities'. Some of these men Heuglin knew from the past. He was going to be confronted with some new names in the company of the Tinnes, and often in a most disagreeable way.

In a chapter entitled *Zustände im Ägyptischen Sudan und am Weissen Nil*, Heuglin comments that, after their visits on the White Nile in the winter of 1861-1862, most trading ships had come back to Khartoum in July having obtained a very considerable amount of ivory using hard-handed ways. Individual well-established companies which, like the boats, always had a large 'military' escort, tried to hunt down the much pursued creatures but with little success. The crew on the trading ships generally used to buy single elephant tusks in exchange for glass beads, iron implements, copper bangles, Indian corn, etc., both on the river itself and on short journeys into the country. Brandy, too, was imported in very large quantities as an article for barter. Gradually, however, the groups of people along the White Nile were so inundated with glass beads etc. that the value of these items diminished considerably. After some time, these barter goods were no longer desired by inhabitants who lived in the close vicinity of the river. In particular the Bari, living in the region of Gondokoro, demanded higher prices for less ivory.[17]

Later in 1869, in his retrospective of the expedition, Heuglin would explain that in the 1850s, the traffic in ivory with the people on the White Nile had from the outset been restricted to the purchase, or rather barter, of ivory, which was at first not of value to the riverain people.[18] This was confirmed by the account of Andrew Melly, a Liverpool trader who in 1850 was wandering about the White Nile region. He states that ivory was not wanted by the natives; it was the elephant meat they were after. The trunks of the butchered elephants were laying with what was left of the bodies for waste on their hunting grounds.[19] In the past, Heuglin had seen ivory only being used for bracelets, small clubs and thrust weapons, trumpets and small pins for tying cows. There was hardly any value attached to this material. For a few handfuls of ordinary glass beads, one could obtain a load of fine ivory.

Ivory was used in the West to manufacture billiard balls, piano keys, knife handles and toilet accessories, and the market for these products was rapidly expanding. This resulted in growing demand for ivory, an increase in the ivory trade and the subsequent scarceness of it. Because the barter value of beads was diminishing, traders searched for new means to continue their purchases. Initially the traders bought slaves but soon they were capturing the natives in raids on villages and then exchanging them as slaves for ivory. The brutality of the traders and their crew led to an increase in bloody battles with groups of native people who increasingly began fighting back with their lances and arrows. People travelling alone by boat became a victim of revenge. Traders were henceforth compelled to have fewer sailors and other shipmen aboard in order to take on more armed men, referred to as 'soldiers'. Such a flotilla could number 40 to 100 men, forming a well-equipped army.[20] The boats of the Tinnes also carried a large amount of soldiers and were equipped to be able to engage in battle with these so-called 'malevolent natives'.

Because of frequent disputes with ethnic groups, which often escalated into sanguinary confrontations, the traders had to increase the number of escorts considerably. Traders entered into agreement with one native community and, under its guidance, launched a surprise attack on their neighbours in an attempt to catch as many prisoners as possible and abducting them to be used as slaves for bartering elsewhere. At the same time, the available cattle was grabbed to satisfy the wants of the people the traders had made 'friends' with, and to use it for barter trade as well. A caravan of such plunderers, often over 100 men strong, surprised a village, cut down those who attempted to defend themselves, and then transported both humans and cattle to the next tribe, where they exchanged the cattle for elephant tusks, which fetched a price of 60 oxen for 50 pounds of ivory.[21] A crucial part of the profits made by White Nile traders and their ruling caste of Arabian servants depended on the trade in stolen cattle and slaves.[22]

Over time, it became more and more difficult for the White Nile traders to hide their activities due to the enormous expenses, the inflation of barter trade – which at a certain point consisted exclusively of slaves – and the increasing lack of ivory as merchandise in the neighbourhood of the White Nile banks. In exchange for their ivory, the native peoples began to demand increasingly valuable goods such as copper arm rings, brandy and in particular cattle, which they valued most. Sometimes there was a dearth of salt and fine corn or *durra*.

Most of the traders established their fortified settlements, known as *zaribas*, in those districts where native people were not hostile. Common interests could be created by developing friendships with tribes that eventually led to cooperation in robbing cattle in the vicinity. From their fortress-like places, traders organised raids inland, supported by an army of slaves and servants which were housed in the *zariba* itself.[23] During these forays, traders discovered that the more inland they went, the larger the quantity of elephant tusks they could procure. Contacts were first made with the Shilluk in the 1850s, followed by the Jur and the Kresh, who lived further west in the basin of the Gazelle-river. *Zaribas* soon began to appear in the lands of the Azande people, who lived more to the southwest of the Bahr el-Ghazal (see foldout map).

Some Europeans conducted this kind of business on a very large scale. Heuglin provides a list of their nationalities: besides Turks, Copts, Syrians and Sudanese, Europeans – in particular Germans, Frenchmen, Italians, Englishmen and Greek – were involved in this 'respectable profession'. Many of them established contacts with Muhammad Khair, Sheikh of Hillat Kaka, who succeeded in mustering a large number of men and arming them properly. De Malzac (mentioned in appendix 3: Khartoum) sold most of his 'black goods' to Muhammad Khair. Although Khair's place of residence was not tributary to the government in Khartoum, he offered them a yearly toll of cattle in order to be recognised as a sheikh in Kaka. His offer was accepted, as Heuglin recorded in one of his letters.[24]

In 1862, the Egyptian-Turkish authorities introduced a new policy towards the Sudan slave trade. To implement this policy, on 2 August 1862 a new person was appointed governor general of Sudan: Musha Pasha Hamdi. He was 'a most energetic man, a friend of the Europeans, a good administrator and an expert on the situation in the Sudan', relates Heuglin to Petermann, after he heard of this.[25] Both knew each other from the past 12 years when Heuglin, then vice consul of Austria, met him in Egypt and Khartoum several times. This time Musha Pasha invited him to be his companion during a campaign in East Sennār and some Egyptian districts on the border with Abyssinia. Heuglin declined this invitation because he still had hopes of making a journey in the basin of 'the Ghazal'.

Having received an assignment from the Egyptian government with all official backing, Musha Pasha was expected to end not only the mutinies and riots within the Sudanese regiments but also the increasingly widespread corruption within the government administration. He then levied high taxes on land as well as on merchants and shopkeepers. Europeans travelling in Sudan were also heavily taxed. Musha Pasha's merciless taxes would eventually infuriate Alexine Tinne after her return to Khartoum and drive her to her wits' end. Musha Pasha had been given orders to improve the registration of slaves kept by Sudanese people themselves. New regulations regarding sound and reliable ('taugliche') slaves were, as Heuglin argues in 1863, a direct consequence of the upgrading of military ranks. Musha had also been instructed to begin suppressing the White Nile slave trade, but no one believed that this could be achieved.

Complaints had been made by European travellers about their confrontations with slave dealers occurring on the river embankments. They did not have any effect on the Turkish authorities, who were well informed about the matter but held the opinion that this behaviour was beyond their control when they occurred on the other side of the Egyptian borders.[26] After Musha's arrival, however, the government in Khartoum in due time sent three large vessels to Hillat Kaka (Khair's residence) to establish a kind of river police. The commander of this corps had the right to seize any ship suspected of transporting slaves, who would then be liberated.[27] The establishment of control of the river prevented slave ships from delivering their cargo directly to Khartoum, forcing traders to search for other possibilities up the White Nile. They soon found new ways and means to dispose of their booty. Between the river Sobat (an eastern affluent of the White Nile) and Wad Shellal, new areas of distribution were found. After having disposed of their slave cargo, the ships continued their trip to Khartoum without their loads and sailed back to the White Nile in order to repeat their business transactions. By creating new caravan routes on the embankments before they reached the control, their trade ware could easily be abducted as far as Suakim and Massaua at the Red Sea, a route on which there was hardly any control.

Given the government's interests in this trade, and with many civil servants as well as consular agents engaged in this trade, it is hardly surprising that this new policy did not succeed in reducing the slave trade in Sudan.[28]

During the Tinne-Heuglin expedition, Sudanese slavery was to become an international political issue (see appendix 3: Khartoum: centre of slave-trade and appendix 4: Sudanese slavery and the Western world). Heuglin mentions the principal interests of the Egyptian state in the slave trade – slaves could be used as soldiers in the army or sold in order to increase government revenues – in his letters of 1862-1863 and in his review of 1869.[29] What lay behind these interests was the rise of the Egyptian state, its relation with Sudan as its province, and the rise of Sudanese slavery. This trade had in fact been begun by the Turks and Egyptians but it was further developed by traders from abroad, notably Europeans.

CHAPTER 3

Preparations for the journey

Heuglin's list of informants

Heuglin's reason for refusing Musha Pasha's invitation to join him on his campaign to the east of Sudan was that he hoped to fulfill his growing desire to travel to the basin of the Gazelle-river. In his search for information regarding possible routes, he could choose from among the traders or explorers who were then in town and could be of importance to him. During the monsoon, from July to the end of September, Heuglin and his companion Steudner spent many evenings in the company of Europeans, in particular with Thibaut. Before he left for Mount Arash Kol on 29 September 1862, Heuglin also met several Arabs who had just returned from their journeys or were preparing to leave Khartoum in a short while. Even during their trip to Arash Kol, Heuglin was gathering information about possible routes to the Bahr el-Ghazal and from there to the Azande people.

In a paragraph entitled 'Nachrichten über neueste Reisen in den Nil Ländern', Heuglin provides a survey of all the persons he approached for information about the challenges posed by the different possible routes to the Gazelle-river.[1] An extract from a series of letters, the last one dating from 8 December 1862, illustrates with what frenetic energy Heuglin held these interviews. Several of the persons named in his letters to Petermann Heuglin already knew personally. He was well informed about the circumstances and conditions of doing business with the inhabitants and other non-Western parties. Heuglin was now particularly interested in their knowledge about possible routes. Although Heuglin thought the information he received was vague and incomplete, he did not hesitate to submit the results in his letters to Petermann.

In addition to De Pruyssenaere, Heuglin and Steudner spoke with Jules Poncet, who had arrived in Sudan in 1851 with his brother Ambroise and Alexandre Vaudey, his uncle who was then a proconsul of Sardinia in Egypt and had crossed regions of the White Nile embankments and the Bahr el-Ghazal. They also met with Guillaume Lejean, who arrived in Khartoum at the beginning of August. Heuglin wrote to Petermann that Lejean 'works quite diligently and meticulously, but only by compass, and he does not know any Arabic'.[2] Lejean left Khartoum in the middle of October for Abyssinia to fulfill a mission on behalf of the French government.

Then the name of Kleincznik turns up for the first time in Heuglin's writings: 'Johann Kleincznik of Carniola' was a former co-worker of the Catholic mission in Khartoum who was now an elephant hunter. He embarked on a commercial expedition in November 1861 with two sailing ships in the direction of the Gazelle-river. Heuglin relates how Schubert left with Kleincznik on 15 November by boat on the White Nile heading for the southwest. Schubert, who had joined Heuglin's Vogel expedition as a *horticulteur* at his own expense, continued his travels after having met Kleincznik and agreeing to accompany him to his settlement in the Kosanga mountains. Again at his own expense, he left Khartoum for the region of the effluents of the Bahr el-Ghazal in the Azande country. Heuglin was sorry he was not able to say farewell to Schubert.

One may ask why Heuglin himself did not seize the opportunity to join Kleincznik on this trip. Several possible reasons might have prevented Heuglin from joining this voyage. It is unlikely that he was not invited, as he was the leader of the former expedition and was eager to continue his travels southwards. The lack of available means may have been the decisive factor. A notation in *Nouvelles Annales des Voyages* says that Schubert somehow had a personal budget at his disposal and was able to take care of his own expenses.[3] No substantial funds were available to Heuglin after what was left of the sum that had been spent on his trip to the Jebel Arash Kol. Heuglin must have realised by that point that he would be far better off in the company of the Tinnes whose wealth would come in handy. Thibault may also have played a role in persuading him to stay and wait for the return of the Tinnes, who in Khartoum had already hinted that they would go in the direction of the Azande after their White Nile trip. Their search for new adventures suited Heuglin well. Somewhat bitterly, Heuglin would later relate the truth that joining the Tinnes implicated that he as well as Steudner were supposed to take care of their own expenses for virtually everything they needed for participating in the expedition.

For Schubert, the trip turned out to be fatal. He had hardly recovered from his illness in Khartoum when he fell ill again at Kleincznik's *zariba* on the border of the Azande country and eventually succumbed there to fever and dysentery. He was the first European to have compiled a journal of travels to the Azande country, which unfortunately never reached the outside world due to its disappearance after his death.

Heuglin recounts to Petermann what Kleincznik had told him about his proceedings towards the Bahr el-Ghazal. After having landed on the so-called Meshra el-Rek (i.e. port of the river Rek), the vast marsh which was thought to be the source of the Gazelle-river, Kleincznik set off in January 1862 with an armed escort from the south bank of the Rek in a south-westerly direction. For seven days he marched for at least six hours daily through a somewhat undulating plain inhabited by the Dinka, with numerous patches of forest and thicket, many springs and some rain water pools, untill he came to the river Jur with flat banks which were not marshy. This river was still very broad and three to four feet deep. At this point the Jur, which flowed more or less from south to north, received a tributary, the Bongo-river, flowing from the west. On the ninth day, it was necessary to cross another tributary of the Jur, the Kosanga-river, so called after the people living to the west of it. Among wooded hills he followed the course of the river Kosanga for two and a half days, crossing the river several times, which was very rapid, its bed being at different levels. After passing through wide tracts of cultivated land for half a day and again for a day and a half through forest, Kleincznik reached the 'Qolo tribe', as Heuglin writes. Arabs had inhabited these Central African regions for some time, while Westerners only began arriving in the late 1850s and 1860s. Under the Bahr el-Ghazal, Kleincznik met Zubeir, a Khartoum merchant in his trading station, which had been established many years before. Half a day's march further towards the southwest, he reached the *zariba* of Biselli. It was at a day's journey from this spot that Kleincznik would establish his own *zariba*, on the caravan route from the Azande to Hōferat el-Nāhas (see foldout map). He mentioned to Heuglin that Petherick, the English consul, had his *zariba* some days' journey further northeast. Darfur traders travelled in four weeks to the Azande area, bringing with them donkeys laden with copper, which they exchanged for slaves with the Azande.

The second traveller who gave Heuglin information about the Azande was the trader named Kuchuk Ali Agha, who had a settlement in Gondokoro, a place far up the White Nile, from where the Tinnes were returning when Heuglin was writing his letter to Petermann. This trader had a small army of 80 soldiers. Like all other traders he was required to defend himself against the riverain Nile people who were opposing their raids for slaves. Kuchuk Ali Agha related how he travelled from Gondokoro for seven days in a westerly and rather southerly direction through an uninhabited plain and then for six days of six hours' march through the populous country of the Nyambara or Yambara, often quite hilly, covered with forests and with much water. Here, Bari and Mondu were spoken. From the western boundary of the land of the Nyambara, he travelled through the country of the Mondu for four days, mostly via plains rich in vegetation, water and honey. Here his *zariba* was on the farther side of a wide river with rocky bottom and banks, which never ran dry and where crocodiles and hippopotami were to be found. Petherick had also established a *zariba* here. It was said that this river flowed into the Gazelle-river, but it was probably the Jur, Heuglin adds in his letter. From Mondu one needed to travel for another three days to reach the 'Niam-Niam' (the name Westerners used for the Azande tribe), whose territory extended still further south. According to the information received, they were called Makrakà in their own language.[4]

It was in particular during these conversations with Kleincznik that Heuglin's endeavours to enter the Bahr el-Ghazal area, and beyond that the country of the Azande, must have taken shape. The route to be followed had been established. The Bahr el-Ghazal expedition, going to 'Lac No', Meshra el-Rek, Wau and to the Kosanga Mountains, travelled along the same route as was described by Kleincznik to Heuglin.

Heuglin's preliminary trip

Since the Abyssinian expedition had not been particularly favourable to his reputation, Heuglin had to consider carefully his next steps in Africa. Going back to Germany was out of the question. Though he was assured of the support of some influential and important men, he would have stirred up a hornets' nest. What he needed was an accomplishment that would compensate for the Abyssinian mission and would rehabilitate himself. Abyssinia had been largely mapped out and the Royal Geographical Society would send Speke to Lake Victoria in order to establish this water as the source of the White Nile. There was one area in the vast region of northeast Africa that remained to be explored: the Bahr el-Ghazal, whose effluents and sources had not yet been recorded. And then there were the mysterious 'Niam-Niam' people who lived to the south of this river.

However, there was no substantial budget for another expedition available due to the distances covered and the expenses made in Abyssinia. He had reserved some of his budget with the intention of using it later in Khartoum. Together with Steudner, Heuglin dedicated much of his time during the wet season to arranging the research documents from their Abyssinian journey: scientific collections, the sketches he had drawn up for maps and his diaries. They had to go into the details of the events that had occurred during the expedition, as the geographical societies in Germany urged Heuglin, Munzinger, Steudner, Schubert and Hansal to make their evaluation of the expedition.

In September, fresh funds were available which enabled Heuglin and Steudner to make a short explorative tour to the mountain of Arash Kol to the east of Kordofan, southwest of Khartoum, above the Gazelle-river. During this journey, the Belgian Eugene de Pruyssenaere is introduced in one of Heuglin's letters. When Heuglin and Steudner arrived in Khartoum in July, they found out that their direct neighbour was De Pruyssenaere, who was according to Heuglin a restless person, enthusiastic about travel and nature. He shuttled back and forth tirelessly along the Nile from Cairo to Khartoum after his arrival in Africa in 1856 until his untimely death in 1864.[5] It was not long before De Pruyssenaere decided to join them. The account of this trip to Arash Kol constitutes the first part of his correspondence of December to Petermann. Other parts he sent to Germany consisted of a mixture of facts, arranged for the magazine of Petermann, who expected to learn about the latest state of affairs not only in the field of geography but also in meteorology, and the results of his research concerning zoology, Heuglin's specialty, and an analysis of botanic specimens. The most important of Heuglin's contributions to the magazine, however, was formed by his interviews in Khartoum with travellers and traders about their journeys to the Bahr el-Ghazal.

The main object of his trip, as Heuglin argued, was just the restoration of their health. While recovering from their Abyssinian expedition, Heuglin and Steudner continued their scientific work on the western bank of the White Nile by gathering facts on geography, zoology and botany.[6]

They returned to Khartoum on 20 October; exactly one month before the Tinnes would re-enter the town after their White Nile journey of almost six months. Directly after their arrival, Henriette and Alexine Tinne would meet Theodor von Heuglin and Hermann Steudner. Their encounter in Khartoum took place on the eve of events that would create some drastic changes in the relationship between Westerners in Sudan and Turkish-Egyptian authorities.

Stopover in Khartoum

The Tinne party re-entered the capital of the Egyptian Sudan on 20 November at the conclusion of their White Nile trip. They were lodged in a town in which most of the Europeans lived, in the quarter between the Roman Catholic Mission – an imposing block built in the Italian *seicento* style – and the palace of the governor general, designed after the mission, near the high embankment and the garden alongside the Nile. In case of the arrival of persons of note or distinction such as the Tinnes, a consul (if possible representing their nationality) used to take care of their reception and dwellings. Presumably because the Tinnes were Francophone, in Cairo Thibaut had been recommended as the right person to be approached. Their previous arrival in the spring of that year would have come as more or less of a surprise, which explains their encampment in the park on the island. This time they had been able to make all sorts of deals about their reception after their Nile trip.

Because of Khartoum's increasing significance for the trade of ivory and its largely unexplored hinterland, European nations had begun sending over consular agents, after having established consulates in Cairo earlier. Already in 1838, France had installed Georges Thibaut as its consul to Sudan. Britain appointed John Petherick as a consular agent in 1850. Austria followed in 1851 with Constantin Reitz as a vice consul, and the Kingdom of Sardinia with Alexandre Vaudey, a Savoyard, as vice consul in 1851. After Reitz died in 1853, his place was taken by Theodor von Heuglin. He was followed in 1860 by Joseph Natterer, who after his death in 1862 was succeeded by Martin Ludwig Hansal, who had accompanied Heuglin on his Abyssinian expedition in 1861-62.

At the time of the Tinnes' arrival, Khartoum was buzzing with business transactions. However, no substantial banking house was to be found that maintained branches in Sudan from Egypt. The more creditworthy Khartoum merchants acted as accredited local correspondents for the banks in Alexandria. In this capacity they honoured letters of credit and drew bills at sight. Egyptian money, which consisted of piastres, had little value in commercial exchange up river from Egypt itself. The people who dwelt along the banks of the White Nile as far as its southern limits of navigation and its affluents like the Gazelle-river actually were beyond the range of the money economy. Barter was the only way possible for acquiring ivory, slaves and other desired products. The southern Sudanese peoples were initially in particular interested in exchanging slaves for cowrie shells, glass beads and other trinkets. The beads came chiefly from the Venetian glass factories in Murano, then part of the Austrian Empire.[7]

Once in Khartoum, or perhaps even before their arrival in the capital, the Tinnes began writing their family, providing them with their travel experiences. To Jetty, Alexine's tone had somewhat changed after her 'Montagne des Dinkas' letter. The horrifying scenes with the slaves now seemed farther removed. To her niece she continues to write about journeys of which the next would be even more exciting than the one she previously made. On 20 November, she writes:

> You will be surprised to receive a letter from me from Khartoum, returning here hardly was our intention, but having been close to the 4° degree as far as our boats can go, we found the White-river such [sic] terribly far, that we had resumed there to establish our quarter and instead of sending the steamboat back on its own, we returned all together to gather our provisions, bring back Aunt Addy… [to recover] of the fever and the evil of the country and after a month rest we count on leaving again, but well (…) with 60 soldiers, donkeys and a quantity of (…) powder etc. for a new journey on the Bahr el-Ghazal and the Djour (you will find the rivers on the maps) and from there to the Niambara if we can the Niambara east and in the south of Gondokoro (the 4° degree).

This letter, in which not a single word is uttered about her own disease, indicates that at first instance Alexine intended to proceed from a south-westerly direction to the east, from the Bahr el-Ghazal regions ending up in the

Nyambara. While planning this new journey later with Heuglin, this intention must have been the subject of discussion, because the route actually was the one as described by Kuchuk Ali Agha to Heuglin.

To Queen Sophie in the Netherlands, Henriette writes about their illnesses but also the carefree life they enjoyed: 'This sad termination is a pity, as else I should have been satisfied with the lazy everyday life carried on without the bother of money, and absence of care, a damn-me don't care sort of life, which I value very much.' [8]

The Tinnes also instantly started to gather information concerning the goal of their next expedition: the Gazelle-river and the Azande people. At that time, Alexine knew that in Khartoum one traveller in particular would be of importance in making the preparations successful: Theodor von Heuglin. At least two months before his descent from Abyssinia to Khartoum, Heuglin's coming arrival was circulating in Khartoum's news circuit. Also in Europe, one appeared to be informed about Heuglin's movements. In the Netherlands, Uncle Hora-Siccama appears to have been abreast of the expedition and Heuglin's expected arrival in Khartoum. On 7 May, less than a week before leaving for the White Nile, Alexine responds, in a postscriptum of her letter to Jetty, to Uncle Hora Siccama's question of whether she was informed about the German traveller Heuglin:

> Dear Uncle Hora Siccama – I have heard much talking about Mr. Heuglin here, one says his expedition is not successful – there is a Mr. Petherick who is at this moment going from Gondokoro (4th degree) to Zanzibar; his wife accompanies him. [9]

It remains unclear how Alexine came by this information. Petherick himself only cherished the fulfillment of his mission of reaching Gondokoro in order to welcome Speke and Grant and never to travel beyond. Speke and Grant were to take the route going the opposite direction – from Zanzibar to the mainland and then via the principal source of the Nile (Lake Victoria) in a northern direction to Gondokoro and Khartoum.

In Khartoum, apparently almost everyone knew of Heuglin. There are no concrete details pointing to a possible connection between Heuglin's imminent arrival and the Tinnes' plans of going up to the Bahr el-Ghazal region, which Alexine had already suggested during her White Nile trip.

What is remarkable, however, is Alexine's somewhat enthusiastic comment on the coming arrival of Heuglin, brought to her notice by her uncle while she was still busy preparing her White Nile trip.

Both initiatives might not necessarily have been interdependent; an expedition to the Gazelle-river and the Azande was a hot issue in the international geographic world of that time. Going from Khartoum upwards, travellers approaching the White Nile's junction with the Bahr el-Ghazal often wondered where this river with its thick layers of floating plants and trees came from and what new information its source could possibly give in relation to the still burning question of the origins of the White Nile. What we know for certain from his accounts to Petermann is that Heuglin was himself aware of the Tinnes' aspirations for an expedition after their return to Khartoum. One person in particular might have been of importance in this regard: Georges Thibaut. Thibaut had become an acquaintance of both mother and daughter Tinne and was still in contact with his former friend Heuglin, who could be very useful to the Tinnes with their plans for a future expedition.[10]

After their return from the White Nile trip, the Tinnes had to refresh their cash funds. Meanwhile John Tinne kept their accounts and provided them with the recent balance of their credits in a letter which they should have received upon their arrival in Khartoum.[11] In regulating the prices of their provisions and the choice of articles that Henriette and Alexine had to buy from local merchants in Khartoum during the expedition's preparations, Georges Thibaut played a crucial role. Obtaining cash and paying for the provisions for the expedition was a tall order not only for the 'bankers' in this town but also for him. A notebook indicates that Thibaut was to receive 55,720 piastres (around £470, where £1 = 119 piastres) on behalf of 'Mme la Baronne van Capellen'[12], probably in his capacity as agent for a banker in Alexandria or Cairo, where the international banking companies were settled. The notes also indicate Henriette's role as treasurer of the expedition. The expenses that were due for the fitting-out of the Tinne-Heuglin expedition were to be handled by Henriette with money from her own capital and that of Alexine's bequest of 1856, which was to be withdrawn in Khartoum by means of letters of credit. After Henriette's death, Thibaut maintained his close financial relations with the Tinnes via Alexine when she arrived back in Khartoum in March 1864.

There actually was another currency that could be used in Sudan. Besides an amount of Egyptian piastres and other kinds of copper coins, Henriette took with her on their expedition a substantial amount of Maria Theresia Thaler. This ancient silver coin, officially last struck in 1789 during the last year of Maria Theresia's government of the Austrian empire, was accepted as currency in the entire northeastern part of Africa. Also in Sudan, this coin was considered by Arab merchants to be a valuable currency, in particular the proprietors of the *zaribas* in the Bahr el-Ghazal regions, which the Tinne-Heuglin expedition was to call at on its way.[13] Having their home ports in Khartoum and their *zaribas* established in regions often at a great distance from Khartoum, there were only a couple of these merchants, members of the Arabian ruling caste, independent and omnipotent, acting according to their own rules. Tinne and Heuglin were to meet one of them in particular. (Chapter 6 will deal with their encounter with Biselli, which would involve a most unpleasant confrontation with his brutality in demanding high prices for their daily provisions, preferably to be paid out in Thaler).

In Khartoum itself, several dangers were already discernible that were ultimately to determine the expedition's final abortion and the ensuing distressful situations (see appendix 3: *Khartoum*). First, there was the chance of catching one of the prevalent and often fatal diseases. Disease was the first setback that Alexine and Henriette, as well as Heuglin and Steudner, were to be confronted with. On their journeys far away from Khartoum, both Henriette and Steudner had succumbed to a disease that was similar to one described in Khartoum. Second, Khartoum's economic relationship with its hinterlands relied increasingly on the vast trade in slaves by merchants who held office in the capital. The slave trade was witnessed firsthand by the Tinnes during their stay in the Bahr el-Ghazal area and was to be faced by Alexine before and after her return to Khartoum. All slave trade had Khartoum as its commercial centre.

The encounter of November 1862

Heuglin enthusiastically writes to Petermann in a letter sent on 8 December that he had spoken to Henriette Tinne after her arrival on 20 November. 'A very rich Dutch woman, Madame Tinne and daughter, did rent the steamer of Halim Pasha by which she departed in June to Gondokoro (…)'. Remarkably, Henriette Tinne is described by him as the leader of the White Nile trip. 'Madame Tinne', he proceeds, actually wished to fulfill 'the project' of going up to the Gazelle-river and from there to the West. Heuglin tells Petermann he would love to be invited, though, as he indicates, the steamship would have too much draught for the marshy places and its paddles would certainly get obstructed by waterplants.[14]

At the time of the encounter, both Alexine and Henriette had also had a conversation with the Italian traveller Carlo Piaggia during which they proposed he join them on their expedition. In his diaries of his travels in the years 1863-1865, Piaggia relates how he was approached by the 'ladies Tinne' and Heuglin in Khartoum on the eve of the preparations for their expedition to the Bahr el-Ghazal. Piaggia, who could hardly write, calling himself 'humble' and of lower-class descent, wrote out people's names phonetically in his memoirs. Talking about 'Alxin' and 'Heglin', he relates that he was invited by them as well by Heuglin ('Barone Eghlin e il Dott. Subner'), who had already joined the Tinnes. It was 'the young daughter mademoiselle [madamigella] A. Alxin who absolutely wanted to undertake a journey to the country of the Niam-Niam'. Piaggia, however, had a previous agreement with the Khartoum trader Ghattas for an ivory hunt, followed by a journey to the Azande.[15] On his way up, he would later encounter the Tinne-Heuglin expedition near the river Jur, as promised.[16]

On 20 November, the day of their arrival, Henriette writes to Jules van Capellen, her brother, that she is '(…) happy to say Heuglin is going with us,

> He has given so many broad hints of his wish to make this journey
> that at last we told him we could not offer him a place either in the
> steamer or the *dhahabiyya*, but that there were two other boats
> going with provisions, soldiers, and animals, if he liked [sic] to
> have a cabin arranged for him and his friend he was very welcome,
> and I wish you could have seen with what pleasure they accepted it.
> This shows at least what an underline{interesting} [underlined] part it is. We
> shall be [sic] fourteen days reaching the River Gazelle. There we
> shall soon be stopped [sic] for want of water and when all is ready
> to go into the interior I shall send the steamer back with letters and
> Addy can write as often as she likes.[17]

The ardent wish of reaching the Azande

One name given to a group of people comes up frequently in their accounts and letters: the 'Niam-Niam'. To reach the countries to the southwest of the Gazelle-river and encounter the Azande was the primary aim of launching the expedition to the Bahr el-Ghazal. Accomplishing the journey to the Kosanga mountains would imply that the expedition was only a two days' journey from the Azande country, 'their intended goal', as Henriette would later argue in a letter to John in Liverpool.[18]

In the Western world, the Azande already had a legendary status. They were definitely the most intriguing of all the Nilotic and Sudanese people, and to encounter them was the crown on the expedition's achievements.

In one of his letters to Petermann, Heuglin dedicates several pages to the Azande; these were to become the first extensive study on them. All records Heuglin received were fairly unanimous in saying that the whole territory of the Azande consisted of many small kingdoms or chieftains who quickly united for war against a common foe, gathering their vassals and slaves around them. The land was inhabited by a different 'race' than the usual type of 'negro', and also by their slaves. One and a half day's journey to the south of Kleincznick's *zariba* lived a very powerful King (later called 'Sultan' by him) called Mofío. The Diqa, Basa and Qorombo were pointed out to Heuglin as 'tribes of the free Nyamyam who are called Sandé'. Here Heuglin mentions for the first time in travel and ethnographic literature the name 'Sandé' for a large cluster of people, later to be named 'Azande' after their own 'official name'. Then follows a description of habits, customs and some utensils (or *ethnographische Gegenstände*, as he would name them) of the different groups.[19]

In 1865 he would add much new information which he most probably had gathered during an interview in November 1863 with a delegate of 'Sultan Mofio', who had been approached by Alexine (see Chapter 6). In this letter, Heuglin included a paragraph which threw new light on facts about the Azande and their place in Central African ethnography. By searching for ethnographic facts, so far only known by traders who had been crossing through or staying in the country of the Azande, he was able to uncover details about their culture, providing an extensive list of particularities.

Heuglin recounts that sketchy, partly very fantastic tales about the Azande have come to us since the time of the explorer Denham (1822-24) and the first White Nile expeditions in 1839 and 1840, which had gone up the Nile travelling along the Bahr el-Ghazal. The 'Niam-Niam', or according to others also spelled 'Nyamyam' or 'Namanyam', were considered to be a group of people that distinguished themselves completely from other peoples already known. They were thus a different 'race', according to the then predominant theory about human species, characterised with all its various visual particularities.[20]

According to the tales of Arab traders, the Azande were said to be half dog and half man, and to be fond of eating human flesh (Niam-Niam is the ideophone of 'eating'). The first testimony that there were people in Central Africa with tails was given by the Englishman George Browne who, following a caravan of Arab merchants, managed to be the first European to go deep into Darfur (see foldout map). In the narrative of his travels, published in 1799, he refers to tales about cannibalism told by Arabs. 'There is', he writes, 'a remote part of the pagan country, from which slaves are brought, which the Arabs distinguish by the term Gnum Gnum (a sobriquet), whose inhabitants eat the flesh of the prisoners they take in war. I have conversed with slaves who came thence, and they admit the fact.'[21] In 1854, Louis du Couret published his *Voyage aux Pays des Niam Niams ou hommes à qeue, avec le portrait d'un Niam Niam* under the pseudonym Abd el Hamid Bey, with a preface by Alexandre Dumas. The book appeared to be about a faked journey, meant as a fantastic tale. Besides being anthropophagi, the Niam-Niam were equipped with tails, as the writer saw with his own eyes. Though his stories were given no credence, the rumour about tailed people became persistent and was not to be invalidated until 1860 by Guillaume Lejean, who explained the story about the so-called tail. 'The supposed tail of the Niam Niam would be nothing more than the end of a belt which serves for fastening the loincloth of the nyam nyam Blacks passing between their legs from behind. Mr. Charton has received from Mr. Lejean a drawing of that strange belt by which these Blacks veil their nudity'.[22]

The story was also falsified by recent information from Pierre Trémaux who drew attention to it in an article in *L'Illustration*, the Parisian two-weekly news journal, in 1859 ('Des Hommes à queue'), strengthening his argument by using an illustration from his *Le Soudan* (1854), which shows a picture of a chief of a group of 'negroes' from the Blue Nile meeting a king of Sennār. Like his comrades, the chief wears a cloth of hide, hanging down from behind in the form of a tail.[23] By the time Heuglin refers to this story about 'negroes with a tail' in 1862, it had been rendered obsolete.

However, after Browne's account of 1799, the theory that the Azande were cannibals was not referred to as a fairy tale. It received new life by the Poncet brothers, who visited the region in 1860 and published their account in the prestigious *Bulletin de la Société de Géographie*. Petherick, who stayed in 'Niam-Niam' country near Mundo in 1859, confirmed their reputation of cannibalism.[24] The Poncets' and Petherick's 'story' was one of travellers who claimed to have seen and experienced Azande culture themselves. In 1869, the distinguished scientist-explorer Schweinfurth, who became the leading authority on the Azande after his major publications in 1874 and 1875, referred to raids executed by the Azande in 1869, verifying the intelligence of the former two and also of others.[25]

Just before Schweinfurth's publications, there was another confirmation of the Azande's cannibalistic nature. In 1870, Heinrich von Maltzan refers from Tripoli to an interview with one of the Sudanese girls who Alexine Tinne had taken up in her company. She happened to be of Azande origin and she recounted to him 'hideous events' of cannibalism.[26]

At one's own expense

Being invited to join the Tinne company certainly did not imply that Heuglin and Steudner's expenses would be compensated by Henriette and Alexine. From the outset, the expedition had been conceived of as a project of individuals who would each take care of their own part in the organisation and performance of the enterprise. As a participant, each member had to purchase – at one's own expense and according to the available funds – a quantity of soldiers, porters, pack and riding animals, provisions and barter goods, which were thought to be necessary in order to proceed in the best way possible.

Some time after their initial conversation with the Tinnes at the end of November, a letter is sent to Petermann in which Heuglin tells that he will join the Tinnes' 'project' to go up the Gazelle-river with a hired steamer. Somewhat indignantly, he also remarks that the Tinnes' invitation meant for both him and Steudner that they would have to provide for an additional substantial part of their own expenses dealing with the rental of boats, luggage, animals, crew and provisions. From this letter it becomes clear that Henriette Tinne had taken on the responsibility of cashier, as far as their part was concerned.

> For the costs of travelling I have been mistaken; despite all possible advantages which we enjoy thanks to Madame Tinne, I was obliged to take up today another 300 Thaler [provided by Petermann, slipping money into his pocket every now and then]. Some days ago Dr. Steudner received from his mother 140 Maria Theresia Thaler and will accompany me now, but I don't know how he is going to equip himself with such a sum of money, which will be sufficient for only the half of his journey back to Cairo and not even enough for 2 or 3 months living here.[27]

After having extended the rent, the Tinnes had the steamer again at their disposal. However, a great deal of the plans of both parties was *in statu nascendi*, and nobody was sure they were feasible, as is explained in one of Heuglin's letters.

> Despite all difficulties and adversaries we have no lack of courage and I hope that the desire of returning will not come soon, provided circumstances won't force us to. A proper plan was not yet made up by me, however I think to proceed at least deep into the country of the Niam-Niam. When there is a breach open to the West and means and some crew will be left to me, we will see what could be done from there. Possibly nothing at all, but I will be satisfied to remain for a year or so with the Niam-Niam and to cross the meridian of Darfur to the West.[28]

In the last moments of their preparatory activities, one person appears on the stage who would become one of the principal *dramatis personae*. Heuglin recounts to Petermann: 'On 12 January of this year a young Dutchman, Baron Van Arkel d'Ablaing, arrived here from Abyssinia'. After a rather tiresome journey in Abyssinia, he was glad to enter Khartoum and eager to become acquainted with the European community in which Alexine Tinne and her mother played a conspicuous role. The Tinnes were obviously enchanted to come into contact again with the Baron Daniël d'Ablaing, who was actually to become a family member of Alexine's niece Jetty Hora Sic-cama by her marriage in 1869 to Jan Daniël Baron de Constant Rebecque. In her letter of 5 February, Alexine informs Jetty that d'Ablaing would join them to the Gazelle-river, where he had at first planned to proceed to Gondokoro.[29]

'A disorderly and rudderless machine'

The new expedition of the Tinnes and Heuglin was to be equipped in a most ambitious way. They intended to reach the source of the Bahr el-Ghazal with the steamship that the Tinnes had already been offered before and at that time was the only one to be found on this part of the Nile. Its owner, Prince Halim, a son of the former Khedive Muhammad Ali, gladly let it this time again to the Tinnes, the price obviously playing a considerable role. It was known that the Tinnes travelled with what Lejean later would describe as 'un luxe royal'. In the purchase of all that was necessary for travelling according to the comfort the Tinnes wished for, Alexine in particular fell victim to a group of 'coquins' [rogues] in a 'blind trustfulness'.[30] Taking into account that the price of hiring this steamer on their White Nile trip had been over 25,000 French francs[31], the prince was not likely to let slip a second occasion for renting his ship to the Tinnes.[32] In his later recounts, published in 1869, Heuglin tells that this small boat was used as a tugboat for a large sailing ship and would show its substantial benefits regarding time saving and the maintenance of the connection with Khartoum.

For such a journey, firm and competent leaders were needed as well as a considerable number of armed men, servants and beasts of burden and various vessels for the transport of the participants and their assisting company, the crew, dromedaries, donkeys and provisions. After having enthusiastically accepted the official invitation by the two women in the beginning of December, Heuglin and Steudner announced that there was not much time left for preparations. Both knew that in the districts that were first to be visited, the summer showers often started in April. As most of the vessels of the commercial enterprises on the White Nile had already left Khartoum or were at least already fitted out for doing so, the recruiting of a competent crew was to become a tricky problem given that there was a shortage of good sailors and soldiers at that time. For the recruitment of the crew, a specialist, called a *wakil*, was employed. He would have full responsibility for all personnel and had command over the entire expedition. Assisted by the *wakil*, Thibaut had taken care of the purchase of provisions for the Tinnes, the delivery of necessary transport vessels, and beasts of mounts and burden. Heuglin and Steudner were offered the possibility of hiring a transport vessel and engaging 8-10 men for surveillance, which enabled them to spend the money that was left for other outfits. Their instruments for mathematical and physical measurements needed readjustments for which Khartoum was not the right place. Heuglin, however, was able to purchase a 'Sekundenuhr', a ship's compass and a 'Glashorizont', and had an Italian in Khartoum adjust his chronometer. Their wardrobe and footwear were repaired as best as possible. From their previous expedition, Steudner had retained his mule and Heuglin a fine horse for hunting, to which he added a mule and eight donkeys. Expecting the Tinnes to supply most of the provisions of the whole undertaking, they confined themselves to buying some ship's biscuit, corn, flour, butter, rice, coffee, tobacco, candles, soap, wine, brandy, and as barter trade they brought such things as copper wire and copper bracelets, fine glass beads, white, blue and coloured cloth and salt.[33]

On New Year's Day 1863, the expedition's flotilla was composed of the steamship, serving as a 'remorqueur' (tugboat), two large *dhahabiyyas* equipped for luxury travels, and three transport vessels or *nuggar*. Both Heuglin and Steudner were quartered on one of the *nuggar*, which was moored nearby their house in order to have it fitted according to their wishes. On the afterdeck, a small wooden hut with a roof of palm leaves was constructed. It offered just enough room for their two *anqarebs* [Sudanese beds made of bamboo, see Catalogue ills. 8, 8a]. Both ends of the hold were almost completely filled with corn, and in its open middle there was place for their mounts and beasts of burden: one horse, two mules and eight donkeys. On the foredeck was the small kitchen. The *ra'is* or captain and helmsman were situated behind their hut. The two other identical but larger ships contained provisions for the two women, some twenty soldiers, four dromedaries, twenty-five donkeys, one horse and the necessary crew. Ten of the total of sixty-five soldiers were embarked on their boat, in addition to six private servants and 'one female slave for the baking of bread'. Both Alexine and Henriette had at their disposal a Turkish officer with ten men infantry, the captain of the steamer and their *dragoman* [interpreter] Contarini, and Anna and Flore, their two Dutch maids, some Arabian clerks and administrators and twenty mercenaries. The entire expedition, amounting to more than 150 people, stood under the command of the *wakil* Wad Khalid, a Berberine who had wandered about the White Nile for many years as a helper and slave.

All victuals were sufficient for five to six months, while the steamer could be sent back from Meshra el-Rek to Khartoum to provide them all with new provisions. As Heuglin explains just before his departure to Petermann: 'Imagine quite a party, twenty six travellers [not all servants and soldiers included], not agreeably settled on these ships though, but one refrains gladly from any comfort, expecting to obtain a foothold on soil never trodden on by Europeans before.'[34]

Equipping this train of persons involved more than two months of work. There was no lack of money – on the contrary. However, as Heuglin states afterwards, the trouble was the lack in gathering practical information about the regions to be visited, the way they would travel and transport materials on land, the knowledge concerning which barter trade was appropriate in the sense of currency and usefulness, and above all the lack of knowledge concerning climatic conditions. Moreover, at the time of departure, several ships appeared to be in bad condition, in particular the *dhahabiyya* of the Tinnes. Though the expenses made for the equipment verged on the incredible, Heuglin and Steudner noticed that much of the most necessary equipment was missing, while a mass of redundant trash was blocking the way on the quay, and the crew with their captains were mainly just lounging around.

In Heuglin's later account of the preparations for the expedition, he argues that things got out of hand because of the incapability of the Tinnes to organise the expedition. He indicated that between the leading characters – Alexine and himself – there was no communication or coordination regarding decisions concerning what was needed during the preparations. Although close cooperation could only have been advantageous to both of them, the expedition lacked a central gearing of activities. The two women as 'administrators' could therefore easily spend their budget on (their) things, unnoticed by Heuglin or anybody else. From their side, the Tinnes were not likely to discuss their preparations. For both Heuglin and Steudner, putting pressure on the Tinnes for a different approach was out of the question, as this would have been counterproductive and could have jeopardised their participation in the trip.

No systematic plan had been drawn up, nor had there been a clear engagement of the native personnel. The provisions and barter trade for the Tinnes had been bought by the *wakil*, who was under the impression that the journey went as far as the Rek-lake at the Bahr el-Ghazal, and possibly from there some days' journey inland.

Looking back on the preparations in his review of 1869, Heuglin would give a rather negative judgment, qualifying them and subsequently also the whole expedition as 'a disorderly and rudderless machine'. However, in a letter to Petermann dated 27 January 1863, he is looking ahead, not knowing what the future of the expedition would be. He only relates how 'we had to spend on the preparations more time than every one of us had calculated'. Much of the delay would be due to forces beyond their control. Despite many exhortations, many indispensable types of equipment were only ready and delivered long after the deadlines agreed upon. The 23rd of January moreover appeared to be an Islamic public holy day on which nothing could be done.[35]

The delays in the preparations and the sense that the wet season was to arrive in due course urged Heuglin to propose to the Tinnes that he would leave Khartoum some days earlier than they did. At this time of the year a steady northern wind would give them a lead. When on the next day the transportation vessel meant for him and Steudner had been prepared for sailing, the pack and riding animals were loaded in, as well as the victuals.

Finally, on the evening of 24 January, after having transferred the rest of the cargo to their ships, Heuglin and Steudner sailed ahead to a *moqrén* [a spit of land], between the White Nile and the Azraq, from which they would set sail southwards the next day, very early in the morning. The Tinnes and Baron d'Ablaing had promised to follow them within the next two days.

CHAPTER 4

To the Bahr el-Ghazal

Ahead to the Gazelle-river

On 25 January at daybreak, Heuglin and Steudner sailed off from the *mo-qrèn* as the lead of the expedition, accompanied by a volley of rifles from other boats moored in the bay. The northern wind was blowing inshore and at the junction of the Blue and White Nile they had to make use of their oars to keep the boat in the middle of the stream. While turning around the land point the sails unfolded and the broad bow of the *nuggar* cleaved the foaming waves of the White Nile.

It was a fresh day and Heuglin relates how brightly the rising sun was shining. He was sitting, dressed in a flannel coat, before his ship's compass looking to the south and thinking of his country in the far north that he had left behind. Somewhat preoccupied about the near future but cheerful at the prospect of fulfilling his long-awaited aim of reaching Central Africa's unknown regions, he saw 'cheerless Khartoum', with its 'filthy mud huts', rapidly vanishing beyond the horizon. A huge ancient acacia tree, 25° southwest from Khartoum on the eastern bank, marked a point known far and wide to all the ships' men as 'the tree'. Cows were slaughtered there and cut into long strips, which were salted and hung in the tackling to dry. Already Heuglin's group had been provided with meat. His ship had to moor there to allow some crew members to embark. To bring the last passengers aboard, his boat had to touch the tree roots which stood partly in the river at high tide.

The vegetation on the shores, in particular the west bank, was growing more and more luxuriant. The next morning at 4 am they passed the village of Wad Shellal scattered about the eastern bank, a vital link in the trade between Sennār and Khartoum and Kordofan. Most of the houses were of the *tukul* type: round straw huts with high tapered roofs, fit for the hot climate. From this point their route proceeded mainly along the current of the western coast of the White Nile, skirting various islands, one of which seemed to Heuglin to be a small Garden of Eden with its yet undisturbed and enchantingly silent nature. As a zoologist, his attention was soon drawn to the rich varieties of water birds abiding in abundance in the nearby woods along the shores. On 27 January, a precarious moment occurred when the ship ran with full sail onto a sandbank. Despite all the efforts of the crew standing to their shoulders in the ice-cold main stream and the yelling of the half-drunk *ra'is* (the captain), they had to wait for the next morning to free the *nuggar*.

With an often changing but mostly favourable wind, the ships were gradually approaching the junction of the White Nile and the river Sobat. This region, once inhabited by the Dinka, was now deserted, as the Abu Rof Arabs from the North had conquered all their land and frequented this area with pirate ships in search of slaves.

At night the roaring of nearby hippopotami was often heard. On the first of February at 3 am (they continued sailing by night), Heuglin moored at the settlement that had been established by the notorious Muhammad Khair in 1857 as a base of operation for his slave trade, being 'a miserable nest of some 150 *tokul*', inhabited by Berberine women in particular. Because he knew that Khair had made a marauding expedition to 'the Keilak, in the inner lands', Heuglin was eager to speak to him about the results. An encounter between the two, however, has not been recorded. He worked on the map of the river while awaiting 'Fräulein Tinne' on her steamer, who was expected, as he states in his notebook, to track the distances between certain points on the river by now. He was, of course, unaware that the latter was still in Khartoum, delayed by some needed repairs to one boat following an act of sabotage. The surveys of distances were actually made not by Alexine but probably by Henriette Tinne, as the schedule of the time the steamer spent on distances from Khartoum up to other stations on the Nile has been quoted from her diary.[1]

At this point they had yet to observe any trace of the train with the *dhahabiyyas* of the Tinnes. After Hillat Kaka, the wind was still favourable and the company was hoping that the Tinnes' steamer would catch up with them before they had reached the junction of the White Nile and the Sobat, entering the White Nile as its affluent from Heuglin's left.

Approaching the junction where the White Nile makes a bend to continue southwards, to their right the 'Lac No' came into sight. Heuglin describes how they entered the *Sudd*, a region of islands with lush vegetation. For him the 'Sunt', as Heuglin names it, was in fact the most beautiful part of the 'Bahr el Abiad' [the White Nile], consisting of vast marshes of floating forest islands, long but narrow strips of land on which mainly *Mimosa nilotica* (a reed or papyrus species) grows. Small canals between the plant decks provided some opportunity for navigation. It was still the dry season when the tide was low. Within a few months the rainy season would bring along drastic changes.

At an increasingly quicker pace than expected, Heuglin and his company advanced on the third of February, landing in the afternoon on the banks of where the people of the Shilluk lived in order to gather wood and find grass for the beasts. To the great annoyance of the crew, the donkeys kept breaking into the ship's storerooms and eating from the wheat or *durra*. During the night they continued to benefit from a fine northerly wind, arriving at 4 am at the junction of the Sobat and the Bahr el-Zeraf (the Giraffe-river). Heuglin noted that if this pace could be maintained during the coming night and morning, by sunset of 4 February they could certainly reach the Gazelle-river. A lack of wind, however, forced them to enter Lake No, the entrance of the river, almost one day later.

After the small lake, the Gazelle-river divided itself into many canals. The weather being calm, no wind facilitated the speed of the sailing boats on the river's main course. Despite their delay, Heuglin writes on 5 February that the Tinne steamer had not yet caught up with them. With a more favourable wind they succeeded on the next day in reaching the principal village of the Nuer people. The Nuer inhabitants were, according to Heuglin's description, 'the marsh birds (*die Sumpfvögel*) of mankind, genuine flamingos, 5 to 6 feet tall, stilt-shaped, ash-powdered all over, able to stand for hours on one leg, the other raised at the knee, while leaning on a lance.' At their peculiar appearance the crew burst out into laughter, which seemed to amuse the Nuer. The women greeted them frequently, raising their arms high in the air while making 'some ungraceful dancing movements', as Heuglin recounts. Probably because of their numerous company, the Nuer looked askance at them. He adds to their description that their *tukuls* (clay-huts with conical roofs), being built of a clay-cylinder, were peculiarly shaped. Because of a nasty species of fly, named 'Baudah' (bauda = mosquito), in these swampy areas these people roll themselves through ash in which they also sleep. When he and Steudner went for an evening walk in the Nuer village, their feet almost immediately sank into the mud. The summer rains that had started here had changed the level of the Gazelle-river considerably. As far as they navigated the river there was no place where one could possibly disembark, which in other years easily could be done during this time of the year, the marshes being dried out. Apart from buffaloes and hippopotami, in these circumstances big game would not dwell near the river.

Both men planned to settle down and await the Tinne party after arriving in Meshra el-Rek. Meanwhile, they continued sailing up the Bahr el-Ghazal, recording its effluents while holding in their hands the sketch of a map that was later to be published as map 6 of Petermann's *Inner-Afrika* edition.

On 7 February, both men left their ship in a small bark to find a place where they could go hunting, in which they did not succeed. Back in the boats they went on looking for one of the entrances on the map of Brun-Rollet of 1855, which was also not found.[2] They did find two large estuaries, one on the western bank named Maya Omar Effendi, and the other on the eastern bank. The first one had been visited several years ago by seven men belonging to a certain Omar Effendi in search of ivory, but all were killed by the Nuer. The story went that the latter estuary should be avoided. Heuglin recounts that a trade vessel had passed them the day before yesterday from the Jur with sailors saying that it was practically impossible to disembark on the Meshra el-Rek: one had to walk for a day through the marsh before coming to firm ground. The small barks, which both men had used to go ashore to hunt, apparently were made by the Dinkas and proved themselves to be rather inefficient. They capsized easily, after which the boat kept floating upside down, and getting in again was impossible, as Heuglin sighs.

At three o'clock on 11 February they found a recently deceased elephant floating in the water where the river broadened, which the crew tried to drag into the ship under whoops of triumph. In the evening this action had still not been successful despite the combined forces of 24 persons dragging the animal as high as possible to take off its tusks, which were estimated to weigh 100 to 150 pounds each. Later Heuglin recorded in his diary that the excising of the tusks took more than 24 hours in total, in particular because they were unable to find a dry spot anywhere in the vicinity to which the colossal animal, which hung alongside the boat, could be drawn. Axes and knives refused to do their work, and only by performing a kind of operation was Heuglin able to sever the rump from the head; the latter then was dragged into the ship to receive further 'treatment'. In the morning of the 13th, they moored at a place where Heuglin wrote a letter to Petermann in which he explains how disappointing it was to still see no smoke of the steamer or a mast of 'our flotilla'. They found themselves in a swamp forest with acacias, tamarinds and other sorts of trees and 10 to 12-feet high cane and grass. They walked daily through the low water and saw white ant hills and pools with beautiful nymph and lotus flowers. Climbing onto a termite hill and looking out over a treeless ground, they perceived in the distance 'hundreds and hundreds of elephants' grazing in the marsh, now and then raising their trunks and letting out yells, 'their backs covered with numerous small birds'. The noise the men made while walking through the marsh meant that hunting was impossible, except the collecting of ornithological rarities, as Heuglin discovered to his joy.

In this stage of their journey, the tone in Heuglin's letter becomes impatient. The bauda mosquito forced them to stay for four to six hours each day in the water, the nights were humid and cool, the afternoons very hot, and the pack animals suffered immensely. Thus, being able to disembark in the Meshra became a matter of utmost urgency. Again he writes that the delay in the arrival of the steamer is totally incomprehensible for him and seriously disturbing. The crew believed that they could be in the Meshra in two days. On the first day they were to sail, they would pass two large river mouths, the second of which would be the Jur.

While navigating, Heuglin established major inaccuracies in one of the maps drawn up by a previous traveller. In his letter to Petermann he asks who had been responsible for picturing a tableland that extended itself near the Nuer settlements on the Bahr el-Ghazal. It could be seen nowhere, he says, even at a five to eight-mile distance from the top of the ship's mast. A footnote by Petermann in *Inner-Afrika* adds to this remark: '*This states that Lejean's evidence was correct. This tableland on our map had been indicated by Petherick.*'

From everything he had seen and read so far about the Gazelle-river, Heuglin regarded it as an extended marsh whose level rises some feet during the rainy season, and with water of its western effluents slowly running into the White Nile. The water content, however, must have been considerably diminished since 1854-55 when this river had been navigated for the first time by Namen Habashi, Petherick's *wakil* and Coptic merchant, who then described it as a broad stream, in some places even being like a lake. He also refers to the Italian Angelo Castelbolognesi who joined Petherick's expedition in 1856-57[3] and left in his account, edited by Lejean in 1862 in *Nouvelles Annales des Voyages* and *le Tour du Monde* (see Catalogue: introduction), his findings about the level of the stream.

At that time, the ivory trade on the Gazelle-river was in the hands of Turkish members of the Sudanese government, after Petherick had closed down his settlement on the Jur in 1863.[4]

On 24 February, finding themselves in the canal between Meshra el-Rek and the Jur-river, for a time they made little progress due to a lack of wind. Here, near the river Homr, they ran into a *dhahabiyya* of Ali Amuri, a merchant who for quite some time had exploited the Gazelle-river by founding various *zaribas*. After having worked their way through a narrow and clogged canal, they paused again – forced by the lack of wind – at a place where Heuglin started to write another letter to his publisher. The sails they spotted on the horizon had to be those of the expedition without doubt. When looking through his telescope, however, Heuglin recognised a Turkish and Italian flag. The boats were those of the merchant Ghattas from Khartoum with on board the Lucchese traveller Carlo Piaggia, 'one of the most renowned elephant hunters of the Sudan'. Piaggia (who had left Khartoum three days after Heuglin and had started his expedition which would eventually bring him as the first European deep into the country of the south-eastern Azande) said he had seen the steamer and the two *dhahabiyyas* of the Tinnes some 18 days ago at the El Eis island on the White Nile. Contarini, the *chargé d'affaires* of the Tinnes, had told Piaggia to give instructions to the captain of their two *nuggar*, which had stayed behind at Lake No, to sail up with the Tinne flotilla. All of them would be there in three or four days.

Heuglin's hopes to sail into the Meshra the next day were to be realised. On the 26th, they finally reached the first goal of their journey. Thanks in particular to the unflagging energy of their crew, to whom had been held out the prospect of some bottles of date brandy, they could wait here for the Tinne barks to arrive. Once he had unpacked on the island in the Meshra, Heuglin would send back on the empty boats all soldiers they no longer required. He writes to Petermann that 'your' map of the Bahr el-Ghazal leaves much to be desired; many inaccuracies could be corrected by him. Petermann remarks in a footnote in this letter in *Inner-Afrika*: 'Unfortunately Mister Von Heuglin did not seem to have had Lejean's map'.

Meshra el-Rek itself appeared to be nothing more than 'a filthy marshy harbour', as Heuglin puts it, and not the huge lake as presented on the map of Petherick and the number 10 of Petermann and Hassenstein. Alongside the shore some 20 trade barks were laying in a small curve, waiting for their crew to return with ivory and slaves from the inner lands. Around the Meshra some vegetable gardens had been laid out, cultivated by sailors.

During the first night of his stay Heuglin had an attack of fever, which was remedied by quinine but caused a tone ringing in his ears the next day. No fortuitous messages had arrived from the interiors. A manager of Franz Binder's trading company, known to be previously working for De Malzac and having shot with his own hands 'more than 50 negroes', had raided the Meshra and stolen 2000 oxes, as Kuchuk Ali Agha did likewise. Heading in a southerly direction would be impossible in these circumstances, even with an escort of over a hundred men. 'But we', Heuglin notes, 'have always intended to turn into the more western route, at least as far as the Niam-Niam'.

Meanwhile he went on a vessel made of two trees with some Dinkas (the principal group of people of this region of the Gazelle-river) to two islands in the main river. Observing still no sails of the Tinne boats on 2 March, they became very worried, as some time ago a ship of a Khartoum trader had been assaulted and stolen. Six persons had been killed.

The departure of the Tinnes
Back in Khartoum the Tinnes and Baron d'Ablaing had planned to follow Heuglin and Steudner on 2 February with the remainder of the flotilla, consisting of the steamer, two *dhahabiyyas*, one passenger boat for each of the Tinnes and two other sailing boats carrying the bulk of the people, the livestock and stores. These boats and the steamer carried some two hundred persons in all, including sixty-five soldiers armed with muskets, also four camels, thirty donkeys and mules, a horse, and the stores: ammunition, ar-

ticles of barter (including a ton and a half of glass beads, eight bars of copper and 12,000 cowry shells) and provisions for ten months' supply.

Just as they were about to embark on 2 February, Alexine's *dhahabiyya* was found to be rapidly filling with water. They discovered that a large hole had been drilled in her side through which the water poured in as she sank ever deeper with the loading of additional cargo. Expecting Alexine's boat to sink within a couple of hours, her cargo was quickly discharged. As this boat had been hired from the Khartoum government, Alexine and Baron d'Ablaing went off to complain to the Mudir. The Mudir, who had returned with them to the scene, had the vessel mended by the sailors and suggested they go for a three-hour trial run. He gave instructions to go no further than a certain tree outside Khartoum called 'Maka Beg' and to anchor there, to see if all remained safe. The leak continued to be as bad as before. On closer enquiry, the captain was obliged to confess that he and the steersman had drilled the hole to prevent them from going on the voyage.

Once she had arrived in Meshra el-Rek, Alexine would tell her niece Jetty about the great irritation she felt about this incident: 'My captain, who apparently did not very much like to leave Khartoum has made of our boat a 'tonneau des Danaïdes'. Henriette writes in her diary:

> There was again fuss, and the captain of Alexine's boat was made
> to owe he and the pilot had made the hole so as not to go on the
> White Nile which he did not like. The hole was again stopped.
> Four experts were sought for, who all engaged to make us safe, but
> we are now to have another Captain and another crew.

Another two days passed before a new crew could be selected for Alexine's *dhahabiyya*. Henriette was able to visit Addy, who had asked to be left behind in Khartoum. She found her sister gathered with several friends singing in the garden of the house they had hired for her. That evening, Henriette was able to make Baron d'Ablaing laugh at the absurdity of the situation they found themselves in. 'By this fine moon Mr. d'Ablaing and I returned home and we laughed at the idea of being in the centre of Africa, *a nous deux* on donkeys, only attended by an old man, he and a little boy with a lantern!! We were no more afraid of lions and tigers or Negroes than on the downs *chez nous*.' [5]

Finally the Tinne train was ready and sailed from Khartoum on 5 February. In a letter, Alexine tells her niece the day before about the expected departure:

Dear Smous, This is finally our last day in Khartoum. We expect to leave this evening as far as at least one can count on leaving in the Sudan, where at the last moment there are always sailors and servants who are missing and who are to be searched for in all the locations (…) of the town; but after all, if it is not this evening we leave, it will be this night (…). Our intention is always to go further than the boats are able on the Bahr el-Ghazal and then to continue on land in the direction South West, when you look at the maps you will see that there is at the South West of the Equator a large space empty of names, it's there we want to go to. Till where we will go, I don't know. There has been a change in our company. Aunt Ady rests, and we have a place for Mr. Heuglin about whom your father asked me for news, isn't that a coincidence? He had, with a Prussian doctor, returned from a voyage in Abyssinia, not knowing anymore what to do, and looking for an opportunity to undertake new expeditions, they wished very much to explore the White Nile and the West, and envied us that much that we offered them to pick them up on our boats and let them take advantage of the guidance of our soldiers what they did accept with pleasure; they left ahead of us eight days ago, with our luggage and our men. What is rather funny as well is that we travel as far as the Bahr el-Ghazal with Mr. d'Ablaing You know, whom we made a rendezvous with in Central Africa, and who had a philippine in Cairo what he should have said on our first meeting – and the other day, a bahoud, a kind of Turkish soldier, studied us; we wanted to answer him, when he said goodbye in Dutch, and we recognized Mr. d'Ablaing; then I remembered and said to him, bonjour philippine – so I did win.He was returning to Europe, but our example carried him away and he had quickly taken a boat and soldiers and will leave at the same time as we. We will split up at the Bahr el-Ghazal, from where he will proceed to Gondokoro. It is peculiar that the first two Dutchmen who have ever been on the Fleuve Blanc are there just at the same time. And Aunt Addy stays here – she who opposed so strongly against Africa and the Sudan and only wanted to see something European, has suddenly changed.

First she wished to go only to Cairo, and all was settled for her departure, when on the last moment her courage left her and she preferred to stay here – So we have found her a home to which she has moved with 2 negresses to serve her and the servant and the donkey and the horse; [unreadable]...Go back, and to behold the vicissitudes of fate, to see Aunt Addy running a home in Khartoum, and speaking by gestures to her black cook – she finds it a bit *akelig* [Dutch for 'nasty'] – now farewell.[6]

It would take almost ten days for the Tinne flotilla to navigate up the White Nile and to proceed to Meshra el-Rek.

The arrival of the Tinnes at Meshra el-Rek

At last on 8 March, Heuglin and Steudner perceived three or four sails that could possibly be those of the Tinnes. The two concluded that the women would arrive in the evening, provided there was a steady wind. Heuglin tells Petermann that he could not set himself to work in the past few days; the hunting in the marshes and the sleepless nights caused by bauda mosquitos, against which there was no repellent or remedy, caused severe fevers, which even large doses of quinine could not take away. Steudner was also suffering. He did not achieve more than collecting some nice zoological specimens, among which was a very peculiar fish. Finally on 10 March, Heuglin perceived the sails coming nearer and entering the Meshra. This time the boats, which were approaching very slowly because there was hardly any wind, *had* to be those of the rest of the expedition. At 1 pm both men, feverish and weak, crawled into a small bark and began to row through the narrow canal towards the newcomers. After having rowed for almost two hours they reached the first ship. It was their *nuggar* which had stayed behind and had been asked by Contarini to join the others on their way to Meshra el-Rek. It was towing the *dhahabiyya* of Alexine Tinne, followed by those of d'Ablaing and Henriette.[7] Then there came another *nuggar* which was surprisingly towing the steamer, whose paddles had been taken off. This second *nuggar* dragged the steamer which some 50 men were pulling on with ropes and pushing the vessel on with poles. The reason for their journey taking twice the amount of time of a sailing boat was, as Heuglin tells afterwards, not only sabotage in Khartoum but also their progress through the Bahr el-Ghazal which had been exceedingly slow on account all kinds of obstacles they had to overcome and also some daily excursions the two women made during the journey, wanting to enjoy themselves in 'the beautiful scenery'.[8]

The forests of *ambatch* (marsh trees with yellow flowers), which completely blocked up the channels, eliminated the use of the steamer which prompted Alexine to decide to strip it of its paddles and to let it be towed by one of their sailing boats. As this was virtually impossible because of its weight, it was more pushed than pulled. But, as she argued in her letter of 26 March referring to this decision:

> In this country one only needs a will, particularly there where the daughter of the Sultan finds herself on her fire ship.

Besides that, d'Ablaing once tried to shoot a lion which was standing near the water, in which he failed. An identical story was told as Heuglin had regarding 'his elephant': they also ran into a huge dead elephant, regarded by the boatmen as a prize of the highest order, the tusks being worth about £25. Floating in the water, extraction of the tusks was very difficult, as there was no spot of dry land to drag it upon. They also managed to sever the head from the carcass after 24 hours.

At the moment the whole company was putting into the port of Meshra el-Rek, the soldiers on all their ships greeted the company with 'a hellish gun-fire' out of 'perhaps 300 muskets' while on the land heavier guns operated. The whole crew received 'half of the monthly *Baghschisch* (bakhshish = tip)', as well as 150 bottles of brandy, which on the same evening were emptied till the last drop.

The next day the beasts of burden were disembarked and brought to a cattle park of the Dinkas. Meanwhile both women stayed on their boats. It was quickly decided to proceed from here to the Kosanga mountains or possibly to the Azande and to stay there during the rainy season (the *harif*). Now, however, they learned from the tradesmen in this place that most of the barter articles would be of no use here and the support of the large group of soldiers and servants was not customary and thus useless. The quantity of pack animals was not sufficient, only just enough to carry the private luggage of the Tinnes. The *wakil* tried to contact the agents of the present tradesmen to obtain carriers through their mediation. At first the men were promised; soon, however, it became evident that the slave traders were not in favour of complying with this request, and even were opposed to it. In addition, the *wakil*, who had been engaged in slave trading on their route, continuing just after his arrival in the Meshra, appeared to have lost his desire to accompany the expedition. Noting this down, Heuglin adds that his desire to visit 'their land' met all possible difficulties just because in these regions the Khartoum traders were shamelessly creating havoc.

While waiting for solutions to enable them to proceed with the expedition, days passed. They were well aware of the fact that the rainy season would set in ultimately in May (earlier in the mountains) and that the water would rise in April and would soon be impassable for the caravans, and finally that it would be impossible to keep pack animals alive for more than some months in the lowlands before them.

Then d'Ablaing proposed to seize the opportunity to go back to Khartoum with the steamer in order to purchase the missing materials and to return as quickly as possible. Heuglin, expecting him to leave within eight days and to be back in five weeks' time, hoped d'Ablaing would be able to bring back some money for him from the city. He needed some 1000 piasters of glass beads, quite a lot of copper bars and probably some pack animals. When they did not reach Lake Chad (only once is this destiny mentioned by him), he had to dispose of the means to arrange an expedition on his own at a certain moment. 'One has here to make long-range plans; although much could intervene with his plans: qui vivra – verra!'.[9]

After careful consideration Heuglin proposed that the Tinnes – provided they still wanted to undertake a long voyage to enter the unknown interiors – accompany Steudner and himself to the Kosanga mountains only carrying light luggage, not slowed down by this kind of delay. Keeping a pace that would not put too great a strain upon them, one would easily be able to reach the mountains in ten to twelve days and to arrange some appropriate housing there for the rainy season, to hire carriers, beasts of burden and a group of soldiers, sending back more of them to the Meshra, where in the meantime d'Ablaing had returned with all the necessary goods. Once beyond the regions of slave trade, they could in all probability rely on a friendly reception of the inhabitants, and have the prospect of being able to nourish the crew and animals. After having presented his plan, he recounts:

Fräulein Tinne, who has to be considered as the inventor (*Urheberin*) of this total enterprise, seemed not to be averse to this plan; Madame Tinne though declared that she was not willing by any means to curtail herself of the usual comfort she preferred while travelling, having spent such enormous sums of money on this expedition.[10]

The decision was a determined one and appeared to be decisive for Alexine as well. Being a member of the expedition – perhaps having learned from his former experiences during the Abyssinian journey, when the party broke up due to discord – and also largely dependent upon the Tinnes, Heuglin then took the opportunity to make a counterproposal, trying to execute his plan. What if Steudner and he would leave this place to explore the region with their servants and some of the soldiers, who would only bring inconveniences to the two women, and as much luggage as the pack animals could carry? Where possible, they would try to hire porters and to establish housing, to which they could bring their belongings. Then they would send back the animals and most of the crew to the Meshra. His proposal was accepted and immediately effectuated, as every day of lingering on this spot would bring more reverses and complications. Heuglin would cross over to Lau, a place on the mainland which even for Dinka canoes was not approachable. Contarini, taken along from Khartoum as a dragoman, would accompany them for all communication into the Dinka and Dōr languages.

Due to laborious preparations, it took another two days before they could bid farewell to each other and leave on the 23rd at 10 am. The Tinnes stayed on their *dhahabiyyas* moored at a small island named Kyt. They spent the days there walking Alexine's dogs and sojourning in the gardens. After Heuglin and Steudner had left and deliberations about how to proceed had ceased, the Tinnes' stay in Meshra seemed just a quiet period of waiting for them all to return. Alexine found time to write to her family, in particular a lengthy letter to her niece Jetty dated the 26th, which looked back on the trip she made through the marshes of the Gazelle-river:

> And now we are…Yes, oh…where are we? In the most particular place (…) where one arrives following a route even more particular. After having followed the Ghazal for 3 to 4 days (…) it appears to stop: one arrives before brushwood and weeds (…) but it is only a marsh and there is a small passage which is like our smaller

slooten [Dutch for ditches] as the one which runs alongside your garden at Meerdervoort (…) the steamer has been sent for again, dragged by a sailing boat (…) Mr. Heuglin and the Doctor waited for us for ten days – we count on disembarking and leaving as soon as possible; but despite all our efforts we have not been able to procure porters – so here are our plans, Mr. Heuglin, our soldiers, and our donkeys loaded with what they could carry have gone for 8 or 10 days from here looking for porters and return as soon as they find these, and then we are at a place which combines the conditions wanted for passing the rainy season which takes 4 to 5 months. Now, as we arrived here, we noticed we were lacking a mass of things (…) Mr. d´Ablaing in the meantime will go back in the steamer to Khartoum in order to get all what we want (…) and then will join us to the interior. The equipment of such a voyage is something incredible – if you imagine we have to take along provisions for ten months – 3000 pounds of trinkets, (…) 800 bars of copper, 12000 cowry-shells and salt for ten months and for more than 150 people, that is incredible – we will see to another 40 soldiers which will bring us on 100 – Mr. d'Ablaing takes 25 of them including our servants, we will have hundred fifty armed men – one says that is sufficient. Adieu then, perhaps for a longer period (…).[11]

She seems to be satisfied that d'Ablaing had decided to join them.

The steamship was expected to be of great help for collecting and transporting victuals. One did not however give it a second thought that travelling back and forth from the Bahr el-Ghazal and Khartoum would take some months each way, which would cause substantial problems, as Heuglin recounts in 1869.[12]

When Heuglin and Steudner said good-bye to the others on 23 March, d'Ablaing had not yet left but would return to Khartoum within the coming days.

CHAPTER 5

Beyond the Bahr el-Ghazal

Back and forth to Wau and Meshra

In their aim of procuring a sufficient number of pack animals, Heuglin and Steudner did not succeed; yet they proceeded on 23 March to Wau and the Kosanga mountains, hoping to hire the necessary number of porters and go back to the Meshra in order to move the whole Tinne expedition forward to Wau. While crossing over the river Rek and a smaller one, their boat suddenly could not go further, as it had become entangled by marsh plants. Holding the guns high in their right hands both men got out and waded through water and reed, following a route with a path which was covered with four to five feet of water. After a while Heuglin felt dizzy and had to vomit.[1] Two and a half hours later they arrived in the village of Lau and stayed there overnight. After having resumed their journey, the road led them in a south-westerly direction where Petherick had established his *zariba*. This place they left for what it was; Petherick himself was at that moment far up the White Nile where he was supposed to meet Speke and Grant. His *zariba* at the Jur-river had already been abandoned.

The scenery gradually changed from marshes to treeless plains and to forest areas where the Jur people lived in small fenced courtyards, casting iron from which they fabricated iron objects, which were becoming renowned for their quality. After eight full days' march, they paused on the 1st of April at a place where one of their guides had acquaintances. Some of their group had remained far behind and there were already some cases of disease. The next day the river Jur was crossed. They walked on through a forest and in five hours reached a village belonging to the people of Wau. After the Fertit or Wau-river they made an encampment at a source where women and children were dwelling; all men had been engaged by Biselli, the owner of the nearby *zariba*, in a war against the neighbouring Dōr, who had attacked another *zariba*. Heuglin explains in a letter to Petermann that these slave dealers, after having settled themselves, demanded substantial compulsory contributions from the people who were made their subjects. This Jur land was so saturated with the usual barter goods – glass beads and copper bracelets – that the daily support of the servants and soldiers demanded at least twice the cost of those in Khartoum. Even enormous payments in copper made it hardly possible to procure porters from the population. Most of the male population were the 'property' of the traders and avoided people who were travelling.

On 8 April, they finally arrived at Wau where Heuglin, who had been consistently suffering from fever for several days, wrote his next letter to Petermann, dedicated to his mission as a scientist. Both men had fallen seriously ill and could not undertake longer journeys. He tells about his hope of receiving from the trader Biselli, to whom upon his arrival he had directly made his request, at least 50 to 60 porters and to return to the Meshra to take up the Tinnes. Our 'expedition machine may be getting too extended and unmanageable, but I hope to reduce it considerably after the rainy season'. He then expatiates on zoological rarities he had seen around him. In order to reach the Kosanga mountains they had to march for 18 hours. There, however, the population had not been able to sow anything this year for fear of the slave traders. Nourishing 150 men and 50 pack animals would probably be impossible. 'That would be seriously bad', he adds. It looked bad for their nourishment as well. They had run out of liquors, bread had become inedible, since there departure there was no butter, and they lived on rice, the results of some hunting, ate *durra* dough and *belilah* (boiled *durra*) and beans, and all that 'just with some salt'. He apologises to Petermann for not having finished his astronomical determinations of places, but he could make up for it in 'the Kosanga'. He would be glad to be back from the Meshra with the whole company, having built rain-proof huts and entrenchements around the camp, but that would take certainly another three to four weeks. And when would Baron d'Ablaing have purchased their new provisions? No, 'the outlook was not brilliant', he concludes. More patience than usual was needed in the presence of the Berberine soldiers and servants, who were already kicking up a row and threatening to pillage the local people after the lack of food for only one day.

On 10 April, he makes a note in his diary about the unexpectedly quick death of 'poor Steudner'. It was on this evening that they had dug his last resting place under a group of trees not far from the river; a grave as deep as possible, safe from floods. Heuglin had the body sewn in a large Abyssinian shawl, and on the grave's floor a hollow was made and filled with foliage. After the entombment the space was covered with wood and bark, on which again much foliage, then earth was laid. Again 'a restless wanderer and researcher of Africa unfortunately did become an early target, while not having been able to pick the fruits of his labour', he states. It was only after his return in Meshra that Heuglin announced Steudner's death in an official correspondence to Petermann. All that Steudner had possessed would be sent to Thibaut in Khartoum by Heuglin, as soon as possible. Fortunately his collections from Abyssinia and Kordofan had been dispatched by Hansal from Khartoum to Germany before the present journey. The rest of his belongings were listed that evening with the servants, the *wakil* and a clerk. Some items would be given to the servants, except for his golden watch and seal ring, which would be handed over to Thibaut. Because his private servants had been paid three months in advance they would fall to Heuglin.

In addition to the account in *Inner-Afrika*, Petermann, possibly thinking it necessary for reasons of providing his public with all the facts of the case, took up a letter written by Heuglin to Heinrich Barth, the German North Africa explorer, containing more details concerning Steudner's death. One of these refers to particularities that will be encountered in Henriette Tinne's death occurring later during the expedition. Steudner had already had some attacks of fever on the island of Rek, which recurred, although in a weak grade, during their marches and in the first days of their stay in Wau. After an attack in the afternoon of 6 April, the patient took in a strong dose of a liquid with *ipecac*, which made him vomit as expected, immediately followed by the swallowing of some 30 grams of quinine in citric acid. During the night his vomiting continued, accompanied by severe diarroehea and at 7 o'clock, though weakened, it seemed he was recovering. At 8 o'clock in the evening they even had a good time together until midnight. When Heuglin rose the next morning before dawn to go for a hunt, Steudner seemed to be still sleeping quietly. On his return he found him still like that, rather quietly breathing, his pulse weak and his face showing a markedly yellow colour. The situation remained the same throughout the day, the night and the following morning, the patient not uttering a word. His breathing stayed quite weak, and, without showing any symptom of pain, he passed away, almost imperceptibly.

Several members of the Bongo, subjects of the Dōr people, had visited him on 11 April. Heuglin describes them as 'a fine, somewhat blended, strong kind of people, darkblack coloured, no negroe though'. With their 'muscular arms, small hands, strong calfs, poorly developed heels and an open, full, more semitic face, the Bongo presented themselves in a favourable way, compared to their neighbours, Dinka and Jur'. The men wore an apron of blue cloth, their upper lip was often pierced and interlaced with rings of copper wire. They carried lances and *trombash* (sickle-shaped knife), one of them had a nicely worked out club and everyone had smoking equipment, a pipe, a small fire tong and other implements. Glass beads were of no interest to them; barn stone chorals and copper arm rings as well as fabrics pleased them more.

In the afternoon came the first vehement hurricanes announcing the arrival of thunderstorms with rain and the approaching season of tropical rainfall which urged them to search for permanent quarters.[2]

On 14 April, Biselli himself came to visit Heuglin, who was surprised to learn that it would take only two to three hours to his *zariba*, though he was told that it would take at least one day to go there and return. As Heuglin was suffering from an attack of fever, however, he was not able to negotiate with him about anything. Biselli gave him some flour, which his stomach could better digest than the sour raw *durra* corn, and two large pans with *merissa*, a kind of beer, and some goats. 'He was known as avaricious, untrustworthy, tattling, although he had the appearance of an honest and honourable chap. He complained to him about bad times, bad business, fierce competition, and about the measurements taken by the government, taxing the personnel and soldiers and in particular about Ali Abu Muri, his neighbour in the *zariba* next to his, who had no discipline among his crew.[3] Finally he promised to deliver a number of porters, not by far the amount the ladies would need though.'[4]

Since Steudner's death, Heuglin's task of collecting specimens was progressing only slowly, due to his weakened condition. Working in the sunshine caused attacks of fever after a while, against which he could only take citric acid. Taking quinine and salicylic acid made him unwell in his head; moreover he was running out of his supply. By sending 20 soldiers to the Dōr, he hoped for corn to use on their way back to Meshra. Already on the 16th they came back, not having proceeded further than the *zariba* of Ali

Amuri, whose *wakil* had offered to shelter luggage, lodge the sick people within Heuglin's group and to sell him as much corn as he wanted for a reasonable price. He also would send some 300 pack animals to Meshra within six days. Heuglin would continue on horseback to Amuri's place, passing by Biselli to inform him about the proceedings. He had been away from the Tinnes now for 22 days and they did not know about his where-abouts.

The soldiers had told him how the Homr and Baggara people, the bravest and most efficient elephant hunters, did their work. Two of them would approach the animals holding their long lances with razor-sharp points while a third one distracted the animals. One thrust in the entrails was enough to kill the animal on the spot. What a difference compared to 'our' hunting, writes Heuglin, in which rifles often failed to kill the beasts instantly. He did not like this kind of game though, despite the fact that there was a shortage of meat. After his cook had hammered on and rolled the meat, cooked it for six hours and roasted it, it was still too tough and dry for his teeth, and the fat was distasteful. It was palatable though if it had been dried for a long time, pounded in mortars and cooked with hibiscus into *melaha*.

He now continued with his ornithological findings, which would be very valuable, and he would take over Steudner's work by collecting botanical specimens. On the 17th, he found himself in Ali Amuri's *zariba* in the place Bongo in the land of the Dōr, having left 'cheerless Wau' and the land of the Jur people. The Bahr Fertit or Wau-river, which designated the border between the Jur and Dōr, lay behind them and they were proceeding in a cheerful state of mind.

In his letter to Petermann written from the *zariba* of Ali Amuri at Bongo on 17 April, he dwells on the vegetation, in particular the species of mimosa and tamarind trees, and describes the difference between the shapes of the Dōr and Jur houses (the first being more spacious and cleaner and having a dome-shaped roof). Heuglin also gives attention to the appearance, decorations and other ethnographic characteristics of the people of these regions. Biselli had shown before in his *zariba* some of his Dōr female slaves, who had paintings of red ferruginous earth mixed with oil ('iron-ochre') on their bodies, and were all wearing a cylinder-shaped piece of wood through their upper lip, which had also small brass ringlets, while others had them through their ear rims. On their hips the Dōr girls wore girdles of less than a hand's breadth, often beautifully braided from plant fibres; in its front and backside a fresh green many-leaved twig was stuck, functioning as an apron. Most of the Dōr, living in the northern part of this land, were missing their four middle teeth, but not the Fertit people, who had their cutting teeth filed into points. The Dōr language differed completely from that of the Dinka and Shilluk and also from the Dar Fertit. The Fertit lived to the west of the 'Niam-Niam'. The Dōr and Jur did not eat with their hands as the Arabs did, but served themselves by using large *conchylia* (shells) as spoons.[5]

Later, in his book of 1869, he would provide some additional details regarding the utensils belonging to the Dōr and Jur cultures (see Catalogue, Introduction). Besides their agriculture and iron production, many Dōr worked on the burning of ceramics such as pipe-heads, smaller and larger pottery and kitchen utensils, often finely decorated with interlaces of straw and twigs. All Dōr were hunters, using lances, shields, clubs and large bows with iron-pointed arrows. In each hut, large nets could be seen, meant for catching put up game. With their neighbours, the 'Fertit' (people living in Dar Fertit) and Azande, the Dōr exchanged weapons, in particular dagger knifes, short sickle-shaped sabres with the cutting edge on the underside, and the *trombash* and small bows and arrows that were carried by the Kresh people. The iron points of these items were finely and gracefully made, with numerous barbed hooks. A Kresh often carried with him some hundred arrows in a bag-like leathern quiver, to be used not only as a weapon but at the same time as barter objects (see Catalogue illustrations 59 and 59a-d). The Jur and Dōr would sell their ironware with profit to the traders in the Meshra, who in turn sold their merchandise to the Shilluk, Dinka and Baggara and further east, on the river Sobat. The costs of living for the expedition group was in the vicinity of Amuri's *zariba* far lower than during their stay at the Jur, where they had to spend more than two loads of the finest glass beads and several dozens of heavyweight copper bracelets and cast metal for 50 people in 14 days for only the most necessary provisions.[6]

On 19 April, he remarks that Ali Amuri's men had gathered more than 400 loads of ivory – more than any trade company had done so far that year. Because battles were raging between 'rebels' and the united armies of the three *zariba* holders – Biselli, Ali Amuri and Kuchuk Ali Agha – Heuglin was forced to hold his group together for six to eight days. In his next letter, he sent a message to Dr. Hartlaub in Bremen announcing his ornithological findings. Leaving Bongo on the 24th, the group arrived after a seven-day march in Meshra el-Rek, thanks to the decision to leave 11 sick soldiers and servants behind and having hardly any luggage. On his way, Heuglin became witness to the atrocities committed by Kuchuk Ali Agha's men who killed five men and 14 women and children because they resisted the slave raid. Afterwards their village was devastated. Some witnesses were found and he took down a precise note of their story, which he planned to hand over to the French consul (Thibaut) once he was back in Khartoum in order for it to be presented to the Sudanese government. Seeing the Meshra already across the river in the afternoon of the 30th, he could not go any further, as he was extremely weakened after severe attacks of fever. The next morning he was taken over the river to the group of the Tinnes. Though he noticed Henriette was very ill, she apparently had been worse and would be now on her way to recovery. They all hoped that they should now be able to proceed with the expedition within four to five days. The 120 porters for the journey to Bongo and Kosanga they found in the coming days, exceeding their highest expectations. But the deal did cost the 'horrible sum of 1000 Thaler', according to Heuglin's notes.

Speke's warning

During Heuglin's absence, the Tinnes had received a letter from Addy who described having witnessed the arrival of Speke and Grant in Khartoum on 30 March. Addy also sent a similar message to Jules van Capellen in The Hague. 'I have still one moment before the post will leave, also to send you some lines to say that the source of the Nile has been discovered… I just have met Captain Speke who arrived straight from Lake Victoria (…)'.[7]

The news that 'the Nile was settled' had reached London one day ahead of the arrival of both explorers in Khartoum, resulting in a reception in their honour upon their arrival, arranged by a representative of Musha Pasha. Addy, who had attended the festivities, noticed that she could be useful to both Englishmen who, as she remarks, spoke neither Arabic nor French.

Addy had chosen not to join the expedition herself; her sojourn in Khartoum, however, had soon become an ordeal for her. In her letters to members of the family in The Hague she complained of 'being tired of vulgar people and savages.' She had hoped to travel back to Cairo but had not felt strong enough to make the journey. In the same letter of 22 February to her brother Jules, she expressed her feelings about her stay in Khartoum:

> Ít is nothing but a mud-hole for frogs. Among the 4,000 inhabitants there are only three women that can speak French: the Consul's daughter, a half-educated child of a Negress, the daughter of a Cairo tailor married to a slave merchant, and her mother-in-law who looks, and perhaps was, an actress. But such as they are very kind and willing to do anything for me, but I am very tired of vulgar people and savages.

That the house Henriette had found for her before they left was deprived of any comfort, having no windows in order to protect her from the omnipresent Khartoum dust, only strengthened her sincere hopes that Henriette and Alexine would return soon.

In the letter she also states her opinion regarding the whole expedition, and refers to the leading and financial role in the expedition Alexine apparently fulfilled:

> Alexine said she meant to go as far as possible to the south-west, and said she hoped to arrive opposite of the land of Fernando Po, but this as well as her intention of going as far as the Cape of Good Hope are all vain boasting which she does to astonish people, and many tell me they surely will come back here in a couple of months as then the rainy season will begin, and they will be glad to come away. Anyway, time will tell what they will do. It is a great pity Alexine has not more reasonable tastes and that she threw away her money in such a ridiculous and useless way, and when there are so many beautiful countries to see she has brought us into this horrid place.[8]

Addy's ordeal during her stay in Khartoum was considerably lessened for a couple of days by the presence of Speke and Grant, to whom she could be useful because there was no one else in the city who could speak English. Inevitably, the subject of her conversation with the explorers was the expedition of the Tinnes who had left Khartoum almost two months ago. After having explained the plans of Alexine as described above, Addy learned that Speke confirmed her opinion that this expedition was a kind of headstrong enterprise. He had been strongly sceptical about the outcome, in particular regarding the effects of the climate which were not to be underestimated. She then seized the opportunity to ask Speke for his opinion on the Bahr el-Ghazal expedition in a letter adressed to her, which she would forward to Henriette and Alexine by the steamer which went between Meshra and Khartoum. Accompanying her letter to Henriette which notified her about her meeting with both explorers, there was another epistle representing a negative travel advice by John Hanning Speke.

In his letter, Speke leaves no doubt at all about the eventual fatal outcome of the expedition:

> Khartoum 11th April 1863, My dear Baroness, As you have shown so much anxiety with regard to your party on the Bahr-al-Ghazal, and have condescended to ask my advice respecting the feasibility of their being able to accomplish a journey which would tend either to scientific or even pleasurable results, I must frankly confess I can see no possibility of either or the other ending satisfactorily, knowing full well the nature of the African climate. I would never dare travel with more than one companion and should even then be careful in my selection of one whom I thought constitutionally fitted to undertake a harassing march.
> With regard to pleasure, sight seeing, and so forth, there is nothing to see anywhere near the Bahr-al-Ghazal of such interests as exists in the region of Gondokoro; indeed the beauties of Central Africa are concentrated within 4 degrees on either side of the Equator where rain is continuous throughout the year. If a Scientific Expedition was the object at issue, every sacrifice, even life, must be risked for its accomplishment. Then porters should be engaged to carry all property – there is no trust in animals – and bartering stores taken in sufficient quantity to last two years at least, for there is nothing of any material importance in a geographical point of view to be gained until a march of five hundred miles has been made South by West from the Bahr-al-Ghazal. At that distance the watershed between the White Nile and the Congo may reasonably be expected to be found, and should anybody be fortunate enough to discover the source of the Congo the greatest credit would be given for having unlaid the last feature of interest in Africa.

I sincerely hope your party may be <u>the means</u> of discovering the source of the Congo. One man or two might do it, more could not, and if they attempted it I would not be answerable for the lives of any.

Pray excuse the abruptness of my style in writing, but what I have said I mean, and I should be sorry to see any ladies attempt an exploring journey when failure would inevitably be the result, not from want of luck (…), but the fearful effects of African climate, which cannot be overestimated. Believe me, Yours ever truly, J.H. Speke.[9]

Although he had not uttered a word in his letter to Addy about Theodor von Heuglin, Speke knew the Tinnes were accompanied by an accomplished and experienced Africa explorer who was capable, in theory, of accompanying the two women and bringing them safely back home. Speke would make up for this omission in a personal letter to Heuglin (see Chapter 6). At almost the same time, he wrote his separate letter to Heuglin proposing that he would proceed on his own southwards. This above-mentioned letter must have been ordered by Addy and drawn up as an urgent message by an authority on this kind of travel, and a demand to Alexine and her mother to return as soon as possible.

Crossing over the Rek

After his return on 30 April from Wau, Heuglin brought the news of Steudner's death. The Tinnes themselves had experienced nothing special; 'only Madame Tinne had suffered several weeks from some disease, but had recovered already.'[10] Ali Amuri had entered the encampment trying to negotiate with the Tinnes; being the only one to offer his services, he was asking 'fabulous prices'.

On 4 May John Petherick unexpectedly appeared on the stage. After having failed to reach the two explorers, Petherick descended the Nile again and was on his way back to Khartoum when he reached the entrance of the Gazelle-river at noon on 24 April and anchored there. It had been a dreadful journey up the White Nile during which he had lost almost all of his luggage, provisions and barter trade worth £3000.

It was his intention to proceed afterwards to port Rek, near the island of Kyt, where he hoped to meet his men in the *zariba* among the Jur; he also felt he could be 'of some service to the adventurous Dutch ladies who were travelling in these parts.'[11]

Petherick relates how on the 5th, 'Baron von Heuglin paid us an early visit':

> At noon we embarked (…) to visit the ladies who were at the *mishra* or port. This was reached in about an hour; so winding was the channel and choked with the ambage and rushes that the progress was from necessity slow. Warmly were we welcomed by the beautiful Miss Tinné, who introduced us to her mother, truly a noble dame. With tact and delicacy the ladies gleaned from me that I was ignorant of our having been mourned for as dead. Though Mr. Baker mentioned there were vague reports to that effect, he had treated them lightly; but now Madame Tinné showed extracts from newspapers asserting that we were no more. Oh, how I wept! well knowing the pain such tidings must have inflicted upon those who loved us.

Besides a newspaper bringing the news of both their deaths, Alexine also showed (or handed over to) the Pethericks some photographs she had taken at Gondokoro, including the one portraying the missionaries.[12]

In his account to Petermann, Heuglin does not give a precise indication of the awkward position in which Petherick found himself at that moment. Everyone believed Petherick to be far up the White Nile where he was supposed to meet Speke and Grant, the glorious discoverers of the source of the Nile. His departure from Khartoum to Gondokoro, where he should have met the two travellers, had been dramatically delayed by a late departure and heavy rains and southerly winds. He just succeeded in reaching the Cic regions, where he disembarked and tried to proceed on land. Struggling with extreme difficulties and dangers, he finally came to the Yei-river and arrived at Gondokoro in March, where the two discoverers, coming from the region of Unyoro in the south above Lake Tanganyika, had just left and were descending the Nile towards the north. Soon it became clear that Petherick had fallen victim to his own self-interest. As a British vice consul and also a trader on the White Nile, he tried, under cover of his mission to bring relief to Speke and Grant, to obtain facilities for the import of a large quantity of arms and ammunition for their defence when proceeding upwards, as there were many turbulent and warlike tribes in the countries bordering the White Nile. The total of his demand was cut drastically by the British Foreign Secretary. The man who was at Gondokoro on 15 February 1863 to welcome the two intrepid explorers out of the blue was Samuel Baker. He had navigated upriver with his wife, driven by the instinct that Petherick's trading interests might prevent his being on the spot at Gondokoro on the momentous day. After Speke and Grant told Baker's version of what had happened on the way up to Gondokoro, Petherick was immediately dismissed as a consul because he had not been able to present himself as he was expected to do. An additional cause of his undoing, however, was the slave trade of which he had been accused. Although he denied this, he only later was able to free himself from this accusation and purify his name.

The main reason for his delay in meeting Speke and Grant, as he must have told Heuglin on 4 May, was the refusal of the Foreign Secretary to fulfill his demand for support in order to accomplish his mission to Gondokoro. Petherick's version of the story was copied right away by Heuglin in his letter to Petermann in 1863 and was maintained in his book of 1869. His sympathy for Petherick was not affected by the fact that he had brought himself into an embarrassing position as a trader-consul. Doing anything in his power to ward off the accusations of slavery towards Petherick, he composed a letter with a declaration of the latter's innocence in Khartoum in May 1864, after Joseph Natterer, Martin Hansal and Georges Thibaut had done likewise.[13]

In the morning of 8 May, a large part of the luggage of the Tinnes was sent to Dambo in the interior. They were waiting for porters from Rek, who would arrive the next morning, after which they could eventually move forward. Heuglin comforted himself with the hope that the time he had lost – once installed in their 'rainquarter' – would be used to his advantage, being able to dedicate himself to his research undisturbed. Petherick had offered the Tinnes his caoutchouc ship, a very practical vessel in the circumstances that could easily carry four to six people together with some light luggage. It could be inflated by means of a pair of bellows in a short time and seemed to be solid and with little draught.

The next day Heuglin noted that the rest of the porters had not yet arrived; most of the 'patients' were recovering, however, and the message came that the steamer from Khartoum was approaching Meshra el-Rek and would be there perhaps that very night. He includes in this letter an ornithological survey consisting of a list of new bird species spotted between the rivers Jur and Kosanga, meant for Dr. Hartlaub in Bremen, and concludes with the hope of finally receiving some news from Petermann, promising to write more within a few days. During the night of the 8th, there was a terrible storm; the next day Heuglin fell ill.

'Little pleasant visits' were exchanged daily between the Tinnes at Rek and the Pethericks. They were impatiently expecting the return of the steamer and a *dahabiyah* from Khartoum. Finally on the 15th, d'Ablaing returned from Khartoum and took care of Heuglin. Among the letters from Europe, he also handed over the letter from Speke about Heuglin's mission to Central Africa, which, as we will see in the next chapter, he was to answer (in French) only some months later during his stay at Bongo.

Petherick recounts:

> This evening they arrived. Baron d'Ablaing informed us about the death of H.H. Said Pasha. Our men from a station in the interior at the Djour joined us yesterday, bringing with them ivory. On the 17th we bade adieu to the ladies, who disembarked preparatory to their start for the interior, which was attempted early the following morning. Like others in this land, the greatest difficulty was experienced by them in getting porters to carry their loads: it was arranged that those who had brought in our ivory were to assist; but even with this addition there were no porters to remove the baggage of Baron d'Ablaing.

On the night of 17 May, there was a fearful storm and rain again. 'We were full of anxiety on account of the ladies. At dawn I received a letter from Madame Tinné: they had suffered much, but would proceed.' Petherick started to see if he could be of assistance in any way, and remained until they left. 'Madame Tinné was carried in a chair neatly constructed; Heuglin was too ill to be moved, and the Baron d'Ablaing awaited porters.' During the next few days, Petherick attended to Heuglin, who continued to be seriously ill. He writes:

> The Baron d'Ablaing was likewise unremitting in his kindnesses to the sufferer; but the news received from the ladies last evening

was of a nature so alarming, that he was compelled to advance, though still without porters, hoping to render assistance. Grain was scarce with the party, and the soldiers mutinied. Miss Tinné, always heroic, made them lay down their arms; but the excitement, fatigue, and exposure to rain had induced fever, and she was prostrated. But very little progress had been made by the fair travellers, so, in all probability, the Baron would quickly rejoin his countrywomen.[14]

Heuglin hoped they would be able to leave the place soon. Petherick assured him that the Bahr el-Ghazal had changed in appearance since he was there eight years before. Back then he could sail for days without seeing any land, and the Meshra was an immense lake; the tide now was at an all-time low and was still dropping.

CHAPTER 6

The reversal of fortune

A forced stay at 'Biselli's'

Shortly before his transfer from the lake at Meshra el-Rek to the mainland on the evening of 4 June, Heuglin writes to Petermann: 'I am still at the Lake Req and have since then lived through quite difficult days. My illness had increased in two days time to such an extent, that I had given up all hope of recovery. Now thank God it goes better.' Besides dysentery he suffered from scurvy and a precarious swelling of his legs; thanks to Petherick's attendance, however, a change for the better had set in and his courage for new enterprises had revived. It was useless to return. Here as well, there had been heavy rainfall. 'I know very well what I am doing… *Es muss sein.*'

On 15 May, additional supplies had come from Khartoum to Meshra. Henriette also bought things she needed out of Petherick's stock, including his rubber boat.[1] The boat from Khartoum also brought articles dispatched by Speke for Heuglin: a letter and a quantity of medicine and two camp beds. In his letter Speke argued that the last issue to be solved in the discovery of Africa was the source of the river Congo and he could imagine Heuglin as the only well-known European traveller there, while working his way from Lake Rek downwards, to be able to accomplish this mission in a glorious manner. In his answer to Speke some three months later, Heuglin argued that he unfortunately found himself not in the financial position to think about such an enterprise; he was hoping though, once having recovered, to enter the regions between the White Nile and the so-called 'Central African Depression' (see below for the letter).[2]

After Alexine had hired 80 porters from the trader Ali Amuri during her stay in Meshra, together with an additional 100 obtained by Heuglin and the 130 porters of Petherick who had just brought a consignment of ivory to the Meshra, the Tinnes broke camp on 25 May. Heuglin was left behind, as he was too ill to be moved. He was supposed to follow the train once his condition permitted him to travel. On 1 June, he met Kleincznik who was returning from the Kosanga mountains, where he had settled himself two years ago, to Lake Rek. Kleincznik had not been able to reach the Azande this time and had left behind Heuglin's former companion Hermann Schubert, who was suffering from a severe disease, and would die soon afterwards. Heuglin proposed that d'Ablaing hired Kleincznik, who was an expert in these regions, as a *wakil* for the whole expedition, which was effectuated after Kleincznik had settled his business at Meshra.

In the evening of 4 June, d'Ablaing transported the sick Heuglin through the marshes in a sedan chair especially constructed for him. The more than 200 loads of remaining luggage arriving afterwards did not, however, contain Heuglin's belongings, which forced him to bear heavy rainfall during the night of the 11th in his wet clothes. He had just begun to recover somewhat, but this last setback caused him to suffer from a new and immediate attack of dysentery. On the 12th they proceeded through land which for the most part had changed into impassable marshes, swarmed with numerous geese, ducks, marabouhs, storches, spoonbills and other marsh birds and waterbirds. In the afternoon they finally caught up with the expedition train, where Alexine had begun to suffer from a severe fever after a vehement storm combined with pouring rain struck their company.[3]

In his account of the events that occurred between the departure of the Tinnes on 17 May and when he caught up with the main group on 11 June, there is a gap in Heuglin's letters in terms of information. This was partly due to his disease, which hampered him from describing any of the events taking place in their encampment before his arrival. Another contemporary source provides us with additional information about what happened in this period. There is a letter by Mrs. Katie Petherick which was published later in 1869 and which mentions an uproar taking place in the encampment of the Tinnes on 23 May before Heuglin arrived on the scene. Baron d'Ablaing, who was then still behind with the last part of the group and taking care of Heuglin, received news of such an alarming nature from the Tinnes that he was compelled to advance, though still without porters, hoping to render assistance. Grain was scarce and the soldiers had mutinied. 'Miss Tinné', as Mrs. Petherick recounts in her letter to a member of her family, 'always heroic, made them to lay down their arms; but the excitement, fatigue, and exposure to rain had induced fever, and she was prostrated. But very little progress had been made by the fair traveller, so, in all probability, the Baron would quickly rejoin his countrywomen.' In a letter to John, Henriette dates this incident 19 May and provides more details.[4]

Preceding this uproar, other difficulties had occurred. Among the men they had hired, there were differences between those engaged in Khartoum (who were Turkish) and those taken on from their neighbourhoods. When the porters (recruited from the native population) complained they had no corn and that the meat they had been given was too meagre, a whole crowd of men threatened to mutiny. The *wakil* who was in charge of Petherick's porters, Abd el Rachman, had no control over them. After Alexine had spoken to them and agreed to feed them better, an arrangement was made that the Petherick porters and their *wakil* should go to their *zariba* where they could collect more corn. When in the night a sudden storm broke out over the camp with lightning, thunder and lashing rain followed by hail, Alexine felt the tent collapse on top of her bed before she was able to get out. Once out of her tent, shivering and soaked, she had to battle a fierce wind to erect it to form some sort of shelter.

The next morning Alexine and Henriette were held at gunpoint by the soldiers they had commissioned to protect them. The men said they would not tolerate the dreadful conditions they had endured during the night, and threatened to mutiny for the same reason the porters had given: they lacked food. Again Alexine got them under control, telling them in Arabic that they had to obey her. At her command the soldiers laid down their muskets. They then lined up and, one by one, entered her tent to ask pardon for their behaviour. Alexine arranged that one contingent of men should go ahead to Ali Amuri's *zariba*, another she sent back to the Meshra to obtain further supplies of provisions. At this point, she was taken ill with fever. It had started suddenly and unexpectedly, but she was soon in a critical state. For three days she rallied, and then her condition worsened with long periods of unconsciousness. For the next few days, she was carried on a stretcher by four porters.

In a letter to John dated 1 July, Henriette prefers to present these events in a positive light:

> Alexine stands the journey very well. She has a stretcher, arranged
> with a canopy to keep off the sun, and her matrasses on it, so that

she rests very agreeably and often takes a refreshing nap. I have a chair. We are each carried by four Negroes. We each have twelve, so they have time to rest. Flore and Anna ride on donkeys. Mr. von Heuglin and Mr. d'Ablaing ride on mules. We now have 120 Negroes for our immediate luggage.[5]

At that time, Henriette had received Speke's letter that Addy had forwarded. She was not impressed and wrote to John about the success of the expedition:

> Once more *en route*, we shall, we trust, arrive safe and sound at the mountain Casinka, where we shall sow our seeds and remain till the weather is again fine and the earth dry. It must be a beautiful country, full of game and the people very good (…) We know the masters of nearly all zeribas [sic] on our route; and they have promised to supply us with wine and all we want. We have already sent off three companies of porters, amounting to about 400 men, with our baggage. They carry but little, say 40 lbs. each, and all on their heads.

On the 7th of June she wrote: 'We are expecting Von Heuglin to join us today; we hope he may be able to go with us; it is so great an advantage to have a scientific man in one's company. Although Captain Speke has informed us that this part of Africa is not interesting, yet a new country always is in some degree, and it is such a pleasure to have a really good map.'[6]

In Heuglin's later account of this part of the journey, there is no understanding and even some irritation regarding the behaviour of the Tinnes. When the whole party broke up in the afternoon of 14 June, Heuglin gives the following description of the way the Tinnes proceeded:

> The ladies had themselves carried in heavy sedan chairs by negroes, which were held in step by a *wakil* with his whip, surrounded by soldiers of the Divan [those who had been engaged from the Turkish government]. A group of agents who had delivered the porters were present; the whole train of over 400 negroes and more than 150 soldiers and servants worked their way on the narrow paths which were spongy and slippery. Because there were not sufficient supplies for this large quantity of people they were

forced to feed the blacks exclusively with beef, which was provided by the agents of Petherick for a high price. Subsequently, and also due to the dampness, the poor negroes, who were already for more than three weeks on their way, without protection whatsoever, were struck by dysentery, which disabled a considerable number of porters. Nobody however troubled one's head about the destiny of these people; many literally were hardly able to drag themselves any further and even received an extra load to carry, until they collapsed.[7]

The Tinnes appeared to be determined to maintain their time schedule, which did not permit an early morning rise. Somewhat irritated, Heuglin mentions that 'because the ladies did not like to get up early and they more-over spent several hours on making their toilet and having breakfast, one could only proceed in the afternoon when the sun was burning, instead of in the morning when it was still fresh.' After having marched for six and a half hours on the 15th Petherick's agent pleaded for a rest for the porters, which, as Heuglin states, was not permitted by the Tinnes, who, seated in their sedans, stated that one was in a hurry.[8]

Finally the river Jur was reached on 19 June. They made their encampment on the embankment, where the top was almost touched by the high tide of the water, swollen and rapid by the recent rains. Here the porters were taken across in three Dinka canoes; the beasts of burden had to swim over and the Tinnes themselves made use of the rubber boat that they had purchased from Petherick for £35. Having arrived on the other embankment, a hor-rendous storm struck them. For the entire night, there was heavy rainfall that drenched both the people and their luggage. While trying to take shel-ter under a leather cover somewhere else on the field, Heuglin, who was able to cross over only much later in the night, and still feeling ill, was forced to endure again the pouring all-invading water. Drenched to the skin, he did not close an eye. It was only at the break of morning that people found him and, as he tells later, if it wasn't for d'Ablaing who helped him to stand up, he would not have been able to change his soaking-wet clothes.

By this time the whole train had been scattered into groups that went their own way to Wau, the place indicated before to all participants as their next destination. As the newly appointed *wakil*, Kleincznik received on 20 June the order from the Tinnes to hurry on ahead of them in order to find a fordable spot at the river Dambo. Kleincznik, however, was suffering from worms ('*Filarien*') and had an insufficient number of soldiers and workmen at his disposal to make the necessary rafts and barracks, in addition to not having obtained a donkey to fullfil this job.

Along the embankment of the inundated Jur they marched for two days, and after having crossed the river Fertit (or Wau) they reached the *zariba* 'Biselli' on 21 June, where they were received with the firing of rifles. Heuglin refers to this part of their journey as a march with hardly any rest, as if one had to catch up with the time that was lost in the last three months.

On their arrival they were overwhelmed by the generous hospitality that Biselli bestowed upon the expedition. Henriette writes to Jules van Capellen how she was charmed by this welcome. 'We asked him to borrow us some doera, but he said that all of us were his guests for twenty-four hours and he behaved himself quite royal [sic].' They, however, would not take advantage of his hospitality, she adds, saying that a small *zariba* would be rented.[9] But Biselli had played a waiting game. Once the expedition had settled itself within his reach he subsequently launched his merciless policy of demanding extremely high prices for everything they needed, annoying and harassing their personnel and soldiers.

In her 1 July letter to John, Henriette writes in a light-hearted tone:

> We take very short journeys and always find a village to sleep in
> about four o'clock. We stop at a place which pleases us and send for
> the Sheik, who gives orders and chooses our host who clears out
> his cattle and his furniture, and we take possession for the night.
> We have always found them kind and willing to quit a little group
> of tukuls. There is always one large one for the cows: here I, with
> Flore, and the dogs put by with the luggage. Alexine and Anna go
> to another, but the cow house has a deeper [?] door so I prefer
> that.[10]

Serious problems concerning the continuation of their journey arose again. News came that the water of the Dembo and Kosanga, the remaining rivers to cross over (the last one even three times), was standing very high and was still rising, with a strong current. Biselli and Ali Abu Amuri, the owners of the *zaribas*, were asking ridiculous prices for the forwarding of their 500 pieces of luggage to the nearest Kosanga mountains, only a three to four-day march from there. Many indispensable items of their luggage had been lost by rain and theft, one quarter of their beasts of burden had perished, and Heuglin was afraid it would be necessary to hire Kosanga porters as soon as his very weakened health would permit. Although they had some shelter and space here, there was no time to lose because it was raining at an increasing rate, causing the water level in the rivers yet to be crossed to rise even higher.

Heuglin writes on 28 June that the Tinnes had drawn up a contract with Biselli, who would deliver 400 loads to the Kosanga mountains for 1600 Maria Theresia Thaler, to be paid directly, under the condition that they would not make a deal with Ali Amuri's people.[11] 'So one gets swindled here! For around 2 hundredweights durra [2 "Zentner" = 10 Kg wheat], which these *zeribah* owners take from their negroes by force, we have to pay 8 thaler', he exclaims. The Tinnes also made a costly deal with Biselli to hire their own private *zariba* for one month; they did not want to travel further for the moment. In her letter to John, Henriette refers to the trader Ali Amuri who by that time had started to bother the expedition more and more. '(…) These traders are raving mad.' After having heard it would not be possible anymore to reach the Kosanga mountains in this season, Alexine became 'infuriated again', and left the *zariba* to search for another place to stay.

As soon as the weather had improved somewhat, Alexine, accompanied by d'Ablaing, who had fallen ill in the meantime, tried immediately to search for a better place for an encampment. They returned, however, with nothing achieved. The Kosanga mountains were never attained by the full expedition and the final charge asked by Biselli for the porters was never paid to him.

Still complaining of sickness and diarrhoea, Heuglin was hardly able to walk more than 300 steps, but he inquired about the possible routes by asking the slaves of Biselli. He continued to make his scientific observations, registering plants that were very rich in oil, while regretting in this context the death of 'our poor Steudner'. On 30 June, slave traders coming back from the Kosanga mountains brought them the message that practically the whole region in between had been inundated, making it impossible for them to proceed further. That upset all their plans, as he concludes, also because their *zariba* began to present an alarming shortage of nourishment. Cereals were hard to get, even at extortionate prices. According to him the whole expedition would be better off splitting up and spreading itself across the region in order to provide for him or herself. Provisions from Khartoum were only to be expected in December. As he explains, he had to purchase food for himself but he hardly could afford to spend another hundreds of Thaler:

> I myself will hardly be able to provide for the most necessary provisions, because I doubt whether I can afford some hundreds of Thaler to purchase what I need most to prevent me from living miserably like our soldiers during the last part of the trip. The lack of copper, fabrics, pearls etc. prevents me also from accomplishing personal trips and acquiring and transporting collections. I never had an idea of the fabulous costs of such an expedition, being relatively not always that high, for my actual financial situation much too expensive though.[12]

There was also the issue of which flag this 'Deutsche Expedition' could use. A German flag did not yet exist. In Egypt they had to travel under English protection and hence the British flag; in Khartoum, as Petherick was absent from his post, they had been compelled to ask for French protection, which had been certainly advantageous. Now he travelled under the Dutch flag. Germany had failed him thus far, he concludes.

On 5 July, he informs Petermann that he had to finish his correspondence while the last caravan was leaving for Meshra, where the remaining ships waited for their departure to Khartoum. Their connection with the outside world would then be cut for several months. The second *wakil* had already been fired, and there was no replacement to be found here. Many people had left their train; the others were protesting about the harsh circumstances. In Heuglin's view, the problems they faced were practically unsolvable as they were on bad terms with Biselli, conditions were not likely to improve due to the lack of food, and there was nowhere to go. Despite these adversities he mentions in his almost daily contribution to Petermann that he is considering various kinds of different routes that would bring them to the regions of the Azande, living to the south. And the scholar speaks, when he gives his critical remarks about the names of the rivers in the nearby region. So Kleincznik had been wrong in saying he crossed the Dōr river after the

Jur, and not the Bongo river; this 'Dōr' had been his 'Wau'. The name of 'Bahr Fertit' for the northern Wau also had to be changed; this river was identical to Poncet's Wau. He feared that week after week would now be wasted by waiting.

The letters of Henriette and Heuglin about the expedition's foregoing events, dated 1 and 5 July respectively, were the last ones to reach the outside world for nearly nine months. With the last caravan that left the Biselli *zariba* for the Meshra, all direct communications had stopped. Alexine was not able to send any letter announcing Henriette's death on 20 July. The promised boats were not to be expected before October, which was to become December. Only late in March the next year when she arrived in Khartoum could Alexine inform Adriana and announce Henriette's death by sending letters to her family in the Netherlands and England.

For a reconstruction of what occurred between 5 July 1863 – when their last letters were sent to Meshra and thence to Khartoum and the outside world – and their return on 30 March 1864, the available information is restricted to a couple of notes by Henriette and Alexine, Heuglin's letter to Speke, his later accounts of 1865 and copies of some notes that have been left in the archives.

In the months following their arrival in Biselli's *zariba*, the whole expedition was forced to remain there until the second half of November. The surrounding land had been flooded, increasing the swamps; the rivers had become impassable; and they also were forced to stay in this spot by their continuing illnesses and weakness.

Shortly after having drafted the contract with Biselli concerning the hiring of porters to the Kosanga mountains and their own *zariba*, Alexine, accompanied by Anna and the sick d'Ablaing, went on her way to find a better place for the expedition at a higher elevation. On her trip she sent to Henriette a small note addressed: 'Madame Tinne' with in pencil: 'Encore une bouteille de beurre… Les gens de Kleinznik partis il y a 3 jours, ont du retourner des bords de Kosanga, qui selon eux est devenu impassable!'.

Henriette answers in a note to Alexine, addressed: 'Mademoiselle Tinne God knows where!!':

I thought of you when the sky got thick but as there was <u>no</u> thunder and very few drops of rain I hoped you were not frightened. We were all asleep when your note came – Mr. Heuglin brought it (…) I will enquire tomorrow if Bucelli means to play us a trick and if so, you may be sure I will move to the Outward Tugul [toukoul]. I send the bottle of butter!!! Mariam must be careful, we have only 4 bottles for all the time we remain here! the dogs are well they eat up <u>your</u> dinner Mr D'Ablaing's and Anna's that is they were well off today (…) I am glad you arrived safe and trust to take care of your dear self for my sake affe[ctionately]. H.T. the Petherick negros are not gone yet 9 (…) [o'clock].

This was to be the last document that Henriette wrote.[13]

Alexine and d'Ablaing returned without having found a better place for them to stay. However, the latter had been positive to Heuglin about the possibility of a new location at a greater distance. Feeling a little better and after having put Kleincznik on his feet again, Heuglin went on horseback on 17 July to the village Kulanda, 18 miles west of Biselli's *zariba*, where a sheikh had his residence near the Kosanga mountains. There were growing disagreements between Biselli's and Amuri's people which threatened to burst out into open hostilities, in which case Alexine's soldiers were not likely to choose in favour of but on the contrary against her and Heuglin. The latter was accompanied by some trustworthy men whom he knew to be somewhat independent of Biselli and had also taken with him some 50 men to build solid straw huts. Three miles northwest of Kulanda, on the high embankment of the Dembo-river amid a forest of high trees called Qaba, they dismounted when night had fallen. The next morning they soon found a suitable place for the expedition at some distance on a higher level. The sheikh promised to send some people who were to make preparations, erecting straw huts, and who would continue the next morning with their work. On the 21st, six large waterproof huts had been built as well as a store-room. Paid with copper materials and glass beads, they were eager to support them also by delivering fresh food. Everything seemed to be going well when in the evening of the same day news was brought by a man who was sent by d'Ablaing; 'the Billet' was notifying them of the sudden death of 'Madame Tinne', who had been suffering but had actually not been in an alarming state, according to Heuglin's last impression when he left the *zariba*. At the same time the messenger who had been sent to Schubert returned, announcing that this second member of his previous expedition had succumbed to dysentery and fevers.

The next day early in the morning Heuglin was on his way back to the *zariba* 'Biselli', arriving there at 4 o'clock in the afternoon in the pouring rain. Henriette Tinne had been buried already on that day under a sycamore, some two miles west of the *zariba*. Directly next to this place Alexine ordered soldiers to build some huts and to set up her tents which she soon moved into. Besides a numerous company of Arab servants, her maids Anna and Flore remained there with her and the lieutenant Abdallah Efendi of the government with 10 infanterists and some 50 Berberine soldiers, of which two-thirds were dismissed soon afterwards due to their bad behaviour.[14]

Shortly after his immediate return to Biselli's *zariba*, Heuglin received a small note in which Alexine stated that she would not like Henriette's death to prevent him from travelling to the Azande country. She asked him to make use of her remaining supplies of glass beads, munition, fabrics, copper, etc. for his next journey, and to indicate to her the quantity of soldiers he would need from her, which she would provide with all pleasure. In the given circumstances, Heuglin thought to accept Alexine's generous offer. Moreover she was so kind as to promise him the largest part of the provisions that were expected to arrive from Khartoum. 'Only one principal problem has to be solved', writes Heuglin as a concept of a letter to Petermann.

> I need to hire from the Dōr (…) some 80-90 porters for a period
> of at least 4 to 5 months, because at the Niam niam [sic] I would
> under no condition be able to get these. I fear that the high price
> of the hiring and the nourishing of so many people will ruin me
> quickly, and I have to take also into consideration the journey back
> to Khartoum, which will cost me, needing a ship with crew, a large
> amount of money.[15]

Within eight weeks, all pack animals and mounting animals, except for some mules, had succumbed to malnutrition and diseases. Sometimes Heuglin was often too sick to move, and neither Alexine nor d'Ablaing were willing, due to their weaknesses, to proceed any further on a new journey to the Kosanga mountains, let alone beyond. Everyone had to cope with the situation at the *zariba* of Biselli, who gave no causes for further complaints in Heuglin's opinion, apart from asking exceedingly high prices for provisions.[16]

On 20 August, Flore, already ill for some time, succumbed to a disease similar to the one that had felled Henriette one month before. Although their encampments were lying at quite a distance from each other, Heuglin made a daily trip to Alexine's place to be of some assistance. Despite the pouring rain and his condition, he partly swam and worked his way to her through fields of long grass.

From this period after the death of Henriette and Flore dates a small note, sent by Alexine to Heuglin, which gives an impression of the state she was in, and the help she needed from him:

> Thanks, thanks and thousand times thanks, my dear Mr. Heuglin, for your attention – it is a joy for me – Because Mr. D'Ablaing agrees to be paid, that's all what is needed, I will give the price to Mr. Thibaut [apparently she thought of leaving for Khartoum in short time] – Anna is not good today, she was sweating continuously and on top of it all, we received an alarm. The fire has come that close to the Zariba, that we had to flee, running to the Khir (…), with the luggage. Till tomorrow, I hope.

A most important opportunity to come into direct contact with the 'Niam-Niam' was created by Alexine. Initiated by Heuglin, who in Khartoum had written about King Mofío who should be approached by the expedition, Alexine had sent some presents in October to Mofio, who was a 'sultan' or king of the Northern Azande. A response came in the middle of November. An ambassador of Mofío holding the rank of Bēqi, or governor of a frontier state, arrived and presented her 'a nicely crafted wooden tub' [see Catalogue: illustrations 25 and 25a]. 'Today a Beqi, i.e. a sheikh of his Majesty King Mofio, has arrived here with some presents of his superior for Miss Tinne, who had sent some time ago people to Mofio', he writes in a letter dated 10 November 1863.[17] The man ('clearly not of the pure Azande race, but a half-negroe') for a while made himself comfortable at her place and told Heuglin he had heard about him and that he was expected to come to their country. For his part, Heuglin presented him with some copper bars and glass beads, of which some were unknown to the Azande.

Heuglin took the opportunity to record many of his new findings regarding zoological specimens, meteorological research and ethnological descriptions of objects of the Dōr and Jur tribes, and provided precious new facts about the Azande. The sheikh's wish was to obtain a double-barrelled rifle from Heuglin, who promised him this provided he delivered a bushman ('*Waldmensch*' or 'a Gorilla-like M'bán'), dead or alive.[18] He also drew up a chart of their vast surroundings, of which later a smaller copy was sent by Alexine to John who made use of it for the map included in his 1864 publication about 'the Dutch Ladies'.[19]

A copy of a letter by Heuglin from Bongo dated October 1863 and addressed to ´Mon cher Capitaine´ indicates that he responded to Speke's letter to him which included his appeal to proceed to the Azande together with the provisions he had sent to the Meshra: 'We are now waiting for our barks which have received the order to enter and proceed to the frontiers of the tribe of the Dōr (…).' He relates how difficult it was to arrive just as far as this area, proceeding from Meshra in the rainy season.

> Madame Tinne and her femme de Chambre have succumbed to the fatigues of the journey and the climate, the rest of the company is still suffering and will not proceed any further. As far as I am concerned, I will still try to go further but I doubt that I will succeed to go as far as the Sisia and Makona (…), despite my best willingness. There are many obstacles, not from the side of the inhabitants, but from that of the traders of slaves from Khartoum who are quite afraid that people get acquainted with their secrets (…).

Then he expounds on the Jur, the Fertit, the Kresh, the Kwolo and the 'Niam-Niam' and some physionomic characteristics of them referring to the 'type of negroe' they would represent to him. Despite the total lack of 'porteurs', he reckons on reaching the Azande by next May. By this time the situation in the Biselli *zariba* would have improved and he would have a better chance of arriving there; *égards* and *obligations* so far did not permit him to continue his route. He doubts, however, that he will find in Khartoum 'sufficient means for another enterprise for the second time, but he has a bit of consolation in the conviction that this small sacrifice at least would have the result of being able to designate a new route for travellers, better than I have now, whose researches certainly will be crowned with enormous success and having discovered a quantity of *nouveautés en zoologie*'. Regarding geography, he relates having had 'at least the result of tracing down a fairly exact map of the Bahr el-Ghazal, and to provide new facts and notes on the Niam-niam countries, Fertit etc. etc. more correct than what we had so far.'

The postscript in his letter announces that he would return from 'the interior' to the Bahr el-Ghazal sources on 9 February and hoped to arrive in Khartoum at the end of March. This indicates that the letter was written after the news on 21 November that their ships had arrived in the Meshra.[20]

The letter reveals that Heuglin would actually have liked to proceed to the Azande on his own but was held back not only by the expenses in this attempt but also by feelings of sympathy. His 'égards' must refer to the situation of Alexine, who after three months must not have shown signs of some recovery; his 'obligations' insinuated that he could not let her return to the Meshra on her own and was obliged to accompany her on her way back. In his way he took care of her, and, as he describes, delivered 'daily game to Miss Tinne's kitchen'.[21]

On 16 November, Biselli was initially able to suppress the uprising against him initiated by soldiers from outside his encampment, but then *his* own soldiers turned against him and within several hours his whole *zariba* was deserted by his former employees, leaving him without any executive power. The slaves sought protection at Amuri's *zariba* and partly at Alexine's privately hired *zariba*, at one hour's distance from 'Biselli's'. In her settlement, Alexine attended to a man who had been severely wounded during the uproar, but she was unable to prevent him from dying. Heuglin and d'Ablaing's soldiers and servants were also eager to leave the place. D'Ablaing went to Amuri's settlement and Heuglin was invited by Alexine to settle himself in the direct neighbourhood of her *zariba*.

The retreat to Meshra

November and December 1863 were spent waiting and hoping for news from their ships that should have entered the Meshra by then. In October, Heuglin was expecting some possible news about the potential arrival of the ships. When they left Meshra in May, the crew had explicitly been ordered to set off with the first northern winds from Khartoum and would have been navigating at the latest in the middle of November on the Gazelle-river. They had also ordered the steamer, whose charter had expired in June, to be re-engaged.

In order to be able to maintain better communications with the harbour and to procure porters as well, Alexine decided to move to Wau. On 4 January, they left Bongo. The bodies of Henriette and Flore were dug out again and carried on donkeys. D'Ablaing left Amuri's place in the neighbourhood and met them on the 7th in a small village. The transport of all the luggage took several days. The soldiers were sent ahead in order to build some straw huts in Wau. Gradually the whole train was rallied again. In the weeks they stayed in Wau, Heuglin was able to work on his research to complete his collections of *naturalia*. He was not able, however, to solve the problem of the provision of porters who could transport his collections to the Meshra and was therefore forced to leave the largest zoological objects behind.

Finally on 10 January, the written tidings came that a ship carrying an additional number of 75 soldiers and provisions had pulled into the port of Meshra after a 45-day sailing trip.[22] A new *wakil* would be on his way to their place at Wau. It was 14 January when the recently arrived group pushed through to Wau by land, accompanied by much shouting and gun volleys. In Heuglin's account, not a single word is mentioned about the arrival of the relief expedition that was commanded on 23 November by Adriana van Capellen in Khartoum. Having left Khartoum for the Meshra at the end of November and arriving at the end of December, the boat with soldiers and supplies for the expedition was, according to Heuglin, the one that had been ordered by the Tinnes and himself to sail from Khartoum as soon as the weather permitted, carrying all kinds of additional supplies. He had expected these ships in October. But he could not know that the promised convoy had been detained in Khartoum.[23]

On 22 January Anna, Henriette's maid for many years and a support and refuge of the family and the last remaining of the two maids from The Hague, died of total exhaustion at Wau.

In the afternoon of 1 February, when the heat was at its highest, they all left Wau and proceeded along the river Jur. It took several days to get the local people to deliver porters in order to transport the entire luggage Alexine was taking with her, including all the belongings of Henriette, Flore and now Anna. After an exchange of copper and glass beads as barter, some leaders were willing to provide the necessary people. Heuglin had hired from Biselli some 40 porters for 6 Maria Theresia Thaler each, a relatively low price as he states, and d'Ablaing took from Amuri's *zariba* as many as he wanted without any problem. With its more than 350 people, the train was again of an extraordinary size.[24]

Among the obtained men, some of whom had been pressed into service by others, there were several that were held in captivity and guarded by the other soldiers. Referring to this situation, Heuglin explains that several porters who had been pressed to join the train were running away. The only solution was to make each soldier responsible for the amount of porters he had to command, and in case one escaped he had to carry the left luggage himself. Alexine's part of the train in particular was inflicted by these troubles concerning men held prisoner during the march to the Meshra, according to Heuglin, who relates that his own group was led by a very capable *wakil* hired from Biselli.

Numerous groups of inhabitants whose lands they traversed seemed to have hostile intentions against them and gathered around the train. After Heuglin had ordered the soldiers not to make use of their rifles, he sent a negotiator who informed him that these people feared they would be carried away by the soldiers of the expedition as slaves. The soldiers, however, were not held back in plundering small villages while passing by.

After having spent the night of 7 and 8 February under a forest of sycamores at Auen they finally reached Lau, with Meshra el-Rek on the opposite side of the river. Alexine had already traversed the river with her company and a part of her luggage on the 10th. Both d'Ablaing and Heuglin then suffered from high fevers, notably on the night of the 12th. A vessel that was promised to bring them to the Meshra did not appear, which they realised only after having made their way partly by foot wading in a weakened state through the water to the place where the vessel was supposed to be waiting for them. After returning by the same route, Heuglin's condition worsened and he was to remain in a state of serious illness almost permanently until his arrival back in Khartoum on 30 March.

When the rest of Alexine's luggage had been transferred to the Meshra on 14 February, Heuglin purchased from Alexine, who was selling as much of her supplies of rifles and ammunition as possible, some muskets to cover the expenses of his porters – some of them preferred being paid out in muskets instead of money – and had to procure the most necessary things for his return journey for ridiculous prices, as he relates.[25] That night, the signal for departure was given and the ships entered the ambatch canal and thereby a rather closed water basin which was at this time full of rubbish and waste. It took them three days to push through the basin using rudders and poles, all the time being attacked by massive clouds of mosquitoes that no nets or smoke were able to stop, and which could even enclose candles in such amounts that the flames would extinguish. They then entered the regions of the *sudd*, which consisted here not of papyrus plants but wild sugarcane and reed. While they were taking in a supply of wood, the barks that had stayed behind arrived, one of them carrying the body of a female servant that the Tinnes had brought from Khartoum and who had died the previous night of 'syphilis' [sic], from which she had already been suffering since entering their service in the city, as Heuglin describes.

The following days they worked their way through increasingly large fields of floating islands of sugarcane and reed. The roots of the plants on these islands were far longer than those previously encountered. Another five days were spent covering a relatively small distance. On the evening of 25 February, they reached the mouth of the Bahr el-Ghazal. The nights had been primarily cold and humid. Many members of their crew had fallen sick again. Everyone was coughing and complaining of the cold.

On the night of 1 March they made good progress sailing, reaching at dawn the bark of Alexine, which had moored shortly before at a place where further progress was practically impossible. The wild sugarcane prevented them in every way from sailing further, and more of these masses of plants were floating into the area each hour. Help eventually came from an officer of a nearby Turkish ship who sent his crew to get the Tinne boat floating again, which took five hours and more than 300 men.

Working their way through the *sudd*, all passengers and crew of their boats were required to assist. When everyone came on deck, there appeared to be quite a number of 'black cargo', according to Heuglin's description. Apart from some 'free negroes' who had taken their chance to join the expedition as servants when they left Bongo, there were more than 40 men and women aboard, including some boys who had been given as a present to Lieutenant Abdallah Effendi with the permission of Alexine. After Effendi had overruled the prohibition of holding slaves, most of the crew had followed his example and purchased girls who they married in the presence of Effendi for the sole purpose of gaining the property of the girls. The lieutenant was asked to take full responsibility for these transactions and to render an account of his actions to the divan in Khartoum. Later in Khartoum, Musha Pasha was to pursue Alexine for her role in this. He made a great fuss, asking for explanations from Thibaut as Alexine's consular person of contact and putting the people involved in prison, giving the impression that Alexine had bought slaves. For her part, Alexine denied having been aware of the fact that her boats had been used by the ships' staff for the transportation of slaves. This made her very upset because her actions were done with the best intentions, as she told John in the first letter she could send from Khartoum.

After passing the river Zeraf and having struggled with a strong adverse wind, Heuglin's boat was moored above the mouth of the river Sobat on 6 March. He had hoped to ascend this river in imitation of his friend De Pruyssenaere, whose investigations he had followed eagerly and whose letters he had forwarded to Petermann to be published,[26] but was unable to do so due to the weak condition he was in. The next morning he set off following the other ships that had gone ahead. With a favourable wind, they now navigated along the embankments of the country of the Shilluk, who had been forced by the Turkish rulers to deliver a yearly tribute of cattle as well as slaves for soldiers. The latter had to be robbed from their neighbours, the Dinka. From his ship, Heuglin witnessed a large-scale slave raid near the sand dunes further inland.

In Hillat Kaka the zariba that Muhammad Khair had left some time ago was now occupied by Egyptians. Heuglin was visited on his boat by a representative of the new inhabitants and was informed about the recent measures taken against the slave trade. He was told that what now happened with the Shilluk was meant to be in their favour because they were protected against raids that had previously been executed by men like Muhammad Khair.

The new policy, however, was impossible to implement because of the lack of manpower, ships and provisions. Slave traders were able to continue with their work, and their boats navigated unhindered on the White Nile. While he proceeded in a northern direction the next day, Heuglin saw many of these boats that had been suspected of looting and robbery.

While entering the next port he heard that the captain of Alexine's *dhahabi-yya* had been ordered to stop four barks that were sailing upstream with the request to deliver a letter to Meshra. When the *ra'is* rowed to one of the boats and received no answer from the crew, he suspected them of slavery and opened fire on the ship after a warning. He then seized the vessel with its cargo, which was to be handed over in Khartoum. The prisoners, however, took the opportunity to jump off their ship.

On the 18th, they moored at Jebel Dinka where a Turkish command with eight soldiers had installed itself in order to inspect every ship passing by for slaves. Alexine had taken on her ship a woman who had been found as a female slave while staying with the *ra'is*. While going ashore, the woman was immediately seized by the *ra'is*, as her former owner. She was liberated by Abdallah Effendi, who captured the *ra'is*.

On 22 March, they were finally past the long layer of water plant islands forming the so-called *sudd*. They began to approach more inhabited regions such as Wad Shellal, which was reached on the 25th. They noticed that this place had been abandoned by its former inhabitants. Most of the straw huts had been destroyed and the marketplace was empty. Heuglin concludes that the pressing tax system of Musha Pasha must have been responsible for its abandonment. Charging the *fellahin* (villagers and farmers) also meant that their properties could be annexed by the government. Heuglin quotes a farmer who said to him: 'Where a Turc sets his foot, grass won't grow anymore'. Thousands of mills in Nubia and Sennār stood still, which were falling into decay. While imposing his taxes, Musha Pasha had doubled the military ranks.

In the early morning of the 30th, the first mountains under Khartoum appeared. Alexine had informed Heuglin she would follow his ship at a slow pace and would not enter the city itself but go ashore in a nearby village or stay in her boat. He heard from a ship passing by that Petherick had set up his tents in a place they had passed by before dawn. The consul Thibaut was already awake and came to greet him, offering him Petherick's house in Khartoum, which was now empty. When the sun rose higher, Heuglin saw the city lying before him and waited for the other boat with Alexine to anchor on the embankment of the Blue Nile.

Back in Khartoum

Meanwhile in Khartoum, Adriana van Capellen had been desperately waiting for months for news from her sister and niece. The last letter she had received from Henriette was dated 1 July 1863, dispatched with the last ship leaving Meshra el-Rek. After having sent Speke's negative advice on the entire expedition, she had expected a sensible reaction to it. However, Henriette, as we know, had not agreed at all with Speke's reservations about the enterprise. It seems instead to have strenghtened her decision to proceed on their terms, having at their side Heuglin as someone whom even Speke would know as a renowned Africa traveller.

Adriana took comfort in the company of John and Katie Petherick, as well as Georges Thibaut. When the boats of the Tinnes were suspected of having been engaged in the slave trade ('the trade of negroes under Dutch flag'), all of them had been chained up at Musha Pasha's decision to put an embargo on them.[27] After hearing nothing at all from the expedition for four and a half months, Addy decided to proceed to action.

> My dear Siccama we let on 23 November 5 boats depart with provisions, soldiers and everything what they possibly would need to return (…)', writes Addy van Capellen on November 28th to her nephew O.W. Hora Siccama at The Hague.[28]

This relief party had reached Meshra el-Rek in December last year.

Rumours began spreading in March that the boats of the expedition were approaching Khartoum. On 14 March, Katie Petherick reported that she received a message about the Tinnes who were navigating towards Khartoum. It was only on 31 March that it become clear that the expedition bore ill-fated news: namely that Henriette Tinne had died in July the previous year. Mrs. Petherick recounts in a letter to her sister dated 31 March 1864, which included a letter to Mr. Tinné, informing him of the sad news 'Poor Madame Tinné is *dead*' and that 'Miss Capellan' had told her: 'I must tell you my dreams: last night I saw my lovely mother and dead sister (…) they held out their arms from the bright clouds to take me there, and I was so happy. Then I awoke, but to sleep again and to dream of Harriet (Madame Tinné) that she was dead'.[29]

By the time the news of Henriette's death had reached Khartoum, the ships had already entered the city and moored at the embankment of the Blue Nile. Adriana was informed that her niece Alexine had retreated to the small dune island named Tuti, which lay between the White Nile and two branches of the Blue Nile. She had decided not to enter Khartoum again and did not wish to receive anybody except for Adriana. Heuglin was lodged in Petherick's house, and d'Ablaing stayed in a house of a Syrian in the town.[30]

Both our protagonists arrived in Khartoum in a miserable state. Heuglin was in a state of utter exhaustion. Not even the thought of joining acquaintances could make him happy. Letters from his homeland did cheer him up somewhat, and there was the recognition of his endeavours, which were flattering but in his opinion unmerited. Rest and a good diet aided his recovery. The social traffic gradually became more enjoyable, and good sleep, which he had missed so much, helped him regain his former condition.

After accounting for all his expenses and the income he had received from Petermann as his intermediary fund supplier, there was a surplus of 50.000 piasters, sufficient for a new journey to be executed. For travels in Sudan, however, this period was very unfavourable. There was still the hot summer season, but the summer rains were going to start soon. Means of transport on land or water were greatly restricted by a dearth of boats and camels, which had been confiscated by the government. The invitation of Musha Pasha to join him on an expedition on the White Nile was postponed because of other priorities such as Musha's campaign against the rebellious Dinka in Sennār and the creation of a new army.

For Alexine, it was more her state of mind than her physical condition that was affecting her. Having recovered from her illnesses, she was still afflicted by anger and indignation about the terrible sojourn in Biselli's *zariba* and the way members of her crew and soldiers had been treated by both Biselli and Amuri. Everyone had been prepared to be confronted with great problems and obstacles but no one, not even Heuglin, had had any idea that their greatest problems would be with the traders instead of the indigenous peoples.

Alexine had also been struck hard by the deaths of Henriette, Flore and Anna. Her letters give the impression that all the details of Henriette's last moments in particular kept lingering in her memory for months to come.

And as if that were not bad enough, directly after her arrival she was confronted by Musha Pasha who accused her of slavery. 'This is a horrible place!', writes Katie Petherick in a letter to her sister in England. 'When the ladies' boats returned from The Bahr el Gazal, they were filled with slaves, and the Dutch flag was the protection. An invalid servant of Von Heuglin's, returned in the boats for change of air, denounced the proceedings of the *reises* (…) and their men. Mademoiselle von Capellan (…) pleads in vain through her Consul for redress – it is a hopeless task: the servant is dead, and no one will bear witness. In the meantime, the slave traders composedly say, 'All the Europeans traffic in slaves, even the Dutch ladies'. 'This fills poor Miss Capellan with grief.'[31]

With Musha Pasha officially accusing her of slavery, Alexine found herself hurt not only by personal losses but by insults as well. This caused her to sink into a depression, with her emotions alternating between grief and anger for months. Before her arrival in Khartoum, she had notified Heuglin that she preferred to stay outside the city itself. The location she found on the island of Tuti gave her the opportunity to cope with the accusations, prepare her case against Musha Pasha and to deal with her depression in almost complete isolation. The first thing she did was to inform her nearest British and Dutch family members about the news of the fatal events that had occurred.

Letters from Khartoum

Just before her arrival in Khartoum and directly afterwards, Alexine wrote several letters to her family, some of which she had written on the boat were sent off the very day of her arrival.[32] The letters show her state of mind, which was overcome by distress, despair and fury. In practically all the letters she explains all the events of the previous months. The addressees are provided with all possible details regarding the diseases that struck and the slavery of which she was accused (see appendix 5: Letters from Khartoum and Berber).

John had already been notified about the news of the deaths by Petherick, who had sent a messenger to Cairo on 31 March to send a telegraph to London; to him, Alexine sent a series of three letters, two of them dated April. The next person to whom Alexine wrote was her Aunt Jemima in The Hague (Jemima Frederica van Capellen, sister of Henriette, who stayed in the house in The Hague until her death on 17 June 1864), followed by her uncle Jules van Capellen one month later. Alexine's niece Jetty was not to receive a letter until late in 1865, after Alexine had reached Suez. Her father, Uncle Hora Siccama, had been sent all the news about the journey and the reasons for its abortion. Since her last letter to Jetty from 26 March 1863, the character of the enterprise had changed from a sightseeing excursion, conveying all kinds of nice and interesting details, to a desperate attempt to survive. All the energy she had left was needed for her case against Musha Pasha, in which she counted on the help of Heuglin and Thibaut.

With 'Khartoum' as the place of dispatch but with no date, she tells her half-brother:

> Dear John, I could not bring myself to announce you those awful news so I asked Mr. Heuglin to do it…Mama was taken from me in the most unexpected and incomprehensible manner. At the Mishra as you know, she had that same rheumatic illness she had at The Hague after our return from the East; but she recovered rapidly and well and was the strong one of the party on the journey, I having the fever, Flore a chronic illness and Anna not being a strong girl.

As the pacesetter of an extremely perilous expedition to the interiors of Central Africa, Alexine obviously realised that she had braved danger. Her *beau idéal* of a grand expedition had been performed at the cost of human lives. She could only escape out of this moral constraint by establishing her mother's death as 'unexpected' and 'imcomprehensible', or possibly caused by 'poisoned bonbons', or the doctor's fault (see appendix 5: letter A. Tinne to J. Tinne, April, Khartoum). Even the deaths of both her beloved maids she tried to construe as inevitable, a result of their weak condition. She used the same argumentation in the case of the death of her aunt Addy, blaming the local doctor for his incompetence. It is as though she is trying to convince others and herself that what had caused these horrendous events was *à force majeure*.

She proceeds by telling John how she and her mother went together on donkeys to see a place where they intended to remain for the rainy season. The next day she came home late to find 'Mama' a little unwell, but they had the table spread by her bedside and had 'a gay meal'. The next day the ague returned. She eventually died because her illness prevented her from taking care of herself, as Alexine states in her conclusion. Henriette's death had 'a dreadful effect' on both Flore and Anna – Flore seemed crushed and Anna, who was a nervous girl, was 'frightened into fits', not so much from grief as from fear of death. As soon Anna felt better, she resumed her usual life walking about and working. Flore, however, seemed to have exerted her last strength – as Heuglin said 'like a lamp that has no more oil'. Her condition deteriorated rapidly until she had a fever almost continually and was nearly always sleeping. Gradually she lost consciousness and was barely alive the last two days. Heuglin, whom she had sent for, tried several remedies, but nothing being effective, Flore died on 20 August in the night and was laid next to Henriette. Anna's nervousness started to rise again. She was convinced that she would die on the 20th of September, the two previous deaths having occurred on the 20th of the two months before. Until that date she was in 'a dreadful state (…) laying crying and screaming of fear'. Seeing her condition grow worse and worse, Alexine said she would not have been astonished if Anna really did die on the 20th. After that date passed, Anna suddenly felt much better. Always fond of eating, she then ate all day long, mainly all sorts of unwholesome things, as her stomach had been thrown out of balance. She wanted to strengthen her body by eating, as she was sure she would die if she went a day without food. 'I tell you', Alexine writes to John, 'you can have no conception of the way she went on murdering her stomach those 5 months', having a continuous diarrhoea while almost permanently eating. In vain Alexine prayed, ordered, and got angry with her while Heuglin warned her; she was either affronted or pretended to listen to them but kept eating on the sly. In the middle of November, Anna developed a violent pain in her leg which kept her lying down for some weeks. In December, when she was up again, the diarrhoea returned. Thinking that a change of air would do her good, they left Alexine's *zariba* and went to Wau. When the tidings came that their soldiers had arrived from Khartoum, they decided to set off on 22 January. Everything was packed when on that very morning Anna slept unusually late. Alexine went to see her several times but did not wake her. When at last a servant went to look closely at her, he saw that she was dead.

Alexine provides almost casually in the next paragraph a crucial reason for her not to return to Europe:

> And now, you will probably ask yourself, what I am going to do, and I don't think you will be very astonished when I tell you I am going to stay in the East – not at Khartoum but in the pretty neighbourhood of Berber, where Mama and I always said we would go and rest after our travels. It is not from a romantic enthusiasm for the East, or from any great excentricity [sic] but from motives which I am sure you will understand, if you consider them well. To return alone, in my empty house… no, I cannot tell you how I shudder even at the idea – it would be like an evil dream – that is out of the question for me. The happier I have been there, the less I could return, and where [sic] I to go elsewhere, in some place I don't care about, and among strange people, my life would be very different from before – my position is quite changed – I am no longer young and so my former enjoyments I would not have, and quiet and freedom which is all I can wish for afterwards I would not have in Europe for though I might keep out the "world" there are a thousand people and things I could not avoid. Here I can live free and quiet, naturally without a daily struggle for it: there are no conventionalitys [sic], no obligations for a European here – I feel at home to a certain degree, having been here nearly two years and know the ways and manners of the people and country, and bad as they are can get on with them.[33]

After having been away from The Hague for more than three years and having gone through a number of events she experienced as ordeals, Alexine concluded that she preferred the relative freedom of living abroad to her life and house on the Lange Voorhout. The house she had once certainly loved she now felt she would experience as a corset.

To her Aunt Jim she sent letters in which she looks back on the deaths:

> (…) I happen to begin John's letter first, and when I had gone through all those horrible details that I hardly bear to write, I could not go over them again – I am sure you will not be hurt as after all, there are only facts which I could but repeat in the same words – I wish to write to you and yet what can I say! – (…) – I can't believe

it yet – it is only at times I can realize it – if Mama had known she
was going to die, I don't think I would have stood the parting – but
she had no idea of it, and I only knew there was danger when she
as gone – she was so beautiful after! – I dreaded to look at her, but
she had such a calm holy expression, that it did me good – but
I can't bear to write about it all yet, and poor Flore's death which
was brought on by Anna's silliness makes me so furious that
I cannot even <u>think</u> of it – the only consolation I had left! – ...it is
too cruel –.[34]

Meanwhile she kept in touch with Heuglin from her island. Dating from the first period of their stay there is a scrap of paper with a message to Heuglin in which Alexine gives her thoughts about what to do with the body of Anna.

My dear Mr. Heuglin, How are you this morning? – Won't you
forget you have promised to hand me over all of the <u>soup</u>? If you
have too much- You could find me at Adolf [?] (...) Would it be
better to leave poor Anna at the Mission (...) to bury her until
I know what her family knows what to do?[35]

Her last proposal was effectuated. She concludes her letter by asking him in the postscript: 'What perfume did you use today? Your letter has a very particular scent'.

In another letter to John, she tells him about the 'shocking state' of Sudan caused by Musha Pasha's policy and asks him to publish something about the shameful way in which 'the Dutch ladies' have been treated (see appendix 5: letter A. Tinne to J. Tinne, April/May 1864, Khartoum). John Tinne would do what Alexine had asked for. He wrote a letter to *The Times* which was published on 12 September 1864.[36]

In another third letter, also written just after her arrival in Khartoum, Alexine demands from John 'redress'.

(...) Teased and unhappy about it and want you to help me to get
redress – You know already by Mama's letters of the 8th July the
shocking conduct of Buselli towards us? – since that time it has
been but a long series of injustices, affronts, hostilities and wrongs

of all sorts from him and Ali Ohmuri's brother and agent; We were complete prisoners, and sometimes they openly attacked our soldiers – I will not repeat all the facts, as most are mentioned in my official "plainte" and Mr. Heuglin's rapports, which I send you enclosed, but Mr. Heuglin was prevented going on with his journey, and I with the greatest difficulty obtained our most indispensable wants; Every time I was too indignant and wanted to punish as I could those wretches on the spot, Mr. Heuglin and the Turkish officer [Abdallah-Effendi] always prevented me, and said, it was far better to have them legally punished in Khartoum; Everybody was shocked, at my return, to hear what had happened, but when I sent my complaint officially through the French Consul to the Pasha, he has shown as clearly as he can that he won't punish them and give me redress! – at first he kept the complaint 2 or 3 days, and then sent it back under pretence his dragoman, though he speaks French perfectly, could not translate it; then he tried to decline interfering on various excuses, so absurd, that he himself was obliged to owe they could not hold, and now is putting off doing anything under pretext that in this season he cannot bring here the guilty parties, which is not true as he has a steamer. I cannot yet legally complain of him, as he has not yet officially refused, but his ill-will is shameful – Besides this when after our letter of the 8th of July showing our destressing [sic] position and asking either a man of the government, authorised to keep the merchants in respect, or at least for a letter of the Pasha to order them not to molest us, and for the steamer, Mr. Thibaut wrote to him for the steamer he did not even answer; that may be as he says that he did not get the letters, but when he came back from Cairo and that the boats were at last setting out to our rescue, poor T. Addy and Mr. Thibaut praying and working themselves to get them off quick, he not only did not give the man a letter as asked, but sought to detain the boats, under the most unjust reason! [37]

Apparently a letter with a request for assistance to Thibaut had been sent on 8 July 1863 which indeed might have been too late for the post from the Meshra to Khartoum. The requested officials who were asked to inspect and prevent the traders from their obstructing and annoying actions could not have been sent by Musha Pasha for that reason as well. The remark concerning Musha's efforts to impede the departure of their boats, which were supposed to return to the Meshra, explains why Heuglin had expected them to arrive already in December.

While Addy wrote her letter announcing the relief expedition, Katie Petherick was a witness of what happened in Khartoum at that time.

> The most iniquitous act has been in the case of the Dutch ladies. Three of their boats had sailed ere the arrival of the Pasha, their *dahabyeh* [sic] remaining, as it was hoped that the steamer might be hired to tow her through the lake, as the ladies are in some trouble; but the Pasha would not let her go; moreover, he insisted upon the tax being paid on the boats which had previously sailed with their papers duly attested under the new regulation of last year. 'Monsieur Thibaut, the French Consular Agent (under whose protection the ladies are) demurred; it was useless, as the Pasha threatened to seize the *dahabyeh* and bring back the other boats; therefore Thibaut paid, under protest…!!.'[38]

In her letters to John Alexine would be continuously hammering at her case against Musha Pasha:

> (…) that I think is such a burning shame, that it must be punished and you who were so anxious about us, must think it shocking – particularly when you know the injustice of the reason he wanted to detain the boats, and leave us to perish for; 3 of our boats had started before he came back and one was on the point of sailing, when he suddenly made a law that all sailors or soldiers going to the W. Nile should pay 100 p.ters per head; but as my boats were gone and one starting, all its soldiers having spent the money they had received, he wanted to force Mr. Thibaut to pay or he would not let the boat go, and would send to stop those that were gone; Mr. Thibaut knowing us in danger and want was weak enough to promise to pay <u>tout en protestant</u> – It is the most horrible injustice for a law cannot apply to what is done before its enactment. He might as well force us to pay for having gone last year; leaving alone the barbarity of refusing us help, and trying to stop the only succour we could at last receive, it was a most horrible injustice and about that I am going to complain at the French consulate in Cairo – He and his people try to tease in every way possible, they

have a spite that quite astounds [sic] me, tried to accuse <u>me</u> of bringing <u>slaves</u>! <u>Me</u> of all people in the world! It is a long story and I am so tired I hardly can write more but I will try to give you an idea of it.[39]

In what evidently is a postscript to the last letter, Alexine adds:

As I had finished my letter I receive the present statement of Mr. Thibaut, and to have it more exact, as the place of a word makes sometimes a difference, I had copied it through – it is now not 503,124 but 611,934 p! – and when it all is paid, 700,000 and more – the whole income of 1864 is gone! I am afraid now that your letter of the 25th of Sept. in which you say "imagine my delight, as well as relief and satisfaction on hearing etc" was written in ignorance of what he has spent, and in the belief that he did not want the £2000 – it is very distressing, everything comes upon me at once! – and it is so <u>uselessly</u> spent; if the journey had <u>really</u> costed that, and what we thought it worth it, we would have had what we wanted but it is only those miserable <u>interests</u> and mis-management that have made the sum so large – For you know what a careful woman of business Mama was, and all this [sic] costs are yet what was foreseen and arranged by her – I have, so to say, spent nothing since her but my daily living and she had calculated the cost of all we ordered, and reckoned, I know, much, much less – my return cost nearly nothing, as this time, not fearing any more quarrels and discomfort as in Mama's time, I hired the porters (…) of <u>themselves</u>, in spite of Buselli, and paid only the real price, a few beads! – and the rest, as I said, boats, soldiers, provisions, had been foreseen and calculated by Mama. It is most distressing for me – I really am most embarassed – I had meant as you know to settle down and establishing oneself costs a great deal; building or buying a house, having things come etc. likewise I see it is almost necessary I should go to Cairo or at least Suez before I settle, for all sorts of reasons, and travelling and living at an Hotel costs too – However I know <u>land</u> in Soudan and Egypt brings up a great deal, and as there is here a Mr. Joyce, who is come from a Company to make plantations on a large scale I will see and hear through him, what I could make of land to cover the first expenses – once established I would live cheap enough, <u>common living</u> is cheap, (generally) and then no dress, no parties, no fires make a difference – but it is the first setting out – and I can't go on hanging about for a year or two! – I must think all this well over, and pray write <u>clearly</u> about all too, perhaps you will suggest me something; Next letters, send me here, and one to Mr. Ruyssenaers to keep till I come, in case I should set off soon, and miss the post here.

Although Henriette largely had control of their budgets while dealing with the expenses to be made, her death did not directly lead to a sudden lack of financial control by Alexine. In a letter sent to Heuglin while in Khartoum, Alexine shows herself to be a treasurer too:

> Hereby (…) the bills and the letter for Mr. Thibaut; – the things to be rectified are the following – 1° Why (…) the expenses raise to 647,173 p. [piastres] the total of the bills only mount up to 465,766 p. – the rest of the sum has to be taken into account – 2° On the bill of the second expedition (…) 47 soldiers have been put, whereas there were only 34 – on the bill to Ayatt he puts 60 rifles, I have only received 34, one for each man.

She finds in total five items to be corrected in Thibaut's accounts, including one [3°] which d'Ablaing has to be charged for, though Thibaut was not blamed for this because he did not know. She appears to be quite preoccupied about the mixing up of bills of d'Ablaing and hers, and wants to have it cleared up before their departure, expecting an answer from Heuglin that he had sent Thibaut a clear response.[40]

From Khartoum, Heuglin kept Petermann informed about all the news, also including his own activities and accounting for all his steps and the care with which he performed his mission. He says he catalogued his collections and those of Steudner, which had been taken along on his entire journey, and to have packed them all for shipment to Cairo. In the letter there is also a remark about Musha Pasha having three steamboats at his disposal which he would like to use, in addition to the one the Tinnes had made use of, for a White Nile expedition. Heuglin had been invited by Musha Pasha to accompany him. 'This invitation really is not too bad', says Heuglin, because it would give him the opportunity to navigate the Sobat. However, Heuglin soon had to join Alexine on her way to Berber and Cairo, so Musha Pasha left alone for Sennār on 24 May, returning on 5 June.[41]

Musha Pasha's case against Alexine

In her defense against the accusations made by Musha Pasha regarding the act of slavery, Alexine stood somewhat alone. Heuglin's acquaintance with Musha Pasha dated from the period he held office at the Austrian consulate. When Musha Pasha became governor general of Sudan, Heuglin had been positive about his capacities and even optimistic about his influence on the future of Sudan's state of affairs. After a while he began criticising Musha's new policy of taxes levied on the Sudanese population, in particular concerning its effects on Western travellers and traders. He also had serious reservations about the motives of Musha's anti-slavery activities. Nonetheless, he seems to have maintained his good relationship with Musha, even planning to join him on an expedition on the Sobat.

His good relations with Musha Pasha may have been what ultimately led to the accusations against Alexine being postponed. After Musha's accusation had been established officially and the people involved had been detained, there actually never was an official process against Alexine. It is highly likely that Heuglin played an intermediary role between both parties to settle the affair. A meeting may very well have been organised in Khartoum between Alexine, Heuglin and Musha Pasha.[42] Eventually Musha Pasha might have satisfied himself with the penalties regarding the taxes paid by Alexine via Thibaut. The complaints against Biselli and Ali Amuri that Alexine lodged directly after her arrival were supported by two reports by Heuglin, who definitely was not willing to put them aside because of his good relationship with Musha Pasha. In September and October 1863, he drew up two accounts on behalf of Alexine in which he recorded the events that had taken place at their encampments near Bongo. Both letters deal with atrocities and unjustitified behaviour on the part of both slave traders. He also noted the facts about the imprisonment and murder of some of their men: how Kleincznik's men had been buying *durra* in the land of the Azande and Fertit at the other side of the river Kosanga when they were surprised by Ali Amuri's elephant hunters who imprisoned them, killing three of them in the process, saying they were tresspassing in 'their country'. As stated in his first letter of 1 September, these events spread panic among his men, leading them to refrain from any further service.[43]

Despite differences in their estimation of Musha Pasha, Alexine appears to have maintained a good relationship with Heuglin, as is illustrated by the following small note which was most likely written during their stay in Khartoum:

Thousand and thousand times thanks, my dear Mr. Heuglin, for your nice interest in me – I am much better, only my throat still hurts and I have renounced on my daily promenade – but I believe I could pay honour to the *pintade* – I think to be almost better this afternoon, and I hope, that I will be able to receive you this evening in a slightly better state than yesterday. Au revoir…[44]

From the dune island of Tuti, Alexine fought her own battle against Musha Pasha's accusations and the incidents of the past eight months, persisting in this for almost one year. First of all there was her case against Biselli, who had taken advantage of the expedition's awkward situation, and Ali Amuri's crimes towards the local people, those who were in her service and her soldiers. Alexine appeared to be extremely affected by these atrocities.

Heuglin was also disturbed by the events near Bongo, of which he had been a witness in October and November the previous year. He personally considered these to be appalling acts towards the native population and points in his accounts to the fact that the behaviour of these monopolistically acting traders ran counter to the freedom of traffic on the White Nile. This freedom had been agreed upon by European and Egyptian authorities in Cairo and Khartoum and had been broadcasted in journals all over Europe.[45] By handing over his two reports in October 1863, he provided Alexine with ammunition for the official complaints against these traders she wanted to make in Khartoum and later in Cairo.

A second indignity suffered by Alexine was the detaining of the expedition's boats by Musha Pasha after their return from Meshra to Khartoum. The high taxes that had been levied forced Thibaut to pay large sums on Alexine's behalf.

And lastly she was never able to clear herself fully of the accusations of her involvement in acts of slavery, which became a source of almost constant indignation and irritation.

On 30 April, Alexine sent an official letter of complaint to Thibaut in Khartoum. She demands, or actually begs, satisfaction: 'Je viens me plaindre à vous et vous prier de me faire obtenir satisfaction des affrontes et vexations dont les negocians [sic] Aly abou Amouri et Buselli se sont rendus (…) envers nous, et de tout ce qu'ils nous ont fait.' This document was signed by Thibaut on 12 May and sent to Musha Pasha together with Heuglin's reports.

The object of her indignation gradually shifted from the slave traders to Musha Pasha. Her letter of complaint addressed to Isma'il Pasha in Cairo contained mainly her accusations against Musha Pasha's conduct towards her.

The three issues made her decide to ask for assistance from her Dutch family. On 8 May, Alexine notifies her uncle Jules van Capellen, who was a chamberlain to King William III, about her awkward situation and begs him for help (see appendix 5: letter A. Tinne to J. van Capellen, 8 May 1864, Khartoum). Accompanying this letter is a short request written to King William III himself in which she speaks of her hope that he would deign to assist her and permit her uncle Jules to explain the nature of her complaints. If he would put in a word in her favour to the Egyptian authorities, she pleads, her situation was likely to change completely. Van Capellen directly approached Ruyssenaers, the Dutch consul in Alexandria, via the Minister of Foreign Affairs and later informed the king, who confirmed that, if necessary, Alexine could count on his protection in the near future.

The fourth bereavement

On 19 May, Adriana van Capellen died unexpectedly quickly after having been ill for three days (according to Heuglin it had been 'typhus'). At Alexine's request, d'Ablaing took care of the further arrangements to be made, and Addy was buried *'provisoirement'* in the churchyard until Alexine heard from Aunt Jim whether she wished the body to be transported to Eik en Duinen in The Hague. From Tuti, she arranged the church ceremony of Addy's burial.

Katie Petherick's letter to her sister on 28 May describes the events preceding Addy's death and afterwards:

> One morning I received a tiny note from her wishing to see me;
> I went at once, she was in bed, and knew me not for a few minutes;
> I saw that she was very ill. I dispatched a messenger to miss tinné
> [sic]; sent for the doctor (…) [who] soon came, and laughed at my
> fears: he said it was only a little fever; but in three hours she was
> dead – the following day was buried. All the Europeans attended
> the funeral of Miss Cappelan (…). Poor Miss Tinné's grief is
> bitter.[46]

By now the news about Henriette's death had reached the Western world. The royal court in The Hague was also informed of Henriette's death via Jules van Capellen. Only after having arrived at Suez could Alexine read the letter from Queen Sophie dated 11 June 1864: '(…) Your whole life you shall miss <u>her</u>, whose whole existence was devoted to yours (…). Tell me of your plans, and when you think of returning to your old house, you will ever find me. Your affectionate Sophie.'[47]

From Khartoum to Berber

After Adriana's death, Alexine made up her mind and decided ('at last', in the words of Heuglin[48]) to go from Khartoum to Egypt via Suakim, and asked Heuglin to escort her. D'Ablaing left Khartoum for Egypt at the end of May, not having been able to recover from his illness. For Alexine and Heuglin, however, it took May and June to make preparations for this journey. Due to obstructions from the Khartoum authorities, Heuglin had some difficulty in hiring three barks.

On the evening of 5 July, he sailed out of the city with a favourable wind. With a feeling of relief, Heuglin said farewell to the capital of Sudan 'for ever', as he exclaims.[49] After an auspicious journey, Heuglin reached Berber's palm gardens on 9 July. Alexine had been delayed and arrived nine days later. Meanwhile, Heuglin had started negotiations concerning the camels and drivers they needed to cross the desert from Berber to Suakim. When complications arose because of the lack of animals, provisions and people, Alexine had 40 camel loads sent ahead to Cairo. Back in Khartoum she had been forced to stock her quantity of corn and meal, which were not available in Berber, for two months. In the beginning of August, these loads arrived from Khartoum. In Berber, the delay was prolonged because of difficulties raised by the camel drivers concerning the packing of Alexine's loads. Finally on the evening of 6 September, they could leave.[50]

Shortly after her arrival in Berber, Alexine provided her aunt Jemima (who had by then been dead for almost two months) with some important details concerning her mother's death, the way she experienced this and how practical she could be in seriously demanding circumstances. The letter illustrates her state of mind and exhaustion after the trip (see appendix 5: Letter A. Tinne to Jemima van Capellen, 5 August 1864, Berber). In this letter Alexine referred to her changing relationship with d'Ablaing, who by then was on his way back to the Netherlands. Presuming that he would pass by her aunt once in the Netherlands, she anticipated his version of the story about what had occurred during her mother's last moments. At that time he had been unkind towards her and therefore had fallen short of her expectations.[51]

On the same day she wrote to her uncle Jules, Jemima's brother, from Berber about Adriana's last moments. While adding all kinds of daily needs, she establishes her view regarding the present situation in Sudan that European civilisation there was waning (see appendix 5: Letter A. Tinne to J. van Capellen, 5 August 1864, Berber).

> The Sudan is in a shocking state – I ask myself every day, if time has not gone backwards during my stay at Bongo, and if we are got [sic] back to the good old time when a European ambassador had to dismount and prostrate himself before a Turkish common soldier – Seriously I could not have been more astonished if I found Holland en pleine féodalité, burning Jews, and people who say the world is round – I cannot imagine how the influence of Europeans, that has been so slowly and firmly established, had changed so in one year – Is Europe got so weak? – or Egypt so strong? – (...) Now everything is reversed (...) everyday the Europeans at Khartoum had some new insult to complain of (...) Musha Pasha has seized some merchant's servants, Petherick's amongst others, and put them to torture to try to make them witness against their masters. Petherick's have been twice insulted by soldiers (...) –
> And now I have something to ask you which I hardly dare to do – I think you will find it strange – but both Mrs. Heuglin and Petherick who are here advise it me...the Food is scarce as I told you, and I heard there has been a sort of a famine in Egypt, and it is so annoying having every day a vulgular [sic] hunt for your dinner... I want you to send me a quintal of stock-fish, as much of *rook-vleesch* as will keep for three months, salt butter for three months, and 3 or 4 *comijnde-kaasen* [cumin-cheese] – I would like the *rook-vleesch* to be taken from the man who always furnishes us, the servants will know who – (...) to be sent by the same boat from Rotterdam she had taken (...) if you think potatoes will keep (...) send a provision of them too – and some *bockum*, those herrings

with eggs – all that had best be sent to the care of Mr. Ruyssenaers, who will forward it to me when I come – (...).[52]

Almost all her personal belongings and those of Henriette, Flore, Anna and Addy were transported by Alexine on her way to Berber, Suakim, Suez and Cairo.[53] Several children accompanied her on the trip to Cairo. The names of Habiba and Abdallah will be mentioned later again, having been described in the letters that Margaret Tinne-Sandbach sent from Cairo. During their journey through the Nubian desert, they stayed in *whadis* like Ras el-Wadi where men, women and children came into their camp, once they had settled down on 16 September. Besides sheep, milk and food they were able to purchase some ethnographical artefacts (see Catalogue numbers: 13-22, 31, 33, 34, 44-48 and 79-80) by bartering with tobacco.[54] In the evening a thunderstorm released masses of water from the surrounding rocky hills, streaming into the valley and their place. Because Heuglin had given his two tents to Alexine, he was forced to take shelter under a large piece of leather that was used to cover the rugs he had taken along.

Late in the evening of 23 September they halted under sycamore trees near Suakim, arriving in Suakim itself the day after in the afternoon. Heuglin soon realised that this place would bring another serious delay. Alexine took possession of a private house at the customs, and he found some barracks. They expected a steamer to come around mid-October, but its arrival was delayed day after day. Alexine decided to go Jeddah where there was more frequent traffic of steamers to Suez. There, she hired an expensive sailing boat which could only be prepared for sailing on 23 October. This time she went ahead 24 hours before Heuglin, who had to find a boat for himself that could leave on the 24th. Five days after their boats had moored in Jeddah, the French consul in Egypt visited them, then the English consul did likewise. Both procured separately their tickets for the boat trip from Jeddah to Suez. Their steamer named Gladiator would leave for Suez on 10 November.

In stormy weather they entered the Gulf of Suez on the evening of the 20th and were able to proceed to the city two days later. On the boat, Alexine had caught a cold because of the chilly weather. Their return journey from Khartoum had taken five months. At the customs in Suez, Alexine's small group of Sudanese girls and boys caused many complications and was kept in custody, as Heuglin relates in 1869.[55]

The body of Henriette as well as Flore's had been buried provisionally in Khartoum. On Alexine's departure for Berber and Egypt, both bodies were dug out again and transported on camels, presumably in the tin coffins she is referring to in her first letter in April 1864 to John. From Jeddah the bodies were shipped to Cairo, and from there to the Netherlands. After having received no notification from her aunt Jim or her uncle Jules, Adriana's body was definitively buried in Khartoum's graveyard.

Stopover at Suez

In Suez, Alexine read all the letters that were responses to those she had sent from Khartoum and Berber. They included the news about Jemima van Capellen's death, which made her feel 'wretched', as she writes on 4 December to Jules. She relates that she was received by someone from the consulate in Alexandria as soon as she arrived at the port of Suez, thanks to the fact that Jules had written to Ruyssenaers demanding his attention to her arrival in Suez. Ruyssenaers sent a telegram to John in Liverpool about her arrival. In a postscript to Jules, Alexine adds that she received a letter – 'a very odd one' – from Anna's brother asking her to send the body to put a stop to rumours that were apparently circulating concerning the death of Anna. 'I don't understand how the presence of a body dead since a year can stop any calumnies as no autopsies can be made nor in what it concerns my reputation but as I proposed I must keep my promise and thereon I wanted to tell you, though it may be an indiscretion on their part entre nous it is not a great expense or trouble to me as it wont probably cost more than 20 fl. it is so light.'[56]

On reading Alexine's remark that she had not telegraphed or written to John because Ruyssenaers had told her he was *en route* to visit her in Cairo, Jules copied her letter and forwarded it on 18 December to John, who might have read it just before his departure for Marseille.

In Suez, Alexine wrote more letters looking back on many events that had taken place. From their content, it is obvious that she considered the string of deaths to be the work of destiny and that she was simply ill-fated. All these events were a 'succession of misfortunes, which generally happen at long intervals'. It all was 'too cruel, and it well required all the kindness expressed in the letters of you all, to cheer a little the gloom of my arrival.'[57]

By grouping all the deaths together with Jemima's, which had nothing to do with her expedition, it became possible for her to establish a series of the most inconvenient events that almost seemed to pass by, with herself as a spectator who could be blamed for nothing. Even the cause of her mother's death was not to be found in one of the illnesses prevailing in the Bahr el-Ghazal surroundings; it was the doctor who had made errors, and something poisoned she had eaten.

After having arrived in Suez and then Cairo, the expedition had come to an end. The companionship of Alexine and Heuglin lingered on, however, for some months. Their sojourn between mid-December and Heuglin's departure for Germany in mid-February can be considered an aftermath of the entire enterprise.

In a small note to Heuglin, Alexine indicates their changing relationship:

> I just went to telegraph in order to know why you wrote me nothing, fearing that something did happen, when your letter came, I was afraid (…) [that you had fallen ill], having seen you leaving that indisposed and I am satisfied to see you at least go better – in Cairo you could take more care of yourself than you have been able to do since a long time – I still have a cold and not well and in a hurry to leave this wretched hole of a place – everyone here is more or less ill and Tolba the day before has delivered from a little girl who did not survive, and she is herself is in great danger – You are complaining I have no more commissions to give you, but believing you to be free of my importunities if badly knowing my usual indiscretion; I have yet several things to ask you – 2 small lanterns, proper for oil or candle, of a size as mentioned on the enclosed paper, for being placed in the house (…) 3 pair of red shoes, size included, "les piques [cotton tissue] de <u>chit</u> [chintz] very ordinary for a dress of an arabian woman, rose or yellow or blue – 40 "piques" of fabric <u>very ordinary white</u>, for a "chemise arabe" (…) the small "chemise intérieure" called aragi (…) I send you a piece of <u>chit</u> not for the colour, but to show you the sort of fabric (…).[58]

This letter illustrates how Heuglin had been engaged in the business of daily things around her and to what extent Alexine liked to be dependent upon him. Having no money at all at his disposal, Heuglin had entered into her service – a kind of tenure in which he was supposed to deliver all kind of services to her, including doing shopping. Their relationship had changed from companion travellers – an adventuress and a scientist – into something close to that of a patroness and a servant in her employment. As a wealthy lady, she ordered him from Suez to do some shopping in Cairo.

From Suez, Alexine had also charged Heuglin with the dispatch to Jules van Capellen concerning the death certificate of his sister Adriana, which had just been released by the Dutch Consulate General. In his letter to Jules dated 27 November, Heuglin writes that they arrived on the 23rd from Jeddah in order to offer his services to 'Mlle. Tinne' who 'thanks God, was recovering from the fatigues of her miserable journey'. 'She hopes her brother will be coming this winter in Egypt and I am convinced that his presence will much contribute to her consolation –.' [59]

To Uncle Jules, Alexine writes from Suez on 4 December 1864:

> I cannot write much as I and all my Sudan have been taken ill by the cold we found here and suffer from coughs, ophlamy [ophtalmia] and fevers... It was absolutely necessary for me to buy some clothes and things before going further... But although I would not like to enter Cairo again, this place is so miserable that as soon as Mr. Heuglin! is able to find me a house <u>outside</u> Cairo! I will go there and stay probably till I have found what would suit me definitively –.

She complains of the cold in Suez: '...[This] is quite incredible and is the cause of my shocking bad writing to you as my hand is quite paralysed and my head feverish with a bad cold – I pass my days in bed, rolled up in a blanket, and dread to stretch a hand out – the blacks are ill too.'

Still in Suez, she provides crucial information to her Uncle Siccama in a letter dated 16 December:

> [It was] a very disagreeable voyage from Berber through the desert of Souakim – firstly I was suffering and weakened, and regarding the chameliers [camel drivers] who are a bad race of people (...) they caused me unbelievable troubles. You will understand that

I am sure that it is embarrassing for me to return to The Hague and if I had to I would leave the place (…) I prefer the Orient what I love and know – (…) the Sudan is something else.

And she describes how she had terrible confrontations with the camel drivers: 'Each morning there were horrendous disputes how the camels were to be charged', and how they had to defend themselves with arms against raids by *sheiks*.[60]

Her remark to John about the way she would experience taking up her previous life in the society circles turns up again in a letter to Jetty, in a different form though. Since more than one and a half year she had not written to her. From Suez she tells of her being conscious of her aging during the past years. After apologising for this delay in her correspondence, Alexine ('it would have brought up all the painful details') refers to Jetty's face which by now is gradually fading away in her memory. Like everyone one has to face his aging, 'I myself am totally rimpled up. But you, you are not aged at all, without any doubt changed much though. I would like to have a photograph of yours.'[61]

After three weeks, Alexine and Heuglin could leave for Cairo, with their cargo containing the two bodies of Henriette and Flore, their other luggage and her 'children'.

A letter written by Jules on 15 December 1864 announced John's intended visit and was read by Alexine when she had arrived in Cairo and John had already paid his first visits to her: 'John! is preparing to start Eastward and will be with you before long. He is in fact the only person who can afford you what your complicated affairs and arrangements will require.'

CHAPTER 7

A pause in Cairo

Tidings from Cairo

Having been permanently sick since her arrival in Suez on 23 November, Alexine finally moved into a house in Cairo some three weeks later. Eager to leave Suez – this 'miserable and cold place' – she had ordered Heuglin directly after disembarking to search for a house outside the city, in 'Old Cairo', the quarter alongside the Nile embankment. Alexine's outspoken wish of staying in the old quarter, at some distance from the city, was identical to her choice of not remaining in Khartoum itself after the return of the expedition. Here as well, too many memories of the near past would fall upon her when seeing the places where she had stayed with her mother and aunt. With her group of Sudanese girls and boys she moved into her new home. Alexine had shared her isolation with others who experienced themselves under her guidance as being associated with each other.

In 1865, Old Cairo was still a quarter on its own, at a distance of some two kilometres from the city. The house Heuglin would find for her in December 1864 was meant to be temporary, because she intended to look around for a lot on which she could build a large house that would accommodate her wishes. She waited for John's arrival to make visits to parcels that were offered for sale. From this point, one had a fine view across the Nile to the pyramid of Gyzeh, with two small islands in between, of which the larger one had been connected by French engineers with a *pont volant* to the pyramid quarter under the regime of Muhammad Ali.

A decisive moment in Alexine's life had arrived. The Bahr el-Ghazal expedition had been aborted; she had succeeded in accomplishing her return journey to Egypt from Sudan with an immense amount of luggage, including the two bodies of Henriette and Flore. Surrounded by some twenty people, constituting her *troupe* of men and women, and boys and girls, from now on she remained in her house most of the time, avoiding entering the city. In the expedition's aftermath, she appeared unable to come to her senses about the events of the past and her present state, which would enable her to outline her next steps. In defining her new future, she expected John Tinne to fulfill a crucial role. Retreating in her house, she waited desperately for him to arrive. From Suez she had written to his wife Margaret: 'I am daily expecting John now, and start at every railway whistle… It will be like a dream to see him.'[1]

Eyewitnesses: Wilhelm Gentz, John and Margaret Tinne

Contemporary sources indicate that Alexine Tinne did not really recover from the ordeals she experienced during the expedition. In Cairo, all the events that had caused her pain and anger accumulated. She appeared not to have gotten over the deaths of her mother, her two Dutch maids and her aunt Addy, all having occurred within eight months' time. This grief at her losses and the successive accusations by Musha Pasha that she had been engaged in slavery and his obstructions during her departure from Khartoum, followed by her laborious retreat to Cairo via the Red Sea, had generated a mood in which bitterness prevailed.

Two sources provide us with accounts revealing significant details of Alexine's stay in Cairo. Particularly in Margaret Tinne-Sandbach's correspondence, valuable descriptions are found of Alexine's state of mind after her arrival in Cairo and the role Heuglin played in the first weeks they both stayed in Cairo. This source offers us a glance at her companionship with Heuglin and the moments they still remained in contact with each other.

These letters, dating from Margaret's arrival in Cairo on 13 January 1865, are the account of an eyewitness who was somewhat critical of Alexine's behaviour. John Tinne, Alexine's *chargé d'affaires*, kept a diary of his visit to Cairo in a small notebook in which he described his frequent contacts with her and the way he ultimately failed in his mission of persuading her to return to Europe.[2]

17 Portrait of Margaret
Tinne-Sandbach

Courtesy: Tinne Family Archive
Date: ca. 1860
Dimensions: 14 x 8 cm. Crayon drawing

One additional source delivers other important information. Presumably during John's visit, Alexine had a meeting with Wilhelm Gentz, a German artist and writer, who had just returned from a journey to Nubia.[3]

Both eyewitness accounts reveal Alexine as a rather complicated person with a headstrong character who had become a stranger to European society and had subsequently changed in appearance, adapting herself to a life in Arabian or Oriental style.

Meeting Gentz

The encounter between Alexine and Wilhelm Gentz, a German traveller and artist, must have taken place before 16 February 1864, most likely sometime before that date, possibly in January 1865, while Heuglin was still around in Cairo. On 16 February, Margaret Tinne mentions in a letter to her son: 'She has given Papa 2 large boxes full of Africana curiosities & they are to be sent to Liverpool by Boat…'. Gentz describes her ethnographic collections still being displayed in several places in her house. He sketched portraits of members of her company (see illustration 18).

Gentz had been introduced to Alexine by Heuglin, whom he might have met in the *Kneipe* which, as can be read below, was visited in particular by Germans during their stay in Cairo. In case he was not yet informed about Alexine's presence in Cairo, Heuglin would certainly have drawn his attention to her, proposing that he visit her. Thereafter, Heuglin organised a meeting between the two of them. (See appendix 6: Tidings from Cairo, Gentz, 1869.)

Heuglin and his Kneipe

Apart from Gentz, Heuglin met other visitors from Germany in Cairo, specifically from *Schwabenlande*, his native region. The German writer Max von Eyth tells in his *Im Strom unserer Zeit* how he met Heuglin in Cairo in the beginning of December 1864. In search of a decent meal, he passed on his donkey by a pub ('Kneiplein'), which was then located between the quarter of the Esbekiyeh to the mainstreet, the Muski. This place was run by a certain Meyer, a German, who served German beer 'at 18 Kreuzer a pint'. For a German like Eyth, Meyer was 'a comfort in the desert of existence', but for 'an Englishman or Frenchman an enigma, and for the religious Moslem a stone of offence and vexation'. Through the window, Eyth perceived the figure of 'Von Heuglin, the renowned Africa researcher and traveller' whom he had been introduced to a few days earlier when Heuglin had arrived from Khartoum accompanying the remnants of the aborted Tinne expedition. The mortal remains of Madame Tinne and her maid had been left in Suez together with the rest of the luggage consisting of collected specimina of birds, other animals and stones. As a matter of fact, Heuglin then was still making the necessary preparations to bring this 'silent caravan' over to Cairo. He had to go over to Suez the following day to take delivery of this 'luggage'. The geologist 'Professor Fraas from his beloved Schwabian country', who was also staying in Cairo at that time, had already been invited to join him on that trip. 'You know what? Go with us!' Heuglin had suggested to Von Eyth, while insisting on having another pint with him. The account of this voyage is unfortunately restricted to the mere fact that the next day they took the train to Suez.[4]

The aftermath of the expedition took more of Heuglin's attention, however, than just caring for 'the luggage' in the broadest sense. Alexine still needed his assistance, but actually just for a short period of time. The few notes she sent to him show no indication that she was undergoing serious setbacks. The fact that they had returned safely to Cairo meant that her dependency on him might have created a certain bond between them, but not a kind of friendship. Alexine realised that she owed her survival to a great extent to Heuglin's indefatigable efforts to take her along some two thousand miles to Cairo. On her way back to Cairo, she writes him to value that he takes a great deal of pity on her. Once in Cairo, however, living on her own and making plans for the future, including the building of a castle-like house, would put their relationship severely to the test. Their participation in an expedition to remote regions had come to an end. Alexine made up her mind about what her next steps would be, and what might possibly be the further use of having Heuglin around her. She would make very clear to her stepbrother John what Heuglin meant for her in the near future.

18 Etching, representing 'Les Nègres' of Alexine Tinne's suite.
Illustration in *L'Univers Illustré*, 1865.
Illustrated are the sketches by Wilhelm Gentz, made during his visit to A. Tinne in Cairo, January 1865.
Date: 1865
Dimensions: 22 x 28,5 cm.

NÈGRES DU SOUDAN, de la suite de M¹ˡ
I. Ptah, négresse du Fertit; — II. Bérilla, Abyssinienne; — III. T
VII. Dong

Tinne, dessinés au Caire, d'après nature, par M. W. Gentz. (Voir page 807).

se gallas; — IV. Joll, indigène du Denka; — V. Nègre du Dar-Nouba; — VI. Nègre Niam-Niam. —
gène de Gondar — VIII. Nègre du Darfour.

Margaret's letters and John's diary

Margaret Tinne-Sandbach (see illustration 17) writes to her son Herman about her first impression of Alexine's house in Cairo: 'Just opposite her window is a very good view of the Nile & the Pyramids beyond – & the Boats of the country with the white sails look so pretty (...)'.

The letter is dated 16 January 1865. After a journey of two weeks from Liverpool across the Mediterranean to Egypt, John and Margaret Tinne arrived in the harbour of Alexandria on 11 January 1865. Alexine had sent two of her servants, Abdallah and Ali, ahead to Alexandria in order to meet John and Margaret. Abdallah would carry a blue veil in his hand, she had announced in a letter. Directly on the day of his arrival, John had a meeting with Mr. Rowlatt of the Bank of Egypt and on the 13th with Mr. Colquhoun, British Consul General, in Alexandria. In his diary, John notes that they went to Cairo on the 14th and proceeded directly to Alexine's place in Old Cairo. After having spent their first night at Alexine's, they preferred to continue their sojourn in the Shepheard's Hotel, then known as the best hotel for Westerners, which was close by. For over four weeks, from the first day they were reunited, there was frequent contact between John, Margaret and Alexine, as well as Heuglin.

Both John and Margaret wrote in telegram style. John, while recording his daily experiences in his diary, writes for his own use; Margaret inserts into her correspondence to her two sons remarks that sometimes consist of only a few words. She informs her sons in a very direct way and often rather emotionally about the events going on and her reactions to things and people. Margaret's moments with Alexine reveal her very personal view on her behaviour. Because of their multitude of impressions, John's diary and Margaret's correspondence are irreplaceable documents revealing what was going on with Alexine at that time and Cairo as well (see appendix 6: Tidings from Cairo, Letters Margaret Tinne-Sandbach. Notebook John Tinne).

During their visit, John was to be almost constantly occupied by looking after Alexine's affairs. Besides arranging meetings at the British consulate in Cairo and the Dutch consulate in Alexandria, he even visited a reception organised by Isma'il Pasha, viceroy of Egypt, possibly for Alexine's public relations regarding her case against Musha Pasha. In his notebook he does not mention anything personal in particular. In his notations he largely deals with appointments, noting down the results, and writes to a lesser extent about his experiences.

Like a reporter, Margaret recounts in detail about the time she is spending in Cairo, and particularly her moments with Alexine. She wrote remarkable lines regarding the moment she sees Alexine for the first time in years. John and Margaret had been led to her house when suddenly a door was opened and 'poor Ali [Alexine] appeared – pale as death – drawing her breath quickly but not a tear! I cant cry she said but oh I am so glad to see you'. Margaret's first impression was that she looked 'like parchment – but gradually became to recover her looks'. In her appearances there is '(…) a softness & sadness which is not to be wondered at – & a careworn look – but when she is amused & laughs she is like her old self.'

In her impressions of Alexine's behaviour, Margaret's tone is sometimes cynical or critical, and at other times full of sympathy and love. 'She is a strange mixture sometimes so fascinating & so nice you cannot but love her – and other times so strange – so obstinate & such exotish [?] ideas about things & so reckless that one gets almost out of patience with her – she says she has lost all her courage and is afraid of every thing – but she does not seem to me afraid of any thing – .'

   After a week of visits, Margaret writes to Bertha on 25 January 1865 about the way Alexine rides on her donkey: 'You will be amused to hear that Alexine now intends to ride again – (…) on a donkey. She is too old – besides it is not consistent with Arab costume – but what is – is that the ladies ride astride on the Donkeys – their long black silk coverings however hide them so completely that it does not much show – .' On that day Alexine showed them around Old Cairo in a carriage.

In passing, she mentions in the beginning of February some lines about Alexine's plans for the near future: '(…) she says she wants to buy a place before we go that papa may so far see her settled – Yes I said – but in [the] mean time you make yourself ill which I think you do – Oh she said if I have to be ill – if I am what does it signify I can only die – & what matter if I do!'.

It was around this time that the relationship between Alexine and Heuglin came to an abrupt end. After having engaged him in the business of organising daily things for her, she suddenly could no longer tolerate his presence. After an argument with John and Margaret, she reluctantly agreed to their proposal to pay him a sum of £200. Margaret is critical of Alexine's behaviour in this regard: '£ 200 (…) – for <u>all</u> he has done for her & <u>how it is done</u> she says that her purse is £ 200 lighter her heart £ 200 lighter too – for she no longer feels (…) an obligation to him.'

For reasons of health, John and Margaret were forced to leave Cairo quickly and to move over to Alexandria where they arrived on 8 February. Margaret makes very clear why they left the city: '(…) Thank Goodness we have come here – There is a feeling of freshness & clearliness [sic] that is quite reviving after that pestilent menagerie of a Cairo.' Alexine's ethnographic collections, meanwhile, had been packed so that they could be shipped to Liverpool.

All efforts on the part of John to take Alexine with them on the boat – either to Liverpool or The Hague – were in vain. On 24 February, John and Margaret left Alexandria on the ss America, without Alexine.

On Alexine's choice to remain in Cairo, Margaret expresses her incomprehension. 'It is a strange idea to see a young creature like her thrown among a lot of strangers & living in such a way, when she has friends who would cordially welcome her & where she has comforts and luxuries at her command which she throws to the wind & she is always saying "<u>what a poor person I am</u>"! But I must stop this dismal strain.'

Alexine's pursuit of Musha Pasha

At the time of Alexine's arrival, Musha Pasha remained in Cairo where he was in direct contact with Isma'il Pasha, the viceroy of Egypt. Both of them had by then taken notice of Alexine complaints, which Thibaut had forwarded to the viceroy, enclosing Heuglin's testimonies. Soon it became clear that both Pashas were far from being impressed. Isma'il chose the tactic of delaying, putting aside the documents and postponing all decisions on the matter. Alexine's pursuit of Musha Pasha had been supported – behind the scenes – by the King of the Netherlands and was fought out on a high diplomatic level, with consul Ruyssenaers as a vehicle of Alexine's anger and Dutch irritation. Ruyssenaers must have felt himself incapable of bringing Alexine's complaints further in a sustainable and comprehensive case that considered both the *pashas*. Alexine, however, remained tenacious in

19 Alexine Tinne with Abdallah
and Jasmine, Cairo
Courtesy: Tinne Family Archive
Date: 1865
Photo: E. Désiré, Cairo
Dimensions: 14 x 8 cm.
Albumen print

her endeavours to receive 'redress'. This must have bred bad blood with
Isma'il Pasha. Although he was on his guard, confronted with an issue that
might involve a more or less open diplomatic and even royal interference,
Isma'il Pasha counterattacked by accusing her for a third time of slavery.
Even when Musha Pasha died of smallpox in his palace in Khartoum at the
beginning of February and the 'culprit' had left the stage, both parties still
regarded the affair as not having been closed and far from 'settled'.[5]

However fierce her indignation might have been, viceroy Isma'il Pasha must have been well aware of the fact that she did not have a very strong case at all. In stating that she had been unaware of the fact that her boats had been used by the ships' staff for the transportation of slaves, she only proved that she had failed as the leader of the expedition in effectively controlling her ships' crew. Regarding her arguments concerning the tax levy and negligence on the part of Musha Pasha with respect to her accusations against the traders, the viceroy actually must have taken offence. It provided him with one more reason for pushing aside the case which she demanded to lay before court.

In March 1865, Petherick arrived in Cairo to present a long memorandum on the injustices inflicted by Musha Pasha in an alleged attempt to drive European traders from the country and to establish an Egyptian monopoly. It was then commonly believed that this tax was designed to destroy the European traders, though few of them were left because their fortunes and activities were greatly in decline by 1864. His complaints were confirmed 'by one who had no interest in the country to bias her – Miss Alexine Tinné', as Colquhoun, the British consul general, stated to the Foreign Office.[6]

However, it is hard to believe that Alexine and Petherick were in good company in their case against Musha Pasha. Petherick at that time was engaged in a fight with fruitless results. His position had been weakened considerably after his failure to meet Speke and Grant after their discovery of the sources of the Nile. And there were also the lingering accusations concerning his dealing in the slave trade; although consistently denied by him, it was only in 1872 that he was able to refute them entirely. There was an impressive list of persons who made these accusations against Petherick. There were charges by officials such as Joseph Natterer, the former consular agent of Austria in Khartoum, the governor general of Sudan in Khartoum and an official declaration of two consulates, signed by Europeans in Khartoum and sent to the consul general of Britain in Cairo, stating his involvement in slave trade. To ward off the charges made by Natterer, Petherick, then still a consul, had an extensive correspondence with him, resulting finally in a statement by Natterer in 1862. He declared that at the time of his accusation in 1860 he had not been well informed about those carrying out traffic in slaves and that therefore 'not the slightest imputation was intended to be cast upon him'. Petherick also communicated in 1862-1864 with Heuglin, Hansal and Thibaut and extracted documents from them stating that the charges against him were false.[7] Despite these declarations and even one in which the Foreign Office announced that there had been no real evidence of his participation, he was initially unable to purify his name. It was generally well known that traders on the White Nile permitted their agents to seize and sell slaves, being partners in the profits indirectly. These facts worked to his disadvantage. When it was proved that his agents were engaged in slave trafficking, everyone assumed that Petherick himself was not an exception to this kind of criminal habit. As the official representative of his country, he moreover had failed to provide the government with proper information concerning the conditions in Southern Sudan in time. His first official dispatch to Her Majesty's government on the slave trade was dated 24 May 1862 – two years after Natterer had reported about these ongoing events to his government.[8]

It is not clear for how long Alexine persevered in her efforts to buy a parcel in order to build a house. Her situation in Cairo became gradually more awkward. Having entered her house in December 1864, the rental period of four months was to expire before May; her complaints against Musha Pasha were disregarded and the charges against her were sustained. To make matters worse, her endeavours of creating her own place became fruitless. When noticing that Alexine aimed to build a palace-like home in Cairo, Isma'il Pasha must have decided to undermine all her ambitions of settling down. Being blocked in her purchase of a suitable piece of land, Alexine had to dismiss her architect Deibeck. Before the expiration of the rent of her house, Alexine must have made up her mind to leave Cairo on a sailing trip on the Mediterranean; a plan she had already referred to in her conversations with John and Margaret.

One note has been preserved which presumably was written in the short period between John and Margaret's visit and her departure. It gives an impression of the fragile and uncertain state of her body and mind. An epidemy of cholera was then prevalent in Cairo. Alexine seems to be quite preoccupied with her own health and that of some members of her company. She tells how to administer '(…) chlorodyne of Collin Browne': '(…) directly 20 drops of chlorodyne in a glass of water to be taken and repeat after twenty minutes (…) till cured – cramps, vomitting etc. etc. 'cholera' (…) 60 drops of chlorodyne not to be taken in water every twenty minutes till perspiration begins (…) Between the doses of chlorodyne every twenty minutes it is good to give some Chartreuse on a piece of sugar (…)'.[9]

CHAPTER 8

After Cairo

The final journey

With the departure of Heuglin to Württemberg, the story of the Tinne-Heuglin expedition to the Gazelle-river comes to an end in mid-February 1865. Being restricted to this period of time, this book will only superficially glance at their lives before the expedition and after, when both our protagonists entered the last episode of their lives.

Alexine must have left Cairo before the summer of 1865. At Alexandria she hired the steam yacht 'Claymore' and settled herself with her dogs, Arabs and 'negroes' and an Egyptian crew to visit Crete, Greece, Italy, France, Sardinia and Malta during the summer of 1865, crisscrossing the Mediterranean Sea and drawing much attention wherever she went on account of the number of her black attendants.

After John and Margaret had returned home in February, no correspondence seems to have taken place for some months. On 20 October 1865, she wrote John from Naples, thanking him for a letter of credit of £400, which she apparently had asked for, either by letter or telegram. In this letter she states:

> I must, of course, return to Egypt, but in the meanwhile I cannot tell you exactly yet what I shall do for the present. I had meant to spend the winter in Naples, but since my arrival here the cholera has been officially declared. Now I am a bit afraid for myself but I don't like at all the idea of going through all the trouble and anxiety I have had with sick people in my house in Cairo, and the gloom and disturbed state of a town suffering from cholera.[1]

From Naples, John was asked to purchase a sailing boat for her. When he finally was able to buy one (named 'Seagull') built on the island of Wight, England, it was sent to Rotterdam. With the assistance of Jules van Capellen, it was registered as a Dutch ship at the Yacht Club of Rotterdam, named 'de Meeuw' and sent with a hired Dutch crew, headed by Captain Wilhelmie, to Toulon, where Alexine had just arrived after a trip to Sardinia and a longer stay in Nice. The new yacht which sailed into Toulon's port, however, appeared on closer inspection not to have the size agreed on; it was smaller, and by far did not weigh the promised 200 tons. After some harsh reproaches to John about the unfitness of 'de Meeuw', Alexine finally crossed over from Marseilles to Algiers (via Tanger and Tunis), where she arrived on 11 October and found herself a residence in the nearby village Mustapha. After the earthquake in January 1867, Alexine helped wherever she could in the city. The fact that her grandfather Van Capellen had bombarded the city, then a nest of pirates, in 1816 together with a British squadron, gave Algiers a place in the family history. After having read Duveyrier's *Les Touareg du Nord* which had been published in 1864 and also *La Langue Tamachek* by Hanoteau (1860), which was an introduction to Touareg grammar, a new grand ambition began to occupy her mind: penetrating towards the south from the borders of Algeria into the Touareg country.

In the meantime she granted Captain Wilhelmie's request to have come out from the Netherlands his wife, daughter and son to join him, as well as the spouses of some other members of the equipage. Together with Alexine's company of 24 people the entire party (see illustrations 19-21) consisted now of the captain and his family and the Dutch crew which partly was joined by their wives (Metson, the steerman, Petersen, the cook, Cornelis ('Kees') Oostmans, Körver, the carpenter, Bongma, the sail-maker, Van Zanten, Piet Petersen, Ruesch, Dintelaar and Lorentzen, all sailors, and Dulitz and Ary Jacobse, both ordinary seamen).

Before entering the desert from Algiers, enormous preparations had to be made. Alexine had 'de Meeuw' sent back to Malta, asking John to put the boat up for sale. The caravan, consisting of over sixty camels and three horses finally left Algiers in November 1867. Alexine was in high spirits. She rode on one of the three camels which had a palanquin attached to the saddle, protecting the rider from sun and sand. However, beset with problems like arguments between the crew, delays and, eventually, harsh weather conditions, the journey from the beginning became a deception. As they came near the confines of the French dominions, such bad news came in about the unsafe state of the Sahara that it was thought advisable to change the direction of the route. She decided therefore to go back to Constantine and from there to the port of Philippeville. Here the caravan disbanded. After having traversed the desert for six months, Captain Wilhelmie was glad to return to the Netherlands with his family and most of his sailors. With her followers, Alexine embarked again, visiting Malta, but returned soon to the North African continent, where she landed in Tripoli in October 1868. Her encounter with the Africa travellers Gerhard Rohlfs, Gustav Nachtigal and also Heinrich Freiherr von Maltzan brought her to a final decision to have another try at reaching Touareg country from Tripoli. Alexine stayed in the company of Rohlfs in Tripoli from 13 December 1868 to 20 January 1869; with Nachtigal she passed several days in Tripoli and 71 days (27 March – 6 June) in Murzuq.

Some remarks made by Nachtigal in his travel account are worth going into here. Later, Rohlfs would publish his impressions of the situation of Alexine and her train of people. Nachtigal describes her as: 'a lady [who] filled him at first with awe and respect', with 'aristocratic seemingly cold features and distinguished reserved bearing'. It was not until the end of January 1869 that everything was ready for her expedition. The Dutch consul Emile Testa himself saw the expedition off in Tripoli. Her party consisted of people who had joined her since her Upper Nile travels, Algerian women, Arabs from Tunis and Algeria, freed slaves who hoped to make their way back to their homes under her care, and Adolf Krause, a young German who had recently reached the continent. The city had been full of rumours about Alexine's wealth, and she already had been given the name of 'Bint el Re', or King's daughter. Two Dutch seamen of Captain Wilhelmie's group, Kees Oostmans and Ary Jacobse, were among her numerous 'followers' (their diaries fortunately were recovered after their deaths at Wadi Berdjong; a second one by Oostmans has recently been discovered in the Tinne family archive).

Alexine's caravan, consisting of 70 camels and a train of 50 people, proceeded only slowly on account of the large amount of luggage; it took a full month to arrive in Murzuq. Here they halted for a long time. Alexine writes to John: 'I intend to stay here pretty long for I have great plans. I recently got very favourable information, which induces me to go to Bornu, but I still want a good many things for this expedition. In the meantime I shall visit the Touaregs, if one of their chiefs will lend me his protection'. She decided to go on to the Fezzan capital Murzuq, where Nachtigal met her again to discuss further plans. 'Fräulein Tinne lived in the mainstreet as well, in the middle of it, some houses further, in a large building (…). I found her in the company of her beautiful, old, huge dog, which I believe was her most faithful friend in her entourage. [She was] quiet, serious, distinguished, as ever, though more heartely and warmly than in Tripoli'.[2] Both Alexine and Nachtigal wished to travel to Bornu at the end of the summer after having first undertaken a shorter journey. Nachtigal wished to visit Tibesti despite warnings of the dangers of travelling in that district. Alexine had cherished the same idea but was dissuaded from attempting it and, instead, began arrangements for penetrating the interior, trying to gain access to the Touareg region. Before they could leave Murzuq, both travellers came down with a fever in May. Alexine developed appendicitis and became dangerously ill. After sixteen days she began to recuperate, thanks partly to Nachtigal's advice on a suitable diet and the use of narcotics to ease her pain and help her to sleep.

While in Tripoli they had a talk with Ali Riza, the governor general, who had told them that he had no influence at all beyond his own frontiers, with the single exception that if either of them wished to visit the Touareg country, he could help them through Ichnuchen, who was his friend and leader of the Touareg Asgar, at Ghat. Accordingly Alexine wrote suitable letters and received a friendly reply from this chief saying that he would himself be visiting a *wadi* during the summer and offering to accompany her. Realising that she should have enough to last her several months, Alexine wrote to John with a request to send her Theresia Thaler to the value of Fr. 45,000 to her banker in Malta, who would send them on to Mr. Testa, the Dutch consul in Tripoli. She also asked John to send her Fr. 15,000 immediately, so that Abdallah could make purchases in Tripoli. When questioned by John if she trusted Mr. Testa, she answered: '(…) one sees such strange things as one advances in life and particularly in the East where consciences are proverbially elastic that one does not know exactly what to think. A man may not be capable of a very bad action, but weak and led by others into doing an indelicacy, and that is what I most fear.'[3]

On the day Nachtigal started from Murzuq for Tibesti, she proposed they start a short journey to a *wadi* where she was to meet this Ichnuchen. On the evening of 5 June, Nachtigal accompanied her through the west gate of Mur-

20 Photo, representing members of A. Tinne's
suite, in the house at Algiers/Mustapha
The photo, presumably made by Alexine
Tinne, represents Abdallah with Biija (wife
of Ali) and Rosa [?].

Courtesy: Tinne Family Archive
Date: 1866/67
Dimensions: 16 x 22 cm.
Albumen print (colour-washed by A. Tinne)

zuq to the camp that her people had made outside the walls, and took leave of her 'with very warm farewells, since during the common sojourn in Murzuq I had learned to value the heart and mind of this lady very highly'. The next day Nachtigal left for Tibesti and heard no more of her until he was returning again through Fezzan, when a fugitive brought 'the shocking news of the slaying of my comrade Alexandrine Tinne through the shameless treachery of the Touaregs'. In the weeks after his return to Murzuq on 8 October, Nachtigal was able to reconstruct a clear picture of the course of events after talking to and questioning witnesses.

After having met the Touareg chief as arranged, Alexine was told he was not yet ready to proceed to Ghat, so he turned her over to one Murabid Hadj Ahmed Bu Slah, who had instructions to return with her to Murzuq to assist her in her preparations there and then conduct her as far as Ghat. While they were in Murzuq again getting a caravan organised, Alexine was visited by eight Touaregs of Ichnuchen's following. One Hadj es Scheik alleged that they were also to give her any possible assistance and suggested travelling westwards with her. Being treated with all kinds of politeness and respect, Alexine was very pleased with the prospect of such travel companions. These Touaregs left Murzuq at the same time as her caravan, and remained in sight of it day and night. Her caravan advanced slowly because, as Nachtigal recounts as a result of his own experiences two months before, she had admitted men in her company of whom no one was willing to work. Many of them seemed to take advantage of her and moreover were continuously quarreling with each other. Besides suffering from attacks of gout Alexine at that time had also an inflammation of the eyes which often made her lie down on a bed in her tent for hours. Once outside on her camel, she was forced to wear a bandage over her eyes for protection from the sunshine.[4] Due to her disease, she was not able to maintain order in her group.[5]

On 1 August, the men were getting ready to leave Wadi Berdjong (the women's camp was nearby), when a dispute began – 'doubtlessly by pre-arrangement' – between two of the Arab camel drivers over the loading of their animals. Meanwhile, both the Dutchmen were ready, their camels laden, with their firearms hanging from the saddles. Kees Oostmans, who was near the quarrelling men, interfered in an attempt to restore peace. Nachtigal writes: 'This attitude must have given the conspirators the occasion they were seeking to carry out their scandalous plan'. The quarrellers turned upon the Dutchman, protesting against his interference. When the dispute escalated, Hadj es Scheik suddenly sprang in with his lance raised and threw it at Oostmans with the words 'Why do you meddle in the dispute of Muhammadans?'. When Oostmans fell dead on the ground, it brought about the confusion that the plotters were aiming for. Ary Jacobse leapt on his camel to ride to his comrade's aid but, struck by a sword on the back of his head, he fell on the ground and was subsequently stabbed with a lance. In no time, the whole camp was in a state of chaos. Women rushed from their tents screaming, and slaves thought their last hour had come. The wild tumult drew Alexine from her tent and subsided somewhat at the sound of her commanding voice, and then suddenly, as Nachtigal recounts, 'the poor defenceless lady at whose life it all was aimed, found herself in the thick of the fray surrounded by angry Arabs, cowardly or conniving servants and violent Touaregs.'

'It was an Arab who was the first to raise his hand against the defenceless lady (…) with a blow of sharp weapons on her neck and shoulder, but he did not fell her to the ground. There came a blow on the forearm by a servant of Hadj es Scheik before she collapsed from loss of blood. She lost consciousness mercifully soon and was dying by mid-day.'

Alexine's company was sent back to their tents with the promise that 'not a hair of their heads would be touched, for they were only out for murdering Christians'. They were later provided with camels and water and permitted to return to Murzuq. The Touaregs and Arabs opened the chests and bales of luggage, and were very disappointed to find only a relatively small amount of Thaler. Two Arabs who had entered her service in Murzuq then tied a rope around Alexine's ankles, pulled her aside and, 'under gross mockeries', started to strip her of her clothes. While they did their work '(…) she moaned softly'. The Arabs and Touaregs hastily dispersed in various directions, leaving the less valuable articles strewn about on the sands.[6]

Abdallah, who had been one of her most faithful companions for five years, was able to retrieve John's last letter to Alexine, but it was in a tattered state, its date having been torn off. Returning to Murzuq after collecting supplies in Tripoli, he hastened to the scene of the murder and recovered some of her personal belongings. The third page in John's last letter contains the following: 'I often think to myself, "Poor, poor Alexine! Is she never to find that blissful abode, that heaven on earth, she is in search of?" (…). It is a strange

21 Photo, made by A. Tinne of members of her suite, in the house at Algiers/Mustapha.
From left to right: Ali (sitting), Piet Petersen (standing next to him), Dulitz (?), Kees Oostmans (at the column), Habiba (sitting in front of the column), Fourré (sitting next to her), the two veiled wives of Ali: Biija and Rosa with Jasmine, sitting in between, Hermann (H. Körver, the carpenter?) standing next to Capt. Wilhelmie (at the column to the right), Abdallah (leaning against the other side of the column) and 'Baas' (J. Lorentzen ?).

Courtesy: Tinne Family Archive
Date: 1866/67
Dimensions: 16 x 22 cm. Albumen print

infatuation, that dream of your childhood to see what that 'blank space' in Africa contains. Will it reward you when it is accomplished?'[7]

The rest of the story concerns the rather inept attempts of the Fezzan and Tripoli authorities, led by Testa, to find and try the guilty parties. After many months of delay, the case was tried in Tripoli. Nachtigal later learned that the Touaregs had managed to put all the blame on the Arab camel drivers and had implicated a local official at Murzuq, who had been particularly helpful to them, as instigator. According to Nachtigal and others such as Testa, the Touaregs had conceived this whole affair for the sake of money and other valuables, and used the Arabs as accessories in the plot.[8]

Some details have later been added to or corrected in this account. During the investigations and trial in 1870, different versions of how Alexine, Oostmans and Jacobse had been mortally wounded were told. Although Nachtigal was an expert on this regions and had made thorough investigations by interviewing witnesses, he had not been an eyewitness. During the trial, which lasted from January to April 1870, one name in particular appeared to be crucial: Bu Bekker, a young Touareg chief determined to spite Ichnuchen whom he presumed to have taken a fancy to Alexine, who presumably was her assassin.[9]

Before Alexine left Murzuq to fulfill her ardent desire to meet the Touaregs, her company consisted of two Dutch sailors, three Sudanese servants, three female servants, ten male servants (with wives and children), fifteen camel drivers, one Tunisian, two local inhabitants from Murzuq, three male slaves and one female who had run away from their proprietors and found asylum with her, and some more ex-slaves.[10] Almost all of them were, according to Rohlfs, hanging around her because of their interest in her as a benefactress. They were useless for this perilous journey. Rohlfs had tried in vain to talk her out of the idea of entering the region of the Touaregs with this train of people. He proposed instead that she choose a set of professional people in Tripoli. It was Rohlfs who made a sharp analysis of Alexine's motives and how they caused her demise:

> As always on her travels without a fixed plan, she finally had
> decided to proceed to Fessan and Bornu, but at the same time also
> having the intention to go for Ghat, in order to visit the there
> remaining Touaregs. In vain I tried to dissuade her to take along

those large French water tanks made from iron, which obviously were very practical for the French troops in Algeria, but which for an individual traveller on his journey would cause the greatest danger, because those would arouse the rapacity of wild tribes. (…) Alexine Tinne would not let herself be persuaded.[11]

In his summary of Alexine Tinne's travels, Rohlfs is merciless in his judgment: 'Thus the Tinnean enterprises were shipwrecked altogether, once by carrying a train along which was too immense, the second time by the richness of this lady which had become too well known'.[12]

The Tinne family's correspondence paper with black edging, used initially as a sign of mourning for Henriette, remained in use for some time after 1870, having received an additional significance after Alexine's death.

Some uncertainty remains about the photo equipment that Alexine had carried along during her Africa travels. Alexine used a camera and all that was required to process photographs on the White Nile journey. At Heiligen Kreuz, she recorded portraits of the missionaries. These photos – presumably made on glass negatives and made into albumen prints on the spot – were handed over to Petherick at Meshra el-Rek.[13] In 1869, Petherick told John Tinne he should be grateful for 'photographic views of Gondokoro and the Bahr el-Ghazal', which could indicate that Alexine had had her camera with her during the expedition.[14] Of her stay in Cairo only one photo has been preserved (see illustration 19). It was made by a Cairese photographer named Désiré. The camera she evidently had used on her previous White Nile and Bahr el-Ghazal journeys could have been out of order or lost during her return from Khartoum.

The subsequent pictures which have been preserved are of a later date and were made during her travels of 1866, 1867 and 1868. They represent members of her group (see illustrations 20, 21 and 22) and are a clear indication that she was in the possession of photo equipment. Due to their size and personal additions (the use of watercolours), these images were arguably taken by her. She may have bought this equipment on her boat trips around the Mediterranean Sea when she called on Crete, Naples, Malta, Toulon and Marseille, continuing her journey on the second boat to Tanger, Tunis, Algiers and Tripoli. Supposing she purchased new equipment, she most likely would have done so in France. The camera she used after the start of her journey in the Algerian desert, where she took several photos of her group, might have been identical to the one she purchased during her Mediterranean trip. Presumably she left this camera behind in Tripoli and proceeded to Murzuq. After her arrival there, she wrote a letter to John on 3 April with a long list of numbered items she wanted to have purchased and transferred to her. Number 8 reads as: 'un appareil photographique Dubroni [sic], if its price does not exceed Francs 100, if it is as easy to manage and small as the papers say, and requires scarcely any [maintenance?] – if not, it must be accompanied by directions.'[15]

After her death in 1869, John Tinne's sons Ernest and Theodore were sent to Tripoli to gather her belongings and clear her house. They used the camera to take ambrotype-pictures of her house and of some Touaregs, who as chiefs were attending the inquiry sessions following her death. While making photographs of her house in Tripoli, they made use of 'Alexine's Derboni Camera', as described on an adjoining piece of paper (see illustrations 89 and 90).[16]

In his letters Ernest writes how delighted he was in finding this equipment at her place. It was either the camera she had ordered in her letter and which meanwhile had been delivered in Tripoli, including a proper manual which both sons used while operating it, or it was the camera (a different type of Derboni) she had left behind in Tripoli. This equipment was not found among the belongings that John's sons had brought from her house to Liverpool.

Heuglin's reproaches

As an experienced Africa traveller, Heuglin was a full member of an expedition that was led by two women who were determined to maintain their *haute bourgeoisie* lifestyle and corresponding pace as much as possible. Though it was an expedition, hastening was fundamentally wrong to them. Accompanying Alexine meant delay after delay.

Indeed, the predominant tone in Heuglin's later account of the expedition, titled *Reise in das Gebiet des Weissen Nil und seiner westlichen Zuflüsse*, is different from the one he used in his letters in 1863-64. Between the lines, and sometimes even more explicitly, Heuglin in 1869 sounds somewhat cynical

22 Photo, representing
A. Tinne and the
female equipage of 'de
Meeuw' in the house
at Algiers/Mustapha.

From left to right:
Ary Jacobse's wife,
Habiba (servant since
1862 and Abdallah's
wife), Jasmine (with
Habiba's hand on her
shoulder), the wife of
'Baas' (J. Lorentzen?),
Biija (wife of Ali),
Saada (sitting next to
her), Alexine Tinne
(standing, 'en profil'),
Catharine Metson-Don
(the steersman's wife),
Mrs. Wilhelmie and
daughter, 'the cook's
wife', Mrs. Petersen
(wife of the cook's
brother Piet) and Rosa
(wife of Ali).
The photo was made
after Alexine had
placed the group with
herself in position.

Courtesy: National
Archives, The Hague
Date: 1866/67
Dimensions: 18 x 23,5 cm.
Albumen print

about the way the Tinnes organised and maintained the enterprise. Sometimes he even sounds reproachful of Alexine Tinne. He presents himself here as a scientist with a mission. He is straightforward in his account, has a precise view on what had occurred, and remains a detached registrant of the drama of the Tinnes as well as his own, which included the death of his companion Steudner and his own struggle with diseases. When Heuglin describes the last part of the trip to Cairo, his annoyance cannot be hidden.

The amount of £200, reluctantly presented to him by Alexine as compensation for all he had done for her after the expedition was aborted, presumably would not have mollified him given that he had been thrown on his own resources during the two years' time of the 'Tinne'ische Expedition', which essentially had been an enterprise of 'everyone for himself'. As we will read in the Epilogue, another criticism arose regarding the edition of the *Planteae Tinneanae*. According to Heuglin, the names of Henriette and Alexine were erroneously mentioned as the collectors of many items and the provenance of some specimens were wrongly attributed to them.

The news of Alexine's death, occurring on 1 August 1869, might have reached Heuglin before the time his book was presented. On 18 August, the news of her death was sent by telegraph from Tripoli to Europe – too late to be mentioned in the foreword by Petermann, dated 5 August.

During his expedition to the Gazelle-river, Heuglin mapped out new geographical facts, drew sceneries with animals and peoples, and collected ethnographic material. His primary goal was to fulfill his scientific ambitions, despite the loss of his friend Steudner. However, this mission was disrupted by the unfortunate circumstances that befell the expedition, which had forced him to make an untimely retreat. This resulted in another dent to his reputation. Although he had 'a good story' for not having been able to enter the Azande country, he was later to be confronted with reproof for a second time. His critics argued that he did not live up to the expectations many had of him and that, despite the dramatic events that occurred, he should have seized the opportunity to push further into Central Africa and accomplish his mission. This confirmed the opinion of many that Heuglin was a scientist and not 'a real man of action'.[17] The vehemence of the reaction to Heuglin's failure to reach the Azandes can only be explained by the considerable national ambitions that lay behind the expeditions in Africa. While these ambitions were often cloaked under the pretext of the importance attached to discovering geographical information – the main purpose of this type of expedition – they point to the increasingly nationalistic undertones that dominated the subject of the exploration of Africa.

Heuglin subsequently had the opportunity to write about his experiences, which enabled him to re-establish his position in the scientific world to some extent once he was back in Germany. He did not neglect to mention that much of the new information concerning the region beyond the Gazelle-river he had received secondhand. As a man of science, he was willing to state that he had derived most information about the Azande from interviews with Khartoum traders who had visited these peoples and the deputy of Sultan Mofío in November 1863. The fact that circumstances forced him to stay near the borders of Azande land, depriving him of the opportunity to prove the veracity of these statements, must have been an immense frustration. His account actually did not attain more than the level of facts and figures delivered to him by others who had reached the regions he himself had wanted so much to enter.[18]

Though the expedition brought him serious troubles, sicknesses, grief and frustration, in some respects it was a successful enterprise for Heuglin. Apart from the collection of zoological, botanical, geological and ethnographic specimens he had gathered, he was able to complete a map of the Bahr el-Ghazal region that was far better than the ones drawn up previously by other travellers, thanks to the information gathered by him in anticipation of 'the Tinnes' project' (his own words).

No matter how disappointing the actual results of the expedition might have been for Heuglin, he is acclaimed in Petermann's foreword of 1869 as the experienced traveller who mapped out for the first time the whole basin of the Gazelle-river in a scientific manner. He may not resemble some more fortunate and famous adventurers, but his accomplishments are first-rate, argues Petermann, who intended to create new opportunities for him.

In 1870, Heuglin was asked to join an arctic expedition heading for Spitsbergen, followed in 1871 by his participation in a Polar expedition to Nova Zembla. His publication *Ornithologie Nordost-Afrika's, der Nilquellen und Küsten Gebiete des Rothen Meeres und des nördlichen Somal Landes* is the result of his research during the journeys he made between 1860 and 1865, illustrated with 'portraits' of birds in sublime watercolours from his hand.

He returned to North Africa in 1875, visiting Massoua on the Red Sea. This research resulted in 1877 in his final publication: *Reise in Nordost Afrika. Schilderungen aus dem Gebiete der Beni Amer und Habab nebst zoologischen Skizzen und einem Führer für Jagdreisende.*

At the turn of the year 1873, he became involved with Petermann and Adolf Bastian in plans concerning a Congo expedition, which in the end took place in 1874 without him as a participant. He declined an invitation the next year to join a Russian expedition, likewise a possible assignment as a curator of the zoological collections of St. Petersburg Academy. He was waiting for an appointment in Germany, but one which would have fit his capacities and merits was never found by him or offered to him. In the spring of 1876, however, he was invited to Cairo by Georg Schweinfurth, director of the Khedival Society to discuss a possible scientific appointment, but the conversation resulted in nothing.

While completing his last extensive study of 1877 (*Reise in Nordost Afrika*), he suddenly became unwell. A pulmonary infection coming on top of his illness proved to be fatal, and he passed away on 5 November of that year.

The outcome of the Tinne journey on the White Nile
This study began with the question of whether the Tinnes harboured an unspoken ambition to be hailed as Central Africa's first (female) explorers.

The White Nile journey of the Tinnes had an ambiguous character. On the one hand, it was meant as a pleasure trip, but on the other hand Alexine in particular appeared susceptible to the suggestion that an expedition be made of it that would proceed further, even to Lake Victoria. If no disease had assailed her at Gondokoro and if the White Nile rapids had become navigable, Alexine and her mother would have discovered the source of the river before Speke had arrived from the south. Acclaimed as foremost discoverers – of the feminine gender! – they would have been accorded the kind of eternal fame that was bestowed upon Livingstone and Stanley. But given that this did not happen, the results of their journey cannot be defined as those of a discovery expedition, for the region around Gondokoro had already been largely explored before 1860.

One accomplishment they did achieve, however, was that of being the first European women to navigate up the White Nile and pass the magical 4° latitude. Several months later, Samuel Baker and his wife Florence Finnian ascended the Nile and reached this place in order to carry out a reconnaissance with Speke and Grant. John Petherick and his wife Katie, who were on a similar mission but had departed earlier than the Bakers, were considerably delayed. The Bakers arrived in Gondokoro on 2 February 1863, four months after the Tinnes had stayed there.

The results of the Tinne-Heuglin expedition

Regarding the expedition to the Gazelle-river, both mother and daughter Tinne from the start cherished a more or less outspoken ambition to be hailed as Central Africa's first (female) explorers of the regions of the Azande, beyond the Bahr el-Ghazal. However, in this attempt as well, they were to fail, as the expedition did only succeed in collecting new information on the geography, but they were unsuccessful in their efforts to reach the Azande.

Heuglin was able to compose a map of the basin of the Gazelle-river from information gathered largely secondhand. Although he made an excursion to the Kosanga mountains which had not yet been mapped out, Arab and European merchants had preceded him in these areas. Some Europeans had been exploring these regions, staying near the borders of the Azande countries or even entering them. Two of them have been mentioned in the preceding chapters: Johann Kleincznik of Carniola, as Heuglin names him, who had settled himself some years before, and Hermann Schubert, who had stayed at the same place and kept a diary which was lost after his death.[19] And Petherick had established one of his *zaribas* in the direct neighbourhood.

The abortion of the expedition to the Bahr el-Ghazal was partly due to considerable differences between the participants in their experience with Africa. Both Tinne and Heuglin had gained experience in travelling in Africa, although there was a considerable difference in the *amount* of experience they had. In November 1862, when they met and started to prepare their expedition, Heuglin had already been in Sudan for several years and was therefore an experienced North Africa traveller. By contrast, Alexine and her mother had just arrived from their first journey in Central Africa, which had lasted only six months.

As can be concluded from their letters written before the disastrous end of the Bahr el-Ghazal expedition, Henriette and her daughter both had a strong belief in their ability to go anywhere they wanted. Before leaving on their journey, they hardly considered diseases or the occasional obstacles they might meet en route. When illnesses occurred, they dealt with them in their letters as if they were a nuisance that should hardly be considered as part of their enterprise. This belief in being able to accomplish a journey supported by all kinds of conveniences, which no traveller – let alone a female traveller – had done before, was rooted in their wealth, which provided them with the conviction that they could arrange any kind of travel enterprise.

The 'disorderly and rudderless machine' that the expedition was in Heuglin's words had been largely constructed in the Tinnes' naïve search for adventure. At a critical moment in their journey, Heuglin came up with a plan involving a more professional approach to proceed with the expedition. He proposed to continue in a small group without the usual luxury and redundant luggage, which would have reduced the twin problems of finding porters for the huge quantities of luggage and searching for suitable places to stay for the hundreds of members of the expedition to manageable proportions. If his proposal had been accepted, the entire enterprise could have been more successful. Of course, the decision to continue the expedition after Henriette's death would still have been a difficult one. There might have been a realistic chance, though, that Heuglin and Alexine would have proceeded to the Azande region, leaving the remains of Henriette there and picking them up on their way back to Khartoum.

However, here as well, just as in case of their White Nile journey and their crossing of the 4° lattitude, the Tinnes can be attributed a most particular place in history: that of being the first European women in this remote part of Central Africa.

Alexine's personal evaluation
Stories of Alexine's heroic deeds were widely reported on by the French, German and British press during her lifetime. In the US as well, accounts of Alexine's accomplishments appeared. In the last year of her life, she received – rather unexpectedly – attention from the women's suffrage move-

ment in the person of Lydia Becker. John wrote to Alexine in Tripoli on 13 January 1869 that Becker was interested in meeting her.

A certain ambiguity about her goals and mission in life can in fact be read into Alexine's remarks during her lifetime. John's last letter referred to her dream as a child of visiting the blank space in Central Africa which was based on a juvenile interest in the continent. From what she herself explained about the incentives behind her actions, we can safely conclude that Alexine regarded herself mainly as a profound lover of travel. To her nephew Harco Hora Siccama, who proposed to publish part of her letters with annotations, she explicitly states that she had had no intentions to conduct explorations while travelling in Africa:

> [I want to let you know] that I feel myself incapable, being beyond my strength to write the accounts which would be demanded. Then you know how my poor mother and I have undertaken this journey, not to be celebrated, nor to stand out from the rest, but just simply being tourists for our own pleasure. Without doubt I would be happy when in some way this journey could be useful to my country which I love so much, as you will know, although I left it long ago, but the celebrity which is now attached to my name so far has been extremely awkward to me – as if we have made all these travels to get talked about and I would not like to confirm that idea by a publication. It would embarrass me much when I would appear to draw directly the public attention. However, if you really believe that what we have seen and done is worthy to be related, I would propose you a choice which would have the same definitive result without the inconvenience which would make me suffer. That is to gather the documents which you would think to be necessary in order to make a whole which only would be published ten years after my death (…).'[20]

Sooner than Alexine had requested – i.e., less than two years after her death – Hora Siccama would do as she had asked for. In 1871, a review of Alexine's life and travels – described more or less as exploits – appeared in *Le Tour du Monde* with extracts from letters that Alexine had sent to the editor, Edouard Charton. After her arrival in Toulon in the spring of 1866 to fetch the boat that John had purchased and sent to the harbour, she had been approached on the quay by the magazine to become a correspondent to record her next experiences. She accepted the assigment, which she fulfilled until her letter from Murzuq dated 3 April 1869. In the article with a biographical overview, Hora Siccama is mentioned as president of the [Dutch] Public Accounts Committee and provider of all kinds of data concerning her biography and the travels she made before she left Cairo for her Mediterranean trip.[21]

She makes an even more explicit self-evaluation while sailing along the coast between Algiers and Tripoli. This trip must have provided ample opportunities for contemplation and retrospection. In a letter to John dated 23 May 1868, Alexine gives the following statement, which seemed to look ahead to what was to come:

> (…) If anything were to happen to me, during my travels, if I would be killed, which is a reasonable possibility, people might say, "she deserved it, that's what happens with all that travelling, poor Alexine, what a way to die etc", but you will not do that and you will not lament me. I have never understood the happiness of growing old. I always found something sad in it – even under the happiest circumstances and I don't find the thought of dying happily and courageously, by a knife wound or a gunshot, frightful, instead of dragging through a boring life, as I have seen many. Maybe it is shocking to think this way. If you hear today or tomorrow that I have been sent to the other world, then don't think my last moments were lived in bitterness. Overall I have been content about my life – I have lived well (I hope you don't read this to mean I have lived shamelessly). I have had fun. I am in no hurry to die – but if it happens, fine – a short life, but a happy one![22]

These words seem to represent more than some sort of effusion of reflections. A moral testament has been left behind, with a more or less clear indication of a self-chosen destiny. Her words, however, contradict John's words in his last letter to her, which referred to a different aim of hers: a 'blissful abode, that heaven on earth, she is in search of …'. What John was referring to was the first stage of the Bahr el-Ghazal journey when Alexine expected her 'dream of her childhood to see what that blank space in Africa contains' to be realised. That dream, however, had already been disrupted by the heavy blows that 'Fate' had inflicted upon her. After her mother's death, the house that Alexine grew up in – where she had once slept under maps of Africa in all security and luxury, and where she had lost herself in reveries – rapidly sank into an irrevocable past for her. She fled into a kind of fatalism in which she expected her own death to come at any moment.

After the unfortunate ending of the expedition, Alexine thought it too 'embarrassing' to return to The Hague. Her memories of her family and social circles there only confirmed what a 'boring life' she would have if she returned. And life presented her with more unpleasantness: in a letter to Jetty from Suez, she confessed that she was (already) 'rimpled up'. There obviously was 'no happiness in growing old'. Advancing age seemed to Alexine to be something that was best avoided. It was better to die 'happily and courageously'.

After four years of almost continuous travelling, Alexine's aspirations began crystallising into a new form. She had been the pacesetter of an enterprise that had caused the deaths of four beloved people. Since this dramatic outcome, journeys had become interwoven with death in Alexine's mind. From this point on, she could only consider voyages that were meant to offer some sort of redemption. She remained on the move, contempting death, and ready to be sent to 'the other world'.

Her journey to the Touaregs seemed to create just the opportunity for her to fulfil her desire to travel as well as to look death in the eyes. Having read *Les Touaregs du Nord*, Alexine woud most certainly have been aware of the 'religious intolerance' that Duveyrier had warned of. This phenomenon could become 'unsurmountable cliffs' in the hands of a bunch of 'distrustful and egoistic' people.[23] Duveyrier himself had contracted a dangerous disease on his return, from which he barely recovered at home.

Alexine Tinne in a historical perspective

When she was 29 years of age, Alexine decided to accept Dutch citizenship. Because she actually was of British-Dutch descent, her daring deeds have been described both from the British and Dutch point of view. Her life and travels, however, have been considered to be more appropriate to the Dutch historical context (as the *Freule* [=unmarried noble Lady] from The Hague) than the British.

In his diaries, David Livingstone refers to the Tinnes on their journey up the Nile:

> (…) All the great men of antiquity in short longed to know the fountains whence flowed the famous river, and longed in vain – exploration does not seem to have been very becoming to the other sex either. Madame Tinné came further up the river than the centurions sent by Caesar, and showed such indomitable pluck as to reflect honour on her race. I know nothing about her save what has appeared in the public papers (…), but taking her exploration along what was done by Mrs. Baker, no long time could have elapsed before the laurels for the modern re-discovery of the sources of the Nile should have been plucked by the ladies.[24]

Livingstone's rather incorrect view of what the Tinnes had accomplished would prove decisive for the highly hagiographic character of the accounts of both women until far into the twentieth century.[25]

In 1960, a Dutch biography of Alexine was published. This was followed ten years later by the publication of an English biography. The latter includes a concise description of the Bahr el-Ghazal expedition, primarily based on documents in the Tinne family's archives in England. References were made to other documents in Dutch archives, but the biographer made insufficient and inaccurate use of them and of Heuglin's accounts.[26] The Dutch publication, which was somewhat critical of Alexine, had not consulted the English archives nor Heuglin's writings.[27] This biography was doomed to be inaccurate, too. In her introduction, the author Clara Eggink remarked that she was not given access to the Tinne family papers, owned privately by three descendants of John Tinne, despite repeated requests.

Although the two biographies cover the Bahr el-Ghazal expedition, they are far from exhaustive with respect to all consultable sources. In both biographies, the last journey leading to Alexine's death in the Libyan desert receives more attention due to more extensive use of the available historical documents.[28]

In her biography, Eggink is critical of Alexine's travels on several points. From the point of view of science, her travels did not yield any clear achievements. The Tinnes travelled, as Alexine herself described, merely for their own pleasure. Eggink's conclusion was that while Alexine might have been an exceptional woman – undeniably independent, courageous, and possessing a lust for travel combined with an artistic streak – she was also a stubborn lady who obstinately and inflexibly pushed ahead with her plans, recklessly putting her life as well as those of her fellow travellers at stake. Due to the travels Alexine wished to undertake, her mother, her aunt and two chambermaids had passed away.

In the Netherlands, Eggink's view produced an outcry of indignation. The board of the Royal Dutch Geographical Society was of the opinion that Eggink's book did not do 'justice' to 'Freule Tinne'. On its request, therefore, two articles on Eggink's biography were published in the Bulletin in 1961.[29] Brummelkamp and Jongmans, two geographists, provided their view of the life and travels of Tinne.

After reviewing Eggink's study of 'the woman to the image of whom we look up with admiration', Brummelkamp could only conclude that Eggink 'delivered us a tremendous desillusion'. Eggink 'has torn the halo around the beautiful head of Tinne'. And Jongmans admits to being 'confused' upon reading Eggink's biography. Both men searched in the accounts of Nachtigal, Rohlfs and Duveyrier for descriptions of her that would correct the negative image created by Eggink. In Nachtigal's account, Brummelkamp retrieved words of appreciation and compassion regarding Tinne's death that produced an impression 'quite more sympathic than the scorn and contempt which Eggink poured out over the murdered Haguean woman'. However, Brummelkamp is forced to come to the conclusion that 'numerous explorers exposed themselves to exactly the same dangers' and that he would not consider 'a Haguean woman who remains sitting in her boudoir' more praiseworthy.

In his own perusal of writings by people who knew Alexine, Jongmans discovered that Rohlfs was in fact critical of the way the Tinnes travelled. Thus both geographists were unable to counter Eggink's criticism decisively. They were of the opinion, however, that Eggink went too far in her criticism. Regarding Alexine's journey in the Libyan desert, Eggink wonders: 'if one should not ask himself if she indeed saw herself enwrapped by a cloak of invulnerability or that she possibly was in quest for death?' In response, Jongmans considers her observation as 'utterly false'. According to Jongmans, Eggink was too carried away by the events in which Alexine revealed 'a different mentality'. 'The A.T. of later times appeared to have improved her life', as he argues.

Eggink's biography significantly altered the image of Alexine Tinne prevailing at the time. The articles by Brummelkamp and Jongmans were meant to restore her image to that of 'a person, whose image we look up to with awe'. Jongmans established that Eggink 'rightly settled with myths'. However, the new image she created did not match Alexine:

> Although she was not a second Florence Nightingale, although scientific purposes were not underlying her travels, although she had not come to Africa in order to liberate slaves, there is no reason to deny her all qualities, or to portrait her as an eccentric lady, who is no better than she should be and as an injudicious, imperious, heartless creature, who would sacrifice every one to her whims and fancies.

Jongmans seeks a result which could lay somewhere in between. Nor did Alexine Tinne represent anymore a woman with mythical proportions who had accomplished supernatural achievements, nor had she been an eccentric broken adrift who just did what she wanted to do.

The truth about Alexine Tinne may be somewhere in between the two extremes portrayed by Eggink and Jongmans. However, this statement needs to be refined. For instance, one cannot deny that she was 'an eccentric lady'. 'Injudicious' she was to some extent, but certainly not 'heartless'. She could behave 'imperiously'. That she 'improved her life' after the expedition to the Gazelle-river, as Jongmans maintains, would actually imply that she had previously sacrificed 'every one to her whims and fantasies', as Eggink argued.[30] Obviously, this latter opinion strains the truth, because Alexine was in fact responding to her mother's travel mania as well. However, due to her role as the life and soul of the expedition, she was without a doubt partly responsible for the loss of four lives. Some feelings of guilt therefore must have pursued her, making her refrain from re-entering the civilised world where she would have to deal with all kinds of questions concerning the traumatic events of the expedition and her role in it. Not for nothing did Alexine find it too 'embarrassing' to return to The Hague.

This study argues that Alexine Tinne during the Bahr el-Ghazal expedition changed from an adventuress who travelled for pleasure into a traveller who realised that the path to 'adventure' inevitably turned out to be paved with personal dramas and reversals. When leaving Cairo in the summer of 1865, Alexine still had not fully recovered from the traumatic impact the journey had on her personal life. Some of her strong character traits – including stubbornness, irascibility in the fact of setbacks or unjustified accusations, and a rare kind of perseverance in her will to realise her ambitions – would become predominant in her later actions. Alexine could boast of at least one commendable achievement: in an era when Central Africa was considered to be practically inaccessible, she undertook not one but three journeys of a substantial kind, demonstrating her capacities as a female traveller.

She remained astonishingly wealthy. Capital remained the motor of her relentless travel hunger, just as in the earlier days when she travelled extensively with her mother. One thing, however, became clear: there could be no question anymore of tourism or a pleasure trip in Africa. When still alive, Henriette Tinne-van Capellen appeared to be as adventurous as her daughter, despite her age. Initially, a certain silliness had facilitated their hunger for adventure. They paid no heed to Queen Sophie's warnings about 'savage Africa'. Little did they know then that savage Africa had something ominous up her sleeve for both of them. After the loss of her mother – who had been a facilitating and supporting figure in Alexine's life – her character seemed to become less controllable. Once her pillion rider had fallen off, she became rudderless.

Death could no longer be defied but became almost inevitably a travel companion. After the Bahr el-Ghazal expedition and during her later travels after Cairo, Alexine began to develop a fatalistic attitude. Travelling remained her obsession, but being *en route* was forever associated with death.

Can we compare Alexine's desire to travel 'still further' to the mountaineer's pursuit of an 'ever higher' mountain? To some extent, yes, but there is a clear difference. Mountaineering is an athletic and challenging pastime that sometimes triggers excessive behaviour. If a mistake is made or a particular risk is underestimated, death is the result. In this sense, the comparison works. But when the mountain has been conquered, the mountaineer returns to civilisation in triumph, while for Alexine, travelling was not a sport – she was not engaged in performing or achieving something that she could take pride in after her return. On her final voyage, she simply travelled through the Libyan desert as far as possible; she might arrive in Bornou, perhaps even further. She realised herself that this kind of travelling would soon drive her towards death, for which she had no fear. Such an end was to be preferred above a prospect that made her shiver: growing old, even under 'the happiest circumstances'.

Epilogue

The Plantae Tinneanae

During the first stage of their journey, Theodor von Heuglin and Hermann Steudner often searched for good spots where they could gather samples of species of fauna and flora. As was usual in those days, scientists were engaged in the practice of acquiring knowledge about phenomena in several fields of science. Following the tradition of practically all other Africa travellers (until deep into the twentieth century), Heuglin was a lover of hunting, which was opportune in assembling zoological specimens. Although he regarded zoology as his principal field, he also devoted himself equally to the study of ethnographic and floral specimens. After the death of the botanist Steudner in Wau on 10 May 1863, he took over the task of collecting plants and flowers in the Bahr el-Ghazal area.

The most favourable season for practicing botanic research was the summer when the rains produced a sudden outburst of luxuriant vegetation. Unfortunately, he was struck by fevers and diarrhoea at that time and was forced to abandon this job. It was only when the dry period had set in and most of the blossoms and flowers had already vanished that Heuglin could continue his task. Although he worked rapidly, he had little time left. His endeavours only resulted in some eighty samples for his botanical collection. He wrote to François Unger, then professor of botany in Vienna, to arrange for the plants to be displayed at the Imperial Herbarium in Vienna. The well-known botanist Theodor Kotschy was asked to write the descriptions for the exhibition.

At the same time Heuglin demanded from Kotschy that, by accepting this collection, he took the obligation to publish a list of the newly discovered plants and flowers in order to launch its publication, and to return the drawings which Heuglin had made of the prepared samples. It was only by chance that Heuglin found out that the collection had been exhibited in the Wiener Herbarium and that in 1867 John Tinne had helped to publish the promised book on the collection. In that year, Karl Gerold Sohn in Vienna had been commissioned to publish *Plantae Tinneanae*.[1] On the front page it was clearly stated that the book was dedicated to 'Sa Majesté Sophie Frédérique Mathilde Reine des Pays Bas', or Queen Sophie of the Netherlands, who by then had stopped sending letters to Alexine beseeching her to return home.

The book is a beautifully executed work with an introductory text and descriptions in both Latin and French. After a short introduction and dedication by John Tinne, there is a chapter written by Kotschy on the importance of the collected specimens.

> It is only by the Tinnean expedition that the vegetation of the Bahr el-Ghazal has been more especially brought to the knowledge of botanists, by the sketches made by Mr. von Heuglin during the journey as well as by the collection of plants which he found there… the plants which have served as basis for the presented work were collected and pressed during the Tinnean expedition, in part by Alexandrine Tinne, in part by Mr. von Heuglin. Botanists will ever be grateful to Mr von Heuglin for the services which he rendered to science after the death of the indefatigable and ill-fated Steudner, in collecting plants in the vicinity of Bongo as well as on the Bahr el-Ghazal (…). Mr. von Heuglin dispatched from Khartoum a package of plant specimens with some butterflies and beetles, and in a letter to Professor François Unger, asked him to arrange for getting the plants described and afterwards for placing them in the Imperial Herbarium of the Court of Vienna (…). Having been assigned the task of making the descriptions, I wrote to Mr. von Heuglin to ask him to let me further details of the material of which I was to prepare the publication. He very obligingly acceded to my request and during a visit to Vienna gave me as complete a verbal account of the plants as was possible for a naturalist untrained in botany.[2]

Apparently Kotschy, after having ascertained that there was a large number of new species, had proposed to John Tinne that a publication of the collection be issued. He even went so far as to submit to Tinne some drawings that he had prepared of some of the plants. This effectively persuaded John (and Alexine) to play a substantial financial role in the realisation of this luxuriously edited publication.

In his publication of 1869, Heuglin provides a comment on the book. After admitting that the *Plantae Tinneanae* was a most delightfully laid-out book containing a list of species of plants and flowers, 25 hand-coloured plates and illustrations of 33 species and their descriptions, he delivers a damning accusation. In several descriptions of the collector and the location the items were gathered, the name of Alexine appears where this was actually impossible. Moreover, according to Heuglin, Kotschy cites erroneous locations where samples had been picked by Heuglin, and even mixes up geographical names. Referring to Wau, for instance, Kotschy describes it as a river that flows from the Bahr el-Ghazal, to which Heuglin responds that this is 'utter nonsense!!'. When Heuglin wrote these words in 1869, Kotschy, a celebrated Austrian botanist who had travelled in Sudan in 1836-8 and 1839-40), had been dead for three years.

In his book, Heuglin has harsh criticism for the omissions and erroneous identifications. He also accuses the Tinne family of plagiarism. It was he, instead of Alexine, who had gathered most of the plant specimens during their expedition:

> After returning from Egypt I offered the collection to the Imperial Herbarium in Vienna and delivered it to the well-known botanist Dr. Th. Kotschy, who committed himself at once to publish a catalogue of the small collection as well as a description of the new species, thereby making use of the drawings which I made of them (whereafter they should be returned). Years later I happened to find out that the plants actually were deposited in the Viennese Herbarium and that the brother of Miss Tinne took care of their publication under the title "Plantae Tinneanae".[3]

Although Kotschy had mentioned both Alexine and Heuglin as the plant collectors, Heuglin seems much aggrieved by the title of the publication, which suggested that the Tinnes had been the main collectors. In addition, his drawings had never been returned to him. Kotschy's description of him as 'a naturalist untrained in botany' might have also aroused some irritation with Heuglin. John Tinne had actually used similar terms to describe Heuglin in 1864.[4] Heuglin's irritation, however, appears to be somewhat exaggerated and may reflect a dissatisfaction that lay deeper – a remnant of the past. Somehow the impression cannot be avoided that in his *Reise in das Gebiet des Weissen Nil* of 1869 he tried desperately to shake off the weight of the Tinnes, their shadows overhanging the Bahr el-Ghazal expedition. In his book, he presents *his* narrative of the journey, which was tellingly not described as the 'Tinne'sche' journey but rather as his own '*Reise*'.

Appendices

The White Nile excursion of the Tinne party

On 11 May 1862, Alexine Tinne, Henriette Tinne-van Capellen and Adriana van Capellen left Khartoum, after having obtained, with the help of Thibaut, a steamer belonging to Prince Muhammad Abd al Halim, one of the relatives of Saïd Pasha, the former governor general of Sudan. Louis de Tannyon, employed as an engineer on Prince Halim's steamer and also as his French huntsman-in-chief, acted as captain of the steamer. The price of this rent was 25,000 French francs, the equivalent of £1000. The large *dhahabiyya* they were able to hire with it had once belonged to Alfred Peney, a French doctor in Khartoum who had died the previous year on an expedition with Andrea Debono at a point above 4° latitude up the Nile. In this boat a large quantity of clothes, books, Alexine's drawing materials, some examples of her photography, and presumably her photography equipment (her camera and all that was required to process photographs) was packed. With the four boats being dragged by the steamer, they would search up the river for a suitable residence during the wet season. Having left Khartoum, they were at first delighted with this part of the river, as it was different from that above the town, comparing it with 'Virginia Water, near Windsor'.

During their ascent up the White Nile, two problems arose that were to present themselves to Alexine far more intensely the next year and would become decisive for the results of her stay in Sudan. While talking about their journey up the Nile, the Tinnes in Cairo were well-informed about the chance of becoming seriously ill in and beyond Khartoum. To travel around either of the Niles meant also that one had to face the increasing hostility of the native people who were trying to defend themselves against the raids of private armies maintained by Arabian and Western traders. From Khartoum, travelling upwards meant that the phenomenon of slavery would occur more frequently. Having followed the course of the river to the 13th latitude, Alexine sent a letter to her niece Jetty from a place called 'Montagnes des Dinkas' or Jebel Dinka (see foldout map) in which she mentions her actual experience of the slave trade that took place particularly in this region on an unhampered scale that was hitherto unknown. Because a new law was to be introduced in July 1862 obstructing the import of slaves to Khartoum via the Nile, already before the summer the slave trade had been shifting to areas of the Upper White Nile where the Tinne party was working its way up to Gondokoro.

What she saw in Jebel Dinka was the worst atrocity she had yet encountered in Sudan. After an uproar during the night in which slaves escaped but some were captured again, she went the next morning to see if she could purchase some of them to set free. She returned, having achieved nothing. The scenes of people being dragged away, slain and chained for transportation upset her greatly.

On 17 June, in a long letter to her niece Henriette Hora Siccama ('Smous'), Alexine writes about her dismay.

> At that place I saw for the first time <u>the trade in blacks</u>… Never in my life I have I been so astonished and horrified – I have heard one spoke of it, as everyone has, but never I had an idea […] of the cynicism with which it was done – (…) All the Arab merchants and most of the Europeans are (…) hunters of negroes, laying villages into ashes, plunder everything, taking hundreds of negroes with them in boats, in which one brings them into cachottes in the countries of the Viceroy, for though the anti-slavery law is perfectly zero in these remote regions of the government, one though (…) simulates to respect it (…).

Returning in the evening to the spot of the mêlée of slaves and hunters, she was approached by a woman. '(…) A woman who held a small child took my hand and said to me something which was translated. It was a prayer to me to obtain from her master the favour to see her other son and her mother who belonged to another merchant'. After some inquiries, Alexine was told she could purchase all four of them. 'I have them still with me, and when we shall pass through their part of the country I shall set them free again.' The next morning, two old women who said they were abandoned by their master because they were too weakened to be sold asked her on the same spot to be placed under her protection. The six released Dinka people disappeared, however, while they were still camping near the Jebel, which Alexine perceived as ingratitude and which made her weep. She tells Jetty she also purchased a 'petite négresse': 'a small Abbysienne, of 10 to 12 years, whose name is Goulba and promises to become a fine beauty…'.[1]

There was no question anymore about building a house. This Nyambara country presented her with 'scenes out of the temptations of St. Antoine'. Later Henriette would also relate to John Tinne that besides Alexine, she and Adriana considered these people much to be pitied. For once, she presents a different tone than her almost permanently light-hearted depictions of occurrences. They saw the native people being ill-treated by Arabs and Europeans alike, both of whom enticed them on board their boats and then carried them off as slaves.[2]

There is an element of irony in Alexine's efforts to free several slaves in Sudan. The provenance of the enormous capital behind the Tinne name – the flourishing sugar trade established by her father by means of slave traffic in the Dutch and British West Indies – must have been well known to Alexine. This capital had increased substantially with the huge profits in cane sugar in the West Indies during the 1830s, which received a further boost in 1835 from the British government when companies were compensated for giving up their slaves on the plantations, who had been mostly imported from West Africa. In using a substantial sum of money to purchase a number of slaves in Jebel Dinka,[3] Alexine was spending capital that had once been earned at the cost of slavery. In her letters, Alexine never explicitly referred to the provenance of the capital she was entitled to use, but one could argue that, in addition to compassion, some feelings of guilt forced Alexine to buy out some of these people once she had witnessed the miserable conditions these 'slaves' were kept in.

Already before Alexine's purchases of slaves, Henriette had returned to Khartoum on 28 May in the steamer to arrange for an extension of the rental period and to stock up on provisions. The others, meanwhile, remained in Jebel Hemaya, close to the Jebel Dinka. Although the voyage required five days going up the Nile against wind and stream, the return trip took only thirty hours. In Khartoum, it was necessary to have the steamer repaired; this occupied a month, owing to the dilatory and haphazard way of working. Henriette stayed in town during this period. On 17 June, Henriette left

Khartoum, returning on the 21st with a *dhahabiyya* and an additional *nugger* [large broad-beamed boat] to carry the vast quantity of extra supplies attached to the steamer. She had completed all her arrangements and secured the safety of her daughter and sister by taking along forty additional soldiers, 'the slave trade making travelling on the river dangerous'.

During Henriette's absence, Adriana complains to Hora Siccama in June:

> (...) the meals are bad here (...). We thought to stay here for six days and now the steamer already has left for one month. I hope to see you back again. <u>If I will return</u>, I will go find me an apartment or a house of my own – for I get tired of dragging me behind the Tinne's. They pay me so little attention. It is as if I am a burden to them and I can't stand the fatigues as they can. I would like to stay quietly outside (...). Your loving sister, Addy v. C.[4]

On her return, Henriette found out that Alexine had been terribly ill for several days. After her recovery from diarrhoea, Alexine was busy saving animals including a six-month-old panther, which received a collar of one of her large dogs and was placed in a cage. On the same day, she succeeded in securing a porcupine. She had a large crocodile killed and stuffed and caught a large monkey which later escaped. After breaking up the encampment on Mount Hemaya, they proceeded up the river on 7 July.

Their next halt was in Kaka, a village belonging to Muhammad Khair, an Arab trader who, as they discovered, had conquered a surrounding part of Sudan. When his money failed him, he had his armies destroy the surrounding villages and kill the men, stealing their flock and selling the women and children as slaves. When they stopped at his village, he was reluctant to receive them at first, seeing that they had Turkish soldiers on board the vessels. But then he approached the women with royal honours and believed Alexine to be the favourite daughter of the Sultan. He even offered to proclaim her Queen of the Sudan, as John Tinne enthusiastically recounts in 1864. However, in a letter of 18 November, Henriette presents a different version of their meeting with Muhammad Khair. She mentions that Alexine had been asked by Khair to become his bride; a story that lived on after her death, when her person took on almost mythical proportions in some literature.[5] 'He has yet offered (...) our Alexine as Sultan of the country ('Sultan du Pays') provided we would supply silver [Theresia Thaler] for having nourished his soldiers. We have refused (…).' In a letter dated 13 July, she writes: 'Khair proposed us to become his associates – that is to adjust him with money, to find arms and nourishment, and he would conquer all that remained of these poor devils and give us the title he now takes himself – Sultan of Sudan!'[6]

They stayed in Kaka for a week and then sailed up the river. Somehow the news had gone ahead that the Sultan's daughter was coming up the river. In the region of the shore where the Shilluk resided, they had to make a stop. They had been warned about them by Khair. '(…) No wood left for the steamer to proceed', as Henriette writes, '[we were] obliged to stop, the sailors were dreadfully afraid to go ashore to cut the wood, we sent an officer and 10 well armed men to guard (…) Alexine, one Shillook was informing if the Sultan had sent his daughter.'[7] After Alexine had given him beads and cotton fabrics, she was asked to help the Shilluk conquer Muhammad Khair, which she refused, even though she was now offered the title of Queen if she would assist them in their war.

Approaching the confluence of the Sobat – a large river running below Kaka into the Nile on its eastern bank – they were determined to steam up the river as far as it was navigable. The voyage occupied them for more than a week. They saw ostriches and a great number of giraffes, but they didn't get close enough to shoot them. They had heard that giraffes were very good eating. They did partake of part of an immense elephant given to them by the hunter who killed it and considered the meat very nice. The crew did not succeed in killing any hippopotami either, which were also considered to be 'very good eating'.[8] After this excursion, they continued up the Nile and arrived at the Bahr el Ghazal, 'a large and sluggish stream' flowing from the west and passing into the small Lake No, which they did not enter. The White Nile here took a bend, nearly at right angles southward. The windings of the Nile were very circuitous above Lake No and the currents very strong, rendering the navigation dangerous. An accident happened at one of the rapids. The steamer failed to pull up the two heavily loaded boats, so both had to be towed up by the sailors on the banks, who were all in the water, when the rope broke and the boats went floating down the stream. A Janissary, Osman Aga, 'a strong Turk', jumped into the river to swim with a rope to the bank, but sank immediately. One can assume he had been 'seized with apoplexy'. His body was recovered and everything was tried to resuscitate him, but it was all in vain. He was buried with all possible Moslem honours and ceremony. He was washed with a new piece of soap and wrapped in nineteen yards of calico, and perfumes were burnt beneath his body. All the clothes he had died in were thrown into the water, and the crews followed the corpse, laid in a new mat, to the grave, which had been dug under a large sycamore tree on which an inscription was cut marking the spot.

Another stop was Heiligenkreuz or Sta. Croce, one of the stations of the Austrian Roman Catholic missionaries, where they arrived on 4 September. Their previous stop may have been Ghata Shambé, just above the missionary station, the former *zariba* of Franz Binder, who in March had left his station to return to his homeland, Transsylvania.[9] In Heiligenkreuz, the rising tensions accompanying the ivory trade had led to hostile incidents, notably between the Dinka and the traders. Diseases and deadly confrontations had decimated the number of members of the Austrian Mission. Most of the group had already succumbed or had left the place when the Tinne party arrived. Alexine is supposed to have made photographs here, including of members of the Mission, which were handed over to Petherick some eight months later en route to the Gazelle-river in Meshra el-Rek. According to Henriette, Alexine showed the missionaries some photographs she had taken. They both visited the chapel at Heiligenkreuz and experienced 'the beautiful voices of these Tyrolian men' as 'very impressive in this terrible loneliness'.[10]

Out of the thirty that originally formed the mission, only three missionaries remained, among them Francesco Morlang.[11] The three men left with both women on the steamer for Gondokoro and then down the river to Khartoum. From Heiligenkreuz, Alexine undertook an eight-day excursion to explore the interior. In addition to Morlang, she was accompanied by her waiting maid Anna, Contarini, fourteen porters to carry them in chairs and nine boys and girls to carry their luggage. After having stayed in Heiligenkreuz for 11 days, they continued on to Gondokoro. Stopping in a village of the 'Chers' [Sere] en route, they considered the place the most beautiful they had yet visited and cherished the idea of returning there and building a residence, if further up the river did not suit their tastes. They proceeded to Gondokoro, where they arrived on 30 September. As sailing boats did not usually make their appearance there until January, it was a surprise for the inhabitants of this small town to see three boatfuls of people. This was followed by another surprise of being visited by three European 'ladies' from Khartoum. Actually, the Tinne-van Capellens were the first Western women to visit this place, the most southern town of Sudan.[12] In Gondokoro, the Tinne company saw the last remnants of the mission there which was founded by Knoblecher (originally Knoblehar, a Slovene with a Germanised name). As pro-vicar apostolic of the Roman Catholic Mission to Central Africa Knoblecher founded this mission in 1852 and another in 1854 at a point between Shambé and Bōr which he named Heiligenkreuz.

Several excursions were made, of which one was on a road traversing through a rich plain covered with large trees 'like an English park', and with thousands of herds of cattle and flocks of sheep and goats belonging to the Bari tribe, 'a fine and sturdy race of blacks, warlike and easily offended', as Henriette writes to John.[13] They had been informed that the river was not navigable above Gondokoro, but they were not satisfied without seeing for themselves. They succeeded in steaming upwards for five hours until a range of hills, called Belinian, was reached. Beyond this point they were unable to proceed, hindered by the cataracts. They must have known that in the far south of the Nile there was the station Faloro, the residence of the notorious slave dealer Andrea de Bono who five months later would be the first European to carry out a reconnaissance with the discoverers of the Nile source, Speke and Grant, who were then descending from Lake Victoria down the Nile.[14]

In her letters to John during this period, Henriette appears to be concerned about Alexine's health. 'Regarding Alexine (…) she won't take necessary precautions against the cold and the heat.'[15] Just after this remark was written, sickness struck Alexine. And after their return to Gondokoro, all three of them and nearly all the men of the three boats were attacked by fevers. Alexine also suffered from exposure to the sun and was more seriously affected than the others. Although quinine was the only remedy in her case, it did not stop the fever from returning at intervals of two to three hours. Thereafter, it returned again with great force, this time attended with delirium and lasting twelve to fourteen hours. This kept her chained to her bed. After a week, she partially recovered. Being obliged to return to Khartoum, the whole party embarked on 22 October.

When they passed the village of Muhammad Khair, they saw that it was in ruins. The Shillooks, whom he had hunted and oppressed, had at last fought back and defeated him. Khair had fled to the Nuba mountains. Looking back on the trip in a letter dated 18 November written in Kaka, Henriette Tinne writes: '(…) our speedy return was caused by illness which of course made it less pleasant but all our invalids are getting better under the influence of a dry North wind and I feel in good spirit to talk of a most interesting and uncommon voyage (…) undertaken under the most favourable auspices and the most unfavourable time of the year (…) having a steamer made us completely independent (…)'.[16]

The flotilla headed by the steamer sailed back to Khartoum. Making their way up the Nile to Gondokoro (excluding stops and detours) took the Tinnes 360 hours, but returning to Khartoum took only 170 hours. When approaching Khartoum, the boats carrying the Dutch flag passed some vessels under the British flag sailing upstream with Samuel and Florence Baker on board, on their way to Gondokoro to meet Speke and Grant. They saluted each other with a volley, and kept up a mutual waving of handkerchiefs until out of view.[17]

Khartoum in the summer of 1862

Letter, Guillaume Lejean, 14 August 1862, Khartoum.

A witness of the arrival of Heuglin wrote a letter to the editor of the *Nouvelles Annales des Voyages* on the 14th of August 1862 in which he also referred to the departure of Alexine Tinne. The letter contains news about 'the German expedition in Central Africa'. This notification was published anonymously as an extract of 'a letter addressed to the Editor'.

> I am now in Khartoum (…). Before I will tell you about myself and give you interesting news about the geography and the history
> – Mr. Von Heuglin and Steudner are in Khartoum: they are preparing themselves to go to the White Nile, by land. Mr. von Heuglin arrives from Abyssinia with a most superb harvest; a map of Lake Tzana, and another of the region of the Ouello-Galla, another of the countries of Gallabat and Guedaref (…). Mr. Munzinger has passed through here some days ago, returning from Kordofan where he has tried in vain to travel to Darfur. The Sultan has answered on his request with a very friendly letter in which he promises him help and protection till Fasher (…), but not any further. (…) Both Mr. Munzinger and Kinzelbach have left for Massua, by Berber [in footnote: Mr. Kinzelbach has just arrived back in Germany]. Mademoiselle Tine [sic], the eccentric and resolute traveller, has left for Gondokoro on the small steamer of Halim-Pasha, rented for 25.000 Francs, with an ambitious fitting-out. She is now on the Sobat (…).The slave dealers present themselves here more than ever. Muhammad Khair, dressed in his red cloth, a sign of his Egyptian appointment, after having conquered the Shilluk, has delivered to the Dinka of the North a blow in which he has fully succeeded. Please follow this on your map. He

has left for Kaka and has marched to the East, while the Arab chef
Abou-Ruf [Rof], left for Goulé, and marched to the South-West:
the ships of the slavers of Khartoum, cruising on the White Nile
and Sobat, and cut the retreat of the poor black people. All have
been dragged away, almost 4.000 captives; a country with an
extension of two French provinces has been depopulated cleanly:
they have split the booty. Simple soldiers have got some sixty heads
of blacks as their part in the loot. Resistance was impossible: the
men of Muhammad Khair wore leather armour-clads and other
clothes of the middle-ages, impenetrable to the weak arms of the
Dinka. This blow, of which the offenders were Egyptians, arose
the appetite of the slavers in Khartoum, and recently an expedition
has left on camels for the South to make a second one in the same
area. While Europe chats about and feels sorry for the fate of the
negroes, Britain, as usual, acts. The British consul, Mr. Petherick,
has arrested the principal slavers: he had his own Vékil [agent,
deputy], guilty of treason, thrown into prison. There is now terror
in the slavers camp: Mr. Petherick's men are almost openly in a
rebellious state; he has asked, from Gondokoro, where he is now at
this moment, for 120 men reinforcement; one fears for his life.
Mr. Petherick has received some injustice in the past; which he
redeemed in a noble way. He has, on his turn, destroyed the
European piracy on the White Nile. All the Europeans involved
stopped and tried to wash their hands; there only remain on the
river the brothers Poncet, who are without any reproach. In total,
piracy does not diminish, for the reason that the Egyptian prefect,
Muhammad Khair, today has reunited for himself all the ships of
the river, an amount three times more than before.[1]

One might be inclined to point to the French explorer Guillaume Lejean as
the most likely author of this letter, given that he was the only French traveller at that time in Khartoum's neighbourhood. Moreover, Petermann notes
that Lejean had mentioned the sum the Tinnes had paid for the rental of the
steamer in a letter to V.A. Malte-Brun (then editor of the *Nouvelles Annales*). This arguably indicates Lejean as the author of this anonymous letter.
According to Heuglin, Lejean had arrived in Khartoum on 17 August 1862,
but the letter would suggest that it was a few days earlier.

Khartoum

Khartoum as the threshold of Central Africa

As the centre of all commerce in the vast region between Lower Egypt and Sudan, Khartoum had a strong economic relationship with its hinterland, notably the White Nile and its tributary, the Gazelle-river. Situated at the junction of the White and the Blue Nile, practically all caravans crossing from north to south and west to east had to pass by the town. The two Niles brought plenty of products from the southern regions: ivory from elephants, hippopotami and rhinoceroses, Arabian gum, gold-dust, ostrich feathers and, of course, slaves. On the great Nile, these goods were taken along from Khartoum to Cairo and Alexandria and further to the Mediterranean Sea, where most of the goods were distributed to European countries or exchanged for European products.

After Egypt's conquest of the Mamluk dynasty in 1820, the new viceroy (or *khedive* or *pasha*), Muhammad Ali, introduced Turkish rule under the command of the Turkish Sultan who held seat in Constantinople. After its definitive conquest (in 1821), Egyptian provided Sudan with a governor generalship that covered the provinces of Dongola, Berbera, Khartoum, Sennār, Taka, Fazogli and Kordofan. Shortly after, a military settlement was established at the confluence of the two Nile-rivers. This settlement was given the name 'Khar-toum', which meant 'elephant trunk' in Arabic. Situated in the middle of the desert as the centre of the armed forces in Sudan, the garrisons were soon surrounded by shops and shelters for officers, administrators, suppliers and merchants. A market grew, attracting people from the vicinity with products from the countryside which could be exchanged for Egyptian merchandise. As many caravan routes led to Khartoum, within a few decades this settlement and village became a town and a commercial centre.

During the 1840s, Westerners began to flow into Sudan. A mixed company of foreigners, mostly Frenchmen and some Austrians, arrived in Sudan after having been invited by Muhammad Ali, the viceroy of Egypt. Ali had a keen eye for the foreign expertise he needed. Though Europeans from different nations travelled to Egypt and attempted to reach the more southern regions by following the Nile, the presence of Frenchmen was primarily a consequence of their engagements in Muhammad Ali's governmental service. The Turkish Empire was opened to free commerce in 1838 – at least on paper. After Ali's death in 1849, a change took place. Around 1850, Sudan was opened up to foreigners and the hunt for ivory began.[1] From seven different European countries, all kinds of people descended into Egypt to work their way down to Sudan. Khartoum represented the last station of Turkish-Egyptian and of Western civilisation. Reaching the city meant one had arrived at the frontier of Central Africa.

In the 1850s, Khartoum was still a small town with one-storied flat-roofed houses built of unbaked clay or mud. The building of the earlier traditional buildings – the 'tokul' – with their high conical roofs made of straw was prohibited due to the danger of fires. Khartoum's streets were narrow and dusty and unhealthy as well, being made of tamped powdery earth. Squares hardly existed. When the sun reached its zenith, shaded spots were hard to find in town. Some spacious houses had large courts and luxurious gardens with *doum* and date palms and shady Egyptian fig trees, tamarinds and accias crowning high above the enclosing walls. At the foot of the houses, various types of sailing vessels laced themselves into rows along the riverside. On the side of the Blue Nile stream stood the stately white-plastered palace of the governor general, with its high walls and windows, and next to it a roofed-over, many alleyed bazaar. Nearby was the building of the Austrian Mission with its enclosed garden, followed by Turkish coffee houses, shops of Greek merchants, governmental warehouses and the barracks of the Egyptian army with a hospital. In this trading centre was the slave market; there were two of them before 1862. The renowned French traveller Paul Trémaux, visiting the town for the first time in 1848, called Khartoum 'queen of the Oriental Sudan, like once Timbuktu was for the Occidental Sudan'.[2] Its row of buildings alongside the river with its high banks made an austere impression on him. According to Trémaux, the headland at the point of confluence of both rivers must have once been higher, but the form was still reminiscent of the trunk of an elephant. A small cataract up the White Nile created in his eyes the only lively accent in the sad and monotonous surroundings of the town.

The account of the American traveller Bayard Taylor dates from the early 1850s and describes the city as it was then, which must have been in an almost identical state as when Alexine Tinne saw it for the first time less than ten years later. According to Taylor's impression, the town was larger than any of the cities of Upper Egypt. It extended for about a mile along the bank of the Blue Nile. The part next to the river was mostly taken up by the dwellings of Beys, men ranked as under-*pashas* in the Egyptian administration, and other government officers and wealthy merchants. When the north wind rose, their gardens showered the fragrance of their orange and mimosa blossoms over the whole town. Nearly half of the population of the place were slaves, brought from the mountains above Fazogli or from the land of the Dinkas up the White Nile. Their houses in the town's outskirts were springing up like ant hills. Taylor records dryly that in the way these houses were built and streets were created, no efficient plan whatsoever could be found. His point of comparison was most probably the efficient grid-street patterns in the US. Each household surrounded its property with a mud wall, regardless of its location with respect to others, and in going from one point to another, one was obliged to make the most perplexing zigzag movements. Not venturing far on foot but preferring to sit on a dromedary, all the mysteries of lower life were revealed to Taylor from his lofty post. On each side he looked into pent yards to detect how 'the miserable Arab and Negro families lazily basked in the sun during the day with their swarms of children sitting in the dust', or looked into 'the filthy nests where they crawled at night'. The slaughtering of animals, bought and sold on the nearby market, took place every morning on the banks of the Blue Nile, east of the city. Here the sheep, cows, goats and camels were killed, skinned and quartered in the open air. It was not unusual to see thirty or forty butchers at work on as many different animals, each surrounded by an attendant group of vultures, hawks, cranes, crows and other carnivorous birds.[3]

In 1855, Alfred Brehm published his *Reiseskizzen*, which represented the results of his travels as a German zoologist over eight years. Writing about the Europeans in Khartoum, he remarks that they were the scum of each nation. 'We noticed with disgust that the entire European community almost without exception consists of scoundrels, impostors, villains and murderers'.[4] In Brehm's opinion, all Europeans in Sudan lost in some way their native virtues. Out there in Khartoum, they did not work for any common interest but only pursued their own. Cut off from their roots, life in Khartoum was disappointing, even miserable, so everyone had to make it comfortable just for himself. Being chained to this harsh joyless existence, they had to live out their days. If someone was overwhelmed by a fatal fever, his relatives brought the body to some place outside the town and left him there in the sands of the steppe. Then they would return to his house in order to divide his properties, all the time bringing cheers with well-filled glasses. No tears were shed on his death.[5]

The description of Khartoum in Didier's popular book *500 Lieues sur le Nil* was also less than flattering. Stipulating its lack of architectural quality, Didier wrote: 'Absolutely not a remarkable or beautiful city, but merely a metropolis of the desert and the heart of Africa'.[6] Didier counted between 30 and 35 thousand inhabitants in Khartoum. According to the German naturalist Robert Hartmann's observations in 1860, the town then numbered 40,000-45,000 inhabitants, though this remained a guess, as there was no sufficient method of measuring.[7] Heuglin estimates that the town housed more than 45,000 in 1862, indicating that within a few years' time, the number of inhabitants had grown considerably.[8]

Only a small number of Europeans resided in Khartoum. In 1861, Petherick mentions some 25 residents who were principally engaged in commerce.[9] In the summer of 1862, Heuglin counted some 40-45 European residents, while Baker counted about 30 in June of that year.[10] According to contemporary accounts of the town and its characteristics, Khartoum offered very little in the way of comfort for Westerners. Hartmann describes in 1861 how even the best houses had leaking roofs. During the wet season, many a roof would partly tumble down or collapse, with even baked clay walls dissolving under the pouring tropical rainfall. Each house was crawling with 'vermin': centipedes, big cockroaches, large spiders, ants, lizards, bats, scorpions, snakes and termites. Strangely, Hartmann adds to this category 'swallows'. The lower class lived in houses of mere clay which had no stories.[11] What is striking is that remarks about 'crawling vermin' are not to be found in any account of French or British travellers. This observation remarkably seems to be restricted to German travellers (Hartmann, Alfred Brehm in 1855, and Heuglin in 1863 and 1869).

Khartoum: centre of the slave trade

The discomfort of living in Khartoum was nothing compared with the rising tension after 1860 caused by the ivory trade. In his extensive review of 1869 regarding the Bahr el Ghazal expedition, Heuglin provides an explanation for this change in the ivory trade in the White Nile regions. The main cause of the rapid decline in the relations between the native people up the White Nile and Arabian merchants, Turkish authorities and European traders was the devaluation of one barter in the ivory trade, in particular beads, which necessitated the use of another, more valuable barter, namely slaves. Regarding its effects on Khartoum, where most of the traders and merchants had their offices, the deteriorating relationships outside Khartoum had their immediate effects inside the town.

From the beginning of the 1860s, relationships between Europeans in Khartoum underwent a change due to developments in business and politics. In his account of 1863, Hartmann, who was also an explorer and ethnographer, gives a striking example of these sudden shifts in relations and even friendships in Khartoum, which were due to the increasing and often harsh criticism by Europeans towards European traders. Hartmann's account was based on a journey he made accompanying the young Baron Adalbert von Barnim (then 19 years old) across the Bayuda steppe from Dongola to Khartoum and up the Blue Nile. Von Barnim died in Roseires, and Hartmann took the body to Europe for burial. His account was also a study of the people of the Nile valley.[12]

Hartmann provides a detailed description of his encounters with 'the European colony' in Khartoum in 1860/1861. It consisted of people from Italy, France, Germany, Malta, the Levant coast and Greece who in their own countries had not accomplished anything meaningful in their lives and were staying in a sort of self-imposed exile here, looking for a way to make a living. They became merchants, speculating in ivory and slaves. In the years following, they became more and more blunted by Khartoum's miserable conditions and degraded into a group of scoundrels of the most dreadful kind, according to Hartmann. Due to the increasing amount of freebooters who were then making raids involving murder and plunder along the White Nile, Hartmann observes that every bit of confidence and credit in the European community had vanished and that a debauched speculative craze was reigning everywhere.[13] After an enthusiastic account of his cheerful meeting with Alfred Peney, the well-respected French physician who had been Khartoum's doctor since the beginning of the 1840s, Hartmann recounts the story of the decline of Alphonse de Malzac, known as the 'King of the White Nile', who Peney had met. According to Heuglin, De Malzac delivered his 'black trade' [slaves] to Muhammad Khair. His life, death and burial made 'a dark painting', in Hartmann's words. Initially a successful trader on the White Nile dealing with ivory, De Malzac's later success was achieved only by deeds of widespread cruelty and injustice.[14] After having killed a Berberine servant who had had intercourse with one of his favourite female slaves, he had been prosecuted by the Egyptian authorities and was forced to go in hiding. Hartmann found him staying in the building of the Austrian consulate, which had offered him protection. Though well versed in De Malzac's bad reputation, Hartmann accompanied Peney who visited the man as a doctor. De Malzac eventually succumbed to his fevers on the evening of 25 April 1860. In July 1862 Heuglin would indignantly tell Petermann that it had been an outrage that De Malzac, whom he was acquainted with in the past, had been sheltered by the Austrian authorities and died as an Austrian citizen, a status he was not in the least entitled to according to Heuglin. He adds to this a particular detail to the atrocities committed by this Maltese trader: he had shot his Berberine servant after having tied him up to a tree decorated with 'negroe-skulls'.[15]

The economic significance of De Malzac and other White Nile traders was largely eclipsed, however, by that of a small number of Arab traders. All had connections with Khartoum – which was the harbour of all the *nugger*, the boats which departed from there and unloaded their cargoes of slaves directly in the city. This trading practice (which will be covered in the next appendix) was to continue up to the arrival of Musha Pasha in May 1862, when a new rule of the Egyptian Sudanese authorities came into force. Until then, Europeans working in the mixed trade of ivory and slaves were able to earn their fortunes, although they were never as significant as those attained by Arabs such as Ghattas (a Coptic merchant), Biselli, a trader from the *maghreb* (the coastal area from Tripoli to Marocco), Kuchuk Ali Agha, an Albanian trader, and Zubeir Rahma Mansour, who was to become the dominant figure in the overland trade between the Azande, Bahr el-Ghazal, Kordofan and Darfur and the biggest slave dealer of them all.[16] Besides accepting cattle and ivory as barter, all of these Arabs were known to be eager recipients of Thaler, the Austrian silver money. In the story of the Bahr el-Ghazal expedition, it will be revealed how these Arabian traders were feared invaders of the entire region of the White Nile and its affluents, provoking hostilities among the inhabitants of the Gazelle-river basin in order to subjugate them with their bands of armed men. These traders established mutually recognised monopolistic 'rights' over the various routes. During the 1860s, an increasing amount of settlements of these 'Khartoumers' lay stretched out in the countries between the Dinka and the 'Niam-Niam', as the Azande were then called. On Heuglin's map, Ghattas' *zaribas* have been indicated. In total, a dozen *zaribas* can be seen on the map, including those established by Europeans such as Petherick.[17] The Tinne-Heuglin journey, while traversing these regions with its train of people and supporting materials, was at the mercy of these traders, primarily due to the huge amount of Theresia Thaler that Henriette and Alexine carried with them.

Khartoum's diseases

Contemporary accounts describe the chance of dying from diseases as an ever-present danger not only for the population of Khartoum but for that of all Sudan. Khartoum had the disadvantage of being the unhealthiest part of one of the unhealthiest regions in the world. From the southern frontier of Nubia, where the tropical rains begin to fall, to the tableland of Abyssinia in the southeast, and as far up as the White Nile then had been explored, Bayard Taylor saw Sudan in 1854 as being devastated by fevers of the most malignant character. In his account, the summers were fatal to at least one-half of the Turks, Egyptians and Europeans who made their residence there. Parts of the native population also succumbed to disease, although the mortality rate among them must not have been as high. Taylor arrived before the rainy season, the relatively healthiest part of the year, and yet of all the persons he saw, three-fourths were already complaining of some physical 'derangement'. The hospital was filled with cases of fever, dysentery and small-pox. According to his information, travellers could not agree on the reason for the prevalence of disease in Sudan. Some attributed it to the presence of 'infusoriae' [infusion of animal life] in the Sudanese water, yet Taylor says he drank the pure, mountain-born water of the Blue Nile, which was always filtered beforehand. He was inclined to side with Joseph Ritter von Russegger, the Austrian geologist who had been in Sudan since 1838 and who attributed the diseases entirely to the miasma arising from decayed vegetation during intensely hot periods. The country around Khartoum was a dead level. Behind the town, the White Nile curved to the east, and during the inundation its still waters extended even to the suburbs, almost insulating the place.[18] Dal Bosco, procurator of the Veronese Mission in Khartoum, wrote in 1858:

> The climate of Khartoum is commonly acknowledged to be unhealthy, owing to the fact (…) that the town is low-lying. Although present all the year round, the malignant evaporations are increased during the rainy season by the stagnant water, and much sickness is caused. During that time, which lasts three months, fatigue, lack of appetite, drowsiness and heaviness of head, oppression of the stomach, sleepless nights, gloomy days, are the melancholy and usual effects of the unhealthiest atmosphere. Few are immune, even among the natives, but these painful inconveniences are as nothing to those that follow – burning fevers, acute illness, dysenteries and the like which bring sudden death.[19]

In his extensive account of the Von Barnim journey, Hartmann mentions a fatal disease that was hovering over Sudan. Hartmann connects this particular disease, which he calls *Wechselfieber*, to his experiences in Khartoum, adding that it seemed as if this disease, 'the scourge of Tropical Africa', had chosen this place as its residence. The summer rains, the rich but marshy vegetation along the Nile and its tributaries, together with the merciless sun and hot temperatures were all given as concrete causes of this fever. It could deteriorate into a high, deadly kind of fever. In and around Khartoum, a distinction could be made between one-day and three-day fevers. Both could prolong themselves and return persistently, undermining all physical force and energy and eventually causing death after weeks or even months. People in Sennār compared this fever with 'a worm which gnawed around in their bones'. Usually the fever would stop by swallowing large doses of quinine. Not infrequently, a *Wechselfieber* of a simple kind would degenerate into a more pernicious sort. The intervals between fever attacks would become shorter and the fevers themselves nastier, leading often to a sudden death. For Hartmann, it must have been clear that the chance of catching these fevers outside Khartoum was not lower than inside the town. Travellers making their passage through the Bahr el Ghazal's swampy areas put themselves in the perfect conditions for catching this *Wechselfieber*.[20]

The combination of the diseases and the tension between the different groups of people in Sudan was to create the most unfortunate conditions for the Tinne-Heuglin expedition.

Sudan

Sudan: from peaceful coexistence to breeding ground for conflicts

Not only people became more concerned about the future of Sudan, while creating favourable possibilities for the western world, but one also began to reflect on what had happened during the rise of the Egyptian State. Gradually conscientiousness was growing of the Turkish occupation of Sudan from 1820 (to 1881), which became in the eyes of the Western world a representation of the last venture in colonial expansion undertaken in the name of Ottoman Power on and beyond the frontiers of Islam. The term 'Egyptian' was not used in those days. The political power in Cairo was focused on colonizing Sudan and was exerted by a Turkish-speaking body. Hence the Sudanese, and Europeans staying in the Sudan as well, called the rulers of the country 'Turks'. Sudan was Egyptian only in the sense that it was a province of Egypt, a dependency of the Ottoman Empire in Constantinople, the seat of the sultan to whom the Khedive in Egypt, in the function as a viceroy, was subordinate.[1] The Egyptian rule which Muhammad Ali, the first viceroy, worked out for Egypt and Sudan as a general of a Turkish army was *de facto* the Turkish rule. At the same time, Muhammad Ali, who was of Macedonian origin, tried to free himself from the Sultan's power and establish his own rule within Egypt. This was only possible by defeating the Turkish empire in battle, which he failed to do. Nonetheless, he was able to found his own state as a kind of empire and to create a new administrative and military establishment based on the example of modern Europe.

This process of modernisation was accompanied, and indeed fostered, by an increase in the number of foreign visitors, both Europeans and Americans, to Sudan. While very few Europeans had visited the Sudan before 1820, after the Turkish conquest, foreign visitors were admitted. They came in small numbers as travellers, traders and missionaries. Frenchmen were highly esteemed by Muhammad Ali, who engaged them as technical experts, consultants and employees of the administration in his governmental service. The Khedive organised two expeditions on the White Nile, for which he engaged Europeans. In 1839-1841, Georges Thibaut and Joseph-Pons d'Arnaud navigated up the river in the company of Ferdinand Werne, reaching a spot a few miles above Gondokoro where they met the Bari.

Before 1850, during the last years of the progressive government of Muhammad Ali, after Westerners had been given access to Sudan, there was at first a rather peaceful coexistence between the representatives of the different European nationalities and the Turkish and Arabian inhabitants. To Western European countries, the commercial opportunities offered by Africa and in particular Sudan seemed enormous. Westerners and Arabs alike entered the Upper Nile area in approximately the same period. The Arab merchants had an advantage, supported as they were by the local governments and networks of the public administration. They operated everywhere as monopolists, dividing whole provinces among each other like feudal properties and creating veritable small empires where they exercised their exclusive commercial privileges as well as their self-designated right to decide about the life and death of the native peoples. By contrast, the Westerners – unpopular from the beginning, feared and closely watched, financially rather weak – had to operate in a hostile environment, often forced into making humiliating deals and relying solely on their courage and their spirit of enterprise to survive.

The groups of native people in the southern part of the Nile were treated by all foreigners – Turks, Arabs and Europeans alike – with scorn. The first contacts between the foreigners and the southern native inhabitants up the White Nile – the Bari and Shilluk, who were easily accessible from the river – were in the early years quite amicable. This friendliness, however, was soon to be spoiled by a justified suspicion on the side of the ethnic groups which finally culminated in open and bitter hostility.

Among the Westerners, this contemptuous attitude towards the pagan Africans was encouraged by the flourishing slave trade and its Islamic sanction.[2] Among slavers with a reputation of performing the most vicious deeds, Alphonse de Malzac, Nicolo d'Ulivi[3] and to some extent Andrea de Bono stand out. The latter, who was a British citizen, subdued the Makrakà (as the south-eastern Azande were called) in a heavy battle in 1861. Several traders, however, were known for showing at least some integrity while doing business with people on the White Nile. Their names were actually never officially associated with the slave trade. Some of them figure as minor characters in the story of the Tinne-Heuglin expedition (e.g. Franz Binder and the Poncet brothers). Their fortune seemed quite ephemeral, being subject to the results of a commerce that did not offer alternatives and guarantees. And those who would like to save something of their revenues had to find the opportunity to abandon after many years Sudan for ever, because once having left this area there was no fortunate return possible.

Tempted by the huge profits to be made, the Egyptian government initially tried to impose a monopoly of the ivory trade. After much protest, however, it was obliged to lift the restrictions it had implemented and tolerate the European merchants who immediately took over the Nilotic trading area. In due time, the fever of greed must have taken possession of even the most phlegmatic ones, as everyone rushed southwards. Nubian vagabonds descended on Khartoum – some in order to earn advantageous salaries as servants or sailors, others in an attempt to get an interest, as small as it may have been, in the ships' cargo before it left.[4]

It was a golden age for Arab and European merchants alike. However, for the latter it came to an abrupt end. By 1867, European traders were forced to leave Sudan and from that time on would no longer play any role in its commercial life, the control of which fell to Turks and Arabs from Egypt and northern Sudan.

The stream of traders rushing to these territories in search of ivory, increasingly tempted the inhabitants either by ruse and guile or fraud and deception, in order to lay their hands on this precious material. Urged by the growing competition, a few of them began to create posts near the effluents to the right and left of the White Nile, to the territories of the Nyambara. They settled themselves on the banks and up in the marshes of the Bahr el-Ghazal, which were unknown regions and not even violated by the Turkish rulers. The Gazelle-river basin proved to be the most fertile for hunting elephants. As the proprietor of settlements in the territories of the Jur, Bongo, Mittu, Madi and Azande, the Coptic merchant Ghattas was in 1860 by far the richest and most successful ivory and slave trader. When the Tinne-Heuglin expedition sailed to this area in January and February 1863, the slave trade in this region was at its peak.

Arab traders in particular penetrated further into the basin of the Nile, establishing their commercial stations among peoples whom were then known as anthropophagites or cannibals. It is no wonder, then, that these men were considered experts in the fields of geography and ethnology for their regions and that travellers like Piaggia and Heuglin sought their company in order to learn more about Sudan.

The traders were soon followed by members of the Catholic Mission. An 1846 decree of the Pope Gregory XVI established the Apostolic Vicariate of Central Africa. Its principal mission station was in Khartoum, founded in 1848. When the Austrian government opened a vice consulate in Khartoum in 1851, the consul was instructed to protect the interests of the mission. The group of missionaries was composed of a mixture of nationalities (mostly Italian and Austrian). In 1854, a new mission was established at a place up the White Nile and called Heiligenkreuz. In Gondokoro, further up, another mission was built the following year. After many missionaries in the three stations died as a result of disease or violence, in 1862 the few survivors decided to go home and the stations were closed.[5]

Until the beginning of the 1880s, the monopoly on the slave trade remained in the hands of the Turkish-Egyptian authorities. As Heuglin describes, the authorities were involved in the trade primarily to collect revenue in the form of tribute and to swell the ranks of the Egyptian army. The new and ambitious *pasha* Isma'il, who entered office in Cairo in 1863, was intrigued by the possibilities of expanding in particular up the Nile into the vast hinterland of southern Sudan. By taxing and discriminating against the already weakened European traders, Isma'il gradually established Turkish authority over the Nile trade. Free from any local European control, Isma'il advanced up the Nile to build an African empire for himself. By paying lip service to British demands for an end to the slave trade, Isma'il Pasha was able to receive large British loans in order to finance his ambitions of making Egypt an internationally oriented nation and realising an imperial expansion up the sources of the Nile and further to Uganda.[6] These British financial funds, which were furnished in exchange for Egyptian anti-slavery policy, gave a considerable boost to Egypt's economy as well as its geopolitical stature. The Western struggle to eliminate slavery in Egypt and Sudan was, however, doomed to continue for decades, as domestic slavery, which was legally recognised by the Egyptian-Turkish authorities, remained an institution in both Egypt and Turkey.[7]

Seemingly the British commercial and humanitarian interests had been successful with the Suez Canal, opened in 1869, as its most important feat. The collapse of Egypt's finances in 1879 due to Isma'il's loaning policies and the country's subsequent bankruptcy led to his departure. This accelerated Egypt's political and economic decline, resulting in the British occupation of Egypt in 1882. The awakening of radical Islamic forces forming the Mahdi's revolutionary army in 1883 can be regarded as a consequence. The Jihad which then started on a massive scale brought the successes of the Mahdi's and closed off Sudan until 1898. After his victory over the Mahdi in the battle of Omdurman and the recapture of Khartoum General Kitchener, out of piety towards the numerous deaths who had fallen during the mass slaughter in 1885, decided to rebuild the town after having it razed to the ground.

Sudanese slavery and the Western world

At first, Western traders appeared to be willing to deal with slavers. This kind of cooperation was regarded as part of the ivory trade, which was the main reason for many Westerners to be in Sudan. Before 1862, only rumours existed about Westerners dealing directly with slavery, which were largely ignored. The three principal international geographical magazines, *Petermann's Mittheilungen*, the *Bulletin of the Royal Geographical Society* and the *Bulletin de la Société de Géographie*, frequently paid attention to the issue of slavery in Sudan. The mapping out of the geographical discoveries meant that also the *zaribas* and the names of their holders, who were potentially slave dealers, were discernable. Heuglin's map of 1865 was the first to reveal this fact in its entirety, covering the vast region to the south of Khartoum.

Participation in slavery by western traders was only slowly to be exposed as 'a crime to humanity'. The change in estimation and appreciation must have grown in a couple of years. Illustrative of the western attitude towards the traders, whose names were by 1860, though not yet known to the public, connected to the slave trade, is the fact that some of them published their exploration or travel accounts, either as a separate publication or as a contribution to these renowned geographical magazines.[8] As already mentioned, Alphonse de Malzac, one of the principal Western slave traders, died in Khartoum in 1860 while under the protection of the Austrian consul. Heuglin met him during his consularship when De Malzac still held a prominent position among the ivory traders. In traveller accounts, in particular one by Carlo Piaggia, having joined De Malzac for one year as his chief elephant hunter, in 1858 he had been already denounced as slave dealer.[9] His 'fame' only in 1860/1861 became to be judged by his contemporaries as a success which was achieved by cruelty and injustice towards the indigenous people, exploiting the chaos of internal warfare, also between the Africans themselves. Just after his direct participation in the slave trade became publicly known in France, De Malzac was able to publish a contribution in the renowned *Bulletin de la Société de Géographie* about the results of a journey on the White Nile.[10]

The fact that Europeans were among the major participants in the White Nile slave trade was something unknown to the general public in the West. Information about the Sudanese slave trade barely reached the Western world before 1862. Whatever was published on this matter in geographical magazines only reached a small group of professionals involved in new discoveries. Neither the public opinion was influenced by the separate books, published before and just after 1860 by travellers who did not deal with slavery in Sudan and the role Europeans played, though describing their bad behaviour (Brehm and Dandolo already in 1854 and 1855, Petherick in 1861, and Charles Didier in 1856, who stated in his *500 Lieues sur le Nil*, about their presence in Khartoum: 'Europe is represented by the scum of the nations').[11] One page in Didier's book refers to the crimes and misdemeanours of Europeans and mentions the ivory trade but not the slave trade, intending to be a sort of guide for European lovers of travelling.[12] However, in his two studies on Sudan, the influential and authoritative Count d'Escayrac de Lauture made no mention of the slave trade being practised.[13]

Western public opinion was possibly not 'ready' to deal with this phenomenon in an African region that was more distant than the coasts of Western Africa, which were still providing some slaves for Western colonies. After slavery was abolished in the United States in 1863, all the energy of the British Anti-Slavery Society could be directed towards northeast Africa. From 1863, Sudan began to attract more attention from British official and public opinion as being a region where the slave trade was still being conducted on a grand scale. After a while, the protests of the Foreign Office and the Anti-Slavery Society brought about tangible results. Since the European travellers had become sources of news, even consular reports relied on their accounts, while European traders, participating in this trade, had a good reason to conceal the facts from the eyes of Europe. In his *Journal of the Discovery of the Source of the Nile* published in December 1863, John Hanning Speke never mentioned a word about the slave trade which was abundant in the regions he walked through while returning to Gondokoro and Khartoum. In his second book, *What Led to the Discovery of the Source of the Nile*, published in 1864, he devoted one out of 373 pages to the atrocities committed by the White Nile traders. In *A Walk Across Africa* published by his companion James Augustus Grant in December 1864, much more space was devoted to the question of the slave trade that both had seen. Thanks to the controversy between Richard Burton, who questioned the correctness of Speke's story, and Speke himself, Sudan's slave trade was brought to the British public attention. Samuel Baker was the first British writer to draw the attention of the British reading public to the White Nile slave trade in 1866.[14] From that moment on, the question of the slave trade began to also attract more attention on the diplomatic front.

Letters A. Tinne from Khartoum and Berber

Letter A. Tinne to J. Tinne, April 1864, Khartoum.
Only two fragments are left of a letter that evidently must have been written to John from Khartoum and was possibly dated April 1864, repeating to him the story of her mother's deathbed, though providing new particularities:

'(…) [ta]ken with [u]s every[thin]g [you c]ould imagine of comfort and little luxuries, and as the rainy season had not quite set in yet, and the villages so near that we could always be established before the showers, we had nothing to suffer from the weather. Mama arrived and continued well at Buselli´s Establishment from where you had her last letter; there we had many troubles and vexations, but she did not care so much about them except for me, who was so indignant at them; being calmer and not understanding the language she did not take it so much to heart as I did – On the 10th we went together on donkeys to see a place where we intended to pass by the rainy season – it pleased us, and we spent there a pleasant day, rambling in the woods, and making all sorts of plans for our future establishment there – The next day I made an excursion with Anna to a neighbouring Establishment and came home late finding Mama a little unwell, so she went to bed as soon as I came back and we… [top half of letter gone] …better – we had not the slightest idea of anything (…) on 16th she took the quinine Mr. Heuglin had ordered but unfortunately there seemed to be something relaxing in its composition, for many people who took it immediately had diarrhea [sic], and it gave it to Mama too, and made her very ill – from that time she had a burning thirst which augmented till the last, and from time to time wandered a little, though general perfectly sensible; her thirst was dreadful, nothing could satisfy it; we gave her cold tea, wine and water, lemon essence and water and arrow root with wine – the 17th she was a little better and had some chicken broth which she took with pleasure – the 18th and 19th she was in about the same state, thirsty and irritable but sensible and taking interest in all happened around her, even in a gazelle the chasseur had brought and such little things. It now seems strange but nor she herself nor we had yet any fear; – the night of the 19 […]…[on another half sheet, evidently from the same letter:] (s?)aint – Nobody expected it, nor Flore who knew her so long, nor Mr. Heuglin who is nearly a doctor; what her illness was we cannot imagine; Thank God it was not an illness of the country, which would have made it still bitterer for me by thinking I engaged her to come [Alexine had been the originator of this expedition!]: she never had ague or dissentery [sic] which are the two main causes of death of the country. I have racked my head to imagine what it could have been and have seriously thought whether those bonbons I told you we were eating the first days, and which were of those coarse chalky bright-coloured sort, often made up with acids and metallics [sic] have not, if not poisoned at least caused that irritation in her stomach? Her burning thirst, her saying several times 'I feel as if I was poisoned' and a similar case I read in the newspaper suggested me that idea – I keep the remainder of the bonbons to have them examined by a doctor – Mama was buried on the 22nd at the very spot we had so gaily been to see… [other side of fragment] …precaution on our side, it need not in the least have happened. And that is such a bitter cruel thought. Flore had had since a long time an illness of women of her age which weakened her gradually; she was very much fatigued at the Mishra by Mama's illness, was ill herself afterwards, and not well recovered when we set off – A little care and rest would then have put her in state to bear what happened afterwards but nor she nor we thought her so ill and she went on doing her usual service, and a thousand things, like going out in the sun, wet, night etc etc Nothing to her healthy person but which were too much for her and brought on the ague – She was getting a little better when Mamas last illness knocked her down again – Anna had always been well till she got wet in an unfortunate excursion she and I did a few days before Mama got ill – she took cold and had some attacks of ague, which seemed better when she again got wet in that excurs[ion]… [next fragment in her handwriting]… on Saturday 22nd January everything was ready, all her things packed up when on that very morning she slept unusually late; I went several times to see, but would not wake her, till at last, the servant ['who watched her', scratched out] looked closely and saw she was dead! – I had a tin coffin made to be able to transport her, but it was impossible, being dead so recently; so I h[ad her] temporarily buried and left a soldier to guard the grave (…) – I need not tell you, of course, that I have the coffins of Mama and Flore with me; I would not have come back without – You will imagine dear John whatever this letter may be; I wished to tell you all: – All that happened. – and hurried through it trying not to think of what I was writing or I could not have done it –.' [1]

Letter A. Tinne to J. Tinne, April [?] 1864, Khartoum

In another fragment of a letter to John [no place or date either, but possibly sent from Khartoum in April or May 1864], she gives an explanation of the 'slavery' on her ship of which she had been accused:

'Some soldiers of Buselli [sic], came to my service, with their familys [sic]. Among Muhammadans you know, marriage is not so important as among Christians, a woman treated as a wife is considered a wife, and if she is a slave becomes free by having children; Most people have half-wives of that sort, which seems considered quite respectable, and so having conditioned that she would only bring wives and children, no slaves, I was satisfied. Then some of my people notwithstanding our strict forbidding had got Negro girls and lived with them; when the time of our departure approached, they were obliged to own it, and as they were in other respects good people (you must not judge them Europeanly of course) I thought the best was to make them marry the girls legally after the Mussulman rites; it seemed to me more moral than taking the girls away from them, and they thereby were made free and members of the Muhammadan society – But those who had little girls and boys, who they evidently intended to make slaves of, I took away – Since my return, the Government has been making a great fuss, putting the people in prison, asking explanations from the Consul and disbelieving them, in a most insolent way, and implying that I have brought slaves with me! – To understand fully the spite and malice of their [sic] you must know that large caravans of chained slaves are brought by the Divan to make soldiers of – that slave trading goes on actively in town – slaves who know the abolition law, claim their freedom at the Divan, are by fine, restored to their masters! (I beg your pardon, writing so bad, but I have got an attack of fever, and want to finish my letter). – Now dear John what I want you to do is this – most of the things in which Mousa Pasha has so badly behaved I cannot legally complain of – but I know those Turkish functionaries are very afraid of publicity and attention being called on their doings – so could you not, without saying my name of course, publish something about the shameful way in which the Dutch ladies have been treated, with extracts of my letter – besides my own case, you may mention the shocking state the country is in, by Mousa Pasha´s fault. He has put such taxes in all the little industrys [sic] of the country that they have stopped; there is not a <u>mat</u> or a basket or a bit of cotton stuff to be had! He keeps 20.000 soldiers, for whom all the grain and meat is taken by force, so that food is nearly unprocurable and at terrible prices – all the camels of the Cairo road being taken for the use of his soldiers, no merchandises have come since many months and there is complete lack of everything – (I am ashamed to write so, but my hands tremble and I can hardly see) – Large quantities of slaves are taken to increase his army – many villages that I left a year ago flourishing, are ruined and deserted by the shameful taxes; – Khartoum is like a desert, nothing is to be had – and then the taking all the silver makes that the people can hardly live, and is most ruinous for rich people. Do you understand what I mean dear John? I am sure you will be indignant against that horrid man and help me against him. I can not tell you yet what I will do – I may have to go to Cairo to make complaints, in that case I will go by <u>Suakin</u> and the <u>Red Sea</u> and stop in Suez, as I do not wish to see Cairo again; I am not in Khartoum either; I <u>could</u> not see it again; I am in an island called Touti, opposite, where T. Addy comes and sees me 2 or 3 times a week – it is a horrible little place, but conveniently distant from Khartoum. If I go to Suez, I will feel quite near to you –.'[2]

Letter A. Tinne to J. van Capellen, '8 May 1864, Khartoum'

On 8 May, Alexine notifies Jules van Capellen about her situation, begging him to help her: 'Since my sad return I have had no courage to write except to Tante Jim and John, so that you will be astonished to receive a letter from me.' She complains of Musha Pasha's insolences. 'It wears me out, I cannot stand at this moment those perpetual vexations.'

She asks him to deliver her complaints to the King, who might say a word in her favour to the Egyptian authorities, which would change the situation for her. She felt the traders should be punished for their behaviour towards the members of the expedition.

'The Governor General is doing everything to make them escape free (…) and refuse me redress […] to prevent the merchants violences (…) and to forbid them molesting us (…) after months of delay [?] our boats were at last able to come to our rescue…[a] shameful injustice (…) he refused to let the last boat go (…) unless Mr. Thibaut paid for us a certain tax he had no right to ask us, and particularly as it was made <u>after</u> our boats were gone; but Mr. Thibaut was forced to submit to the injustice or to let us perish in want and danger. – Since my return he has on every occasion shown his ill-will and malveillance, and even tried, by misinterpreting things to make me … for a slaver! [I will] return insolence for insolence (…) he is a bad arrogant man (…) trying to tyrannise Europeans whose independance off ends his pride, like the infortunate Soudaniens he is crushing and ruining, quite a despotic Turk of the older times, hating and doing harm to all those who do not crouch for him – and so I have thought of applying through you to the King. – if you feel any reluctance to ask a favour, I reckon on telling me so, I will understand the feeling, but if you do not mind, I would wish you to expose all this to the King and tell him I beg his Majesty's protection. It is a sort of recommendation from the King to the Viceroy of Egypt, expressing that I will may meet [sic] with civility and justice etc. etc. The more pressingly and strongly the King will say this, of course, the better.'

Whether this should be done by the King himself or by his Minister of Foreign Affairs, she did not know. 'Though Pruyssenaers is not a bad man, and is obliged as consul to defend me, he is, entre nous, always so full of commercial and diplomatic schemes, that he rather neglects the affairs of his countrymen…'. She included in her letter a copy of the official complaint ['plainte'] she sent to the Pasha through the French consulate here, with Heuglin's reports. She expects that 'her own King would not abandon me, he would not refuse…Mr. Heuglin says one has a right to claim protection from one's Ministry of Foreign Affairs, and that would be the only thing to do if the King will not do anything.' Although she as well had sent a 'complaint of the unjust tax' to 'Cairo' (Ruyssenaers), on which she received no answer, she could not '<u>legally</u> complain', adding the fact that 'Musha Pasha has not yet <u>officially</u> refused to do me justice'.

The King's recommendation applies to 'the want of courtesy as well as to the injustices':

'After those six dreary months at Bongo, I had a dreadful voyage back, very different from our luxurious and comfortable journey coming – but I did not mind of course, it seemed only in harmony with my feelings – the negroes were hostile, having been horribly ill-treated by the merchants lately, and deserted their villages as soon as they saw a caravan coming, taking all the provisions with them and filling the wells with sand before they left, so after a fatiguing day's march we had sometimes to dig half the night before a drop of water could be obtained, and we soaked the wet mud – as no donkeys or horses can live in the Djour country because of a certain fly that kills them, all my people were on foot, even my little Abyssinian girl, some sunk down of tiredness on the way, and as to leave them would have been certain death, and our half-starved caravan could not stop from want of food (fancy how difficult to feed 450 people in a hostile country!) they had to be dragged on in a most shocking way – That return was awful – I am now living in a village opposite Khartoum as I could not bear to go back to that place I had left so gaily and which contains so many painful souvenirs of happiness – T. Addy comes and sees me every other day; I found her looking astonishingly well and even <u>pretty</u> – she has yet such a youthful appearance – Unfortunately these last days she caught cold and is now in bed, but the Doctor says it is nothing. As soon as I can finish all those vexations of which I write and settle my money affairs with Mr. Thibaut I will leave for Berber, and from there will have probably have to go to Cairo before I can settle down quiet, which is my ardent and only wish – I will probably go by Souakin and the Red Sea, and remain at Suez, as I do not wish to go to Cairo it is for the same reasons that I could not go back to Khartoum (…)'.

She asks Jules to prepare Ruyssenaers for her arrival in Suez. 'I send T. Jim a little map Mr. Heuglin made, and on which are marked all the places we were at – but he could not, for some scientical reason I do not remember, put the latitudes and longitudes and says you can, with a Nautical Alma-nack- and the result of his observations published in the <u>Geographische Mittheilungen</u> of Dr. Petermann it would make it more clear – I beg you pardon for writing so bad, but an attack of fever came on as I was writing and I wanted to continue but my hand shakes and my eyes burn.'[3]

In a postscript, she asks for Jules's understanding for having asked money from the merchants of her ships as a punishment for transporting slaves, hidden in the forecabins of their ships, thereby severely criticising Thibaut.

'(…) Perhaps the rumours of Khartoum might have reached The Hague, that Mr. Thibaut has ruined us! – which, naturally he could not, but has made a dreadful mess with the money he had (…) so that I hardly have enough to live here and not know how I shall travel. Debts are so bad amongst these (…) here, that I rather suffer privations than invade [?] myself in disagreeable affairs –.'

Letter A. Tinne to Jemima van Capellen, '5 Aout 185[sic]4, Berber'
Shortly after her arrival in Berber, Alexine provides her aunt Jemima (who had been dead by then for almost two months) with some important details concerning her mother's death, the way she experienced this and how practical she could be in seriously demanding circumstances. The letter illustrates her state of mind and her exhaustion after the trip.

'I have just received your letter of the 4th of August [1863!], and am painfully astonished that you and John have not yet got the letters I wrote to you [sent in April 1864 from Khartoum] – How you could have heard the tidings before the arrival of my letters is incomprehensible, as I wrote them <u>on the boat</u>, coming down, and sent them off the very day of my arrival, the 30th March – Nobody could have written before, as my boats being the first who came down, nobody could have known anything before I came, and I say, the letters were ready written and sealed, to despatch as soon as I arrived – (…) have been detained on the road and somebody else's arrived sooner – You must have heard the tidings in a very indirect way –.' She apologizes about not to have written her after the letter dated 30th March. '(…) But I could not – I was so sick of horror, that I laid for days on my bed, trying only not to think.- There was something too <u>monstrous</u> and unearthly in such a crush of sorrows – and then I got very ill – Aunt Addy, who had been well for a whole year, dying at my return! – Your sorrow will be dreadful, but I think even you cannot imagine the unspeakable horror it was for me (…) She is gone too – They are all gone! – it was too horrid – and those awful details that I have now <u>four times</u> gone through! I used to tell her that one of the most dreadful things I felt was seeing all those familiar objects and things who [sic] belonged to those one loves, abandoned and useless; and that after arranging Mama's well known clothes and little things with Flore, and poor Flore's things with Anna, and then Anna's. I had to come back alone and take care of all their luggage, and we cried as we looked at the things about the room – A few days afterwards I was arranging her luggage! (…)'. In this letter to Aunt Jim Alexine tells: 'Mr. d'Ablaing at my request has written all the details so I need not and will only say she is buried provisoirement in the Church yard till I hear if you do not think she would have liked to be transported to Eik en Duinen of which she was so fond. I have packed all her trunks as well as I could and will send them to you from Suez. I took out two gowns which I knew she wanted to give to some people who had been civil to her, and so I thought right to fulfil her intentions; I have also got her little negress Rosa with me and will send her to school at Cairo if she does not run away from me, as she is a wicked little girl – and I could not keep her by force, as we cannot acknowledge slavery. I made the Doctor give me a description of her illness [Addy's], as I regrette not knowing what Mama and Flore had (…)'. Beforehand though the analysis of the 'doctor', being the one who treated Henriette on their journey, was rejected by her as well as by others in Khartoum like Mrs. Petherick, who called him 'a murderer'.

She had been disappointed in d'Ablaing, as she tells aunt Jim:

'You will probably soon see Mr. d'Ablaing and will be naturally interested to see one who can tell you so much, but I must tell you, quite confidentially of course that you will not find him as you would expect one who has been with us so far and in such trying moments – Though I believe a good fellow, he was not nice the last times of Mama's life, she and I were quite vexed with him sometimes, and he was so unaffectionate during her illness that after her death there came a coldness between us, which lasted ever since – (…) However painful details are, one always want them, and so I send you a little map Mr. Heuglin made of the country we were in, the only map that exists of course, and on which I have marked the spots at which all happened – The orange stinge [?] is the Meshra where we waited in our boats so long – the red line is our route as we came and went – the blue is Abua Se (…), where I was so ill after the rebellion of the soldiers and we remained a long time; I think Mama calls it Afry in her letters dated from there – the green is Wau where Anna died, the yellow Buselli's Establishment and the scarlet mine where I went afterwards and poor Flore died – Mr. Heuglin says somebody must put in latitudes and longitudes to make it clearly – We could not, not having proper… instruments, I forgot what – Bongo is the name of the tribe we were in, a branch of the

Dōr tribe – I am now at Berber, having had great trouble to get away from Khartoum, from negligence of Mr. Thibaut, with whom it is impossible to terminate any affair – (…) Will you tell Anna's family, her body has come from the interior and I have placed it in the interior of the Catholic Church till I know if they wish to have it come to Holland – if not, she shall be buried at Khartoum – and in the enveloppe is some of her hair, that I though they would like to have.' [4]

Letter A. Tinne to J. van Capellen, 5 August 1864, Berber

In a letter to uncle Jules dated '5 Aout 1864, Berber', she recounts the last moments of her mother and proceeds to the order of the day:

'It occurs to me that if poor Aunt Jim is now so frequently ill – she might perhaps not be able to open my letter when it arrives, and so have thought in that case to ask you to do so (…)'. She will repeat to Jules what she wrote to aunt Jim. '(…) It is <u>too</u> dreadful […] you can't know the horrors I have felt (…) She looked quite young yet, the only change I found in her, the great augmentation of that certain <u>distraction</u> she always had (…) that made her sometimes not answer when spoken to, it was so strong now, that she would often stop in a phrase, forgetting the beginning, and ask the same question over again often, and forget names and words – otherwise I say she looked better than when I left her, and her hair had increased wonderfully – Afterwards people told me that sort of mental weakness was since she had heard the news, and it seems since that time she had l'imagination frappée that she must die too, and that killed her – everybody blamed the treatment of the Doctor…I send you some of her hair, I as afraid it might affect T. Jim too much if I send it directly to her. I am since some days in Berber waiting for camels and corn to set off to Suakim, the road to Korosko [is] nearly shut up by the want of camels which are all taken by the troops who come (…) in daily, besides my not wishing to go down the Nile; the way by Suakim is shorter and better, they say, but the annoyance is if there are no steamboats between there and Suez I must take a boat of the county [?] which are very bad and slow. Or go to Massaoua and cross over from there to Aden; – The Sudan is in a shocking state – I ask myself every day, if time has not gone backwards during my stay at Bongo, and if we are got [sic] back to the good old time when a European ambassador had to dismount and prostrate himself before a Turkish common soldier – Seriously I could not have been more astonished if I found Holland en pleine féodalité, burning Jews, and people who say the world is round – I cannot imagine how the influence of Europeans, that has been so slowly and firmly established, had changed so in one year – Is Europe got so weak? – or Egypt so strong? – (…) Now everything is reversed (…) everyday the Europeans at Khartoum had some new insult to complain of (…) Musha Pasha has seized some merchant's servants, Petherick's amongst others, and put them to torture to try to make them witness against their masters. Petherick's have been twice insulted by soldiers (…) -

And now I have something to ask you which I hardly dare to do – I think you will find it strange – but both Mrs. Heuglin and Petherick who are here advise it me…the Food is scarce as I told you, and I heard there has been a sort of a famine in Egypt, and it is so annoying having every day a vulgular [sic] hunt for your dinner…I want you to send me a quintal of stock fish, as much of rook vleesch as will keep for three months salt butter for three months, and 3 or 4 comijnde kaasen [cumin cheese] – I would like the rook vleesch to be taken from the man who always furnishes us, the servants will know who – (…) to be sent by the same boat from Rotterdam she had taken (…) if you think potatoes will keep (…) send a provision of them too – and some bockum, those herrings with eggs – all that had best be sent to the care of Mr. Ruyssenaers, who will forward it to me when I come.'[5]

Tidings from Cairo

Gentz, 1869

Only a few days after his first visit to Alexine, Gentz's attention was drawn to a lady who was passing by in a carriage and waving to him. Gentz relates about his visit to her as follows.[1]

'One day, while promenading in the *Grand Allée* of the Schubrah, where all the fine carriages of the harems of the Grand Khedive of Egypt and the Pashas were rolling by in state, a friendly motion of a hand and head in one of the carriages greeted me, and I perceived that it came form a veiled lady, enveloped in dazzling silk. My astonishment was great, for I lived for many years in Egypt, and knew the stern customs that bind oriental ladies.

I first thought it an intentional and jesting mystification, until I learned from one of the accompanying servants that the inmate of the carriage was Miss Tinné. I had made her acquaintance through Heuglin, at the time of her grand expedition to the region of the Gazelle-river, at the same time that I made the acquaintance of the English Consul for Central Africa, who, with his wife, was ascending the river by orders of the English government to meet Speke and Grant on their return [Petherick]. After years of hardship they returned again into the regions of civilisation, and I was the first European who had the pleasure of congratulating them, on their return, at their success in overcoming so many terrible difficulties!

Miss Tinné was at that time extremely low-spirited. She had lost her mother and aunt on the fatal journey, in consequence of the deadly climate, and by whom she was ardently loved. And Dr. Steudner, her physician, whom she greatly esteemed, became also a victim, as did one after another of her faithful European maids. Death had robbed her of nearly every dear relative, and taken from her all the European connections. She seemed determined to leave things in this condition, and repeatedly declared that she would never again visit Europe, although her step-brother had kindly hastened to her assistance and escort.

She stood firm against all enticements in this direction, and was maturing a plan to build a castle near Cairo, on the island of Rhodes, in the Nile, where the gardens of Ibrahim Pasha were proud in the beauty of southern vegetation. For this purpose she had engaged the services of the architect of the Viceroy, Franz Deibeck, a German from Wiesbaden; he had built the royal palace of Ghesirah [where the Tinne party stayed before in 1861/62], and she desired him to present plans to her, showing them to John when he was there. She was also negotiating with a celebrated architect for Moorish styles, my friend for many years, who was unfortunately snatched from a field of great usefulness by an attack of the fearful smallpox.

In her plans for building Miss Tinné ran into the most eccentric styles. Nothing was sufficiently fantastical or labyrinthine for her. The Arabian architecture, with its windings and involved arabesques, and the irregularity in the height of adjoining rooms – with its projections and ranges of columns – was well calculated to satisfy this desire. The Viceroy of Egypt, however, who did not fancy this Holland lady for a neighbour, interfered with her architectural plans. She had brought before him an accusation against the Governor of Khartoum on account of ill treatment received at his hands, and demanded his dismissal. The Viceroy did not wish to grant this request, although the injustice done the lady was clear. This was the main interest in not wishing her to make a permanent settlement in Egypt, and especially so near to him.

As nearly two-thirds of the land in that region belongs to the Viceroy, and almost all the remaining third to mosques, there was no difficulty in exerting such an influence on the owners that Miss Tinné could not secure ground enough, in any acceptable place, for her proposed castle.

It is difficult to describe the labyrinthine confusion of oriental cities to one who has never seen them. I myself, having lived in many of them, could not again find the dwelling of Miss Tinné in Old Cairo, although Heuglin had conducted me there the first time. But the native smartness of the donkey boys of Cairo helped me out of my difficulty. These boys with their donkeys are like the cabs and cabmen of European cities.

As I was groping about in Old Cairo, peering into every street to discover some sign of Miss Tinné's house, one of these donkey boys, with large sphinx-like eyes, said to me, "Effendi, are you looking for the Dutch Countess?" for by this title the generous lady had acquired a reputation among the donkey owners of the old city. The Egyptians are born tormentors of beasts, and especially of the poor donkeys. Induced by her warm and sympathizing heart, Miss Tinné had taken some of the half-murdered animals from the boys, to nurse and care for them. This fact had become known, and thus it happened that very soon from all quarters sick donkeys, and other mangy and worn-out beasts, were sent to the "Dutch Countess" to be cured. Her mansions bid fair to be turned into a donkey hospital, when she was at last obliged to refuse admission to any more patients.

On the outside Miss Tinné's house resembled a dilapidated ruin. I was led through the dark passages of the lower story, taking the place of our cellars, of which there are none on the Nile, and arrived, by the attention of my little Egyptian guide, in an open yard, where I could again breathe freely. The dark azure-blue sky, and the golden crowns of three lofty palms lighted by a burning sun, lent to the ruin-like structure that picturesque tint that artists so rejoice to find.

On some stone steps in the open air, which led to the dilapidated rear buildings, some monkeys were sunning themselves. Little negro slaves, boys and girls, lay in the warm sunshine on the ground; large negresses from Sudan inquisitively stuck out of broken window panes their woolly heads, with brilliant eyes and teeth. Long-haired Nubian greyhounds, trained to the chase of the gazelle, came jumping and playing toward me. An old white-haired Berberine, such as is usually found tending the doors in Egyptian houses, received my card, to announce me to the mistress of the strange establishment.

Having soon returned, he led me into a second court, where I passed by large open rooms containing an immense collection of curiosities illustrating the manners and customs of the Central Africans; it required no less than fifty camels to transport these from the interior of Africa Among these were curious weapons, stuffed birds, antlers of antelope, horns of the rhinoceros, and all the household utensils of the various tribes of the Sudan. These were lying around still unarranged.

Miss Tinné comes to meet me; she wears an oriental turban wound round her head, and an Egyptian dress, with long flowing sleeves of changeable grey silk; this was thrown over a black mourning dress. Her feet were covered in Arabian style with long morocco boots. The tall, beautiful, pale figure, affected by grief and sickness, with her decidedly intellectual features, and easy, refined manners, could not but leave a pleasant impression on every one.

Her reception room, into which I was conducted, was an ancient harem, one side of which was composed entirely of windows. From the outside it was not possible to look into the room, because the windows were covered with finely carved and grated bow window frames; through these a soft and delicate light was shed into the room, which produced a sort of mystical charm. The floor was composed of inlaid marble of various colours, and the ceiling of wainscoting, adorned with fancy carvings in the Turkish style.

All around the walls were the usual Turkish divans, instead of chairs, the frames of which were formed of wood of the palm tree. In the centre of the room were a few peculiar low seats, resting on three supports, and most whimsically carved; these were from the land of the Niam-Niams. The only piece of European furniture was a small, modest wooden table, on which was a large Arabian lantern, such as are to-day in use among the Turkish Pashas. By the side of this were scattered the books and drawings of Heuglin.'

As Gentz relates, for him as an artist, this visit to Alexine was of the greatest interest, because it afforded him the opportunity to produce sketches of the many slaves of every tribe from the most inaccessible regions of Africa.

'She yielded to my wishes in this respect with great readiness and kindness. Among the girls I especially observed one young creature about fourteen years old, of the tribe of the Gallas, which is celebrated for its beauty. She might have sat for a model of a queen of her race. The children hastened to show me their arms and breasts, that I might admire the scorpions, serpents, and crocodiles that were tattooed on them in the most unique and fantastic forms.

These eighteen [!] remarkable specimens of the black and brown races Miss Tinné informed me had voluntarily followed her; because in their wild native land they were continually exposed to the fearful cruelties of the never-ceasing slave trade. From a missionary who had seen her in the interior of Africa, I learned that she had often taken a severely wounded slave on her own beast, and herself waded for hours in the deepest mire. She certainly had a most sympathizing heart. While I was sketching her negroes she would sit in Arabian style on the floor, looking at me, and seemed never to grow weary in recounting to me her adventures. The extensive marshy regions about the sources of the Nile appeared to have recalled to her memory her early Holland home; the boundless green meadows on which her young eyes had rested rose vividly to her eyes. Indeed, she complained of being sometimes satiated with verdure, and longed for the dry and yellow sands of the desert.'

While Gentz sketched her 'negroes' (see illustration 17), Alexine recounted her adventures. Concluding his interview, Gentz depicts Alexine as a somewhat eccentric woman, indulging in her own secluded world of Oriental-like fantasies:

'Miss Tinné had withdrawn into a species of solitude, and seemed desirous of shunning the ordinary world. Her heart filled with an undefined longing after something. She first seeked a future in building a fairy-like, oriental home in the midst of the Nile (…). She took pity on creatures, animals and people (…), cutting herself off from all European associations, surrounding her by servants and arrangements that would as far as possible keep her in the interior of Africa. She seemed for a time to devote herself almost entirely to the task of indulging these beings in whatever they might desire. She kept a perfect swarm of them around her, and thus erected a little world in her own domain [and] was (…) so willing to yield to all Oriental ways that she permitted her chief servants to have several wives, as is the custom all over the East with those who are rich enough to keep up an establishment.'

Margaret Tinne-Sandbach's letters and John Tinne's notebook

The first days till the end of January 1865
Staying in the Abbatto Hotel in Alexandria, Margaret Tinne writes on 11 January 1865 how 'Papa' went to Mr. Ruyssenaer who was not in but brought back a letter from Alexine.

'(…) She seems very glad that I have come – & expect us to live in her house in Old Cairo. She is afraid I will be horrified at her menagerie (…) I don't care what it is if it is clean!! but I am afraid Alexine has become so accustomed to dirt (…)'.

In her letter she repeats what Alexine said in a letter to her and John: 'I cannot believe that I am going to see you both (...) I think of nothing else – it seems like a dream – and I am afraid something will happen to prevent the reality'. Before leaving for Cairo at 9 am the next morning, they went to see Ruyssenaers, who told them a great deal about Alexine. He had gone to Suez when Alexine had arrived and found her living in a house without doors or windows, dressed à la Egyptienne, 'in a sort of common grey cloth, a turban of the same material and a veil except over the Eyes –'. Ruyssenaers had told her to take off that 'horrid veil (...) for Gods sake'. When first she arrived she looked 'like parchment – but gradually began to recover her looks'. She was sitting on a 'wooden bench full of holes' and to Margaret looked to be in 'utter poverty'. Even the house she had in Cairo was supposed to be 'a miserable place – a tumble down old ramshackle hole'.

Ruyssenaers also related to John and Margaret that many people went to see Alexine, but that she herself returned no visits, '...[nor] goes out she says on account of her health – Mr. de Lesseps – the Suez consul man – & 4 other French gentlemen went to call last week & came back quite fascinated with her – There is a Russian Lady also who often goes to call on her – The Lesseps party had some trouble to find her – & when they did find the house – met 2 hideous negroes at different points on the way upstairs who only shook their heads when asked any questions – They were astonished to find her in such a desolate place –.'

From the beginning, Margaret seems not only to be somewhat critical of Alexine and her household; she also expresses her doubts regarding the way Alexine behaved herself in daily life. Margaret expected her to have a different attitude towards John and her because of all the misery she had gone through. In one letter, this opinion is revealed very clearly. About their visit to Alexine on the 15th – the three of them had not seen each other more than four years – Margaret recounts:

'(...) after having walked through dark ruinous – ghost like places – a door opened & poor Ali [Alexine] appeared – pale as death – drawing her breath quickly but not a tear! I cant cry she said but oh I am so glad to see you – then she took us up a lot of stone broken stairs thick of dust (...) into her sitting room, a long narrow room with things like square thin coops all round and 2 of them with matrasses on – stuffed with hay which are made by yeomen (...) working in a top room of the house – they are all

Dhum [?] matrasses or in time to be covered with red silk – she sat down with a hand of each of us in hers & said Thank God – thank God – I am afraid if I shut my eyes & open them again to find you gone. Do you remember I was afraid once I might go mad – I hope now I shan[']t go mad of happiness – this was about 4 & we sat & talked till 10 – without stopping & in fact never done ever since – there is a rumble floor in this room – partly covered with loose mats & rugs – Alexine (…) eats but once a day – at sundown – such (…) dinners she has & I do believe sometimes eats nothing – she says she has lost the habit of eating as sometimes she had nothing to eat – It is marvellous how she is alike to tell the things she has gone throu[gh] – Mr. Rowlatt told her today he would himself give her £ 500 for a history of her adventures, she is very thin & pale – (…). [There is] a softness & sadness which is not to be wondered at – & a careworn look – but when she is amused & laughs she is like her old self – we slept at her house the first night & the bed was very clean – but I could not fancy unpack my clothes there & besides we found we were in her room & bed – she said Everything is clean! You see there are cupboards – Yes there were but so full of dust & flies & no appearance of her negroes knowing how to clean them to <u>our ideas</u> – she gave us some coffee without milk & some bread & Butter for Breakfast but it was such an evident effort to her – so papa said we would bring our luggage here [to Shepheards Hotel] and sleep there – and I spend the days with her (…)'.

Margaret's tone sometimes gets rather cynical and critical.
    '[Alexine] has adopted Eastern costume as she could not bring herself to put on stays & crinoline or tie up her few hairs under a fashionable little hat –'. She was dressed in 'a thin chemise – a habit-skirt – a purple woollen skirt – a black tunic & once (…) a sort of grey silk gabardine tied round her waist & with a girdle – & a pair of soft white leather high Boots. When she goes out as she did with me yesterday she puts on her veil – having only her eyes to be seen & over all – a black silk mantilla – she looks like a nun.'

To her son Herman, Margaret writes on the 16th:

'[Alexine] is (…) thin & pale & quiet, but otherwise not altered'. '(…) She has gone through most wonderful adventures – Fancy her attacked by Bedouine Arabs in the Desert. Putting all the luggage round in a Barricade (…) sitting each with a gun in their hands and she with a revolver – ready to fight for their lives – Then she was for 7 days & nights on the Medea [steamer from Suakin to Suez] in an open Boat – sleeping on the top of her luggage with her 5 dogs [two of the five still remained from The Hague; her beloved Matushka (see photos 7, 8) had died on her White Nile trip] and her negroes around her – she lives here in an (…) down house in old Cairo – but she does not intend to stay there – she is going to buy a house – she has buried her mother & Flore for the present at Cairo – But when she has a plan of her own she will have them buried there – Just opposite her window is a very good view of the Nile & the Pyramids beyond – & the Boats of the country with the white sails look so pretty – we went across the Nile on Saturday to look at a palace (…) – I don't think it would do for her – it is so damp. She was very pleased with the Photographs – (…) Alexine has 5 negro Boys. 3 Girls. 2 old women – one man – 2 or 3 Egyptian servants 5 dogs & a monkey.'

In the following days, both John and Alexine made visits to places where a lot of land had been offered for sale. 'Mr. Heuglin came to see her yesterday & we rowed across the Nile to look at a palace of Zerif Pacha which is to let – with a jardin –.'

Heuglin's relation with Alexine receives some attention in Margaret's accounts. Although she appears to be '(…) uneasy at Mr. Heuglins charms – Alexine is very grateful to him for he has been unremitting in his kindness & attention. – But it is as a man of business – she would like if possible to [provide him] some employ much at a distance than for him to hang on here – He is very civil but nothing more – Papa went yesterday to call on Mr. Petherick & said he found Mrs. Petherick much quicker than he expected for we were told in Alexandria that she was rather cracked – Mr. P. [Petherick] came to A's house today & he and papa talked for 2 good hours – I was better pleased with him than Mrs. P. but I don't think she would break her heart never to see them again – she talks constantly of Gmama [only Margaret uses this nickname for Henriette] and Aunt Addy – she has buried GM. & Flore since she came to Cairo – only temporarily –.'

During their encounters with Alexine, more practical affairs were to be dealt with. Ruyssenaers had told her that the government would not admit 'keeping the corpses [of Henriette and Flore] above the ground – that if she would not bury them the government would do it in spite of her – so they are for the present [buried] – we have not seen where as yet but she said she would show us – the house she is now in she has taken for 4 months and I dare say in time she will be more comfortable…She had no table – but a tray put on a stool in Eastern fashion off which we eat our dinner – most of her luggage is not yet arrived – she intends to buy a piece of ground – alter or build entirely a new house – after her own fashion & have a very pretty garden – to have an English – or Dutch Housekeeper & an English Gardener… She said yesterday Oh Margaret – how I shall miss you when you go – it is only now I begin to find out how lonely I have been – it is such a relief to talk to you & John & feel I may trust you & that you care for me – for poor Allys sake I am very glad I came.'

While giving her a helping hand, Margaret makes clear that she is worried about John being too engaged in Alexine's affairs.

'Tomorrow morning I am going with Alexine & our dragoman (…) to get some garments for Alexine – her wardrobe is very limited – she bought some stockings at Suez – but for the rest each article as she takes it off is washed immediately – she has an old washer <u>man</u> at the top of the house who does nothing but wash. The mosquitoes bite me most furiously & make me itch like mad – they don't touch papa – He said he must come to sleep here – for he must have some rest of mind – some relaxation from the constant strain & excitement of being with Alexine [apparently John spent some nights in Alexine's house] – If I could write like a steam engine I could not tell you all, I would like to do – It is difficult to give you an idea of how Alexine pours out her thoughts and feelings (…)'.

Writing to her sons, she repeats the stories Alexine told them about her return journey.

'She was 25 days crossing the desert from Bulue to Souakin – & was twice attacked by the Bedouins – she [made] <u>her people</u> make barricades of her luggage – expecting the Bedouins every moment to break in on them, arrived at Souakin – she was 7 days and nights in an open Boat on the red sea – sleeping on deck – surrounded by her dogs & negroes – arrived at Jeddah the sailors refused to take her (…]). 'That if a storm came on the bodies should be thrown overboard – so she had to go back to Souakin & wait till a steamer passed which brought her to Suez.'

And in another letter she recounts; 'Poor Ally gave us a long [account]…of her mother's death & Flores – she said the last 2 days H. [Henriette] was not conscious – she could not bear to sit by her & see her die – and as F. did not know her [?] she used to go in about every hour to see how she was going on – Oh my poor old Flore – she said & 2 Big tears rolled down her cheeks – I hoped she would have had a good cry – but no – it could not come – I am sure it would do her good & perhaps if she comes on these scenes again it may have the effect. She has had no one before to talk to in the same way – one thing I notice is that she hardly ever writes [?] as she used to do (…)'.

If John had in mind to persuade her to come back to Europe, Alexine, on the very first day of their arrival, must have dispelled this idea as a complete illusion. In the diary he kept during the whole journey, he relates how on the first day of his visit he walked with Alexine, she in 'Turkish costume', and how they [together with Margaret and Heuglin] made a tour in a boat to the island of Rhoda where the palace of Shariff Pasha was. This place was for rent. The rest of the day he spent in her house where he met Heuglin ('again'). Visiting his house, John received much geographical information from him and examined his collection of guns, swords, daggers, cups of rhinoceros horn, fish, bird skins, etc.

One of the first days he went out with Alexine, John felt 'very weak & tired & overpowered by the heat of the sun'. He walked with 'A. to see plots of ground as the site for a house –.'

Then John becomes a bit tired of Alexine's company. '(…) It is always difficult to hide ourselves away from Alexine, who has so many excuses to keep us with her.' In a garden, he gathered a bouquet for Alexine who was 'much affected'.

John was willing to devote his time to Alexine's case against Musha Pasha. On the 19th, he went with Mr. Colquhoun to be presented to the viceroy [the khedive Isma'il Pasha] in a private audience; the audience, however, was postponed due to the viceroy's indisposition.

On the 21st, a note came from Mr. Colquhoun stating that in consequence of the continued indisposition of the viceroy, the audience was postponed until further notice.

On 24 January, John had a skirmish with Alexine. She was not pleased with 'the Rhoda house' they had previously seen and which was to let. 'There seems much difficulty in pleasing her', he writes in his diary.

He gives a helping hand for the refurbishing of some furniture in Alexine's house. On the 25th, he went with Heuglin to the bank to draw '£50 & for divan & curtains.' On the same day he drove to Old Cairo and went with Alexine to look at garden and land that had been 'rehabilitated and belonged to Abdullah Pasha'. 'There is also good land surrounding it, covered with good crops (…) the garden is acres 12, the property 20 (…) was only able to examine the outside, examined plans by Mr. Deibeck for Alexine's house.'

One day, John went with Heuglin to see another side of Cairo, '(…) called Embaba – poor places', leaving Alexine at her home. 'A busy & fatiguing day'.

On 23 January, Margaret gives a description to Herman of the members of Alexine's household:

'(…) I am sitting waiting for our Dragoman Skandee who is gone out to old Cairo to bring in 2 of Alexines negro girls in the carriage – as she never comes into Cairo she wanted them to see something of it – as they are two wild little blackies who know nothing – we took them all through [?] the Bazaar – (…)'. Then she tells Alexine has got for her a 'washer man', and '(…) one of her servants is one of the soldiers she had at Khartoum – a Brown man – his name is Wadi – Adam – or the son of Adam – then she has Abdullah a big black fellow of 6 feet high – 5 negro Boys – 2 old women & 3 girls – All the old women do is to cook food for the dogs – she has 5 dogs & they all sleep in her bedroom at night – such great big brutes – she has a goat – a Turkey & one chicken – what amused those girls most was seeing themselves in a big looking glass – they laughed & chuckled & danced about. The ceiling of Alexines sitting room is of carved wood and the sparrows have built their nest in it & are constantly flying about the room – there is a capital view of the Pyramids from her windows.'

To Bertha, Margaret refers to the way Alexine rides on her donkey:

'You will be amused to hear that Alexine now intends to ride again – (…) on a donkey. She is too old – besides it is not consistent with Arab costume – but what is – is that the ladies ride astride on the Donkeys – their long black silk coverings however hide them so completely that it does not much show – .' On that day Alexine showed them around in Old Cairo in a carriage.

From the end of January till their departure

Soon after her arrival in Cairo, Margaret fell ill. Having diarrhoea, she was consigned to her hotel room where she laid for days on the sofa, surviving 'on chicken soup – rice water & powders.' To her son Jim, she explains about her staying in bed:

'Papa will write (…) if <u>he has time</u> – for Alexine takes him on the go continually'. 'Today he is gone to Alexandria on her affairs – and wont be back till tomorrow – so I have the pleasure of my own society – for I am not alike to go to Alexine – I have not been well for more than a week with Diarrhoea – I doctored myself for some days but as it got worse instead of better I was obliged to get a Doctor and he will not let me leave my room (…)'. 'Today & tomorrow Ali will be without either of us (…) she will not be lonely – for she has no end of visitors of all nations – Papa has finished <u>his</u> business with her – but is run off (…) going with her to look at <u>places</u> – wonder if she will find one she likes (…) She does not like paying money. The Divans which for economy she stuffed with tow – (…) one does with cotton / she has covered with rich silk – for which (…) she has to pay £ 50 (paid by John, according to his diary) – she had them made & remade 20 times and of course the people charge for this (…) & she says she wont pay for more than <u>once</u> (…) but she will be obliged – for she did not know what she wanted & ordered all these things herself – she certainly needs some one to manage her affairs – but it will not be easy – she is so forceful & so obstinate – (…) everything for nothing.'

Margaret ends her letter with: 'I close it now – just telling you how surprised I have been by a visit from Alexine (…) – she came in from old Cairo on a Donkey to see how I was – because papa was away & I was ill – she had her big black negro and the Egyptian servant Ali with her – but I persuaded her to go back in a carriage – I was <u>so</u> surprised when I saw the door open and <u>an Arab woman</u> walk in! – It really was very kind of her for I know how she hates coming to Cairo.'

In her letters to her children, Margaret appears to be a prolific writer, confined to her bed in the Shepheard's Hotel. On the very same day she wrote about the visit she received from Alexine, another letter is written (in the evening):

'8. p.m When I had written thus far the door opened and to my utter amazement who should walk in but Alexine. She who had vowed nothing should ever induce her to enter Cairo or Shepheards Hotel again. I told her I felt very grateful to her and fully appreciated the effort she had made at which she was very pleased & said: – It <u>was</u> an effort – (…) – but I could not think of you all alone & ill & John gone to Alexandria for me – so I got a donkey & came to see how you were – Her big Abdullah was with her – and Ali her Egyptian servant – she said she would go back in a carriage & Heuglin ['he makes fine drawings'] came up & said he should go & see her safe home – He did not think it right at this time of night in this country to let her go without – she was very unwilling – he should go – said it was so <u>un-independent</u> – as if she could not do without him – and would not know how he knew she was here – He said all the house knew! – she had wanted me not to tell anyone she had come – I do not despair of her someday coming round – she was (…) [in] our room and said [it] is a long time since I have seen so civilized a room. How nice it looks – she had had no dinner and would not have any thing not even a Bisquit in my room- she told me one of the old negroes had gone mad – then she qualified it & said she [i.e. one of the old negroes] went into hysterics and passions – but all the rest are so frightened they wont sleep in the room with her – they say she is a <u>witch</u> – & she goes walking about the house with a stick & beat any one she can lay her hands on – Alexine is protected by her dogs! – She is a strange mixture sometimes so fascinating & so nice you cannot but love her – and other times so strange – so obstinate & such exotish [?] ideas about things & so reckless that one gets almost out of patience with her – <u>she says</u> she has lost all her courage and is afraid of every thing – but she does <u>not</u> seem to me afraid of any thing – .'

On the 27th, Margaret writes also to her 'dear Girls': 'Papa is gone to Alexandria on Alexine's affairs (…)'. The previous day 'he had been all day with Alexine looking at places none of which pleased her (…). She is so difficult to please and so unwilling (…)'.

Almost every day John and Alexine, often accompanied by Heuglin, made either excursions in the neighbourhood or visits to see land that was being offered. At the end of January, Alexine's relationship with Heuglin was becoming an issue in the conversations. On the 27th, Heuglin told John he would leave Cairo because he could not 'get on with his work'. The next day John left Cairo by train to Suez and Alexandria, complaining on the 28th in his diary about staying at a place: 'night rest disturbed – kept awake by dogs barking (…) till 4, the cats- then cocks, then goats – sticking sheets (…)'.

Finally on 31 January, John was invited to attend a ball organised by the viceroy Isma'il Pasha on the anniversary of his accession to the throne. He was, as he describes, 'ill-prepared, first having an inflamed gum & face' but not being able to resist the opportunity of seeing the novel sight [the Pasha's new palace]. He relates how he '(…) was presented today to the Viceroy by Mr. Colqahoun (…). His Highness is a short fat man with grey eyes which peer into you from time to time & seem to try if he can take advantage of you.'

On that same day he writes: '(…) Alexine called on Margaret at 5½ PM. She had been out from half past 6 in the morning & had had nothing to eat all day – 1st Febr. After having written letters – out to Old Cairo & saw Alexine who had had fever during the night but is now better.'

While being busy with excursions and 'plots of land' for Alexine, John was gradually focusing more on other affairs in order to solve some urgent problems in her household and her near future.

On 2 February, he went 'out all morning with Heuglin, looking in Turkish bazaar & jewel setting shops – streets crowded to cramming (…) – an orderly mob (…) – saw Mr. [F]rantz, architect & heard [about] his [plans] for business with Alexine. Mr. Heuglin gave me the following. (…) Aedemone mirabilis, named by Kotschij, Vienna'. The next day he '(…) intended to have gone to see Pyramids with Mr. Heuglin (…) [but the night had been] very stormy – so much dust this morning, blown up by wind & filling the air like mist…Alexine came to Shepheard´s this Evening – I took her home again (…) had a vain [?] discussion with her on business.'

While still staying in bed, Margaret writes on 2 February:

'Here am I still enjoying my own room & tomorrow. I (…) have a full benefit of it for papa.

I hope we have nearly completed one good thing and that is getting her negroe children to school – now they do nothing but scamper up & down the house laughing & screaming & making dirt pies (…) – Dogs – Rats – preserve me from living there – How Alexine can <u>choose</u> to live here I can[']t think – at which she laughs.'

On 6 February, John went to the station 'at 7½ am for Pyramids with Heuglin (…) with Prof. Dr. Fraas, (…) dealing with many historic details (…)'. The day after he had an interview with Ruyssenaers regarding: 'Alexine's complaints against Soudan traders and Mousha Pasha. Ruyssenaers seems very willing to take actions and forward copies of the papers with the complaints (…)'. The day before John had noted down in his diary: 'News of Mustapha Pasha's death'.

In arranging her affairs with their departure coming into sight, the issue of Alexine's nationality turned up. John apparently tried to force her to make a choice between English and Dutch citizenship. On 12 February he went 'to Old Cairo – long discussion with her about nationality – she came to hotel in Evening & finally determined to give me instructions to obtain Dutch nationality for herself.'

The next day John went again to 'Prof. Fraas [who] informs him he has discovered the large deposit [?] at an hour & half walk distance from the Sphynx (…) embedded in a range of hillocks.' Then he went with Colqahoun to Alexine to explain to her 'the difficulties of a procedure [of her complaints] against Musha Pasha, as a foreigner in Egypt.'

In what appears to have been a short statement, likely meant for John, Alexine expresses in a note dated '3 Février 1865' her wish for '(…) an intelligent perfectly trustworthy man and well acquainted with the State of Egypt who shall be paid in a way that I do not scruple to employ him and whom I may consult on the value and management of land, who will help me to select a site of land, take the necessary steps for purchasing it and who will help me to build a house and manage my land and garden, and who will obtain any information or take any steps in general I may require, for instance claiming a servant from the police. Alexine Tinne, Vieux Caire.'
  This note was joined by another one: 'I wish you, my Dear John, most

particularly to make informations about some concern which will increase my means, <u>without</u> endangering my Capital, and in which I will risk only the sum I put in, great or small. Alexine Tinne.'

In one of Margaret's letters (dated 27 January), an interesting detail is provided regarding the interior of Alexine's house. Referring to 'Lanes Book on the Modern Egyptians' she writes: '(...) Get it & look at the fron-tispiece – it is an exact representation of Alexine's sitting room – the Divan & Table – which is the stool (...) tray on it, in the corner – she has not g[o]t the curtains (...) yet – tho' she has got the material – and for that & the mag-nificent silk which she has covered her tow stuffed Divans with– she has paid £50! –.'[2]

When looking back on what Alexine had gone through in the past one and a half year, one of Margaret's letters to her daughters shows some pity on her and presents Alexine's view on her near future:

'Sunday, I suppose you are all at tea now – Poor Ally is rather bothered by this 3 times repeated [?] accusation of her for slave trading – now specially made by the Egyptian government – I hope & tell her that it is only to tease & bother her – but she says suppose they send me to the galleys – wont people in England think it a great shame & what will you do? I tell her they wont do that – but they may make it unpleasant to stay here – she says she would not care if they cut her hand off – she does not care for dying but it would break her heart to leave Egypt & if she is obliged to do so – she will either go to Syria – or Java – or buy a Yacht and live in that – that she hates the sea & is always sea sick!! – so you may imagine the style of our daily conversation.'

On the day she says to be recovering [2 February?], Margaret writes a letter that presents a revealing insight into the ongoing events:

'My dear girls (...) On Sunday afternoon I felt better & Dr. (...) said I might dine out with Alexine – but I felt so ill before I got there & all the time I was there & before I got back to the Hotel & was in such violent pain I thought I was going to have an inflammation. It lasted all night & all Monday I lay on the sofa all Monday too ill to do anything but lie with my eyes shut groining with the pain.' 'The doctor came twice a day (...) mustard plaisters (...) mustard food & Butter Castor oil (...). Today I am certainly better (…).'. 'Last night Alexine came to see me & if she is not soon ill it will be a miracle [?] to me. She had been all Monday & Tuesday from 6 in the morning till the evening (…) looking at places to buy – & when she came here at 6 last night she was completely done & told us she was so poorly on Monday night she could not come here – and <u>so tired</u> yesterday that she sat down & went to sleep in the garden of one of the places she went to see – she says she wants to buy a place before we go that papa may so far see her settled – Yes I said – but in [the] mean time you make yourself ill which I think you do – Oh she said if I have to be ill – if I am what does it signify I can only die – & what matter if I do! – '.'(…) She receives all sorts of perfect strangers who consider her one of the curiosities of Cairo at present – There is a place of 60 acres she wants to buy because she thinks she can grow cotton & make money – forgetting that there is great deal more than the mere growing to be done before she can make anything by it – she is bent of having Franz the Architect in the place who does all the Viceroys work to build the house – Papa gets completely at his wits end sometimes – and then she tells me how nervous John is – worse than me – what is the matter with him? The Dr. says Old Cairo is very unhealthy – she says she does not believe it & she does not care if it is – Nothing can be unhealthy for her after the Soudan – and she can get land cheaper there than in many other neighbourhood – In fact a wilful woman must have her way and there is no use arguing with her – perhaps when she has thrown away a few thousand pounds she will be willing to listen to the advice of older heads who have lived in the country for years – but at present she thinks she knows all about the country & people quite as well if not better than any one (…) Both Heuglin and Mrs. Petherick say she is ill transposed (…) but I must do her the justice to say that however we have opposed her fancies she has always been most perfectly good tempered & patient & good natured to both Papa & me (…).

All Alexine's Mousa Pacha affairs are gone in letter [to the] Dutch Ministre [sic] at Constantinople (…). Papa must not bother his head anymore about it – Somehow things get (…) awfully slow here – As to one staying till all Alexine's affairs are settled its nonsense – One might stay altogether & her mind is <u>so busy</u> – she has every day some new things to talk about. She was here on Tuesday – but I have not seen her since – <u>Even she</u> does not like to face the suffocating clouds of dust – (…)'.

After having written a few lines more, Margaret adds: 'Alexine came here for an hour to talk (…) Papa went with her & did not come home till close on 12 so you may think <u>how</u> they talked – (…). She is so restless & changeable in her plans – very determined (…) in the main – but so capricious in the details – we thought we had got it so beautifully managed for the American Mission to take the children & how she wants to get rid of the 2 old women & wants them to take them as well – witch & all!!'

She drops some names of people (Mr. Colgahoun, Petherick, Rowlatt and a certain Mr. Mon…[?] 'who has lived here more than 10 years') who had been asked to be of some assistance in clearing up Alexine's affairs, but 'she thinks she knows a great deal more (…)'. 'Responsible is Mr. Rowlatt to Papa -for a certain fixed salary – He is to give his answer tonight – & then we shall see if she approves – ' She was difficult to please – 'the Comtessa as Alexine is universally called here'.

Visits to the pyramids were made. After such a visit Margaret explains that 'A[lexine] will be busy with Mr. Ruysenaer & the Mousa Pacha affairs – .'

On 7 February, John repeated his visits with Heuglin and a Mr. Wright ('the English Clergyman'), going to the Pyramids.

Alexine's ethnographic collection was going to be packed and shipped to Liverpool. The short description reveals that her collection consisted of an ivory trumpet which, however, would never be donated to the Public Museum at Liverpool.

On 16 February, Margaret tells Herman: 'It is a very confusing journey. Regarding Alexine's spirits – 'she is in uncommonly good spirits & seems very happy with her dogs & the blackies for company – '. 'All Alexine's luggage from Kartum is come & the large white donkey Mama used to ride – LA's horse. She has given Papa 2 large boxes full of African curiosities & they are to be sent to Liverpool by Boat – but I don't know when. Among them is an immense long ivory trumpet – about 6 feet long – I picked up a few shells near the Red Sea (…)'. 'It is very bad here – (…) & the smells & the flies are disgusting – Altogether this beautiful country has made me ill – and the doctor says I must go away – so we leave Cairo tomorrow – sail from Alexandria on Sunday or Monday – for Trieste (…).'

For reasons of health, John and Margaret had to leave Cairo and move to Alexandria where they arrived on 8 February, and they stayed for a longer time than Margaret announced in her letter, perhaps to be able to make preparations in anticipation of their return journey. Margaret makes clear that in leaving the city her health was concerned: '(…) Thank Goodness we have come here – There is a feeling of freshness & clearliness [sic] that is quite reviving after that pestilent menagerie of a Cairo.' John would return frequently to Cairo in order to arrange Alexine's affairs.

In the beginning of February, the relationship between Alexine and Heuglin came to an end. In the letter above, Margaret writes:

'Alexine has at last relieved herself of Heuglin – He wanted her to keep him as the man of business to which she decidedly objected – but she wanted the Vice Roy to do some thing for him – (…) as she has made herself an object of annoyance to him by the complaints she has made, he was not very likely to do. Papa told her that the proper way was to make him a handsome present in money – Oh she said No! that would affront him and besides it would take it from my house building – .' After a discussion she more or less reluctantly agreed with the proposal to give 'a present of £ 200'. Margaret's comment is harsh on Alexine's behaviour: '£ 200 (…) – for all he has done for her & how it is done- she says that her purse is £ 200 lighter her heart £ 200 lighter too – for she no longer feels (…) an obligation to him – when she was here so tired out last night – after her long day & (…) nothing (…) since the night before we made her have a glass of wine & water & I offered her some of my chicken soup which she declined. I can fancy Harriet saying quite right too – nasty stuff – .'

The time of their departure was approaching. In his diary John takes down that on the 16th, Alexine signed an agreement with American missionaries for the care of her 'negroes' [crossed through]. '…A[lexine] signed agreement for taking charge of the negro children – had long conversation with her in Old Cairo & bid farewell to the house (…).'

On that day John celebrated his 58th birthday. '[On the] 17th Alexine came to see us off at the Railway.' – 18th 'D'Arnaud Bey called with his map of White Nile Exped[ition] & gave interesting information.' Actually, the French explorer Joseph Pons d'Arnaud was asked by John to inscribe some geographical notes regarding the White Nile, which have been preserved at the end of the diary booklet.[3]

On board the steamer *America* from Alexandria to Trieste, Margaret writes a letter dated '24th February 1865':

'Alexine came to the Railway at Cairo to see us off – to our great surprise & I don't think she can have liked it – for the people all crowded around her – (…) – for from the twitching of her eyes I am sure she felt our going – Before that she laughed (…)'. She was grieved about the way Alexine was living. 'But it is useless grieving – or arguing with her – so I'll say no more about it (…)'.

On the same day ('On board the Austrian Lloyds Steamer America 24th Febr. 1865'), John writes to his children:

'Dear children, we left Cairo on friday evening 17th and Alexandria Saturday afternoon the 18th. We hope to reach Trieste tonight (…). I assure you we are both of us very glad to be out of Egypt. I did not go entirely with the idea that we should have completely unalloyed [?] pleasure but I was hardly prepared for the full amount of anxiety I have had on Alexine's account, and I could hardly have thought I should have been so much put out of the way by the annoyance of the country, dust, flies & dogs, besides other plagues. (…) I have no desire to return to Egypt again – Alexine asked me the last words she said: "Won't you come back to see me?" Of course if it was a duty & she in danger, must do so, but I will not go back of my own free will. I am very sad & distressed at her determination to remain, not for any danger she incurs personally but for the utter want of proper domestic arrangements and her inexperience how to set things right altho' she believes herself very clever & wise. She is now looking out for a place to buy & perhaps she maybe so lucky [?] in finding one to her liking, she may at last give up the thought of living in Egypt but is impossible to say at present what will happen, so we must all live in hopes for the last. She came to see us off at the Railway and has been very often at the Hotel to see Mama who was not able to go out & I think she showed some emotion when we parted, so perhaps a change may come over her when she finds herself now completely isolated. For her late companion Mr. Heuglin was also going away from Cairo. It is a strange idea to see a young creature like her thrown among a lot of strangers & living in such a way, when she has friends who would cordially welcome her & where she has comforts and luxuries at her command which she throws to the wind & she is always saying "what a poor person I am"! But I must stop this dismal strain. You must excuse me for expulsing my feelings for out of the fullest of the heart the brother [?] speaks; it is however just as well you should all know how things are with Alexine & you need not of course mention these to strangers.'

APPENDIX 7

Petermann's maps of 1865 and 1869

This chapter throws new light on Petermann's coloured foldout map (see foldout map) and the progress made in discovering the geography of this Bahr el-Ghazal region that Europeans were so eager to explore. The two maps indicated in the title above refer to two editions of the same map. Both maps indicate the route that the Tinne-Heuglin expedition took in 1863, but the route discovered by the explorer Piaggia was omitted by Petermann, the publisher, and by Heuglin, the author. A poignant detail, because the Italian Carlo Piaggia, a friend and competitor who had also been invited to join the Tinne-Heuglin expedition, succeeded in 1863 in doing what Heuglin desperately wanted to accomplish: to enter the Azande country. The story behind these two maps tells us much about the underlying competition that began to develop among European nations in the discovery of this part of Africa.

Orazio Antinori's account

The large foldout maps that are attached to Heuglin's publications of 1865 ('*die Tinne'ische Expedition...*') and 1869 (*Reise in das Gebiet des Weissen Nil...*) are a good example of Petermann's fine cartography. Exquisitely drawn by Bruno Hassenstein, Petermann's mapmaker, it may be qualified as one of the finest maps to have been published in the *Mittheilungen* since the magazine's start in 1855. All the details of locations with their names and routes followed by explorers have been rendered as clearly as possible and with painstaking precision; its layout and colours reveal a considerable decorative quality.

When Heuglin drafted his map of the Western basin of the White Nile, only a few maps of that part of the region had been published. In March 1862, a map of the Bahr el-Ghazal by Guillaume Lejean appeared in *Nouvelles Annales des Voyages*, which was a result of his journey in February-April 1861. This map, together with those of the brothers Poncet and Petherick, provided much new information.[1] In *Petermann's Geographische Mittheilungen*, part of Lejean's account was included, although this was not accompanied by the map.[2] Strangely, in his accounts Heuglin does not refer to Lejean's map.[3] Of the maps that had been published previously, he only mentions the one drawn by Petherick in 1861. The information on this map was, according to Heuglin, 'not very reliable' and the distances between the mentioned stations 'too high in their records'.[4] These maps were worked out by Petermann in six separate maps and published in November 1863 in *Inner-Afrika*. At that time, Heuglin was in Bongo with Alexine Tinne.

As Petermann states on 8 July 1863, he expected Heuglin to send him a sketch of the Bahr el-Ghazal region containing the necessary information to complete the large new map he had planned of the whole White Nile area. This map was to replace the six separate maps representing parts of the region that were to be published in *Inner-Afrika*.[5] The last written accounts of the *Tinne'ische Expedition* describing the route he and Alexine had followed from Biselli's *zariba* in Bongo all the way to Suez were delivered by Heuglin to Petermann by post in December 1864 or possibly in January 1865; they might have included a large part of Heuglin's sketch as his contribution to the new map. In May, after his return to Stuttgart, Heuglin was able to assist in accomplishing the final draft of his part of the White Nile map, which was eventually published by Petermann as an appendix to the final chapter of the *Tinne'sche Expedition* in the *Ergänzungsheft* nr. 15.

The information that Heuglin provided Petermann on the Bahr el-Ghazal region was limited to the western part of Petermann's new White Nile map. Besides the accounts by Heuglin, Petermann mentions those written by Franz Morlang and Wilhelm von Harnier as being the most recent information concerning the White Nile region to the southeast.[6] Room had been made for the drawings of some ethnographic objects from the Bahr el-Ghazal region, which Heuglin had sent from Khartoum before he left on the Tinne expedition.[7] The list of routes taken by explorers also included the journey of the Italian marchese Orazio Antinori, who, accompanied by Piaggia, departed in November 1860 from Khartoum to the Gazelle-river.

When Piaggia fell ill, Antinori continued his way to meet the French Khartoum trader Alexandre Vayssière in his *zariba* at Wau. When they were returning to Khartoum Vayssière died in May 1861. The account of Antinori's journey was published by Petermann in 1863; at that time, Heuglin was on his route accompanying the Tinnes.[8] In 1868, Antinori wrote an account including his own map of his Bahr el-Ghazal journey, which also indicated the itineraries of Petherick and Heuglin. The main subject of Antinori's travelogue is the journey that Piaggia had made in 1863-65.[9]

Piaggia's route

Heuglin's *Reise in das Gebiet des Weissen Nil* of 1869 contained his story of the Bahr el-Ghazal expedition with some introductory remarks by Petermann. This was accompanied by an exact copy of the map of 1865. For this edition, all the previous accounts of 1863, 1864 and 1865 had been more or less rewritten. The addition of an exact copy of the White Nile map of 1865 leads to the conclusion that in 1869 both Heuglin and Petermann apparently held the view that no new facts had to be added to the map of 1865. Why did Heuglin omit Piaggia's route of 1863-1865 from his 1869 map?

Around 1860, representatives of five European nations were attempting to make discoveries in the Western basin of the White Nile. The Italian Carlo Piaggia was also working his way through the marshes and rivers of the Bahr el-Ghazal area in order to enter the Azande country. While staying in these regions, he was approached by Heuglin who was at that time held up in Bongo, near the Kosanga mountains. In a letter, Heuglin forwarded to Piaggia in September 1864 his intentions to proceed into the Azande country, and asked him to meet and accompany him on his trip. Piaggia sent a response which, however, was lost. From this fact, recorded by Piaggia in his diary (see Chapter 3, notes 15, 16), it may be concluded that Heuglin was well aware of the results of Piaggia's journey.

In 1868, three years after his return, Piaggia finally received serious attention in national geographical circles in the recently established kingdom of Italy. Orazio Antinori, founder of the Società Geografica Italiana in Florence in 1867, was the first to draw attention to Piaggia's efforts by recounting his story according to his yet unpublished diaries.[10] It was not until Antinori's publication in the first edition of the *Bollettino della Società*

Geografica Italiana in 1868 that it became clear what a significant role Piaggia had played in the discovery of the Bahr el-Ghazal region. In that same year, Petermann wrote a review of Antinori's account of Piaggia's journey.[11] In this review, Petermann, who was the first scientist outside Italy to comment on Piaggia's observations, appeared to be critical about their significance. Antinori is also subjected to Petermann's negative comment.

Why was Petermann so critical of Piaggia and Antinori? We argue below that the way he treated Antinori's account of Piaggia's diaries has to be viewed in the light of what Heuglin in Petermann's opinion had accomplished. More precisely, Petermann's criticism might very well point towards Heuglin as the principal reviewer of Antinori's article.

Antinori's account of Piaggia's diaries

Besides referring to his own journey of 1860-61 in his article, Antinori devotes some 60 pages (of 94) to Piaggia's journey into the Azande country. In his diaries, Piaggia noted down a whole range of peculiarities of the regions he was travelling through. Besides information regarding fauna and flora – in particular specimens of trees, complete with their Linnaenean nomenclature (Heuglin did likewise in his travel accounts to Petermann in the same period) – he recounts the customs and habits of the Azande, to which most of Antinori's article is devoted. A finely drawn map accompanies Antinori's article. On the map, almost all journeys in this large area have been indicated (with the exception, strangely enough, of Giovanni Miani's journey in 1859 up the White Nile) in coloured itineraries. The route Piaggia took in 1863 and 1864 actually enters quite deeply into Azande country; it in fact touches the area that Georg Schweinfurth was to enter almost five years later.

Piaggia gives a description of the Azande villages and the way their huts were built up: conically all the way from the base to the peak, lacking the upright round mud walls observed in the villages of the Shilluk, Dinka, Jur, Dōr and most of the other peoples in this part of Sudan, but still sharing similarities. After recounting Piaggia's itinerary, Antinori sums up Piaggia's observations of the habits and customs of the 'Niam Niam'. Both Antinori and Piaggia never mentioned the name 'Azande', which Heuglin had already used in his 1862 publication. Quoting from Piaggia's diary Antinori presents in separate chapters successively the 'customs of the Niam-Niam' in 13 pages, and the journey into the country of the Azande with reference to those made before by Petherick and Lejean. In an appendix, Piaggia's examples of Azande vocabulary are compared with those that Lejean and Petherick had recorded in their publications.

Petermann's review

In his review in the *Mittheilungen*, Petermann partly reproduces Antinori's article by translating whole paragraphs and summarising other parts. He restricts himself, however, to a summary of what Antinori recounts regarding the life of Piaggia, the route he took, a shortened version of his observations concerning flora and fauna and the water levels in the Meshra el-Rek, comparing this with Heuglin's observations. Then he discusses Piaggia's vocabulary. Petermann judges Piaggia's list of Azande words and expressions to be far more extensive than that of Lejean and Petherick. The latter only compiled a small dictionary of words in 1861, which he recorded in 1859 during his short stay with the Azande in the southeast.

In his chapter entitled '*Piaggia's Reise zu den Niamniam, 1863-1865*', Petermann recounts a journey of 'an Italian, belonging to the lower classes, under the name of Piaggia, who penetrated to the Niamniam, partly by order, partly under the protection of an ivory trader from Khartoum [De Malzac].' Beginning with his childhood in Lucca, Petermann tells how Piaggia first set foot in Egypt in 1852. Working in Alexandria as an artisan repairing tapestry, weapons and clocks, he finally earned so much money as an applier of lacquer on carriages that in 1856 he was able to leave Alexandria for the Nile, which he ascended as far as Khartoum. In November of that same year, he went up the river again to the Rajjaf mountains in the Bari regions with the French trader Delphine Barthélémy, who later in 1862 joined Eugène de Pruyssenaere for Gondokoro and died in 1866 en route to Sudan from Egypt with a consignment of goods belonging to the Maltese trader Andrea Debono. In 1857, Piaggia entered into the service of De Malzac, who had a *zariba* amid the Cic near Ghaba Shambé (see foldout map), as an elephant hunter. Petermann gives Piaggia credit for resigning his job and leaving De Malzac and his gang already in 1858, as De Malzac's name was later tarnished by criminal charges. In February 1859, Piaggia travelled back to Italy, where he would leave his ethnographic collection of weapons and utensils acquired along the White Nile in previous years to the Museum of Natural History in Florence. He was back in Khartoum again in September 1860 to accompany the marchese Antinori two months later to the lake in Meshra el-Rek and the Gazelle-river, visiting also the country of the Jur. On 28 January 1863, eight days after Heuglin left Khartoum ahead of the Tinnes, Piaggia undertook his journey to the Bahr el-Ghazal, proceeding further southwards. As told in Chapter 4, they both arrived in Meshra el-Rek on the same day (10 February 1863). At that time, Piaggia had a contract with the Coptic trader Ghattas allowing him to enter via Ghattas' *zariba* under the river Jur into that part of the Azande country that was ruled by the chief Tombo.

After having declined Alexine Tinne's second invitation to join her expedition, he left Meshra el-Rek on 22 March and marched in four days and three nights to the establishment of Ghattas, a stretch of 120 miles in a southwestern direction. His haste turned out to have been unnecessary because he was forced to wait in Ghattas' *zariba* for seven full months. After a while he became inclined to accept the Tinne offer to enter the 'Niam-Niam' regions after all and wrote a letter to the Tinnes which was lost, as he later reported. Eventually on 2 November, he was able to leave with an escort of 95 of Ghattas' men and 200 porters, finally making his way into the Azande region in the south.

Although he was a not a man of science, Piaggia was eager to note down new phenomena in nature as Heuglin did. He noticed, for instance, how some specimens of trees such as the bread fruit tree (*Bassia parkii*) decreased or increased in numbers, as did some acacias that were also growing in the country of the Jur. The inhabitants of the Mandu mountains – notorious for their opposition to any elephant hunter who tried to pass by – shot their arrows from far above, causing three casualties and several injured men in Piaggia's train. Piaggia tells about the wailing of the wild beasts during the night and the deafening cries of parrots during daytime. On 14 November 1863 he finally reached the village of Tombo, the northeastern outpost between the Jur-river and the White Nile of the vast empire of the Azande, which actually constituted of a conglomerate of peoples. Piaggia was the first European to reach this point in Sudan. Chief Tombo was depicted as a man in full manhood, long and slim, with proud but not savage looks, strong limbs and a dark olive, bronze-coloured skin. His luxuriant hair was frizzled and adorned with multi-coloured feathers, which were arranged in a bizarre way. His clothes consisted of a prepared, red-coloured piece of tree bark, attached around the hips by a belt. While presenting himself to Piaggia, Tombo carried three lances in his right hand and a harp, called 'kondi', in his left hand (for a similar object, see Catalogue numbers: 4 and 28).

After this introduction to Piaggia, Petermann begins a new chapter entitled 'Einiges über die Niamniam und ihre Sprache, nach Antinori und Piaggia'. His opening sentence is extraordinary: 'The best, what till now has been written about the Niam-Niam, are the notations gathered and composed by Th. v. Heuglin. All written before, including the information by Marquis Antinori, only rested partly on truth, but more often on totally exaggerated and lied messages from the people living in the vicinity or Arab elephant hunters.'[12] He then goes to say that 'Piaggia only confirms Heuglin's notations, though hardly adding anything new to them, and Antinori does not hesitate to justify his former accounts.'

Further on, Petermann quotes Antinori who states that the 'Niam-Niam were not half-human, or half-dog; they didn't have a tail, they didn't kill and eat, like Petherick told, fleeing slaves and dying oldies; they didn't bury cows and eat human beings, neither did they season their soups with human fat (…)'. Remarkably, Petermann claims that according to Antinori, Piaggia denied that the Azandes were cannibals, whereas in the Bollettino article of 1868, Piaggia is described as having been a witness of cannibalistic rituals.[13] In his comment, Petermann not only detracts from the merits of Piaggia's observations, he is also inaccurate in his representation of Antinori's article. He ignores the fact that Antinori actually did not justify his former accounts but denounced explicitly what he alleged before, correcting one detail in his former account of his travels of 1860-61.[14]

Leaving out a substantial part of Piaggia's diaries, Petermann does not give any explanation about his criticism of Piaggia's observations. Moreover, Piaggia's information on botany is considered by Petermann as 'too scanty for botanists to be of some use, and that concerning zoology is far too sparse'. Ending with the vocabulary, he praises the quantity of words collected by Piaggia. Petermann concludes that Piaggia's observations have no additional value whatsoever but never backs this criticism with solid arguments.

Petermann's comment

Reading Petermann's comment, one cannot avoid the impression that Petermann was strongly favouring Heuglin. In regard to his judgment of Piaggia's diaries, however, it is more than likely that there was a close cooperation between him and Heuglin. The latter was at that time the only person in Prussia who was able to judge the value of Piaggia's account and assist Petermann in determining to what extent Antinori's text concerning the diaries should be taken up and criticised.

In 1868, the year of the review, Heuglin's book was in preparation. Heuglin included several paragraphs full of information regarding ethnographic peculiarities of the Azande including several illustrations of their artefacts with descriptions in the text. As he was able to speak and read Italian (the lingua franca of Sudan till the 1870s[15]), he might very well have been asked by Petermann to translate Antinori's *Bollettino* article and judge its value for the *Mittheilungen*. We can easily imagine Heuglin, after reading Piaggia's diaries with their detailed description of Azande characteristics, feeling obliged to mention Piaggia as the first Westerner to visit the Azande but being unable to bring himself to give homage to *all* he had done and worked out. Piaggia's accounts of the Azande actually refer extensively to their customs and their daily life: the organisation of their society, warfare, hunting, matrimonial structures, eating customs, family, ornaments including their 'tattoo' (i.e. scarifications), superstitions, arts and industries, specimens of artefacts (referring to used materials as clay, iron), musical instruments, full moon feasts and dancing. Compared with Heuglin's information, these notations actually contain new and thus unique facts.

Most of Piaggia's botanical observations and all of his ethnographic exploits were criticised but, because Petermann does not quote Piaggia, the reader is unable to judge for himself whether Petermann's criticisms were justified. Moreover, Piaggia's name was left out on the second version of the map. It is as though Petermann wished to ignore Piaggia's accomplishments as a geographer as well.

By leaving out a substantial part of Antinori's accounts of Piaggia's diaries, the author of the review was clearly trying to help establish Heuglin's significance as a geographer. Petermann actually referred to Piaggia's travels as interesting and rich in details, admitting that they had never before been published, but that Heuglin had been more accurate in his 1865 map. For an explanation of this assessment, he points to the names of Mundo and Mundu. The first name appears on his map of Heuglin's expedition in 1865 and the latter on Antinori's map of 1868. Mundu should be Mondu, explains Petermann, whereas Piaggia states that the region where he stayed for two years was named Mundu by the Azande, which differed from Mondu, a location named by Petherick, far more north at the Yei-river.[16] To Petermann it should have been clear that both names indicated a different location.

The fact had been deliberately overlooked that Piaggia had visited a region of the Azande country that had then been completely unknown, enabling him to gather unique geographic and ethnographic information. We therefore may arrive at the justified conclusion of Heuglin's urgent wish to become at all costs the first one to publish extensively about the Azande. In Petermann he found his powerful supporter.

Mapping out the White Nile area: a competition between nations

It is not likely that the final editing and updating of the map slipped their mind, as Heuglin and Petermann were both very meticulous and scrupulous men of science. Neither could they have argued that lack of time had been an issue. The contributions for the year 1868 had 5 December 1868 as the closing date, and Heuglin's *Reise in das Gebiet des Weissen Nil* was ready for printing at the end of August 1869. Petermann, who wrote the foreword to the book in 1869, must have reprinted the map for publication, handing it over to C.F. Winter, the publisher in Leipzig and Heidelberg. This completely identical version could indicate that the issue was raised of reducing the costs of publication. This possibility must be discarded as well as too meagre a reason for omitting Piaggia's name.

Petermann's review of Antinori's account of Piaggia's travels therefore arguably reflects the underlying competition among individual explorers to win the distinction of having made the best discoveries of the geography of the Bahr el-Ghazal regions and the ethnography of the Azande. This competition seems to have been particularly heated between German and Italian geographers. Despite Petermann's reputation as an accurate editor of an internationally praised magazine and Heuglin's reputation as an experienced man of science, narrow-minded nationalistic feelings ultimately prevailed in their course of action.

The decision of denying Piaggia almost any recognition might be regarded as a deliberate and conscious attempt to favour the achievements that 'Prussia' had accomplished so far. At any rate, Petermann's policy of restricting Piaggia's scientific value turned out to be successful. The initiatives in mapping out this region of the White Nile and establishing its ethnographic survey had only started with Heuglin's results. Just before Petermann's review of Antinori's article, the *Mittheilungen* reported on Georg Schweinfurth's extensive journey of two years to the Bahr el-Ghazal regions and beyond.[17] In 1869, Heuglin presented his full account of the Bahr el-Ghazal expedition, accompanied by the map which remained accurate despite the fact that Piaggia's name and route had not been indicated. Five years later, Schweinfurth published *Im Herzen von Afrika* consisting of two volumes about his travels among the Azande and the neighbouring Mangbetu. It was immediately translated into English and became a classic on nineteenth-century Central African cultures.

On the Italian side, the scientific harvest of the accounts of Piaggia and Antinori would be relatively poor. After having received some attention in *Petermanns Mittheilungen*, no renowned international geographic magazine would reserve any room for Piaggia or Antinori's exploits in this region of the White Nile. What was published of their accounts became restricted to Italian circles of scientists and readers. Piaggia himself only delivered his diary notations to the municipal archive in Lucca. In 1941 and 1978 they were published in an annotated Italian edition.[18] Antinori remained merely the faithful and devoted head editor of the *Bollettino* and published some small works on his Abyssinian travels and the local ornithology, a scientific field he cherished as much as Heuglin did. The German, by contrast, performed his task in grand style, publishing his *Ornithologie von Nordost-Afrika*, which was lavished with a number of his fine watercolours and which became a standard work.

Explanatory notes
to the consulted sources

One of the main reasons a full account of the Gazelle-river expedition has thus far never been published was that most of the archival documents on which this account should be based are kept at five different locations (the Tinne family papers, which in 2010 were still being stored in two separate locations near London, the Tinne-Van Capellen files at the National Archives in The Hague, and the correspondence of Alexine at the Royal Library in The Hague and at the Linden Museum in Stuttgart). For unknown reasons, quite a number of small notations – often not more than scrawls in French – sent by Alexine to Heuglin, ended up in two archives in The Hague (KB) and the museum in Stuttgart. As these were not dated, it was rewarding to put them together again in chronological order. In addition, all accounts in the letters by Alexine and Henriette have been written in English and French; those by Heuglin in German and French. Alexine Tinne spoke and wrote mostly in French, also with Heuglin.

In biographies and articles regarding Alexine Tinne, the expedition to the Bahr el-Ghazal has received some attention. These accounts have, however, limited themselves more or less exclusively to either the primary sources in England (the Tinne Family Archive) or in The Hague (the National Archives) and, in case of cross references as well, often inaccurately and too selectively. The story of the expedition has never been written while consulting the entire archive, including the correspondence and accounts by Heuglin, which lead to a consistent and adjoining composition. It is the combination of the experiences both our protagonists have laid down in their writings that throws more light on the actions that were taken.

The Tinne-Sandbach letters and notes concerning Alexine's stay in Cairo create an intriguing picture of her that has so far never been revealed. The generosity of members of the Tinne family in permitting the author to go through all the files led to the discovery of documents (e.g. those of Margaret Tinne-Sandbach and John Tinne's diary of his stay in Cairo) that brought most valuable information about Alexine's stay in Cairo as well as the last days she and Heuglin spent together. These results were most fruitful and rendered a boost to the research. Gaps in her history could be filled, and as a result, Alexine Tinne has definitely received a more outspoken character. Unfortunately the diaries kept by Henriette Tinne-van Capellen during her two last journeys have not been traced, after having been mentioned for the last time in Gladstone's biography (1970), and must be regarded as lost.

In the Tinne family papers, several letters yet unknown, written by Queen Sophie to Henriette Tinne-van Capellen and Alexine Tinne, have been retrieved. Some of them have been taken up in the publication, including other letters written by Alexine Tinne from Khartoum and Berber to John Tinne and Jules van de Capellen and vice versa.[1]

In the archives of the Tinne family and in the National Archive at The Hague, several important letters have been preserved written by Heuglin to Speke, Musha Pasha and other persons. These letters filled in some blanks in the expedition's story and have now been published for the first time.

In his narrative account of the expedition, a distinction must be made between the letters Heuglin wrote during the journey itself which were published directly by August Petermann in 1863 and 1865, and Heuglin's publication *Reise in das Gebiet des Weissen Nil und seiner Zuflüssen in den Jahren 1862-1864*. In this extensive publication of 1869, he tells the main lines of the story, stressing its scientific results, looking back on all the events that took place more than four years earlier. The book offered room for contemplation on the story itself and is sometimes quite cynical or even negative about not only the delays in the preparations but also the events and the progress of the whole enterprise itself. In his initial accounts, recorded in his letters to Petermann, Heuglin is more direct in all the facts and details he encountered in the twenty-three months of travelling. In each letter to Petermann, Heuglin mentions every event during the trip but kept his mind on the main purposes – to bring back extensive scientific information, in particular detailed accounts of new geographical, zoological, ethnological, linguistic and meteorological facts.

Following the line of the expedition's story, this book makes use of both the accounts of 1863-1865, which were drafted as a kind of diary, and the review of the expedition of 1869.

While writing this book, it became clear that the attention devoted to Sudan of the nineteenth century had been effectuated at a rather selective scale. Sudan had been brought into the British sphere of influence from approximately 1870. Some prominent British historians wrote several authorative treatises in the 1960s and 1970s on Sudan's history that focused on the third quarter of the 1800s, before the 'British period' (Gray, Holt, Hill, later followed by Udal and Johnson). In these studies, concise references have been made to Europeans who dwelled there in these years. On the Italian side, historical publications mainly concerning the role Italians played in the exploration of Sudan and the White Nile were written in the twentieth century (Almagía 1957-59, Zaghi 1971, Bassani 1978 and Castelli 1984 and 1987). Regarding the role of German explorers in the period before 1870, German historical literature somehow neglected the crucial presence of Heuglin and Schweinfurth as the avant garde of the German explorers. A similar story is to be told on the French side about the lack of attention to the presence of Frenchmen such as the brothers Poncet, Vaudey, Vayssière and Henri Pacifique Delaporte.

The English and Italian primary and secondary sources, and in addition Heuglin's accounts in *Inner-Afrika* and *Petermann's Mittheilungen*, provided ample and crucial information to deal with Sudan's history in this book. The expedition's entire course has been embedded in a context that may be called 'rich' because of the multi-varying information about Sudan being provided by contemporary and recent writers in various nations.

Acknowledgements

I have been most fortunate to rely on the assistance, support and counsel of a number of persons. I am most appreciative of the willingness of Emily Fabricius and Alexine Strover to allow me so kindly to consult the documents regarding Alexine Tinne, preserved by both of them. I am much indebted to Zachary Kingdon for his unflagging support in the search for Tinne objects in the storerooms of the World Museum Liverpool, to Pauline Rushton (WML) for introducing me to members of the Tinne-family and Emma Martin (WML) for supporting me in the supply of numerous images. My thanks are also due to Hermann Forkl for his great help in my research in the Von Heuglin-collection in the Linden Museum at Stuttgart. The great co-operation of Silvia Zampieri of the Museo di Storia Naturale at Venice and Mafalda Cippolone of the Museo Archeologico d'Umbria at Perugia enabled me to accomplish various inquiries and searches concerning the collections of Piaggia, Antinori and Miani. Angèle Martin, more than once, rendered her kind and invaluable assistance in my searches for Sudanese-objects in the collection of Henri Pacifique Delaporte in the Musée du Quai Branly. At a distance Maria Bozan was a great help in finding objects in the Franz Binder-collection at Sibiu and I also acknowledge with thanks the efforts of Jeremy Coote who introduced me to the John Petherick-collection in the Pitt Rivers Museum in Oxford, and the assistance which Claude Ardouin provided in the Petherick-collection in the British Museum. In Florence Monica Zavattaro introduced me for the first time to the collections which Piaggia brought to Europe. It became a significant moment in my research when Martin Engelhardt presented in the Naturhistorisches Museum at Stuttgart a box with various valuable Von Heuglin-documents. Barbara Plankensteiner was so kind to bring objects of the Natterer-collection in the Museum für Völkerkunde at Vienna to my attention which enabled me to make references to similar items of the Tinne-collection.

I am much indebted to Antoinette Visser of The Historical Museum of the Hague, who more recently sponsored one of quite a number of journeys to England as well as several photo-copyrights, and assisted me furthermore in numerous other affairs.

For the first c.q. ultimate result regarding the manuscript I wish to thank Jan Abbink (African Studies Centre, Leiden) for assisting me frequently by providing his valuable comments on my manuscript. Furthermore I am much indebted to the shrewd and valuable counsels of several persons who were invited to read the manuscript in various stages: Pieter Milder, Petra Timmer, Bastiaan Willink, Loraine Wright and my daughter Eva.

My final thanks must go to my wife Martijntje Terhorst who for so long had to endure my obsession to complete this work. Without her irreplaceable moral support and inexhaustible patience this four-year project would not have been guided to fulfilment.

Source Notes

Prologue
1 Gladstone 1970.
2 Eggink 1960.
3 Kikkert 1980 (1991, 2005), Westphal 2002 (see: Chapter 8, note 28).

Introduction
1 Heuglin, M. Th. von, *Reise in das Gebiet des Weissen Nil und seiner Zuflüssen in den Jahren 1862-1864*, Leipzig, Heidelberg, 1869: 251.
2 This journey was referred to by Heuglin as 'Die Tinne'sche Expedition' in a special edition of *Petermann's Mitthei-lungen* (hereafter: PM) in 1865 (*Ergän-zungsheft* Nr. 15).
3 It is the English biographer of Alexine, Penelope Gladstone (1970), who uses these characteristics in describing Heuglin (e.g. p. 125-126: 'Von Heuglin was offered to join them'; p. 168: 'Alexine found no geniality in her staid companion' and 'she gained little sympathy from him'; p. 213: '...Von Heuglin, whom she had found stiff and unapproachable...').
4 Schweinfurth, *Im Herzen von Afrika*, Leipzig, 1874. His map will be referred to in appendix 7. Schweinfurth's *Artes Africanae* of 1875, containing relevant descriptions regarding the Tinne and Heuglin ethnographic collections, will

be referred to in the introduction to the catalogue.
5 See: Blunt 1994: 16; Blanton 1995: 3, 4; Mills 1991: 5, 6.
6 See: Bassnett (2002: 230), who sum-marises a theory put forward in Rose (1993).
7 This is how this kind of 'scientific discovery' has been described by Schildkrout & Keim (1998: 21). Bunzl & Glenn Penny (2003) deal with the rethinking of nineteenth-century German anthropology, which, charac-terised by a liberal humanism, stood in marked contrast to the Anglo-Ameri-can and French variants. See also Catalogue § The Azande in Heuglin's ethnography.

Chapter 1
1 Tinne, J. 1864: 19. *Proceedings of the RGS*, VII (103), VIII (12-18). The letters by 'the ladies' made him 'the subject of the discussion', as John Tinne states. From O.W. Hora Siccama (Henriette Tinne's brother-in-law) in The Hague, he received an additional correspon-dence for his report (letter J. Tinne to O.W. Hora Siccama of 3 March 1864, NA 2.21.008.01/225).
2 *Proceedings 1863-6*: 18. The expedition John Petherick made in 1858-9 in the

Bahr el-Ghazal area was executed on his own initiative and at his own expense during his vice consularship, when he developed extensive trade activities.

3 Santi & Hill 1980: 15. The Austrian vice consulate's personnel was responsible for the protection of the Austrian Catholic Mission in Khartoum and the missionary stations further up the White Nile (see appendix 4).

4 Letter (in French), H. Tinne to Sara van Capellen, no date, T.F.A.

5 Duveyrier 1874: 561-644.

6 Gladstone, 1970: 7.

7 NA, MvS 3/5346.

8 When John Abraham Tinne died in 1884 he left an inheritance of £121,586,00. After his death followed a serious set back in the family's fortune due to the sugar futures market (Rushton, 2006: 12).

9 Sutherland, 1935: 20. Hora Siccama provided this information for her biography in *Le Tour du Monde*, 9 September 1871.

10 NA 2.21.008.01/220. Some years after Lady Stanhope's death, C.L. Meryon published three volumes of *Travels of Lady Hester Stanhope* (1845) and *Memoirs of the Lady Hester Stanhope* (1846).

11 Some belongings of Alexine Tinne, donated in 2003 to the World Museum Liverpool by a member of the Tinne family, contain the book *Cours Synthétique, Analytique et Pratique de Langue Arabe* published in 1846 in Paris by J.F. Bled de Braine, then the former director of the Écoles Arabes in Algiers.

12 Copy of letter, H. Tinne, 17 April 1857 (NA 2.21.008.01/241).

13 In a hotel in Dresden, Count Adolf Königsmark, who lived nearby, visited them several times. Alexine ended a love affair with him that had been dragging on for two years by writing him a letter on 25 October 1857. Adolf was rejected as a future suitor, disliked by both Henriette and Alexine (correspondence Henriette to Jemima of 15 June 1857 and to Margaret Tinne-Sandbach, 15 June 1857, fragment of 'Polish Diary' H. van Capellen, 19-26 October 1857, T.F.A.)

14 Gladstone, 1970: 69.

15 Cf. Willink, 2007(I): 36-43. Dutch merchants were soon present in this area of potentially rapid growth for trade, establishing the first 'factory' in 1857 in Ambriz.

16 Cf. James, Baumann, Johnson, 1989. Another Dutchman, Benjamin Nachenius, preceded him some years before. In his book *'Herinneringen aan Abessinië en Nubia'* (Recollections of Abyssinia and Nubia), published in 1878, the author had toyed with the idea of travelling to Zanzibar through Galla country. Schuver had read this work and had taken note of Nachenius's intention, but he had clearly not pursued the idea any further. See also Imanse, 2002.

17 Schmidt, 1896; Bacmeister, 1950. In a necrology in 1877, Heuglin is described as 'a serious, quiet, (…) simple man', occasionally becoming a 'cheerful and warm' personality and modest about his achievements (quotation in: Kainbacher, 2005: XIX-XX).

18 Didier, 1858: 43-44. 'His house was a real *ménagerie*, where almost all kinds of animals of the country had been collected, lions, panthers, apes, and others…'.

19 Heuglin, von, *Tagebuch einer Reise von Chartum nach Abyssinien, mit besonderer Rücksicht auf Zoologie und Geographie unternommen in den Jahren 1852 bis 1853*, Gotha, 1857.

20 Munzinger, W., 'Die deutsche Expedition in Ost-Afrika, 1861 und 1862', *Ergänzungsheft Nr. 13 zu Petermann's Mittheilungen*, Gotha, 1864.

Chapter 2

1 According to Krapf, his companion Johannes Rebmann discovered the Kilima Ndjaro in 1848; one year later Krapf was the first European to see Mount Kenia (Krapf, 1860: 543-547).

2 Copy of letter H. Tinne, 11 January 1862 (NA 2.21.008.01/241).

3 Copy of letter H. Tinne, 8 January 1862, NA 2.21.008.01/241.

4 Letter, A. Tinne to H. Hora Siccama, 7 January 1862 (NA 2.21.008.01/220).

5 Tinne, 1864: 4. A quotation from an unknown letter from Henriette. The story of the Nile trip was part of Tinne's book published in 1864 (Tinne, 1864). His description was primarily based on letters that Henriette sent to him.

6 Copy of letter H. Tinne, 8 January 1862 (NA 2.21.008.01/241).

7 Copy of letter H. Tinne, 22 February (NA 2.21.008.01/241), and letter of H.Tinne, no date (T.F.A.).

8 Copy of letter (in French) H. Tinne to S. van Capellen, no date (NA 2.21.008.01/241).

9 Letter (in French) A. Tinne to H. Hora Siccama, NA 2.21.008.01/220. This 'Frenchman' could have been Delphin Barthélémy, Khartoum trader (see: appendix 7 § Petermann's review).

10 Letters Sophie von Württemberg to H. Tinne, January (no date) and June 12th 1862 (T.F.A.).

11 Letter (in French) A. Tinne to H. Hora Siccama, 17 June 1862 (NA 2.21.008.01/220).

12 Lejean, 1865: 113. He refers to 'exorbitant prices' that Alexine must have paid to purchase these women.

13 Heuglin, von, 1869: 10.

14 Heuglin, von, 1869: 9.

15 Heuglin in: PM, 1863: 97-115. A substantial part of these letters, covering the period from July 1862 (just after his arrival from Arash Kol) to 5 July 1863, were published by Petermann in Inner-Afrika, Gotha, 1863 with a short introduction, dated 14. März 1863. Die Tinne'sche Expedition im Westlichen Nil-Quellgebiet 1863 und 1864. Aus dem Tagebuch von Th. von Heuglin was separately published in 1865 as the Ergänzungsheft Nr. 15 of Petermann's Geographische Mittheilungen and included only Heuglin's letters from August 1863 to November 1864, covering the last period of the expedition.

16 Inner-Afrika, 1863 (VIII): 97-116.

17 Gray, 1961: 37. On this part of the White Nile, called Bahr el-Jebel, the demand for slaves was one of the factors that exacerbated these difficulties. Government trading expeditions during the 1840s had spoiled the initial friendly attitude of the Bari (32-34).

18 Heuglin, von, 1869: 12-13.

19 Melly, 1851 (1852 2nd: 92). Melly describes how tons of elephant teeth were lying about the desert, where these animals had died or were killed by the natives for their flesh. He notes that seekers of adventure or ivory were not explicitly mentioned before the mid-1840s.

20 Heuglin, von, 1869: 12-13.

21 Inner-Afrika, 1863 (VIII): 99.

22 Gray, 1961: 54.

23 Heuglin, von, 1869: 14.

24 Negotiations with Muhammad Khair dragged on until 1863, when governor general Musha Pasha invited him to discuss some proposal in Khartoum. Muhammad Khair, however, scented danger and refused to come, further compromising himself by making an unsuccessful attack on the Shilluk and losing most of his Baggara Arab allies in the mêlée. The king of the Shilluk begged the governor general to get rid of this brigand. After his stronghold at Hillat Kaka was taken, Khair fled to Kordofan, where he was arrested by government order and subsequently killed as 'a work of super-interrogation.'

(Hill, 1959: 108-109)

25 *Inner-Afrika*, 1863 (VIII): 100.

26 *Inner-Afrika*, 1863 (VIII): 107.

27 Heuglin, von, 1869: 19-21.

28 Heuglin, von, 1869: 17.

29 More recent research has revealed that a substantial number of African slaves were engaged in a range of different tasks, including females in domestic slavery and males in agricultural slavery. The greater proportion of Ottoman Egypt's slave soldiers were drawn from areas south of the Sahara, inter alia Southern Sudan (Lane & Johnson, 2009: 514, Johnson, 1989: 77, cf. Johnson, 1992).

Chapter 3

1 *PM*, 1863: 105-107.

2 *Inner-Afrika*, 1863 (VIII): 102

3 Anon., *Nouvelles Annales des Voyages*, 1864 (August): 236-237.

4 Information concerning Kleincznik and Kuchuk Aga in *Inner-Afrika*: 105-106. According to the accounts of the expedition of Georg Schweinfurth in 1869-1873 and in particular that of Wilhelm Junker in 1876-1879, the Makrakà appeared to be a subgroup of the Azande, which then became their official name. Although used until the 1890s, 'Niam-Niam' was gradually considered a nickname of bygone times.

5 Eugène-Édouard-Jacques-Marie de Pruyssenaere de la Wostyne (1826-1864) assembled important documentation of his travels on the White Nile regions, which has been compiled in a separate edition of *PM* (nrs. 50 and 51, 1877).

6 *Inner-Afrika*, 1863 (VIII): 97.

7 Santi, Hill, 1980: 21. No further reference is made in this publication to any person regarding the Bahr el-Ghazal expedition.

8 Letter H. Tinne to Queen Sophie, 24 November 1862 (copy in T.F.A.).

9 Letter A. Tinne to H. Hora Siccama, 7 May 1862 (NA 2.21.008.01/229).

10 As a trader in the Sudan, Georges Thibaut (ca. 1795-1869) delivered the first giraffes to the zoos in London and Paris (Santi, Hill, 1980: 21), participated in the first Egyptian expedition up the Nile in 1839-1841 and became a French consul in Khartoum around 1840.

11 'The balance at your credit on the 31st Dec. was £304.7.11 which has been since augmented to £417.12.2 & the balance at Alexine's credit on the 31st Dec. was £823.8.8' (letter J. Tinne to H. Tinne, 9 February 1862, T.F.A.).

12 Santi Hill, see note 7.

13 *Zaribas* varied in size, according to whether they were temporary way stations along a caravan route or small outposts or long-term settlements (Lane & Johnson, 2009: 519). According to Heuglin's description, the *zariba* knew its peculiarities: it had vermin and rats in abundance, and most of its inhabitants suffered from syphilis. Directly outside, near its water pit, the stench was unbearable because of the dead bodies of animals and slaves that were habitually dumped there (*PM*, 1865: 3).

14 *PM*, 1863, *Notizen*: 106. Petermann inserts a letter by Henriette to John Tinne about the White Nile trip which had been forwarded by John to the Royal Geographical Society in London, and from there to Petermann (*PM*, 1863: 155-156).

15 Pellegrinetti, 1941: 164-165. Bassani, 1978: 4-5.

16 Bassani, 1978: 6. Piaggia would later receive a letter from Heuglin from Biselli's *zariba* informing him about the death of Henriette and inviting Piaggia to join him to the Azande country, whereas Alexine would return to Khartoum (Bassani, 1978: 14).

17 Letter H. Tinne to J. van Capellen, 20 November 1862 (NA, 2.21.008.01/229).

18 Tinne, 1864: 30, 106.

19 *Inner-Afrika*, 1863 (VIII): 105-108. In the separate edition of 1865 on the last episode of the expedition, Heuglin gives more results of his 'Niam-Niam'-research (*PM*, 1865: 9).

20 *Inner-Afrika*, 1863 (VIII): 105. We will discuss this subject when dealing with their collections in the catalogue.

21 W.G. Browne, *Travels in Africa, Egypt and Syria 1792 to 1798*, London, 1799.

22 Lejean, G., 'La queue des Nyams-Nyams', in *Le Tour du Monde*, 1861, Ière sémestre: 187-188.

23 Cf. D'Escayrac de Lauture, 1855-1856 (50-53). Aucapitaine, H., 'Les Yem-Yem, Tribu anthropophage de l'Afrique Centrale' in: *Nouvelles Annales des Voyages*, Tome IV, 1857: 58-66. In 1860, Francis de Castelnau, the French consul in Bahia, Brazil, published a remarkable denunciation of these tail stories by interrogating some twenty Haussa men who had been transferred as slaves from Nigeria to Brazil. In their home country, they had lived quite close to the 'Niam-Niam' area. In the account of his Bahr el-Ghazal expedition in 1860-61 (*Inner-Afrika*: 79-83), the Italian explorer and scientist Marchese Orazio Antinori referred to this tail as existing. In Petermann's 1868 survey of the geography of the southwest watershed of the Nile, Antinori's remark on the tail were seen to reduce his qualities as a geographer (see appendix 7: Petermann's maps of 1865 and 1869).

24 Petherick, 1861, I: 469. Cf. *PM*, 1865: 9.

25 Schweinfurth, 1874, I: 517.

26 Maltzan, 1870: 330. After analysing European records including Schweinfurth's description of cannibalistic rituals of the 'Niam-Niam' (see note 25), Evans-Pritchard, an authority on the Azande, stated in 1960 that most of these accounts were not supported by clear evidence. However, '(...) taking all the evidence together we may conclude that there is a strong probability that cannibalism was practised by at any rate some Azande'. Testimony indicated that '(...) the only persons normally eaten were those killed in war or criminals (...)'. (Evans-Pritchard, 1965: 153). In their 1953 study of the Azande, Baxter and Butt refer to the still existing practice of cannibalism by the Mangbetu and Abarambo (Baxter & Butt, 1953: 44).

27 *PM*, 1863: 156.

28 *PM*, 1863, 155-156.

29 Letter A. Tinne to H. Hora Siccama, 5 February 1863 (NA 2.21.008.01/220).

30 Lejean, 1865: 113. He remarks that the costs of the Tinne journeys amounted to 90,000 Maria Theresia Thaler (450,000 French francs), which added enormously to the difficulties encountered by following expeditions on the White Nile.

31 *PM*, 1863, *Notizen*: 106, footnote 2. Henriette extended the hiring of this steamer after having returned to Khartoum in May 1862, implying still higher costs.

32 Samuel Baker refers to this: 'There are Dutch ladies travelling without any gentleman (...). They are very rich and have hired the only steamer here for £1000. They must be demented [sic]! A young lady alone with the Dinka tribe (...) they really must be mad. All the natives are as naked as the day they were born.' In: Gladstone, 1970: 106, quoted from a letter of 16 June 1862, then in possession of a relative of Baker's.

33 Heuglin, von, 1869: 60.

34 *Inner-Afrika*, 1863 (XI): 142.

35 Heuglin, von, 1869: 62 ('*eine regel- und steuerlose Maschine*'). Letter 27 January 1863 in: *Inner-Afrika*, 1863 (XI): 142.

Chapter 4

1 *Inner-Afrika*, 1863 (XI): 151. Appendix B consists of; 'Fahrtenzeit des Remorque-Dampfers zwischen Chartum und Maiet el Jur, nach dem Tagebuche von Mad. Tinne van der Capellen'.

2 Antoine Brun-Rollet, Savoyard trader, was the first European to explore the Bahr el-Ghazal as far as Meshra el-Rek before 1855. Heuglin refers to the map that Brun-Rollet had published in his *Le Nil Blanc et le Soudan*, Paris, 1855.

3 Udal, 1998: 467-468. Also in this exploration, commercial interests prevailed. As one of Petherick's co-travellers, Castelbolognesi's responsibility was to prepare the conveyance of the previous year's ivory collection to Meshra.

4 Heuglin, von, 1869: 122-123.

5 Letter H. Tinne to J.van Capellen, n.d. (NA 2.21.008.01/229).

6 Letter in French from A. Tinne to H. Hora-Siccama, 4 February (NA 2.21.008.01/220). Petherick, 1869, I: 326-327. 'On the 17th [?] we bade adieu to the ladies, who disembarked preparatory to their start for the interior, which was to be attempted early the following morning.' From Khartoum to the Meshra, he followed the proceedings of the expedition closely: Petherick, 1869, II: 31-33, 43, 46, 52.

7 While entering the Meshra, Alexine Tinne was standing on the bridge of her boat like 'the triumphant Cleopatra on The Nile' as Carlo Piaggia describes her arrival (he was already in the Meshra before Heuglin); (Bassani, 1978: 5). Shortly after their arrival, Piaggia was asked again to join the Tinnes (as states Antinori, in BSGI, 1868: 108). Cf. Pellegrinetti, 1941 (169-171).

8 Heuglin, von, 1869: 138.

9 *Inner-Afrika*, 1863 (XI): 149.

10 Heuglin's deliberation and proposal have not been mentioned in his letters to Petermann, taken up in *Inner-Afrika*. It is only in 1869, when looking back more critically on the expedition that he delves into this subject (1869: 140).

11 Letter (in French) A. Tinne to H. Hora Siccama, dated 26 March 1863 (NA 2.21.008.01/220).

12 Heuglin, von, 1869: 141.

Chapter 5

1 *Inner-Afrika*, 1863 (XI): 142.

2 Heuglin, von, 1869: 170.

3 Petherick followed the river and reached Meshra el-Rek in December 1853 as the first European to do so, but he was preceded by a few days by Ali Abu Amuri, an Egyptian (Santandrea, 1964: 23, referring to J. Poncet's 'Le Fleuve Blanc', Paris, 1863: 3).

4 This additional remark in: Heuglin, von, 1869: 171.

5 Heuglin, von, 1869: 172-176.

6 *Inner-Afrika*, 1863 (XII): 159.

7 Letter A. van Capellen to Jules van Capellen, 18 April 1863 (NA 2.21.008.01/229).

8 Letter A. van Capellen to Jules van Capellen, 22 February 1863 (NA 2.21.008.01/229).

9 Letter J.H. Speke, 11 April 1863 (T.F.A.).

10 Heuglin, von, 1869: 181.

11 Petherick, 1869, I: 321-323.

12 Gladstone, 1970: 136. No source given; presumably the lost diaries of Henriette Tinne. In the foreword of his *Travels in Central Africa…* (pp. V-VI), Petherick says he was indebted to John Tinne for 'photographic views of Gondokoro and the Bahar il Ghazal'. These photos are supposed to have been taken by Alexine who could have given them to John before his return from Cairo to Liverpool in February 1865.

13 Petherick, 1869, II: 141-144.

14 See: note 6.

Chapter 6

1 In a letter to John, Henriette explains how Petherick set off too late from Khartoum to meet Speke, and then had met many adverses. He had had 'dreadful ill luck'. Petherick consequently had to retain all he had sent forward for Speke's requirements, '... which was fortunate for us, for we were thus provided with wine, pale ale, tea, soup, pearl barley, Lemann's biscuits, a gutta-percha boat, nay, we cannot say what. It is strange to find these luxuries here, and we enjoy them greatly.' (T.F.A.; Tinne, 1864: 26).

2 *Inner-Afrika*, 1863 (XIII): 162. Petermann refers to 'the letter of 4th June' that Heuglin would have received from Speke. Heuglin responded to Speke in October (his letter opening with: 'Mon Capitaine...').

3 Petherick, 1869, I: 325: '...unprecedented floods...'.

4 Petherick, 1869, I: 327. Tinne, 1864: 28/29.

5 NA 2.21.008.01/227.

6 Tinne, 1864: 30. This map must refer to the one Heuglin drafted, while he used the maps by Petherick and Lejean.

7 Heuglin, von, 1869: 185. In her letter, Alexine expresses her grief about these occurrences during the expedition (letter 4 August 1864 to J. van Capellen, NA 2.21.008.01/222).

8 Heuglin, von, 1869: 185-186.

9 NA 2.21.008.01/227.

10 Letter H. Tinne to John Tinne, 1 July 1863 (NA 2.21.008.01/227).

11 In her last letter to Margaret Tinne-Sandbach dated 1 July, Henriette states: 'At any rate we are in for it, but I would never advise anybody to come here without a vakeel and **plenty** of money! The expense on travel is ridiculous. You are entirely in the hands of a **set**.' (T.F.A.; copy in NA 2.21.008.01/241)

12 In a footnote, Petermann argues that Heuglin then was not yet informed of

an amount of more than 500 Thaler having been sent to him and with the prospect of more to come (*PM*, 1863: 164).

13 Letter in: T.F.A. John Tinne might have retrieved these documents in Cairo or after Alexine's death in 1869 in Tripoli.

14 Heuglin, von, 1869: 189-191.

15 *PM*, 1865: 1.

16 Biselli was to blame for raising his prices permanently, stipulates Heuglin. The later accusations, comprised in Alexine's official complaint against Biselli, were of a different order: his behaviour against the local natives and their soldiers, in combination with that of Amuri's. In her publication, Gladstone erroneously describes their situation as being in Biselli's stranglehold (1970: 147), preventing the party from leaving his *zariba*. All of them seemed to have been quite free to leave but were precluded from doing so, chiefly by the weather conditions.

17 Note (in French) A. Tinne: KB CEN79D40, 14. Heuglin's letter in: *PM*, 1865: 10.

18 Heuglin, von, 1869: 224-225.

19 This map might have been used for the one, appearing as an appendix of the separate edition of *Petermann's Mittheilungen* of 1865 'die Tinne'ische Expedition...', copy of which joins this publication.

20 Letter in: T.F.A. A copy of Heuglin's letter was apparently taken along by him or Alexine to Cairo and from there possibly by John Tinne, in February 1865 or his son Ernest, at the end of 1869, to Liverpool. Cf.: *Proceedings of the RGS*, VIII: 264. For the news on November 21st of the arrival of their ships in Meshra el-Rek: *PM*, 1865: 11.

21 Heuglin, von, 1869: 224.

22 *PM*, 1865: 13: '45 days'; 1869: 228: '40 days'.

23 *PM*, 1865: 11, 13. The 75 'new' soldiers mentioned by Heuglin could have been

hired by Adriana in Khartoum when she organised a 'relief party'.

24 Heuglin, von, 1869: 228.

25 Heuglin, von, 1869: 234.

26 PM, 1865: 14-15, 21-22.

27 Letter A. van Capellen to O.W. Hora Siccama, 6 July 1863 (NA 2.21.008.01/229).

28 Letter A. van Capellen to O.W. Hora Siccama, 28 November 1863 (NA 2.21.008.01/229).

29 Petherick, 1869, II: 31-32.

30 Dispatch from Petherick to Roderick Murchison dated 16-22 May 1864 (T.F.A.).

31 Petherick, 1869, II: 20-2. Katie Petherick writes: 'Upon the Pashá's return from Alexandria the end of last November, the first step he took was to inlay an impost of two months' pay on all soldiers, sailors etc., who were going up the White River, deducting this from their wages; last year he put on one month, it now amounts to three, and as the sailors have work only for about half the year, it is impossible that they can pay, thus it falls on the employers. All Khartoum is in uproar, and the men of the boats have been scattering themselves over the country. Mr. Baker, when he left last year, refused to pay the one month's impost; it remains to be seen how that question will be settled. Petherick asserts that the Pasha should have give timely notice ere a new tax was levied, as all the trader's boats were on the point of starting when the order so unexpectedly was issued. Petherick wrote to the Pasha to that effect, and requested that, at least, travellers might be exempt from the tax; but *no* – he refused, so Petherick paid for Baker, but under protest.'

32 As she states in her letter of 5 August 1864 to Jemima van Capellen (NA 2.21.008.01/218).

33 Letter A. Tinne to J. Tinne, April 1864 Khartoum, T.F.A.

34 Letter A. Tinne to Jemima van Capellen, April, Khartoum (NA 2.21.008.01/222).

35 KB CEN79D40, 15/16.

36 Copy of letter in: Tinne, 1864: 40-42. Making use of Alexine's letters and her official complaint against Musha Pasha, John explains about Biselli and Amuri's 'outrageous' conduct towards the people of the expedition and 'the shocking state' to which Musha Pasha had brought the Sudan.

37 Letter A. Tinne to to J. Tinne, April [?] 1864, Khartoum (T.F.A.).

38 Petherick, 1869 II: 21.

39 Letter A. Tinne to J. Tinne, April [?] 1864 Khartoum (T.F.A.). As Thibaut was absent from Khartoum during the first weeks after their arrival, Alexine's financial affairs could not be arranged, causing her substantial problems (Heuglin, 1869: 254).

40 Archive Von Heuglin, Lindenmuseum, Stuttgart.

41 PM, 1864: 308-310.

42 A small note written by Alexine might be an indication that Alexine and Musha Pasha did meet each other to settle some affairs. 'I just heard...from Mr. Thibaut that the Pasha is so little inclined to do me justice, that I would like to ask you, as you have said, that he should come (...).' She states it will be difficult for her to receive him politely, feeling so infuriated towards him, that she rather wishes that he would not come. 'Could you not tell him I am (...) too ill to receive him?' (KB CEN79D40/2).

43 Two reports, conceived as letters by Heuglin to A. Tinne (NA 2.21.008.01/222).

44 KB CEN79D40/11, 10.

45 PM, 1865: 4.

46 Petherick, 1869, II: 43.

47 During their stay in Egypt and the Sudan until Alexine's return to Cairo, Queen Sophie sent eight letters to the

Tinnes (T.F.A.).

48 Heuglin, von, 1869: 255.

49 Heuglin, von, 1869: 257.

50 Heuglin, von, 1869: 261: Heuglin had purchased his part of the provisions in Khartoum. 'Nicht so Fräulein Tinne', as he relates dryly.

51 Letter A. Tinne to Jemima van Capellen, 5 August 1864, Berber (NA 2, 21.009.01/219).

52 Letter A. Tinne to J. van Capellen, 5 August 1864 (NA 2.21.008.01/222).

53 Alexine must have left some belongings which were of no use anymore. Wilhelm Junker, who travelled in Sudan mid-1870s, writes about dining in Khartoum in 1876 at the Roman Catholic Mission in the company of Isma'il Pasha from a fine set of table silver which once belonged to the 'unfortunate Alexine Tinné', who presented it to Thibaut; after his death it came in the possession of the mission (Junker, 1889, I: 211-212).

54 Heuglin, von, 1869: 273.

55 Heuglin, von, 1869: 290.

56 NA 2.21.008.01/222.

57 Letter A. Tinne to Margaret Tinne-Sandbach, 4 December 1864 (T.F.A.).

58 Note (in French) A. Tinne to Heuglin, n.d. (KB CEN79D40/17).

59 Letter (in French), Heuglin to J. van Capellen, 27 November 1864 (NA 2.21.008.01/230).

60 Letter (in French), A. Tinne to J. van Capellen, 4 December 1864 (NA 2.21.008.01/219).

61 Letter (in French), A. Tinne to O.W. Siccama, 4 December 1864 (NA 2.21.008.01/220).

Chapter 7

1 Letter A. Tinne to M. Tinne-Sandbach, 4 December 1864 (T.F.A.).

2 Correspondence by Margaret Tinne-Sandbach to her children in Liverpool, sent during her stay with John in Cairo from 11 Jan - 24 Feb 1865. Notebook containing the diary of John Tinne, kept during his visit to Alexine Tinne (T.F.A.).

3 Gentz, W., Briefe einer Reise nach Aegypten u. Nubien, 1850/1851, Berlin, 1853.

4 Eyth, 1909 (2006: 160-163).

5 Hill refers to Musha Pasha as 'Mūsā Hamdī': 'The Sudanese chronicler praised the rough pasha whose rule, though harmful to foreign trade, bore lightly on the Sudanese official class dependent for employment on the governorate-general. For the taxpayers, however, the Pasha's death was a relief' (Hill, 1959: 111).

6 Gray, 1961: 165-168.

7 Petherick, 1869, II: 141-143. On May 19th, 1864, Heuglin sent a letter with a denunciation of Petherick's engagement in slavery.

8 Ali, 1972: 22-30. Ali's opinion is based in particular on contemporary correspondence by the Foreign Office in London. Petherick's claim for compensation at the address of the Egyptian government was finally backed in 1869 by the British government, and the accusations were withdrawn in 1872 (Udal, 1998: 545).

9 Note A. Tinne, n.d. (NA 2.21.008.01/222).

Chapter 8

1 Letter A.Tinne to J. Tinne, 20 October 1865 (T.F.A.).

2 Nachtigal, 1879-1881, I: 86.

3 Letter from A. Tinne to J. Tinne, 2 June 1869 (NA 2.21.008.01/224).

4 Diary C.J. Oostmans, May/June 1869 (NA 2.21.008.01/239).

5 Nachtigal, 1870, I: 96.

6 Nachtigal, 1870, I: 97/98. Nachtigal, 1879-1881, I: 467-471.

7 Letter J. Tinne to A. Tinne, no date (T.F.A.).

8 Quotations from: Tothill, 1947: 25-49.
9 Accounts of the trial refer to 'Boubakre' (NA 2.21.008.01/244, 245). In 1898 the French traveller Erwin de Bary discovered that Hadj es Scheik had been identical to Bou-Bekr (Bary, de, 1898: 30, footnote 2).
10 Nachtigal, 1879-1881, I: 468.
11 Rohlfs, 1885, I: 96.
12 See: note II.
13 In H. Tinne's lost diaries, a reference could explicitly have been made to these photos (Gladstone, 1970: 118, 136).
14 Petherick, 1869, I: v.
15 Letter A. Tinne to J. Tinne, 3 April 1869, Murzuq (T.F.A.).
16 The envelope belonging to the glass ambrotypes contains correspondence between E. Tinne and J. Tinne dating from the end of 1869 to the beginning of 1870 (T.F.A.). The glass positives that were made by this camera have been included in this book, after having been scanned. Additional photos, rediscovered in the Tinne family archive, will be taken up in a forthcoming publication regarding the last episode of Alexine Tinne's travels [RJW].
17 Bacmeister, 1950: 415.
18 Lejean (I), 1865: 5-24. Here Lejean published some critical notes on Heuglin's map and his account of the expedition. He refers to the facts he gathered on his trip on the White Nile and the Bahr el-Ghazal, made between December 1860 and April 1861, resulting in the article concerning Castelbolognesi's expedition of 1857. He corrects some facts in Heuglin's account of the expedition of 1865, and goes deeper into the descriptions of the people inhabiting the river regions.
19 In November 1865 Malte-Brun pays attention to this event in his magazine *Nouvelles Annales des Voyages* (Sixth Series, 11th Year: 129-148).
20 Letter (in French) from A. Tinne to H. Hora Siccama, 15 April 1866 (NA 2.21.008.01/219).
21 Zurcher, Margolle, 1870: 289-304.
22 Letter A. Tinne to J. Tinne, May 23rd 1868 (NA 2.21.008.01/224, copy in T.F.A.).
23 Duveyrier, 1864: VII, VIII.
24 Waller, 1874, II: 51.
25 In the early 1870s the first hagiographically inspired biographies were published in the Netherlands (Kan, 1870 and Posthumus, 1874) and elsewhere. In 1871, William Wells published his biography: *The Heroine of the White Nile...* in New York.
26 Gladstone, 1970.
27 Eggink, 1960.
28 Later biographies were largely based on both Eggink and Gladstone's books: Kikkert, J.G., *Een Haagsche dame in de Sahara...*, Amsterdam, 1980 (2005) and Westphal, W., *Tochter des Sultans. Die Reisen der Alexandrine Tinne*, Stuttgart, 2002.
29 Oudschans Dentz, Brummelkamp, Jongmans, K.N.A.G., Vol. LXXVIII, 1961:353-365
30 '(...) She had been the cause that the old woman passed away in this wasting Central Africa and the others left in Khartoum.' (Eggink, 1960: 125)

Epilogue

1 Full title: *Plantae Tinneanae sive descriptio plantarum in expeditione Tinneana ad flumen Bahr El Ghasal eiusque affluentias in Septentrionale interioris Africae collectarum* or *Plantes Tinnéennes ou description de quelques-unes des plantes receuillies par l'expédition tinnéenne sur les bords de Bahr el Ghasal et de ses affluentes en Afrique Central Ouvrage orné de XXVII planches, composé(s)... par M.M. Théodore Kotschy et Jean Peyritsch. Publié aux frais de Alexandrine P.F. Tinne et John A. Tinne.*

2 *Plantae Tinneanae*, 1867, Preface n.p. Translations from: Tothill, 1947.

3 Heuglin, von, 1869: 350-361. Within Germany, Heuglin's irritation with the inaccuracies in the *Plantae Tinneanae* has been presented as very understandable, also in view of Alexine's 'egotism'. Cf. Bilguer, von, "Wie starb Alexandrine Tinne?", in *Naturwissentschaftliche Wochenschrift*. Nr. 49 (5 Dec. 1915): 753-756.

4 Tinne, 1864; 33 ('Von Heuglin [is] not (…) an experienced botanist').

Appendix 1

1 Letter (in French) A. Tinne to H. Hora Siccama, 17 June 1862 (NA 2.21.008.01/220).

2 Tinne, 1864: 8.

3 Lejean, 1865: 113. He refers to 'exorbitant prices' that Alexine must have paid to purchase these women.

4 Letter (in French) A. van Capellen to O.W. Hora Siccama (NA 2.21.008.01/229).

5 Copy of letter H. Tinne to J. Tinne, 18 November 1862 (NA 2.21.008.01/241). In the literature about Alexine's life, this event has been described without mentioning Khair's conditions.

6 Copy of letter H. Tinne to J. Tinne, 13 July 1862 (NA 2.21.008.01/241).

7 Copy of letter H. Tinne to J. Tinne, 13 July 1862 (NA 2.21.008.01/241).

8 Tinne, 1864: 12. This account by Tinne was based on letters from Henriette, which have not been retrieved.

9 On his return journey, Binder passed through the Jur country (see his route on map Petermann), where he assembled a collection of Jur utensils (see: Catalogue for some items). (Kainbacher, 2006: 39).

10 Copy of letter H. Tinne to J. Tinne, 4 September 1862 (NA 2.21.008.01/241).

11 The habits of Europeans in the Sudan have been recorded by Morlang, who kept a diary that was published in 1973 in an Italian translation from the original German (*Francesco Morlang, Missione in Africa Centrale, diairio 1855-1863*, Bologna).

12 Some months later, Samuel Baker and his wife would ascend the Nile to this place, passing the magical 4° latitude. John Petherick and his wife Katie arrived in Gondokoro two months after the Tinnes had stayed there from 30 September 1862.

13 Fragment of letter H. Tinne to J. Tinne, n.d. (T.F.A.).

14 Instead of Petherick, who was supposed to meet Speke in February 1863, a man named 'Mahamed' ('a very black man') approached Speke in full Egyptian regimentals leading a military procession, holding three red flags. When Speke asked why they did not carry English colours, the man replied that the colours were Debono's, who apparently had 'kinglike habits'. When Speke asked 'Who is the Bono?' in the man replied: 'The same as Petrik' (Speke, 1863: 579).

15 Copy of letter, H. Tinne to J. Tinne, August 1862 (NA 2.21.008.0/241).

16 Copy of letter, H. Tinne to J. Tinne, 18 November 1862 (NA 2.21.008.0/241).

17 Baker, 1866: 21. Baker remarks erroneously: 'The entire party died of fever on the White Nile, excepting Mademoiselle Tinné', adding the names of Steudner and others who died during the Bahr el-Ghazal expedition.

Appendix 2

1 Anon., 'Nouvelles de l'expédition allemande dans l'Afrique Central, du Soudan Égyptien et du Haut Fleuve-Blanc', in: *Nouvelles Annales des Voyages*, 1862, Tome IV: 120-123. Cf. *PM*, 1863: 106. In a footnote Petermann

mentions that in a letter to V.A. Malte-Brun (then editor of the *Nouvelles Annales*) Lejean mentions the sum the Tinnes paid for the rental of the steamer. This note arguably indicates Lejean as the author of the above quoted letter.

Appendix 3

1 Santi, Hill, 1980: 13.
2 Trémaux, n.d.: 15-23.
3 Taylor, 1854: 277-278.
4 Brehm, 1855: 230.
5 Brehm, 1855: 168.
6 Didier, 1858: 22-25.
7 Hartmann, 1863: 337.
8 Heuglin, von, 1869: 3.
9 Petherick, 1861: 132.
10 *PM*, 1863: 107; Baker, 1866: 8.
11 Hartmann, 1863: 313-314.
12 Hartmann, 1863: 312-352.
13 Hartmann, 1863: 318-319. It was only in 1869 that Heuglin would confirm that the European community was characterised by 'scoundrels'. Based on accounts written ten years earlier, it is clear that a shift took place in these relationships. In his 1851 travel account *Khartoum and the Niles*, of 1851 (1852) George Melly describes how Khartoum's community of Europeans cherished Western manners and how there was a kind of culture of mutual solidarity (92). Although 'the followers of the Prophet looked upon the supporters of the Pope with supreme indifference', and the followers of Christianity regarded the worshippers of the Koran with 'profound pity', Muhammadans and Christians lived together in a 'state of harmony' and 'amicably' (110).
14 Gray, 1961: 47.
15 *Inner-Afrika*, 1863 (VIII): 99. This detail concerning the 'negro-skulls' used as decorations is curiously similar to the way Kurtz in Conrad's *Heart of*

Darkness (1902) decorated his house. After De Malzac's death, Franz Binder bought his station in Rambek (Kainbacher, 2006: VII; Gray, 1961: 46).
16 Udal, 1998: 469.
17 Gray, 1961: 61-62.
18 Taylor, 1854: 275-280.
19 Toniolo/Hill, 1974 (1975): 38-41 (40).
20 This fever was sometimes treated with a purgative which in the case of Franz Binder in 1861 caused 'a diarrhoea, which later became the dangerous African dysentery' (according to Binder's account in: Kainbacher, 2006: 42).

Appendix 4

1 Ibrahim, Ogot, 1989: 356.
2 Zaghi, 1971: 225. Cf. Melly's remarks in Chapter 2. Zaghi's analysis is based on Lejean, 'Le Haut-Nil et le Soudan', in: *Revue des Deux Mondes*, 16 February 1862.
3 Nicola d'Ulivi, who died in 1852, is an early example of a successful Western slave trader in the Sudan. He was also a renowned collector of natural history specimens, as George Melly – who had inspected his collections in Khartoum in 1850 – remarked (Melly, 1852, II: 126; Hill, 1967: 362).
4 Gray, 1961: 44-48.
5 Toniolo & Hill, 1974 (1975): 1-28.
6 Hill, 1959: 143-144. Du Bisson, a French diplomat, was a strong opponent of Isma'il. Around 1863, foreign trade in Egypt and Sudan became increasingly obstructed, and French influence was waning or even impeded, to the anger of Du Bisson. He wrote an account in 1868 concerning the pasha who he alleged was enriching himself considerably after having succeeded Saïd Pascha in 1863. He confiscated land and became a merchant, industrial, agriculturist, just to accumulate his

treasures from Alexandria to the frontiers of Abyssinia. With cotton he earned in the first year of the civil war in the US 64 million francs and the following year 120 million francs. In 1864, he cashed 144 million francs. All costs of transport etc. were paid for by the state (Du Bisson, 1868: 26/27). 'Il est à present le premier capitaliste du monde' (35). Under the reign of Isma'il Pasha, taxes were tripled or even raised fivefold, according to Du Bisson (53).

7 Ali, 1972: 89-114. Holt, 1958: 34-35. Regarding the Mahdi's overthrow of the Sudan, Ayadi argues that British influence and the excessive employment of Europeans in posts for which they were unfitted usually provoked Sudanese resentment to the pitch of xenophobia, making way for the Mahdi's occupation (Ibrahim & Ogot, 1989: 375).

8 Bono, A. de, *Recenti scoperti sul Fiume Bianco*, Alexandria, 1862. It was only in that year that it became publicly known that De Bono was a slave trader. Also: Bono, A. de, Voyage au Fleuve Blanc, in: *Nouvelles Annales des Voyages*, 1862, III: 5-38 (also PM, 1862; 356). Malzac, A. de, *Bulletin de la Société de la Géographie de Paris*, 1862, II (Planche, Débit de fleuve Blanc et de ses affluents...).

9 Bassani, 1978: 17. After De Malzac's death, no action was taken against his gangs of robbers and murderers. They were able to return to Khartoum without any difficulty. Heuglin states towards Petermann: 'I give you an absolute right to publish in my name what I have told you, and I am even willing to collect further details on the Bahr el-Abiad [the White Nile] of the things that went on there. Mr. Baker, too, seems to have made a direct report to his government of these happenings.' 'By the way', continues Heuglin, 'I must tell you that at the end of July Muham-

mad Khēr, through his brother, handed over to the Government here a kind of criminal rare in this country, a counterfeiter, who was making Maria-Theresien Thaler of tin. You see how civilisation is spreading further and further into Central Africa! No one would have expected to find a gang of false coiners among the Shilluk negroes.' (*Inner-Afrika*, 1863 (VIII): 100).

10 Malzac, A. de, *Bulletin de la Société de la Géographie de Paris*, 1862, II (Planche, Débit de fleuve Blanc et de ses affluents...).

11 In his travel account of 1854 Emilio Dandolo describes the class of Europeans in Khartoum euphemistically as: 'not always flawless in their behaviour and the way they dress themselves' (273/274: 'non sempre irreprensibile di condotta e di costumi').

12 Didier, 1858: 44.

13 D'Escayrac de Lauture, 1853 and 1855-1856.

14 Baker, 1866 in: Ali, 1972: 34.

Appendix 5

1 Letter A. Tinne in two fragments (T.F.A.).

2 Fragment of letter A.Tinne (T.F.A.).

3 Letter A. Tinne to J. van Capellen, 8 May 1864 (NA 2.21.008.01/223). Jules received this letter on 15 August and responded on the 17th that he had approached Ruyssenaers via the Minister of Foreign Affairs (Minister Cremer) by letter and then had informed the King about Alexine's situation. The latter told him he did well to approach Ruyssenaers in Alexandria and had confirmed that Alexine could count on his protection, providing her the liberty that she could address herself directly to the King if necessary (letter J. van Capellen to A. Tinne, 17 July 1864, NA 2.21.008.01/222).

4 Letter A. Tinne to Jemima van Capellen (NA 2.21.008.01/222).
5 Letter A. Tinne to J. van Capellen, 5 August 1864 (NA 2.21.008.01/222).

Appendix 6

1 Gentz, 1869: 601-602. Translated in: Wells, 1871: 112-124.
2 Lane, E.W., *An Account of the Manners and Customs of the Modern Egyptians*, London, 1860 (5th Ed.).
The book was published in 1835. Margaret Tinne would have referred to the 5th edition which has as frontispiece an 'Egyptian room', showing a sitting- c.q. dining-room apparently in a similar arrangement as the one at Alexine's.
3 Joseph-Pons d'Arnaud was engineer in the service of Muhammad Ali for some time. In 1839-42, he made three expeditions to the upper White Nile in search for its source. He succeeded in ascending the river as far as Gondokoro.

Appendix 7

1 Lejean, (1), 1862. In number 129 of the magazine *Le Tour du Monde*, Lejean would publish this map in 1862 with his translation of the narratives of Castelbolognesi. The Poncet brothers published their map of the White Nile, including its tributaries such as the Bahr el-Ghazal, in *Bulletin de la Société de Géographie* in October 1860. Petherick's map was published in 1861 in his *Egypt, the Sudan and Central Africa*.
2 PM, 1862: 218-222.
3 In *Inner-Afrika*, (1863: 147) Petermann states in a footnote: 'Unfortunately Mr. von Heuglin seems not to have been in the possession of Lejean's map'. He is even critical of Heuglin who referred only to Map 6 of the edition *Inner-Afrika* with its presentation of the journey to Meshra el-Rek that Brun-Rollet accomplished before 1856 and had become outdated by Castelbolognesi's 1862 map and Petherick's 1861 map.
4 PM, 1863: 106.
5 PM, 1863: 275-276 (p. 280 mentions 8 July 1863 as Petermann's closing date). On 16 July 1863, Petermann received a map Heuglin had sent him before 10 May. The map consisted of a sketch of the route taken by the expedition and added new information in particular to Map 6 of *Inner-Afrika*, showing Darfur and Kordofan (*Inner-Afrika*, 1863(XII): 153). During his stay in Bongo, Heuglin dressed up a new map including the route to the Kosanga mountains and Alexine's camp on it ('A.T.') of which he possibly made several copies. One of these copies was sent by Alexine, directly after her arrival in Khartoum April 1864, to John in Liverpool as a record of their journey and their stay at Biselli's *zariba*, and another one was sent by her from Berber to her aunt Jemima in The Hague. To complete the sketches he had sent before, this sketch and an additional new one must also have been sent to Petermann during his journey back to Cairo or possibly just after his return to Germany. A large drawing by Heuglin of the Bahr el-Ghazal region could be the definitive copy that Petermann used for his 1865 map (now kept in the Von Heuglin Archive in the Naturhistorisches Museum at Stuttgart).
6 Morlang, F., 'Reisen östlich und westlich von Gondokoro', 1859 (published in *Inner-Afrika*: 116-124); 'Wilhelm von Harnier's Reise auf dem Weissen Nil, Dezember 1860 bis November 1861' (ibidem: 125-141).
7 In the summer of 1862, Heuglin sent

Petermann some drawings of ethnographic objects from the 'Niam-Niam' (*Inner-Afrika*, 1863 (VIII): 107). These drawings were taken up in a separate overview of one page in *Inner-Afrika* (ibidem, 1863 (VIII): 107) and added by Petermann to the 1865 map (*PM*, 1863: 276). Some of these objects still remain in the Tinne-Heuglin collections. They were presumably purchased in 1862 on the market at Khartoum.

8 'Reise vom Bahr el Gazal zum Lande der Jur, Dezember 1860 und Januar 1861, von Marquis Oratio [sic] Antinori' in: *Inner-Afrika*, 1863 (VI): 79-82. The last chapter is titled: 'Erkundigungen über die Niam-Niam, die geschwänzten Menschen'.

9 Antinori, O., 'Viaggi di O. Antinori e C. Piaggia nell'Africa Centrale nord, con carta e profili del socio Orazio Antinori' in: *Bollettino della Società Geografica Italiana*, Anno I° - Fasciculo I°, Agosto 1868, Firenze [parte I 'Notizie su Carlo Piaggia – Viaggi e Ricerche fatte a Antinori sulle Tribù circostanti ai Niam-Niam' (91-105), Parte II., 'Viaggio e Scoperte del Piaggia fatte nelle Tribù del Niam-Niam' (105-134), Parte III, 'Esposizione Geografica di una nuova Parte dell'Africa Centrale' in: 'Rapporto alle Sorgenti occidentale del Nilo' (134-155), 'Vocabulario della Lingua Niam-Niam' (157-165).

10 Bassani, 1978; Pellegrinetti, 1941. Actually, Piaggia's original version of his accounts consists of far more information concerning the Azande than Antinori dealt with in his article in the *Bolletino*.

11 *PM*, 1868: 412-426 ('Das Land der Niamniam und die südwestliche Wasserscheide des Nil. Nach den Berichten von C.Piaggia und den Brüdern Poncet.'). In this same volume, an announcement is made of Schweinfurth's progress in penetrating 'the Niamniam countries' (229-230).

12 Petermann hereby refers to the information in the fascicle 'The Tinne'ische Expedition', Ergänzungsheft Nr. 15 of *PM* of 1865 and in *Inner-Afrika*, 1863 (XI): 105 ff.

13 Antinori in: BSGI, 1868: 105, 124. Cf. Antinori, O. 'Reise vom Bahr el Gazal zum Lande der Jur, Dezember 1860 und Januar 1861', in:, *Inner-Afrika. Nach dem Stande der Geographischen Kenntniss in den Jahren 1861 bis 1863*, Gotha, 1863: 79-84. Besides an account of his 1860-61 expedition to the Bahr el-Ghazal, Antinori devotes a chapter to the 'Niam-Niam' entitled: 'Erkundigungen über die Niam-Niam, die geschwänzten Menschen'. In *Inner-Afrika* (105), Heuglin considered in 1863 this story about tailed people to be a product of too much fantasy. Apparently it was now widely known as a fantastic and obsolete story. In 1865, Heuglin noticed that during his journey in the region near the 'Niam-Niam' country everybody denounced this tale ('Die Tinne'sche Expedition', *PM*, 1865: 30).

14 *PM*, 1863: 83. Although Robert Hartmann expresses his doubts about Antinori's conclusions concerning the Niam-Niam's tail as an existing anomaly (1863: Appendix XXXIII [30] with his review of Antinori's account), he does not reject it right away, but states that further investigation would be necessary (1863: 344-345). Lejean: 'decoration' (Lejean, 1861, and in *PM*, 1861: 234).

15 Toniolo & Hill, 1980: 9.

16 *PM*, 1864: 309.

17 *PM*, 1868: 229. In 1874, Schweinfurth would publish some words of appreciation regarding Antinori's account of Piaggia's observations: '…Marquis O. Antinori has (…) most conscientiously collected Piaggia's experiences and observations in the country of the

Niam-niam during his residence'. 1874 II: 2 in footnote.

18 See: note 10 and Chapter 3 note 15.

Explanatory notes to the consulted sources

1 This diary must be considered lost. Before 1970, fragments of them were used in Gladstone's biography of Alexine Tinne (Gladstone refers to *Journals, Diaries* of H. Tinne: Vol. I-V. covering the period between 27 July 1854 and 9 September 1862). In the National Archives in The Hague, transcriptions – possibly from the hand of Jetty Hora Siccama or her mother – are preserved of Henriette's notations and letters. Most of Henriette's diary notations, used by Gladstone, could be retrieved in these documents. In quoting, reference is made to this last source.

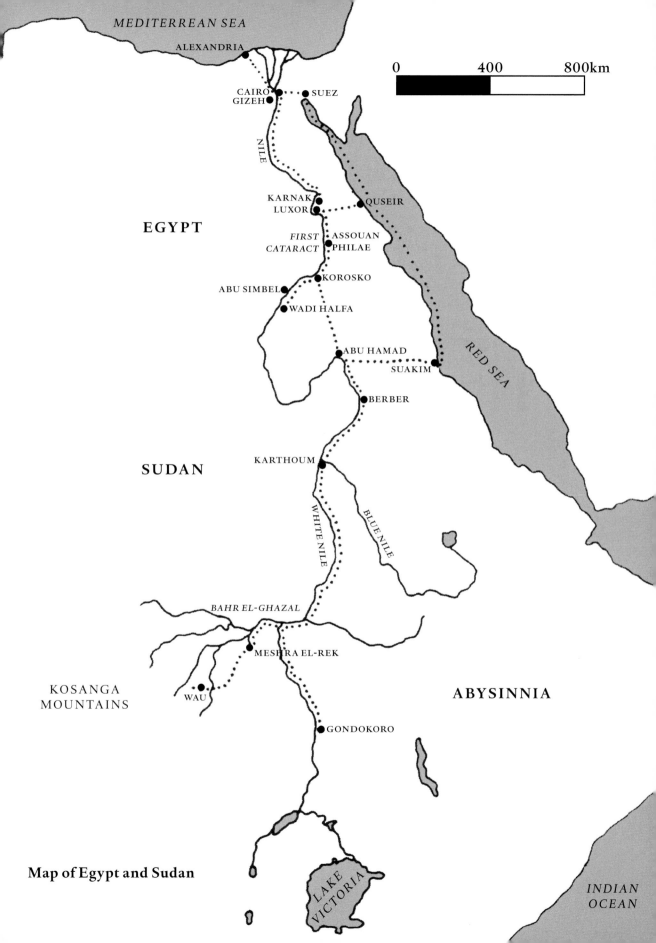

Map of Egypt and Sudan

Catalogue

Ethnographic collections

Introduction to the ethnographic collections

From approximately 1860, the Western world became witness to an explosive growth in ethnographic data coming from all parts of the world. Known as the 'dark continent' on account of its unexplored regions, Africa presented an enticing challenge to European explorers attempting to gather information on peoples that had never before come into contact with European culture. Certain African regions were a treasure trove of scholarly material. Europeans were thirsting for information about the mysterious river named the White Nile, its effluents, its fauna, its flora, its geography and its people. Collecting ethnographic specimens in southern Sudan formed part of this quest to expand the West's scientific knowledge. Those who helped to fill this gap in Europeans' knowledge included naturalists such as Heuglin (a zoologist with ornithology as a specialty) and amateurs like the Tinnes who collected floral specimens on their 'pleasure trip'.

For the most part, these scientific endeavours were motivated by scholarly curiosity. In the following paragraphs, Heuglin's accounts and notations will be put in the context of the development of geographical and ethnological science in Germany. Particularly in view of the period in which Heuglin performed his fieldwork, these discoveries have to be regarded as unconnected to any colonial intentions.

The ethnographic collections

In the months following Alexine's death in the Libyan desert, John Tinne sent his son Fred to Cairo to retrieve the belongings she had left behind. His two other sons Theodore and Ernest went to Tripoli to see that the authorities carried out the necessary investigations concerning Alexine's death and to deal with her properties there. When John visited Alexine in January and February 1865, he had shipped 65 ethnographic specimens collected by her out of Cairo. The following year he donated these items to the Free Public Museum in Liverpool. This collection consisted mostly of what she had acquired during her Bahr el-Ghazal trip, together with some objects gathered on her tour in 1862 on the White Nile. In 1869, several objects that Alexine had assembled on her later Sahara journey, possibly from the area of the Tuaregs, were transferred from her home in Tripoli to Liverpool and donated subsequently to the same museum. Alexine's total collection of 349 items remained preserved at this museum for the next seventy years. But in the night of 3 May 1941, German bombers dropped about 870 tonnes of highly explosive bombs and over 112,000 incendiaries on Liverpool, destroying or damaging buildings and streets all over the city. A 500 pound (225 kilogram) bomb fell on Liverpool's library and museum. Both were burned down, together with a part of the Tinne collection.

Fortunately, the lists drawn up by John Tinne of what was donated in 1866 and 1870 survived the Liverpool blitz. A recent evaluation of Tinne's collection based on a recount of the remaining objects resulted in a list of 133 items. After the first inventory, 52 were selected as definitely or most probably having been acquired during her journeys of 1862-1864.

When Heuglin left Cairo for Stuttgart, he took along all the specimens he had acquired during his five-year stay in Sudan during which he made two expeditions – one to the Bahr el-Ghazal and another to a part of what was then Abyssinia. What he had assembled consisted primarily of zoological and botanical specimens. Heuglin's ethnographic collection, still in Stuttgart, initially contained approximately 40 items and a number of arrows from his Bahr el-Ghazal expedition. Over time, some of these objects have disappeared, reducing the number to 27 items and 70 arrows.

The list of Heuglin's collection indicates that it was meant as a collection of specimens from the regions of the Dōr (or Bongo), Jur, Kresh, Shilluk, Nuer and 'Niam-Niam' (Azande). After he bestowed this collection to the King and Queen of Württemberg, an exhibition was held for which the items were numbered (from 1 to 170) and given a short description of their identification and provenance (e.g. 'Nro. 87. Köcher der Fertit-Neger' [Quiver including over 70 arrows from people of Dar Fertit. See Catalogue nrs. 59, 59a-d]; 'Nro. 105, 106. Pfeife der Djur'; 107, 108. 'Messer der Dor'). In 1998, the identification and provenance of a large part of Heuglin's collection was re-established following a thorough stocktaking.

Heuglin was a pioneer in Germany in the field of ethnographic scholarship. His remarks regarding the Dōr (Bongo), Fertit, Jur, Kresh and Azande and the specimens he attributed to each of them formed the first more or less extensive ethnographic study on Sudanese native people and their culture. The illustrations in his 1869 publication, together with several additional descriptions in 1863 and 1865 and those in the catalogue of the exposition at the Royal Palace in Württemberg, enable us to identify several items in the collection of Alexine Tinne in the museum at Liverpool which had up to now received no proper identification.

We will now look at the way in which the specimens in these collections were purportedly acquired and the underlying reasons for their acquisition, which can tell us much about the contemporary Western view on Sudanese native people.

Collected in situ?

No account provides us with any information regarding an explicit collecting activity by the Tinnes and Heuglin during the first part of their expedition (January 1863 to mid-December 1864).

For one item, though, there exists substantial evidence that it was acquired *in situ* while the expedition was staying at Biselli's *zariba* near the Kosanga mountains. According to Heuglin's account, a wooden tub had been presented as a gift to Alexine Tinne in November 1863 by a deputy of the Azande king Mofío.[1] In Alexine's collection there is one item with an identical description, indicating the southwestern Azande as its origin (see Catalogue numbers: 25 and 25a).

Several items could have been acquired on their return from the expedition. During their passage through the desert from Berber to Suakim, Heuglin writes about purchasing several ethnographic objects while staying in Ras el-Wadi in the regions of the Bisharin and the Funj. These acquisitions could very well refer to several items in the Tinne collections and the Bisharin objects in his 1863 catalogue (see illustrations: 13-23, 31, 44-48 and 79).[2]

The pipe (illustrations 68, 68a-c), described in the 1865 exhibition as coming from the Bongo, is very likely to have been purchased during Heuglin's stay with the Bongo in the autumn of 1863.

For most items, however, it is impossible to determine whether they were collected *in situ*. They could just as well have been acquired in Khartoum, where a thriving market in ethnographic paraphernalia had developed.

Khartoum and its market of ethnographic curios

Khartoum's market in ethnographic objects developed quite soon after the first Westerners began to arrive. A book published in 1851 by George Melly confirms the existence of sellers of ethnographic objects in Khartoum. During his White Nile journey with his father André, a Liverpool merchant and traveller, George relates that every time they visited the governor general in the capital, the outer court of the palace was always full of dealers approaching the visitors with their curiosities.[3] Twice they were asked by Europeans to take along substantial ethnographic collections to Europe. The first time the Savoyard Brun-Rollet offered him his 'entire collection' consisting of 'drums, musical horns, bows, spears, arrows, quivers, clubs and curious iron truncheons, pipes and tea spoons like soup laddles', part of which he requested be donated to the museum in Turin. And another time one of the missionaries at the Austrian Catholic Mission asked André Melly to accept 'about two camel loads of White Nile curiosities'.[4] From Melly's accounts we can conclude that both these collections were accepted by his father. On his way back to Cairo, however, André died. George took along this merchandise, but a large part of it is likely to have been lost during the perilous return journey. Only six items originating from the White Nile – specifically obtained from the Bari people – made it back to Liverpool. Of Brun-Rollet's collections in Turin, only a small number of weapons remain, none of which is thought to be from the Bahr el-Ghazal region.

The transference by Khartoum traders of Nilotic items as a merchandise to Khartoum must have been initiated at an early date: specifically in the late 1840s, when gradually more Westerners began appearing in southern Sudan and the appreciation for 'ethno-curios' increased. With many objects being sent back to Europe, the market for ethnographic specimens grew into a considerable size.[5]

The collection sold in 1854 to the Musée du Louvre in Paris by Pacifique Henri Delaporte, the French consul in Cairo from 1848 to 1854, is indicative of the major role that both Arab and European merchants played as suppliers of 'White Nile curiosities'. Delaporte had gathered a vast number of objects from southern Sudan including zoological items – such as a living giraffe donated in 1852 to the Jardin des Plantes – a series of arms, musical instruments and cult statues. As he recounts in a letter, his relations with merchants trading on both the Blue and White Nile enabled him to gather this substantial ethnographic collection.[6]

There is sufficient evidence pointing to the claim that the harp (or *kundi*) donated by John Tinne to the Public Museum in Liverpool in 1866 (see illustrations 2a and 2b), was purchased by Heuglin on the Khartoum market of ethnographic objects. In the summer of 1862, Heuglin tells Petermann: 'I have sent you a picture of a very pretty kind of mandolin'.[7] The harp was published as an illustration together with other 'Ethnographische Gegenstände aus den Negerländern westlich der Bahr el Abiad' on the frontispiece of *Inner-Afrika* in 1863 (see Catalogue number: 82). The drawing of the harp and the Tinne object in question show a striking resemblance. The harp is assumed to have been acquired around half a year before the expedition departed from Khartoum and was later given by Heuglin to Alexine, presumably in Cairo.

Khartoum's market of ethnographic curios might also very well have been the place of provenance of several other artefacts in the collections of other contemporary travellers. Because Khartoum traders were active in the regions far beyond the Bahr el-Ghazal, the market in Khartoum also procured items from the Dōr (Bongo), Dinka, Jur, Kresh and 'Niam-Niam'. One object – a pipe collected by Joseph Natterer (see illustration 68D in catalogue) – provides confirmation that one could indeed acquire Bongo specimens in Khartoum. This pipe is identical to that in Heuglin's collection (see illustration 68 in catalogue) and can be identified as having a Bongo provenance; and Natterer is not recorded as ever having visited the Bongo region himself.

In addition to Khartoum, Heuglin and Tinne could have purchased several items in the regions of the Dinka, Bongo and Jur themselves. In 1865, Heuglin gives a detailed account of several categories of objects that were produced at that time by these peoples. In actual fact, he was standing close to the production of these artefacts and could have easily purchased several specimens himself. [8]

When ascending the White Nile, Khartoum traders of ethnographic objects had every opportunity to obtain artefacts from the Nilotic people. Having reached Gondokoro, these traders were able to proceed on the right side of the river to the adjacent country of the south-eastern Azande (or Makrakà; see Petermann's adjoining map). Here they could procure Azande items in a region that was far easier to reach than the one beyond the Bahr el-Ghazal, where the Kosanga mountains stood in the way.[9] Travelling in the White Nile area around Gondokoro, Giovanni Miani (see below) was able to gain access to these south-eastern Azande in 1859-60, where he purchased his collection (see catalogue: 2a, 9a, 52d, 57d, 58d).

In the case of one particular knife, called a 'trombash', there is a similarity between the item in the Heuglin collection and the ones purchased by Giovanni Miani, Franz Binder and Orazio Antinori (see illustrations 57, 57a-d in catalogue). Although Heuglin described this particular object in 1863 as a Kresh weapon, in 1869 a similar item is described as having an Azande origin.[10] Miani and Binder acquired their *trombashes* in the region of the south-eastern Azande ('Makrakà'). As with the harp, Heuglin recorded the knife in a drawing and sent it to Petermann who published it on the frontispiece of *Inner-Afrika*. This artefact was in all probability purchased at the Khartoum market of ethnographics, equally to all those having Azande as their provenance (except for 25 and 25a in the catalogue), and being retrieved in the regions of the Makrakà.

Reasons for collecting artefacts

Although not a genuine or passionate *collectioneuse*, Alexine acquired a relatively substantial collection of artefacts which, after the donations to the Liverpool museum, consisted of 349 items. She most probably considered these items as remnants of the journeys she made with her mother in Egypt and Sudan. The company of Heuglin, an ethnographer, might have stimulated her wish to procure these items as ethnographics but to see them later as *souvenirs de voyage*, which she eventually put on display in her Cairo home.

Heuglin gave a more specific nomenclature to the items he acquired. Soon after his return to Stuttgart in May 1865, his collections were displayed in the Royal Palace. The exhibition was dedicated to his entire collection of Abyssinian and Sudanese items, and joined by a modest catalogue of four pages entitled *Austellungs-Catalog der ethnographischen Sammlung des Hernn Hofrath Dr. v. Heuglin.*

With the donation of his collection to Queen Olga von Würtemberg, Heuglin added some descriptions to the specimens which refer to their ethnographic provenance and not in particular to the locations where they had been collected.

As registered in the 1865 catalogue, he donated all the specimens as an 'ethnographic collection' (*'ethnographische Sammlung'*) acquired during his Abyssinian and Bahr el-Ghazal expeditions. As a scientist, he apparently preferred this description to that of a collection of 'curiosities', which these items could very well have been named in those days. The name 'ethnographic collection' indicates that Heuglin regarded these objects as specimens describing the customs and habits of non-Western people. In bestowing the quality 'ethnographic' on them, Heuglin bestowed a scientific status on his acquisitions. At the time of Heuglin's donation, the concept of an 'ethnographic collection' was still just beginning to take root. Gradually, Europeans began to see these objects less as a 'curiosity' and more as something to be studied. In this sense, the 1860s can be regarded as a period of transition. Items from a foreign culture were given a dual value: that of being able to convey interesting facts about another culture, and that of being a rare and unknown example of an exotic culture, which could still be represented as the 'curiosity' value. There even was the possibility of naming them 'ethnographic curiosities' or 'ethnological peculiarities'.[11]

Heuglin's ethnographic contribution

In his enumerations, Heuglin was essentially concerned with conveying as much information as possible to Petermann in order to have it published. In describing the indigenous people and contributing to the geographic knowledge of the area, Heuglin also enhanced the reputation of German research.

In his accounts, Heuglin refers to several different groups of peoples (or in his contemporary terminology: 'Stamm' = 'tribe') as inhabitants of the White Nile basin, including the extended area of the Bahr el-Ghazal. In the middle of September 1863, when staying among the Bongo and Jur people, Heuglin took down his observations regarding the industry, clothes and utensils of these people. He mentions artefacts such as pipes (referring to a drawing that was taken up by Petermann as an illustration on the 1865 map):

> small and decorative, their head is similar to the Turkish pipe, but higher, narrower and on the top somewhat broadened, with a long reed, which has been decorated overall with copper and iron decorations. Both the Bongo and Jur people fabricate benches, smaller and larger, which are made with a cross-bladed ax [see catalogue: 29 and 29a]…and spoons nicely made out of horns of buffaloes or antelopes [see catalogue: 10 and 10a]. The Jur iron forgers make besides the usual lances and digging instruments and knifes also the fine lance points, broad with barbs, which are used not so much as a weapon but more as a barter object and a present in marriages. The bridegroom purchases by 10 to 20 similar pieces a bride from her father, who often provides with these weapons a wife for his son. Mostly the women carry in their girdle a knife without a handle, 12 to 14 inches long, with an engraving-decorated blade and a small button as a finial [here he is referring to a drawing taken up by Petermann in the 1865 map; see also catalogue: 65 [F55266], 65a-c]. Throwing knives have their provenance at the Fertit, Kresh and Njamnyam.[12]

In an ethnographic survey, he later explains the differences between some of the weapons of the 'Sandé' and the Kresh:

> Besides fine lances and arrows, which resemble fully those of the Kresh one fabricates throwing and sabre knives (…). The throwing knives or *Trombadj*, also named *Kurbadj*, do have a length of 30 – 45 centimeters, a grip, winded with cord, and are made from iron, which has at the front side of the blade one or more cross arms or knives, sharply polished. These weapons were thrown in horizontal direction in such a way that it in its flight turned itself around, like the boomerang of the New Zealander. Injuries caused by this weapon are known to be seriously dangerous.

When describing the bows and arrows of the Dōr (Bongo), he provides significant information on two objects in the Tinne-Heuglin collections. He states that the sickle-formed knife, also called 'trombash', and the multi-pointed throwing weapons of the Fertit, the Kresh and the 'Niam-Niam' were not to be found in the Bongo and Jur areas, where he was at that moment.[13]

The Azande in Heuglin's ethnography

During their expedition, Alexine Tinne and Theodor von Heuglin recorded their close encounters with the local population. After the failure of his scientific mission to visit the Azande, he recorded with great interest the visual appearance of the Azande deputy who visited Alexine and him in November 1863 ('not of a genuine Sandé-race, but half-negro').[14]

Heuglin was the first European to gather extensive information on the Azande, a group that in those days had a kind of legendary status. He first obtained information about the Azande from Khartoum traders in the summer of 1862, which he immediately forwarded to Petermann. Both in his descriptions of the Azande utensils and the physical characteristics of the people, Heuglin would be able to provide far more detail in his 1865 accounts, for which he obtained the additional information in the autumn of 1863 from the Azande deputy.

The Azande country consisted of many small kingdoms inhabited by what Heuglin describes as a 'race which represented a non-identical negro-type' ('und von einer nicht vollständiger Neger-Typus tragenden Race bewohnt wird').[15] This race was thought to deviate in some respects from the 'negroe' known thus far. Heuglin notes a marked distinction between the physical characteristics of the Azande type and those of the Nuer and 'the Req', remarking that the last two represented the most pronounced type of 'negro' ('der prononcirtesten Neger-Typus'). This 'type' became less outspoken the further one went down the Jur river and was even completely missing among the Kresh, the Fertit and the Azande.[16] He then gives a detailed description of the physical characteristics of the Azande (hair, skin colour and stature).

In Europe at that time, the field of ethnography began establishing a system of 'racial classifications' according to the vocabulary, manners and customs of an ethnic group along with their physical particularities.[17] Heuglin's analysis of the culture and characteristics of the Azande was based on this kind of classification which emphasised a hierarchy in the different 'negro-types'. The Azande – who were seen as a group that was completely dissimilar to other groups that surrounded it – were considered to be a different 'race'. In addition to Heuglin's approval of their more centralised political structure, it is clear that he accords a more or less intrinsic superiority to their artefacts:

> Their soil is rich in iron, out of which the Njamnjam produce handsome knives, lances, sables and many-edged javelins, also pretty chains, bracelets (...). All their products demonstrate at first sight that these people stand on a far higher level than the people in the East and North, and that the appearance of their throwing knives, sable knives, shields etc...are strongly reminiscent of products from the regions around [Lake] Chad.[18]

Inevitably, Heuglin's evaluation of the Azande people was based on a European-centred mindset that at the time was beginning to establish a hierarchy among the many African cultures.[19]

In his interviews with Kleincznik and Kuchuk Aga in the summer of 1862, Heuglin received important information concerning not only routes to the region but also details about the culture and artefacts of the native people. Heuglin reports to Petermann:

> The Nyamyam are passionate lovers of music and dancing. I have sent you a picture of a very pretty kind of mandolin [called *kundi*]. They also have a large musical instrument, made of banana leaves, and a kind of harmonica, which consists of long pieces of wood to which are fastened transversely sticks of rattan of different lengths; at the end of these sticks are hung earthen vessels, which are struck in turn with a little wooden hammer.[20] Their weapons include iron projectiles resembling boomerangs which are also used sometimes by the Jur, Keredj[21] and Fertit, and Denham[22] gives a drawing of something very similar. They have also a dagger and sword with handles made partly of wood encircled with narrow iron hoops and partly iron wire, which the Nyamnyam make very neatly.

An overview in Petermann's *Inner-Afrika* presented 'ethnographic objects from the region to the west of the Bahr el-Ghazal, drawn by Theodor von Heuglin'. In it, a knife (see catalogue: 82), somewhat similar to the one in the Tinne collection (see catalogue: 50, 50a-b and 51) has been included. With reference to the sabre in the illustration, Heuglin adds:

> Their large sword is only sharp on the inner side of the crescent-shaped blade and on the broad addition on the outer edge towards the point; the rest of the surface is blunt and often serrated.
> A smaller crescent-shaped sword is two-edged. The small, many barbed arrows are thickly covered with vegetable poison.

Towards the end of 1862, Heuglin proposed that an investigation be opened to determine the veracity of the story of the Azande and their 'tails', which by then had already became a virtually obsolete tale. In 1865, he states that he himself had not been able to distinguish one trace of a continuation of the spine ending in a sort of rudimentary tail, and 'no one here prefers to acknowledge the existence of such a thing'.[23]

Heuglin relates the description that the Khartoum traders provided him of the Azande loincloth as part of the male attire:

> The clothing of the well-to-do consisted of a piece of bark about five or six feet long and nearly as wide. When the bark had been stripped off a fine tree trunk of a suitable kind, it was carefully taken off in a piece of the trunk and then put into water and milled with ferruginous clay, until the garment had the appearance and softness of a cotton frock. The Azande women of the north wore no *rahad*, but fresh bunches of leaves fastened to their girdles, while the men had leather thongs, one or two inches wide, which they pass between their legs and fastened to their belts at back and front.[24]

This description was repeated by Piaggia and subsequently published by Antinori in 1868.[25] In their descriptions, however, neither Heuglin nor Piaggia refer to the story of the 'tailed Niam-Niam'.

While Piaggia mentions the phenomenon of cannibalism among the Azande, which then had been broadcasted, Heuglin does not mention the word at all in his 1863 and 1865 accounts. It is only in 1869 that he simply refers to it as an accomplished fact.

'Ethnographische Gegenstände': utensils and artefacts

Heuglin's contributions to the field of ethnography can be placed against the backdrop of some major developments that were occurring in Germany around 1860 in the academic disciplines of anthropology and ethnology. Theodor Waitz and, somewhat later, Adolf Bastian were pioneers in the field of anthropology/ethnology who took a strictly scientific approach to the subject. Data on the particularities of non-Western people were aggregated to identify possible general features of non-Western people as well as the differences between the various non-Western groups. Within this new stream of ethnology, 'the African' received considerable attention.[26] Friedrich Müller's *Allgemeine Ethnographie*, published in 1873, was the first encyclopedic result of these factual compilations of ethnographic records. In 1874, Georg Schweinfurth contributed substantially to the Western world's understanding of the Azande (who were still called 'Niam-Niam') and the Mangbetu (1875). Thereafter, the ethnographic landscape of the Bahr el-Ghazal basin was further unravelled in Franz von Hellwald's *Naturgeschichte des Menschen* (1880-1884) – in which 'Niam-Niam' gave way to 'Sandeh' – and Friedrich Ratzel's *Völkerkunde* (1885-1888), in which some objects from Heuglin's collections were presented.

Heuglin himself, however, did not rework the data he gathered into something that could be seen as a contribution to the more theoretical part of this emerging science of ethnology. As he was operating from within the framework of geography and the natural sciences, he restricted himself to recording the manners, customs, artifacts and physical characteristics of the local people in the expectation that this would be a valuable contribution to science as a whole.

Although Heuglin placed the Azande within a certain hierarchy of Southern Sudanese civilisations, we do not encounter among his accounts any explicit attempt to analyse the extent to which indigenous objects supported the notion of Western superiority. The recent discovery by Westerners of cult statues or 'fetishes' in the West and Central African coastal areas was taken as proof of the prevalence of superstition and the 'lack of artistic skills' among the local populations. This was in turn taken to be indicative of the retarded development of these tribes. In the case of Sudan, however, similar objects appeared to be virtually non-existent.[27] Remarkably, the cult statues that had been acquired by Delaporte and Miani from the Sere and Bari people (in the Gondokoro region) were never the subject of Western criticism. Based on the German anthropological tradition of Waitz and Bastian, Heuglin operated within a broadly humanistic agenda and focused on efforts to document the plurality and historical specificity of cultures.[28]

In his account of the final leg of the Tinne expedition from Khartoum to Cairo, Heuglin devoted more pages to the Azande in 1865. In 1869, he expatiates on the Azande for 13 pages, presenting 14 illustrations of their artefacts. Such objects were in his opinion clearly borne out of aesthetic intentions, since they were unmistakeably the products of careful craftsmanship and technical skill and were moreover decorative and stylish. Although throughout the nineteenth century ethnographic items were regarded solely as instructive 'curios', there was an underlying belief that some of these objects reflected the higher aspirations as artefacts. Far from evaluating these items as work of 'savages' (a word he never used), Heuglin observed a high level of material development. This view predated Schweinfurth's *Artes Africanae* (1875), a book presenting an overview of the material culture of Sudanese people with full-page illustrations of utensils used in the Bahr el-Ghazal region, and in particular of those he had visited in the years before: the Azande and Monbuttoo. Although the title of the book might suggest the use of 'art', this word is not applicable here. Schweinfurth referred to these specimens as *Artes* in the sense of artefacts, meaning *Kunstgewerbe* (arts and crafts, applied arts).

Schweinfurth's *Im Herzen von Afrika*, which described some details regarding Azande cannibalism, was published in 1874. It was directly translated into English, appearing in the same year with the title *The Heart of Africa*, with an introduction by the Africa traveller Winwood Read. The title of his book *Artes Africanae* became in a way almost irreconcilable with the observation of cannibalism; an incompatibility that gradually came into being among circles of ethnologists in the course of the following years.[29]

Alexine Tinne's collection

In addition to being a reunion, the visit John Tinne made to Alexine Tinne in Cairo from 13 January to 15 February 1865 was also an attempt to persuade her to return to The Hague, or possibly to accompany him to Liverpool. Alexine declined his initiative but decided to transfer the largest part of her ethnographic collection, which was displayed around her house (as described by Gentz), by having it shipped by John to Liverpool. On 16 February, Margaret Tinne mentions in a letter to her son: 'She has given Papa 2 large boxes full of Africana curiosities & they are to be sent to Liverpool by Boat…'. Alexine's collections were presumably packed and taken to Alexandria in order to be shipped to Europe on the same ship on which the bodies of Henriette and Flore were to be transported. The cargo was split up later in two portions, one for The Hague (or, more specifically, the cemetery of Eik en Duinen) and the other going to the Public Museum in Liverpool. The following year John would make the trip to The Hague in order to settle all affairs in The Hague. After transferring all the furniture to his mansion 'Briarly' near Liverpool, the house on the Lange Voorhout was sold the next year.

Some objects that were very dear to Alexine might have been kept in her house in Cairo and may have accompanied her to Izmir, Naples, Malta, Toulon, Algiers and her house in Tripoli. Items possibly acquired by Alexine on her last journey may have been retrieved and taken back to Tripoli by one of her servants, presumably Abdallah. Shortly after John Tinne was informed about Alexine's death, he sent his two sons – Ernest and Theodore – to Tripoli to clear out her house. These possessions were shipped to Liverpool and donated to the Public Museum (or Merseyside County Museum) in Liverpool in 1870, along with the remaining items of her collection that John was still in possession of.

Her ethnographic collections had been acquired on several journeys: Syria (1858-59), three Nile voyages (1860-1862), the Bahr el-Ghazal expedition (1863-1864) and her last journey in the Libyan desert (1868-1869). She had taken the objects collected on her first journey and the first two Nile trips back with her to her house in The Hague and left them there when she departed once again for the Nile in 1861. When the house together with its inventory was sold in 1870, these collections were presumably transferred to Liverpool to be donated to the Public Museum together with the items and belongings, found in her Tripoli house (see illustrations: 84-88).

On her White Nile journey in 1862, Alexine actually passed several places she visited with her mother on the trips previously made to Egypt. Objects in her collection that can definitely be attributed to regions in Lower and Upper Egypt above Khartoum might very well have been purchased in locations on the Nile before 1861. Some small pieces of Lower Egyptian origin (still in the Tinne family) are archaeological finds she must have acquired on her first journey in 1858-1859, travelling from Cairo south to Luxor, where she also gathered several clay pipeheads which are of Siout origin (nrs. LWM 27.9.70.36 27.9.70.51-52). There remain some objects from her third journey up the White Nile (20 May to 20 November 1862), one of which might have been acquired in the Bari region in Gondokoro (see catalogue: 42) but more likely in Khartoum, as argued above.

A substantial number of items in Alexine and Heuglin's collections have the Bahr el-Ghazal region as its provenance. What had been purchased in Khartoum before the start of the expedition might not have been taken with them on their journey. In particular, Heuglin was already in possession of quite a number of objects he had gathered on his previous Abyssinian journey. These were most likely stored in Khartoum. Alexine's items were perhaps kept in the house of Adriana van Capellen. After their return to Khartoum, both of them had everything transported to Cairo.

They had two options for transporting their collections. One was to bring the objects along with their other belongings on the ship that brought Alexine and Heuglin from Jeddah via Suez to Cairo. The other was to have a part of the collection sent from Khartoum directly to Cairo. There was in fact a substantial amount of packages and luggage that Thibaut was asked to deliver from Alexine's house in Khartoum to Cairo (see Chapter 'Tidings from Cairo').

A number of domestic objects made from plant fibre and cane came from the Bisharin, the Kababish and the Funj, who lived in the area near Berber between Sennār and Suakim (see catalogue: 13-23, 31, 31a, 44a and b, and 45). According to Heuglin, they both purchased ethnographic objects while staying in Ras el-Wadi in September 1864.[30] These objects must have been acquired by Alexine (Heuglin was by then totally broke) and taken along with her luggage from Berber to Cairo and shipped to Liverpool by John.

It certainly was not Alexine's primary concern to keep close track of the provenance of the objects she purchased. She did not bother to draw up a list of her ethnographic items with their dates of acquisition.

There is no evidence whatsoever that John Tinne consulted anyone, not even Heuglin in Stuttgart, when he set out to list the objects in Alexine's collection. In the list of descriptions of his donations, he wrote down 'Touareg' as the provenance for several types of objects, including a genuine Touareg sword retrieved from her house in Tripoli in 1870 (see illustration: 84). Because this attribution 'Touareg' also occurs in the list of his donation of 1866, before Alexine had visited Libya let alone the Touaregs, we can safely assume that John drew up the list of donations in 1871 in addition to his third donation, which was registered on 27 September of that year. Most of her collections, having been donated earlier without any mention of provenance or attribution, must have been described afterwards, given their numbering. Each of these three lists was signed for by the registrar H. Smith as 'entered in Stock Book'. On 2 February 1871, two more objects from Alexine's collection were donated to the Public Museum and described as 'obtained in the West Indies by the late Mr. P.F. Tinne and presented by J.A. Tinne'. Apparently these two objects had remained in John's house in Liverpool before he decided to donate them in addition to P.F. Tinne's West Indian acquisitions. Both objects originate from the Bahr el-Ghazal region. One is of Bongo origin (see catalogue: 52, 52a); the second one has been erroneously registered as 'Touareg' and regards a 'Niam-Niam' or Azande dagger (see catalogue: 50). This item was already known to be from the Azande from Petermann's *Inner-Afrika* and Heuglin's 1869 publication, which apparently had not been consulted either by John or the curator/registrar at that time.

Several items that were listed in the donations of 1866 and 1870 could not be found and are believed to have disappeared at an early date or during the 1941 bombing of the storerooms. An ivory trumpet that John Tinne sent along with Alexine's collection to Liverpool was never listed in the donations – it may have been kept in the family and subsequently lost. One of the two harps (see catalogue: 4 and 4a) that is missing must be considered lost, more recently.[31]

Recent research shows a striking similarity between the objects collected by both Alexine and Heuglin during the course of their expedition. As an ethnographer, Heuglin was keen on learning more about the local people. He was the only one of the two who took notes on the functions of the various artefacts and the ethnic group that manufactured them. It stands to reason that Alexine Tinne made her acquisitions together with Heuglin and in these cases purchased items identical to what Heuglin purchased. Heuglin may have provided Alexine with items similar to his or not. In particular, Heuglin liked types of forged iron weapons and frequently described them in his accounts. Daggers that can be found in the Tinne collection (see catalogue: 50 and 51) had already been described by him as early as 1863. In his decision to purchase this specimen in Khartoum before the start of the expedition, he might have bought a pair of them (together with the harp; see catalogue: 28, 28a), reselling them at a later occasion to Alexine.

Reference collections

With the catalogue of the Tinne-Heuglin collections, objects from other similar collections with the Bahr el-Ghazal region as provenance can be compared, making it possible to confirm or correct the identity of several categories of objects by cross-reference. In particular, Heuglin's information regarding the provenance of items and the Khartoum market in White Nile curios could provide useful knowledge for identifying similar contemporary Sudanese collections in several European museums.

Other Europeans had already been to the region Heuglin and Tinne wanted to gain access to. The French brothers Poncet explored the region in 1853 in search of trade; their collection of artefacts was sold in 1867 in an auction in Paris.[32] The Savoyard Brun-Rollet visited the Gazelle river frequently in 1855-1856 for barter trade with the locals, gathering an important collection of artefacts which has for a large part been lost. The Italian explorer Castelbolognesi followed a part of the river going to Meshra el-Rek in 1857 and assembled a collection that was dispersed and lost in the Second World War. The British vice consul John Petherick assembled various artefacts when he visited the region beyond the Gazelle river. The Italian marchese Orazio Antinori went up the river in 1860-61. And in the same period as Tinne and Heuglin, the Italian trader and explorer Carlo Piaggia entered the Bahr el-Ghazal region in a separate expedition.

For the most part, the collections of Petherick, Antinori and Piaggia are still preserved in European museums. The same cannot be said of the collections of other explorers. Once back in Europe, many travellers sold their artefacts to collectors of African ethnographic items. The number of private collectors of such artefacts was steadily increasing in those days, fed by the recent discoveries and the flood of ethnographic items being brought to Europe. Once sold, these collections were dispersed among private owners and became nameless. They are now impossible to trace and must be written off as lost forever.

The collectors of reference specimens [33]

Collection of Antinori

Orazio Marchese Antinori (1811-1882) was born in Perugia, the descendant of an old aristocratic family. When the 1848 revolution began, he enlisted in the Liberal army under Garibaldi and fought against the Austrians and French. After the Liberal cause was defeated, he left Italy and went to Sudan via Egypt in 1858. In 1860 he visited Kordofan with the French traveller Lejean and in 1860-61 he travelled to the Bahr el-Ghazal with Piaggia. After his return to Italy, he distributed his ornithological collections to various museums. He became a founder of the Italian geographical society in 1867. In 1871 he and Piaggia went to the Bogo land on the Ethiopian plateau to collect natural history items. In 1871-72 he travelled from Massaua to Kassala. He died in Abyssinia while leading a scientific expedition.

During his Bahr el-Ghazal journey, Antinori was unable to reach the Western Azande regions. The two Azande harps (see catalogue: 28d-g) are likely to have been purchased at Khartoum's market of ethnographics.

Collection of Binder

Franz Binder (1824-1875) was an Austrian trader on the Upper White Nile from 1855-1864 and had a station in Shambé, having bought Rumbek station after De Malzac's death in 1860. He was acting Sardinian vice consul in Khartoum in 1859; in 1864 he returned to Hermannstadt (now Sibiu, Romania) and donated his ethnographic acquisitions to the local museum.

The Catalogue numbers 57c and 58b represent objects Binder is presumed to have acquired *in situ* during his 10-year sojourn on the White Nile. The Azande objects are of East Azande origin, most probably from the Makrakà, an offshoot to the east of the Azande proper.

Collection of Brun-Rollet

The Savoyard Jacques Antoine Brun-Rollet (1810-1858) was born in Saint Jean de Maurienne under the name of Rollet. As a youth, he fled his hometown as a draft dodger under the fake name of Brun, which he later added to his original name. He first came to Sudan in 1831 and died in Khartoum. Brun-Rollet wanted to increase not merely his wealth but was also considering Sudan as a potential exporter of many more products such as sesame, groundnuts and cotton. He was the first European to explore the Bahr el-Ghazal as far as Meshra el-Rek in 1856-57. In those two years, he was Sardinian vice consul in Khartoum. In 1850, Brun-Rollet attempted to interest George Melly (without success) in an enterprise to develop Southern Sudan by means of steamers. Five years later, he recommended the construction of a railway from Aswan southward to the Berber province, where a service of steamers would support the transport of commercial articles.

A major part of Brun-Rollet's ethnographic collection was lost during a transport in 1851. As mentioned earlier, a large part of his collection which he had given to George and André Melly was left behind on George's journey from Khartoum to Cairo. A study of the still remaining pieces of the collection in the Museo Armeria Reale in Turin was published in 1987.[34] In what remains of this collection, no references were found regarding objects in the collections of Tinne and Heuglin.

Collection of Castelbolognesi

Angelo Castelbolognesi (1835[?]-1874) was a native of Ferrara and came to Egypt as a boy. From there, he made his way to Sudan and became an employee of John Petherick, who was then an ivory-buying agent for a Cairo house. In this capacity, Castelbolognesi explored the Bahr el-Ghazal to its upper limit as well as the rivers Rek, Ajak and Jur in 1856-1857. His account was published by Guillaume Lejean. He accompanied Orazio Antinori on an exploration of the region of Sennār in 1859-60. He returned to Egypt around 1860 and later committed suicide in Alexandria.

Castelbolognesi's ethnographic collection, which was of a considerable size, was donated to the Museo di Storia Naturale at Ferrara. A part of it was taken up in the illustration that accompanied the account published by Lejean in 1862 of his journey to the Gazelle river. In 1940, a substantial part was given in loan to the prestigious exhibition 'Mostra d'Oltremare e del Lavoro Italiano nel Mondo' in Naples, and was afterwards dispersed during the Second World War. An impression of what his collection was like was published in 1862 (see catalogue: 83).

Collection of Knoblecher

Ignaz Knoblecher (or Knoblehar) (1819-58) was pro-vicar apostolic of the Roman Catholic mission to Central Africa. A Slovene, his name was originally Knoblehar, though he preferred to use the germanised form. When Pope Gregory XVI instituted the vicariate apostolic of Central Africa in 1846, Knoblecher left Rome for Sudan as a member of the Jesuit Order. He arrived with a party of missionaries in Khartoum in 1848. In the same year, he went up the White Nile on a mission. In 1850 he returned to Europe where he founded a society to assist the mission. After his return to Sudan in 1852 he ascended the White Nile, this time with Angelo Vinco, and founded a mission in Gondokoro and another in 1854 named Heiligenkreuz; both mission stations were abandoned after 1862. On another visit to Europe in 1857, he died in Naples. A small collection is kept in the Museum für Völkerkunde in Vienna. The club (Catalogue nr. 42a) Knoblecher could have obtained when in Gondokoro, where he remained close to the Bari people. At Heiligenkreuz, he developed close relations with the Shilluk.

Collection of Miani

Giovanni Miani (1810-1872) emigrated in 1849 to Egypt as an exile from the Roman Republic. With help from the Egyptian government, in 1859-60 he explored the country of the Bari on the Upper White Nile as far south as the Aswa river in quest of Lake Albert. He then returned to Venice, which then was part of Austria, and he engaged in Vienna in a controversy over the recent discovery of the source of the Nile by J.H. Speke and J.A. Grant. He returned to Egypt as the curator of a zoological museum founded by the Khedive Isma'il in 1870. Intent on exploring the unknown country west of the Upper Nile valley, he left Khartoum in 1871 for Shambé. From there, he travelled to the region of the Uélé, but died during the journey near the present site of Niangara. He was the first to explore the basin of the Uélé river as far south as the Bomokandi river.

Miani donated a substantial part of his ethnographic collections to the Museo di Storia Naturale in Venice (as he himself was a Venetian) and to the Zoologisches Cabinet at Vienna. The collection in Venice consists of what he acquired on his White Nile journey ascending up to Gondokoro before 1860.

Collection of Natterer

Joseph Natterer (c. 1820-1862) began his travels in 1855 to Nubia and Sudan, returning in 1858 with a collection of animals and birds for the Schönbrunn menagerie in Vienna. Appointed the Austrian vice consul in Khartoum, he returned to Sudan to replace Heuglin. He wrote to his relatives that he had made a fortune by speculation and intended to return to Europe to devote himself entirely to the natural sciences, but he died of fever in Khartoum.

The objects in Natterer's ethnographic collection in Vienna come from a wide range of areas along the White Nile. It is questionable that Natterer obtained the pair of Azande daggers (nr. 52b) *in situ* in the region of the Eastern Azande. Khartoum's market seems the most likely place of acquisition.

Collection of Petherick

John Petherick (1813-1882) entered the service of Muhammad Ali as a Welsh mining engineer, trader and explorer. Upon quitting government services, he traded in Arabian gum from Kordofan from 1848 to 1853. When this trade began declining, he transferred his activities to the ivory trade along the White Nile. At this time he explored the rivers Jur and Yalo and arrived at the borders of the Azande country in 1853-1858. In 1858 he was appointed British vice consul in Khartoum. During his leave to Britain in the beginning of 1860, he was invited by the Royal Geographical Society of London to take charge of an expedition to succour J.H. Speke and J.A. Grant, who were shortly expected to enter Sudan from the south. After having misjudged the probable time of their arrival, he later discovered that the explorers had already arrived and were in no need of his services. His failure to meet them did much harm to his reputation. Having shown perhaps excessive zeal in reporting suspected cases of slave trading to the British consul general in Egypt, accusations were made at the address of the governor general in Khartoum that he himself was engaged in this trade. Although the British government doubted the truth of these allegations, Petherick was removed from his post in 1864. (See also Chapters 5, 6 and 7.)

Petherick purchased a substantial number of objects when he led three separate trading expeditions between 1856 and 1858 through Bongo territory, and in 1858 when he visited Azande territory. This material was shipped back to England in 1859, and a large portion of it, if not all, was auctioned for him in London in 1862. This was most probably when H.L.F. Pitt Rivers obtained the items for his collection, which eventually became part of the founding collection of the Pitt Rivers Museum in Oxford. Those objects in Petherick's collection that entered the Henri Christy private collection in 1862 by auction were subsequently acquired by the British Museum during the 1870s.

Collection of Piaggia
Carlo Piaggia (1827-1882) was an Italian trader, mechanic and explorer. He was born near Lucca and came to Sudan in 1856 as caravan leader to some traders (including De Malzac) in the Bahr el-Ghazal region. In 1863-65 he explored the country of the Azande, and in 1876 he travelled to the region of Lake Kioga and the Victorian Nile. He died in Karkōj on the Blue Nile while on a journey of exploration to the river Sobat. Although a man of little learning, he was, besides a careful explorer, also a fine sketcher of Sudan's scenery and its inhabitants (which can be seen at the Archivio di Stato di Lucca). His ethnographic collection is of a considerable size. Those items collected before 1859 are housed at the Museo di Storia Naturale in Florence, while the rest has been preserved at the Museo Pigorini in Rome and the Museo Archeologico dell'Umbria in Perugia. Additional facts about Piaggia can be found in the appendix 7.

An account of the description of the Tinne-Heuglin collections

For the description of the provenance of each item or object in the catalogue, the following research has been made.

With the brief description Heuglin himself provided in 1863, 1865 and 1869, he occasionally indicated the provenance of his collection. Information could be retrieved regarding the ethnic or cultural group concerned. In the catalogue, Heuglin's 'attributions' as well as those made by other authors (e.g. Schweinfurth) have been mentioned as points of reference (Reference Literature). In particular, Schweinfurth's attributions (1874, 1875) and sometimes those by Ratzel (1888-89) were crucial in providing additional information regarding the provenance of the items.

Concerning the nineteenth-century Sudanese heritage which entered European museums in that era in some cases a more or less extensive survey has been published in the previous century.

In 1923-24, a description was published by E.S. Thomas on behalf of the Société Royale de Géographie d'Égypte on the collections of the Museum of the Royal Society in Cairo (founded in 1875 by Isma'il Pasha). The museum closed its doors in the second quarter of the twentieth century. The provenance of some objects out of the Tinne-Heuglin collections could be identified by tracing down similar items in the 1923-24 catalogue.

While drawing up an identification of the provenance of similar objects in the Tinne-Heuglin collections, I was grateful to be able to consult research conducted in Italy. This included Ezio Bassani's 1979 publication concerning the Piaggia collection in Florence, and Enrico Castelli's 1984 book concerning the other parts of Piaggia's collection and that of Antinori in Perugia and Venice. Furthermore, the Pitt Rivers Museum published an important study on its Petherick collection, providing ample descriptions and identifications on the internet (Sparks, 2005, http://southernsudan.prm.ox.ac.uk).

Notes Catalogue

1 'Mid November an ambassador of [the 'Niamaniam-Sultan'] Mofío appeared…[who] brought as a gift a very neatly elaborated wooden tub…' (Heuglin, von, 1869:224).

2 Heuglin, von, 1869:273.

3 Melly, G., *Lettres d'Egypte et de Nubie*, London, 1852. This private edition is essentially a translation of Melly's *Khartoum and the Blue and White Niles*, which was first published in 1851.

4 Melly, 1851 (1852), II: 96-122.

5 For Schuver, see Chapter 1, and note 16. By 1880, the market for ethnographic items no longer existed. Although Juan Maria Schuver does not refer to such a market in his extensive overview of Khartoum's markets, some objects in his collection (housed in the National Museum of Ethnology in Leiden) are from regions he never visited (notably the Azande and Darfur). These were presumably purchased in Khartoum at the market of ethnographic curios, which must have still existed (see: James, Baumann, Johnson, 1996: 269-281; Willink, 2007(2):71).

6 It concerns the collection of Musée du Quai Branly, inventory number 71.1930.54, referring to the series of objects recorded in 1856 as the nrs. 1230-1561. See: Castelli, 1984; 97-114. Sudan-collections of a still earlier date are Cailliaud's collection in the Musée

du Quai Branly, dating from c. 1821, and a collection of White Nile 'curios' in the Southwark Collection of the Cuming Museum in London, dating from before 1840.

7 *Inner-Afrika*, 1863: 107.

8 PM, 1865: 5-6.

9 Another route to the western and southern Azande was taken for the first time in 1869 by Georg Schweinfurth who traversed the Bongo country in a southerly direction.

10 Heuglin, von, 1869: 162.

11 As mentioned in *The Guide of the Society Natura Artis Magistra* of 1864, meant as a leaflet for the Ethnographic Museum at Amsterdam Zoo (Willink, 2007(1): 238).

12 PM, 1865: 5-6.

13 Heuglin, von, 1869: 213-214 and 162.

14 Heuglin, von, 1869: 224.

15 *Inner-Afrika*, 1863: 106.

16 Heuglin, von, 1865: 30.

17 Stocking, 1987: 271. For information on the collecting activities in West Central Africa by European museums and racial theories, see: Willink, 2007.

18 *Inner-Afrika*, 1863: 107.

19 Schildkrout & Keim (1998: 21) date the start of this ethnological hierarchy around 1875, with Schweinfurth's comments on the Mangbetu (1874). Heuglin definitely has to be considered a precursor to this development.

Schweinfurth, whose hierarchical concept had its origins in humanistically inspired German ethnology, has been erroneously associated by Schildkrout & Keim with the rise of colonial imperialism (see Introduction note 10).

20 August Petermann: 'Probably the transverse pieces are struck and not the earthen vessels, which merely amplify the sounds. This kind of musical instrument is found in different forms in almost all places inhabited by negroes, in the whole of S. Africa, Brazil, etc., but also among the Indians of Equador, Honduras, Guatemala, and the Malayans of the Indian Archipelago, Indo-China and other places. Nearly everywhere the instrument is called *marimba*. Illustrations of it are to be found in Livingstone's "Missionary Travels in South Africa" etc.'

21 In a footnote, Heuglin adds: 'The race called by Kleincznik *Kretsch*, who were said to live on the road to Hoferat el Nahas above the junction of the Jur and Ghazal, or on a tributary to the latter flowing due west, is called Kerej. They belong, like the Qolo and Andóqo, to the Fertit race and may certainly be identified with Vayssières Korèk.'

22 Heuglin refers to the first edition (Paris, 1826) of Denham's *Narrative of Travels and Discoveries in Northern and Central Africa, in the Years 1822, 1823, and 1824.*

23 Heuglin, von, 1865: 30.

24 *Inner-Afrika*, 1863: 106, 107.

25 See: Appendix 7, note 9.

26 See: Willink, 2007: 293-299.

27 The non-reference to statues in travelogues on Sudan could provide a possible explanation. After Schweinfurth's illustration of some Bongo cult statues (1875 Tab. VIII, 5, 7), however, no critical comment has ever been published on their visual appearance. See: Willink, 2007: 7-11; also regarding the aesthetic criticism in Western travelogues from 1855-1880 regarding the West Central African cult statues. It was only after 1920 that missionaries discovered that the Azande-manufactured sculptures were kept in secret places (see: Willink, 2011).

28 See: Bunzl & Glenn Penny, 2003. The introduction briefly mentions some characteristics of German nineteenth-century anthropology and ethnology.

29 Regarding the ethnographic specimens of the Azande culture, this observation of cannibalism caused a remarkable tension between their 'inhuman behaviour' and their industriously fabricated utensilia. As Kean would state in 1884: 'The form and ornamental designs of their utensils display real artistic taste (…). Here again the observation has been made, that the tribes most addicted to cannibalism also excel in mental qualities and physical energy.' (*Ethnology of Egyptian Sudán*, 1884: 6). Schweinfurth's conclusion on the matter was as follows: '…Taking all things into account, as well what I heard as what I saw, I can have no hesitation in asserting that the Niam-niam are anthropophagi…' (1874 II: 18). For an authoritative voice on Azande 'cannibalism' in the nineteenth century, see Evans-Pritchard's remarks (in Chapter 3 note 26).

30 Heuglin, von, 1869: 273.

31 In 1878, four objects out of Alexine Tinne's collection were sold to the British Museum by A.W. Franks, a member of the board of the Liverpool Public Museum (see catalogue: 48c, 51, 54 and 55).

32 Dampierre, de, 1991: 92.

33 The following short biographies have been derived from Hill, 1967.

34 Castelli, 1987.

Catalogue
Alexine Tinne collection

List of objects, collected by Alexine Tinne before and during the Bahr el-Ghazal expedition (Jan. 1863-December 1864).

References are made to similar items, collected by other contemporary Sudan-travellers.
A catalogue-number of the Tinne-collection refers to items in other collections by a subdivision (for instance: 2a, 2b and 28c, 28d, 28e, 28f, 28g).

Details, as acquisition date, dimensions, accession numbers, reference literature and the museum where the item is registered, are mentioned in the additional list of data at the end of the catalogue (pp. 425-434).

▲ 1
Pipe
Ethnic group: Bongo (Dõr)
Description: Pipe in black earth the stem bound with flat
 steel and copper wire; stem broken.

▼ 1A
Detail

2
String with pegs
Ethnic group: Azande [?]
Description: Cylindrical pieces of wood, strung upon a leather thong

◄ 2A
Necklet

▼ 2B
Necklet

3
Head ornament
Ethnic group: Shilluk
Description: Headdress of skin and hair from neck of lion [?]

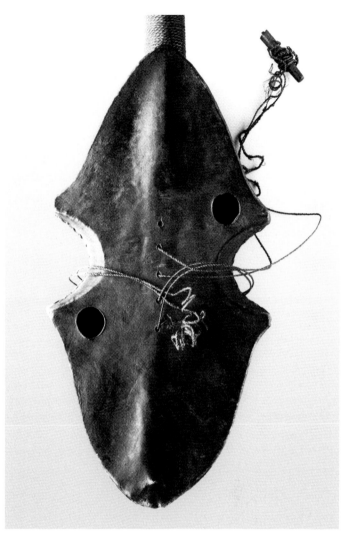

4A+B
Harp
Ethnic group: Azande
Description: harp of carved wood & bark,
with pin of bone to secure the strings of fibre (broken).

5
Canister
Ethnic group: Azande
Description: Canister
of bark, the top and base
of wood

334

▲ 6
Basket
Ethnic group: Azande [?]
Description: Plaited basket with square
woven base, over sewn rim

▼ 7
Bowl
Ethnic group: Bongo (Dõr)
Description: Bowl in dark-coloured earth;
ornamented. Broken.

▲ 8   ▼ 8A
Bed or bench   Detail
Ethnic group: Azande
Description: Bed or bench of bamboo, on base of wood.

▲ 9
Bell
Ethnic group: Azande
Description: Iron bell sounding body with two holes in top and no clapper.

◀ 9A
Bell

▲ 9B
Bell

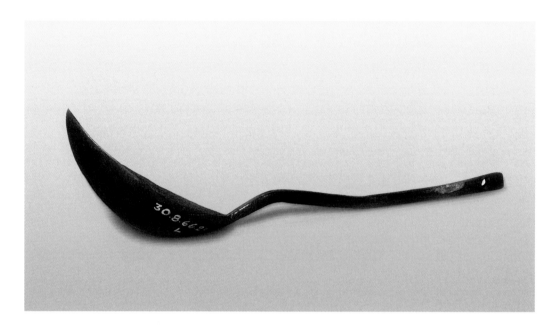

▲ 10
Spoon
Ethnic group: Bongo (Dōr)
Description: Spoon of dark-brown horn [?] with oval bowl and upwards
sloping handle with bend near bottom of handle. Hole in top of handle.

▼ 10A
Spoon

11
Tobacco cake
Ethnic group: Bongo (Dōr)
Description: elliptical block of tobacco, with holes all over top surface, rounded top surface and flat base.

▲ 12
Rope
Ethnic group: Dinka [?]
Description: fragment of rope with two wooden pegs

▼ 12A
Rope

▲ 13
Basket
Ethnic group: Kababish, Bisharin
Description: Basket of cane, circular,
with bands stained red.

▼ 14
Basket and cover
Ethnic group: Kababish, Bisharin
Description: Basket and Cover; cane, oval,
with ornamental designs stained red and brown.

▲ 15
Cover
Ethnic group: Kababish, Bisharin
Description: Cover of a basket; cane,
oval, with ornamental designs stained
red and brown.

▼ 16
Basket
Ethnic group: Kababish, Bisharin
Description: Basket; cane, circular,
coiled panels with ornamental designs
stained red and brown.

342

▲ 17
Tray
Ethnic group: Kababish, Bisharin
Description: tray (or cover) with ornamental
designs stained red and brown.

▼ 18
Cover
Ethnic group: Kababish, Bisharin.
Description: Table-Dish Cover, cane, bound
and mounted with shagreen, coloured straw, and
a coloured parchment topping, conical.

▲ 19
Cover
Ethnic group: Kababish, Bisharin.
Description: Table-dish cover conical; of cane
work; the rim and upper portion stained in red
and black.

344

▲ 20
Cushion case
Ethnic group: Kababish, Bisharin
Description: Cushion or pillowcase, cane,
herring-bone centre & numerous border patterns
stained in red and brown.

▲ 21
Pair of baskets
Ethnic group: Kababish,
Bisharin
Description: two pannier-shaped
baskets in coloured cane.

► 22
Basket
Ethnic group: Kababish,
Bisharin
Description: pannier-shaped basket
in coloured cane, with strap.

346

23
Cup
Ethnic group: North-East Sudan [Funj?]
Description: Gourd cup, the foot ornamented
with coloured cane work.

▲ 24
Animal figure
Ethnic group: people Bahr el-Ghazal
region
Description: Wooden figure of 4 legged
animal, middle of body decorated with
incised linear design.

◄ 24A
Animal figure

▲ 25
Tub
Ethnic group: Azande
Description: Tub, oval-shaped
wooden bowl, exterior decorated
with quarter sections of
ribbed grooves

▶ 25A
Detail

350

26
Pounding-dish
Ethnic group: Azande [?]
Description: Pounding-dish, oval, in wood with two handles,
one perforated for suspension, and footed.

▶ **27**
Harp
Ethnic group: Bongo, Mittu [?]
Description: Stringed instrument
from the Mittoo people – a sounding
board made of cleansed goat-skin
over a wooden frame, supplied with
6 sounding holes, over which
5 strings are stretched.

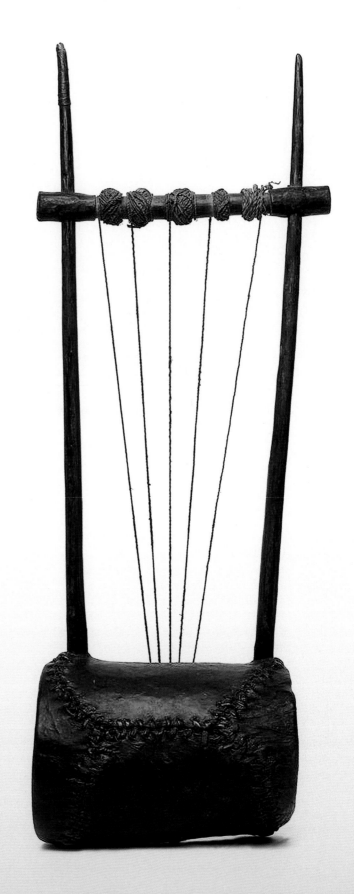

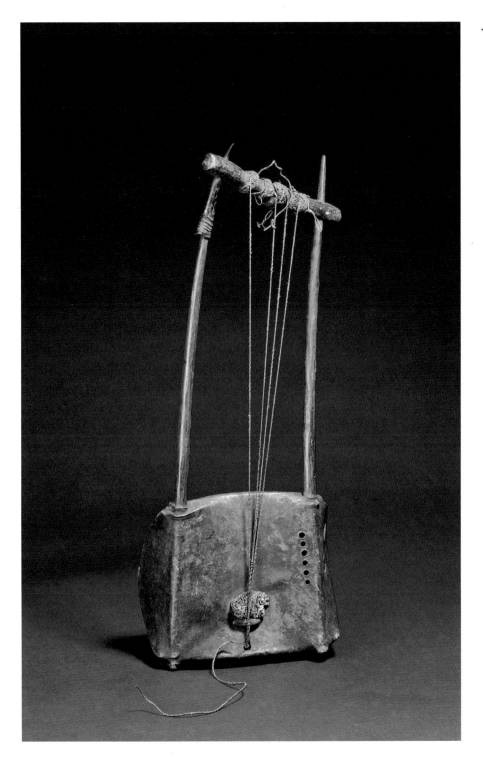

◄ 28
Harp
Ethnic group: Azande
Description: harp of curved wood surmounted
by a carved female head (the ornaments atop
broken off; pins to secure the five strings
of hemp; lower portion of wood, hollow,
covered with leather and having two
circular orifices. Strings broken.

▲ 28A
Detail

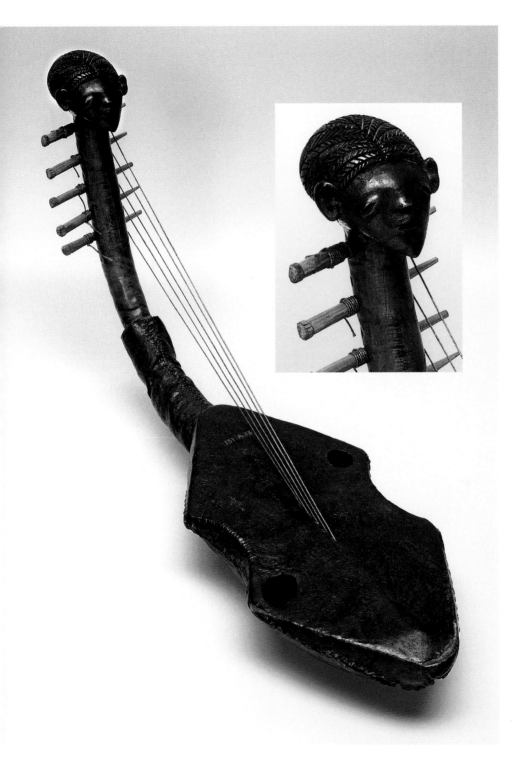

◄ 28B
Harp

◄ 28C
Detail

▲ 28D
Harp

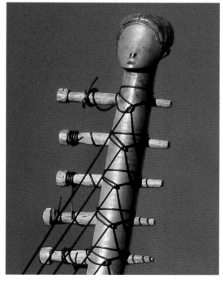

▶ 28E
Detail

▲ 28F
Harp

◀ 28G
Detail

▲ 29
Adze
Ethnic group: Jur.
Description: adze with iron blade

▼ 29A
Adze

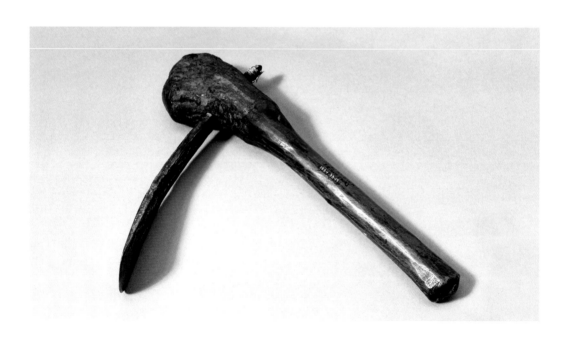

358

30
Bowl
Ethnic group: Bongo (Dōr)
Description: Bowl of black pottery with ornamentation (broken and repaired)

▲ 31
Lid
Ethnic group: Kababish,
Bisharin
Description: Basketry
lid (circular), coiled,
multicoloured (or
platter with foot)

▶ 31A
Detail

32
Hat
Ethnic group: Dinka, Nuer.
Description: Hat, of plaited cane or bamboo, covered with red and blue seeds,
secured by a resinous cement; handle leather.

▲ 33
Girdle
Ethnic group: Bisharin [?]
Description: Girdle composed of strips
of fine leather suspended from a cotton line
dyed red and ornamented with cowrie shells.

▼ 34
Girdle
Ethnic group: Bisharin [?]
Description: Girdle composed of strips of fine leather
suspended from a cotton line dyed red and ornamented
with cowrie shells, red glass-beads and mother-of-pearl
buttons.

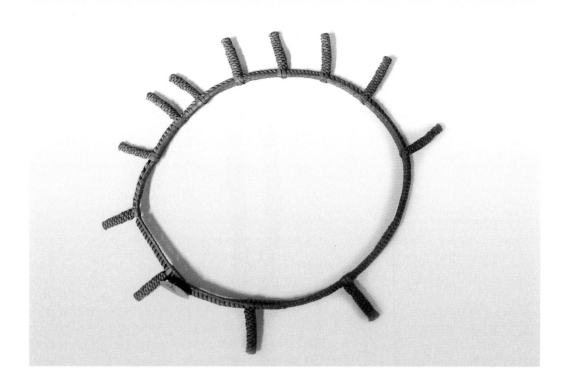

▲ 35
Ornament
Ethnic group: Bari [?]
Description: Ornament for the head, or
necklace, of fine canework, circular with
12 cylindrical projections.

▼ 36
Necklace
Ethnic group: Shilluk (Shuli, Bari?)
Description: Necklace composed of black seeds.

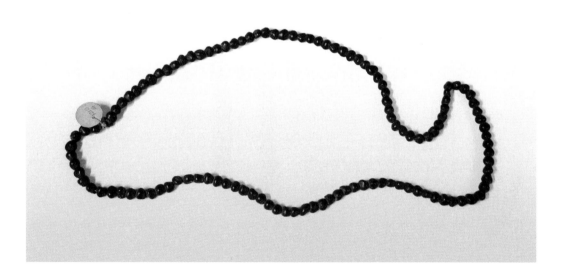

► 37
Necklace
Ethnic group:
Nilotic people
Description: Necklace
composed of black
seeds and beads of
scarlet glass.

364

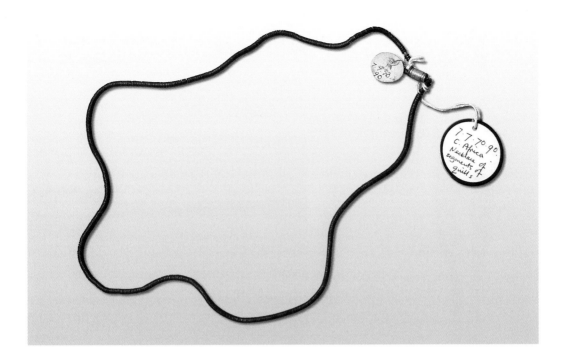

▲ 38
Necklace
Ethnic group: Shilluk, Bari [?]
Description: necklace with black disc
beads (shell).

▼ 39
Necklace
Ethnic group: Nilotic people [?]
Description: Suspender ornament, composed of
four strings of beads in coloured glass, conjoined.

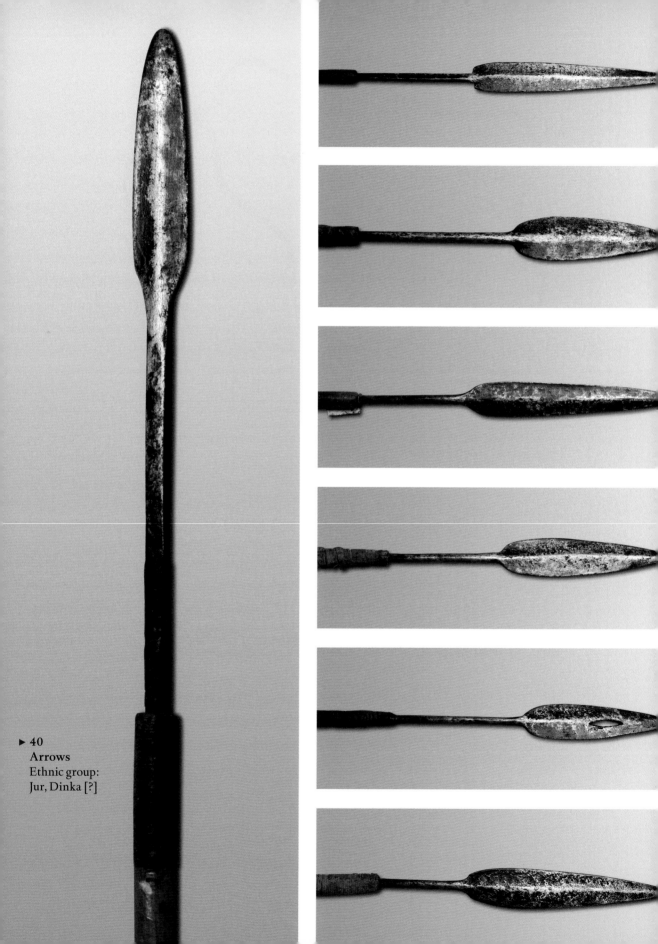

▶ 40
Arrows
Ethnic group:
Jur, Dinka [?]

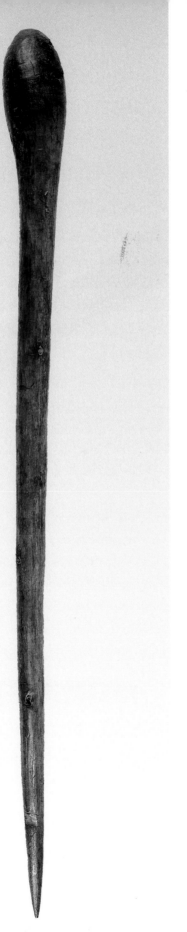

◄ 41
Club
Ethnic group: Dinka
Description: War club of light
coloured wood, with large oval head.

▼ 41A
Club

367

▲ 42
Club
Ethnic group: Bari
Description: Tapered
wooden club with
fibre-bound base or
grip, longitudinal
ridges on lower shaft,
with covering of
woven hemp on
handle.

▶ 42A
Club

368

43
Club
Ethnic group: Bari [?]
Description: Multi-ribbed wooden club with pointed butt.

▲ 44.1
Cover
Ethnic group: Kababish, Bisharin.
Description: cover for table dish,
coiled cane, stained in patterns.

▼ 44.2
Tray
Ethnic group: Kababish, Bisharin.
Description: tray or dish, coiled cane,
stained in patterns.

45
Tray or cover
Ethnic group: Kababish, Bisharin.
Description: tray or cover for table dish, coiled cane, stained in patterns.

46
Basket
Ethnic group: Kababish, Bisharin.
Description: Basket of plaited grass edged with leather and lined with cowrie shells.

47
Girdle
Ethnic group: Kababish, Bisharin.
Description: Girdle made of leaf (palm), seeds, cord (coconut fibre), and enclosed seeds.

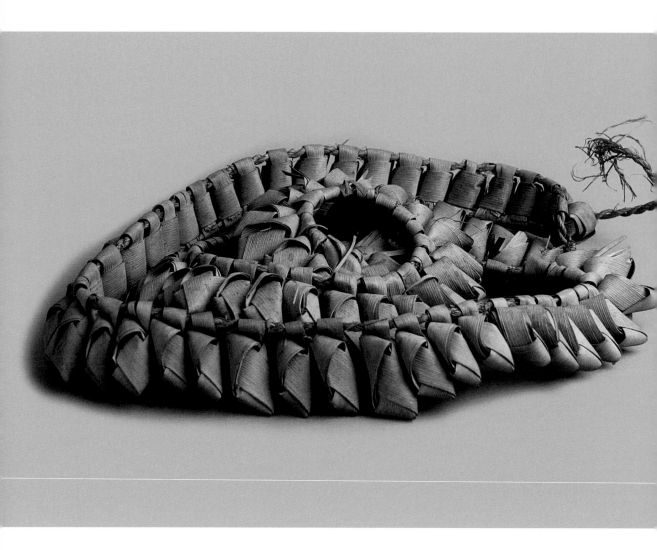

48.1
Girdle
Ethnic group: Kababish, Bisharin.
Description: Girdle made of leaf (palm), seeds, cord (coconut fibre),
and enclosed seeds

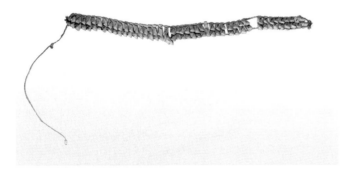

▲ 48.2
Girdle
Ethnic group: Kababish, Bisharin.
Description: Girdle made of leaf (palm),
seeds, cord (coconut fibre), and enclosed
seeds

◄ 48.3
Girdle
Ethnic group: Kababish, Bisharin
Description: Girdle made of leaf (palm),
seeds, cord (coconut fibre).

▲ 49
Throwing knife
Ethnic group: Azande, Jur
Description: Z-shaped
throwing weapon [*Pingah*].
The knife is decorated with
chased work and has a grip
of woven string made of
plant fibre.

▶ 49A
Detail

376

▲ 49B
Throwing knife

▲ 49C
Throwing knife

50
Dagger
Ethnic group: Azande
Description: Dagger with
iron blade, the handle
bound round with wire

◄ 50A
Detail

◄ 50B
Pair of daggers

379

51
Dagger
Ethnic group: Azande
Description: Dagger
made of iron, wood,
wire (iron).

▲ 52
Bench
Ethnic group: Bongo (Dŏr)
Description: Bench, ladle-shaped,
four footed & handled

▼ 52A
Underside of bench

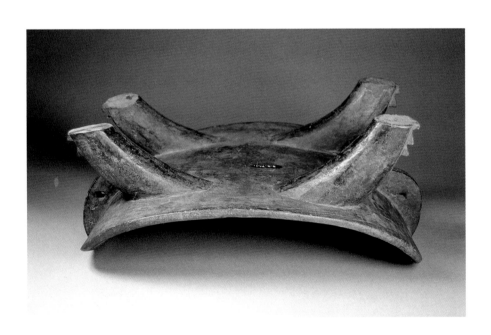

▲ 52B
Bench

▲ 52C
Bench

▼ 52D
Bench

▼ 52E
Bench

53
Bench
Ethnic group: Bongo (Dōr)
Description: Small bench of wood, circular; four footed (one broken and replaced by nail)

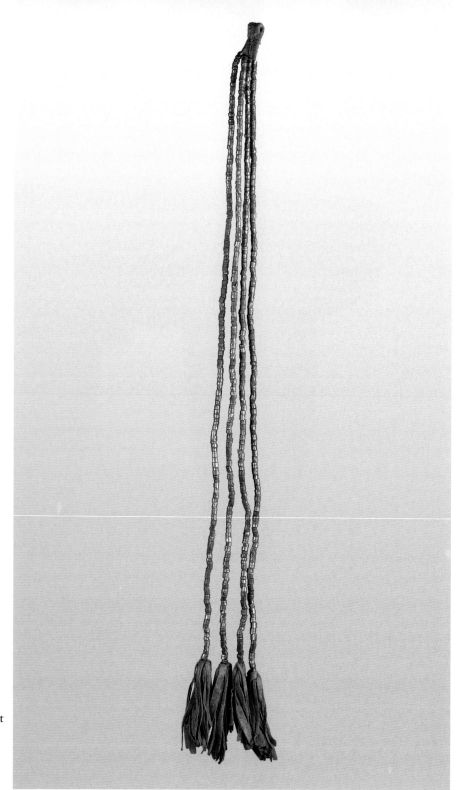

▶ 54
Ornament
Ethnic group: Jur [?]
Description: Ornament
made of iron beads
and red leather.

384

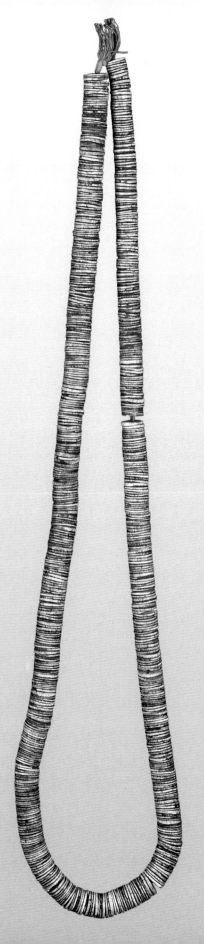

◀ 55
Belt or necklace
Ethnic group: Shilluk [?]
Description: Belt or
Necklace made of beads
(shell), fibre (cord).

▲ 55A
Belt or necklace

▼ 55B
Belt or necklace

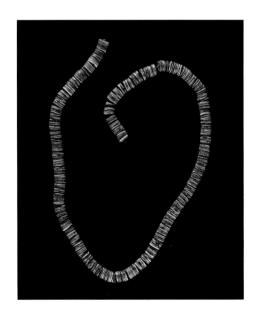

385

Catalogue
Von Heuglin collection

List of objects, collected by Heuglin during the Bahr el-Ghazal expedition (Jan. 1863-December 1864), in the Linden-Museum Stuttgart.

References are made to similar items, collected by other contemporary Sudan-travellers.
A catalogue-number of the Heuglin-collection refers to items in other collections by a subdivision (for instance: 57b, 57c, 57d and 65a, 65b, 65c).

Details, as acquisition date, dimensions, accession numbers, reference literature and the museum where the item is registered, are mentioned in the additional list of data at the end of the catalogue (pp. 435-439).

56
Quiver
Ethnic group: people of Dar Fertit [Kresh?]

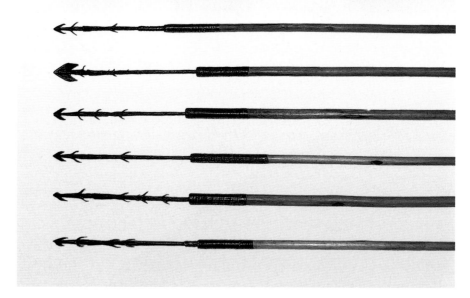

► 56.1
Arrows
Ethnic group:
people of Dar
Fertit [Kresh?]

► 56.2

► 56.3

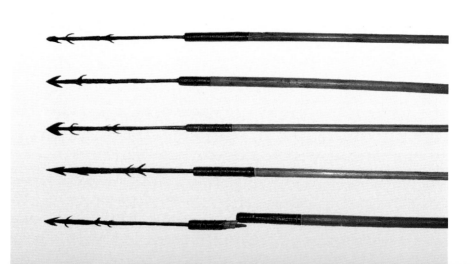

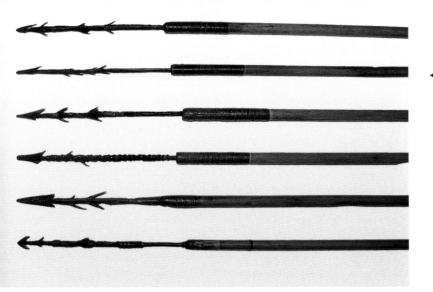

◄ 56.4

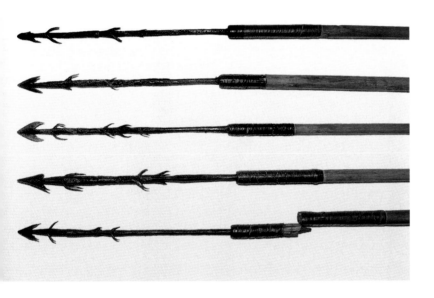

◄ 56.5

◄ 56.6

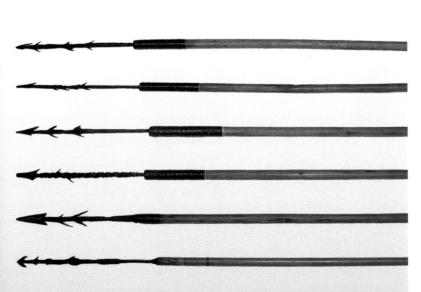

389

57+ 57A
**Sickle-bladed knife
and detail**
Ethnic group: Azande,
Mangbetu
Description: ceremonial
sickle-bladed knife, with
three holes in the blade.
Its middle decorated
with copper band and
twisted iron wire.

390

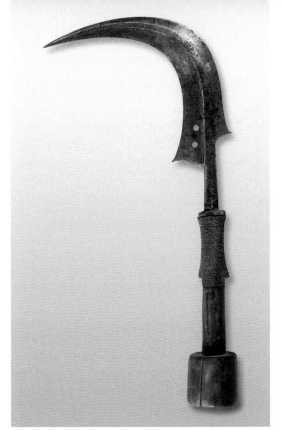 

▲ 57B
   Sickle-bladed knife

▲ 57C
   Sickle-bladed knife

▼ 57D
   Sickle-bladed knife

▲ 58
Throwing weapon
Ethnic group: Azande, Jur
Description: Z-shaped
throwing knife [*Pingah*].
The knife is decorated
with chased work and
has a grip of woven
string made of plant
fibre.

► 58A
Detail

392

▲ 58B+C
Throwing weapon
and detail

◄58D
Throwing weapon

393

▲ 59
Spoon
Ethnic group: Bongo (Dōr)
Description: Spoon of dark-brown horn with
oval bowl and upwards sloping handle with bend
near bottom of handle. Hole in top of handle.

▼ 60
Spoon
Ethnic group: Bongo (Dōr)
Description: Spoon of dark-brown horn with
oval bowl and upwards sloping handle with bend
near bottom of handle. Hole in top of handle.

61
Spoon
Ethnic group: Jur, Bongo
Description: Spoon of
dark-brown horn with
oval bowl and zig-zag
curved handle. Hole in
top of handle.

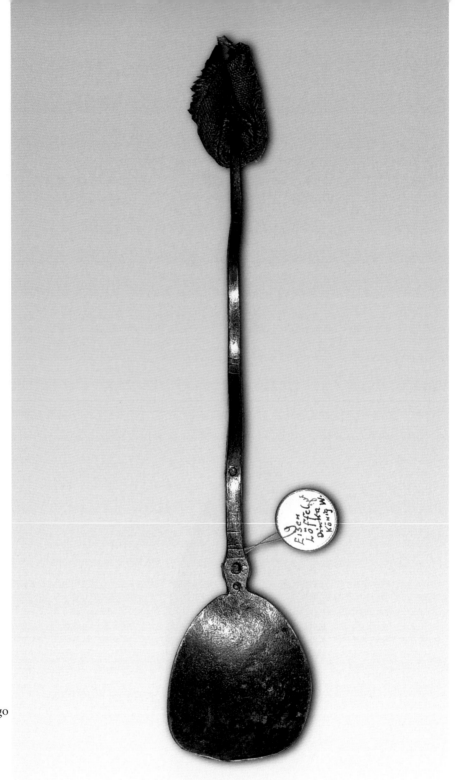

62
Spoon
Ethnic group: Jur, Bongo
Description: Spoon
of forged iron with
zig-zag curved handle.
Hole in top of handle
with cord of woven fibre.

396

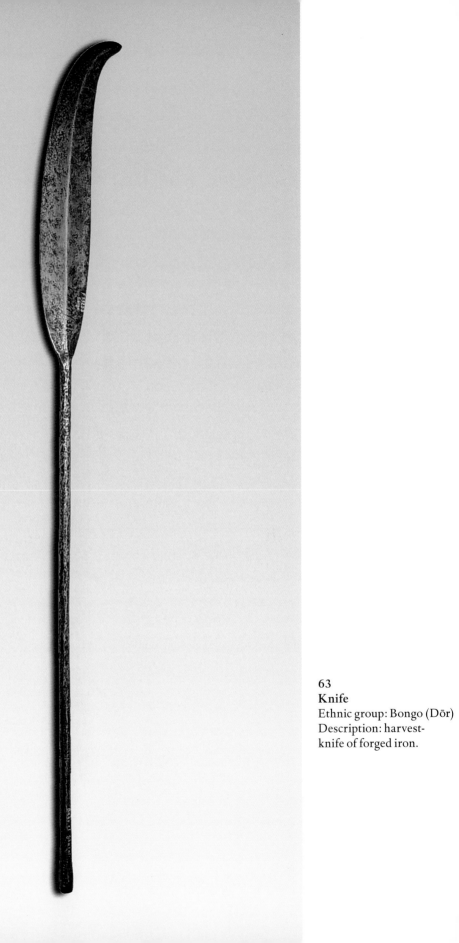

63
Knife
Ethnic group: Bongo (Dōr)
Description: harvest-
knife of forged iron.

64
Spear
Ethnic group: Bongo
(Dōr)
Description: spear for
fishing of forged iron.

▲ 65
'Spear points'
Ethnic group: Bongo (Dōr)
Description: objects out of forged iron,
flat-pointed, meant as money.

▲ 65A, B
'Spear points'

▼ 65C
'Spear point'

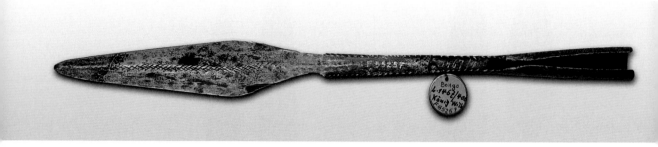

▲ 66
Spear
Ethnic group: Bongo (Dōr)
Description: point with shaft of
forged iron.

▼ 67
'Spear point'
Ethnic group: Bongo (Dōr)
Description: object out of forged iron,
flatted pointed, meant as money.

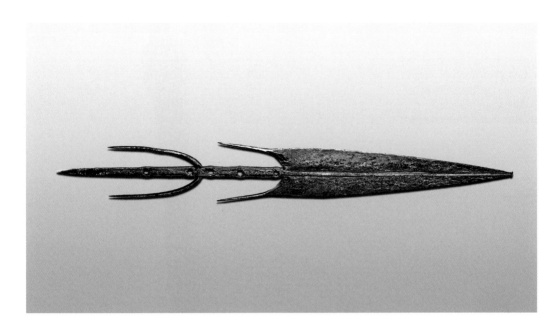

▲ 67A
   'Spear points'

▼ 67B
   'Spear points'

► 68
Tobacco pipe
Ethnic group: Bongo (Dōr)
Description: composite
pipe of clay head, wooden
stem with sculptured
human half-figure on top.

▼ 68A
Detail

402

◀ 68B
Detail

▼ 68C
Detail

▼ 68D
Tobacco pipe

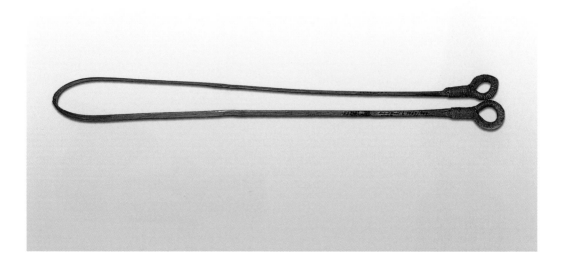

▲ 69
Bowstring
Ethnic group: people of Dar Fertit [Kresh?]
Description: bowstring with cord wrapped
around its ends, stabilised with wood.

▼ 70
Waistband, girdle
Ethnic group: people of Nyambar region [Bari?]
Description: girdle, braided and spun with threads
of fibre, reptile skin stitched at the ends.

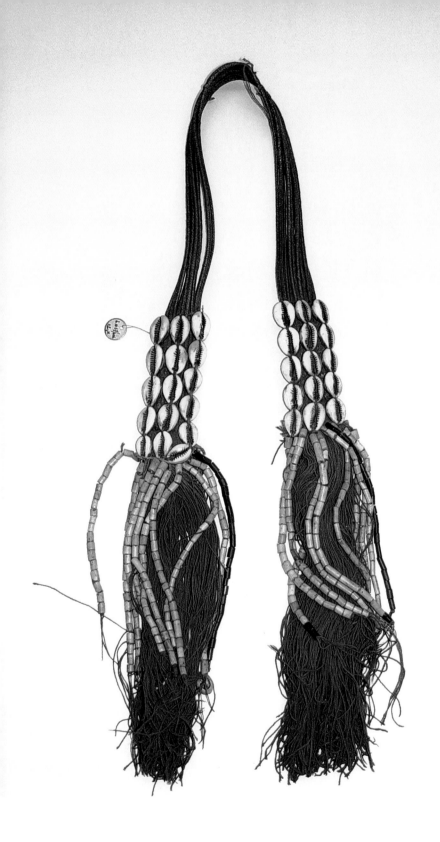

71
Waistband, girdle
Ethnic group: people of
Nyambar region [Bari?]
Description: girdle,
braided and spun with
threads, stitched with
kauri-shells, glass-pearls
(white, blue)

405

 72
Apron
Ethnic group: people of Nyambar region [Bari?]
Description: women's apron of woven fibre,
stitched with kauri-shells, glass-pearls (white/
blue/black/red).

▶ 72A
Apron

406

▲ 73
Waistband, girdle
Ethnic group: Bongo (Dōr)
Description: girdle of dyed and braided,
twisted grass and plant-fibres

▲ 74
Waistband, girdle
Ethnic group: people of Dar Fertit [Kresh?]
Description: girdle of braided fibre, ends leather-stitched

▲ 75
Necklace
Ethnic group: Jur
Description: necklace of twisted plant-fibre with kauri-shells and glass-pearls (blue/white/red),
 the blue ones facetted.

76
Necklace
Ethnic group: Jur
Description: necklace of twisted plant-fibre with glass-pearls (blue/white).

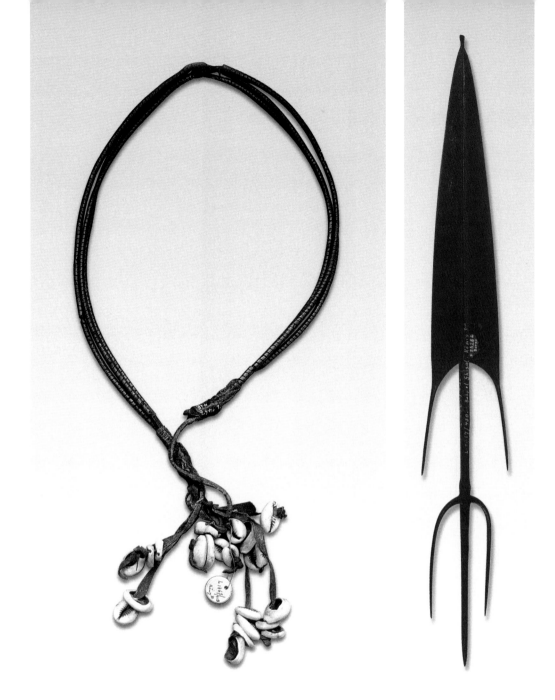

▲ 77
Collar
Ethnic group: Jur
Description: leather collar winded with spirals
of forged copper, kauri's attached at the end.

▲ 78
'Spear point'
Ethnic group: Bongo (Dōr)
Description: object out of forged iron,
flat-pointed, meant as money.

411

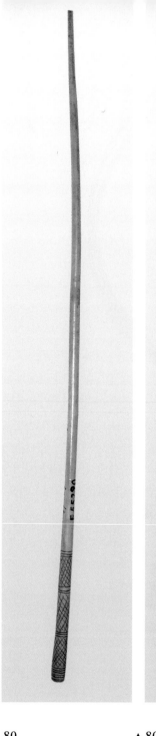

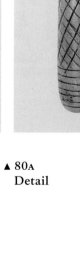

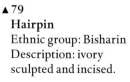

▲ 79
Hairpin
Ethnic group: Bisharin
Description: ivory
sculpted and incised.

▲ 80
Hairpin
Ethnic group: Bisharin
Description: ivory
sculpted and incised.

▲ 80A
Detail

▲ 80B
Hairpin
Ethnic group: Azar
Description: ivory,
sculpted and incise

412

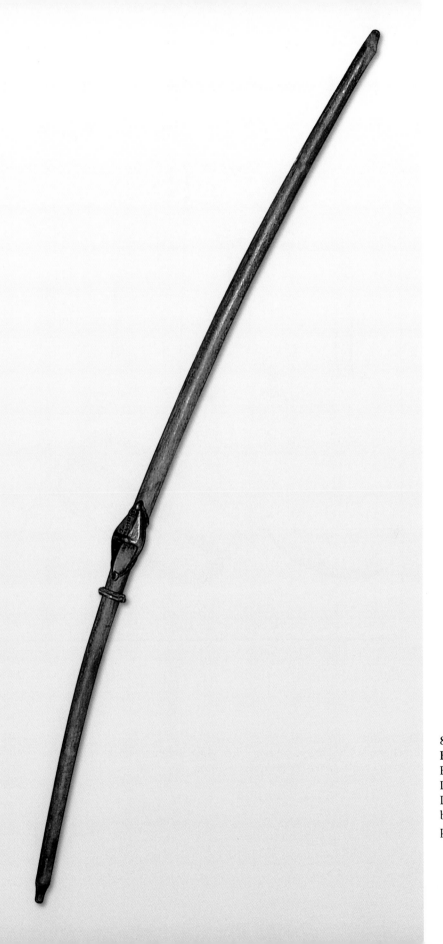

81
Bow
Ethnic group: people of
Dar Fertit [Kresh?]
Description: wooden
bow, cut, sculpted, with
pyrographic decoration.

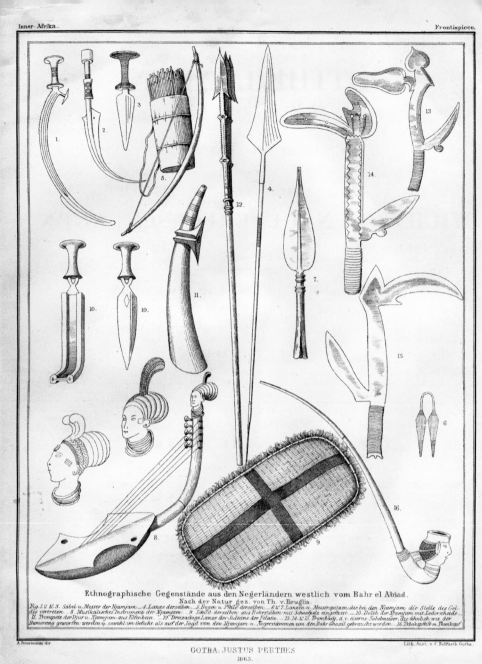

Ethnographische Gegenstände aus den Negerländern westlich vom Bahr el Abiad.
Nach der Natur gez. von Th. v. Heuglin.

Fig. 1.2 & 3. Sabel u. Messer der Njamjam. – 4. Lanze derselben. – 5. Bogen u. Pfeile derselben. – 6 & 7. Lanzen u. Messerspitzen, die bei den Njamjam, die Stelle des Geldes vertreten. – 8 Musikalisches Instrument der Njamjam. – 9. Schild derselben aus Rohrstäben mit Schaafpelz eingefasst. – 10. Dolch der Njamjam mit Lederscheide. – 11. Trompete der Djur u. Njamjam aus Elfenbein. – 12. Dreizackige Lanze der Sultane der Felata. – 13.14. & 15. Trombasch, d. i. eiserne Sabelmesser, die ähnlich wie der Bumerang geworfen werden u. sowohl im Gefecht als auf der Jagd von den Njamjam u. Negerstämmen von den Bahr Ghasal gebraucht werden. 16. Tabakspfeife m. Thonkopf.

A. Petermann dir.

GOTHA: JUSTUS PERTHES
1863.

Lith. Anst. v. C. Bellfarth Gotha.

82
Illustration
'Ethnographische Gegenstände aus den Negerländern westlich vom Bahr el Abiad', in: *Inner-Afrika* (Frontispiece), Gotha, 1863.

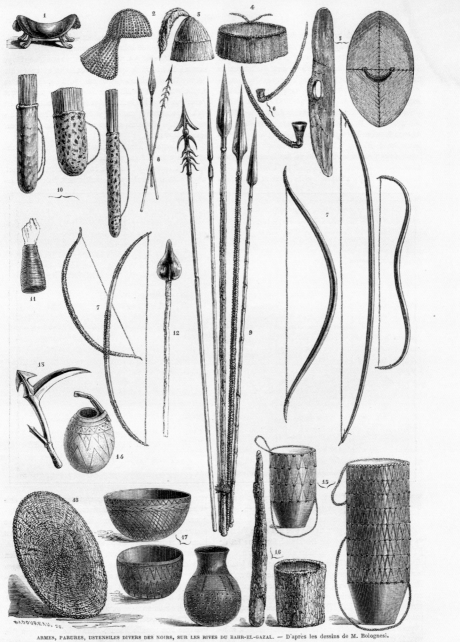

ARMES, PARURES, USTENSILES DIVERS DES NOIRS, SUR LES RIVES DU BAHR-EL-GAZAL. — D'après les dessins de M. Bolognesi.

1. Siége portatif. — 2. Bonnet en *cauris* (cypræa). — 3. Bonnet en paille. — 4. *Rahad*, pagne des jeunes filles. — 5. Boucliers, l'un en bo's, l'autre en peau. — 6, 7. Pipes, Arcs, quelques-uns recouverts de fines et fortes lanières de cuir. — 8. Flèches. — 9. Lances, manche en bambou. — 10. Carquois dont deux en peau de panthère. — 11. Bracelet. — 12. *Molod*, sorte de bêche. — 13. Trombach ou sabre à plusieurs pointes et à deux tranchants. — 14. Calebasse. — 15. *Nongaza*, tambours de guerre. — 16. Pilon et mortier pour le maïs. — 17. *Gazas*, calebasse, et *bournua*, cruche en terre noire ou rouge. — 18. Sorte de *tabaka*, couverture en paille pour garder le grain, le lait, etc.

83
Illustration
'Armes, Parures, Ustensils divers des Noirs, sur les Rives du Bahr-el-Gazal', in:
Lejean, G. (III), 1862, Ill. 'D'après les dessins de M. [Castel]Bolognesi'.

The Tinne collection
Appendix

84
Projectile, Weapon
Ethnic group: Touaregs
Description: Projectile, or hand weapon for cutting or throwing,
with leather-covered handle ("Shing-el-Mingl", a sword to throw at the legs).

85
Pair of sandals belonging to A. Tinne

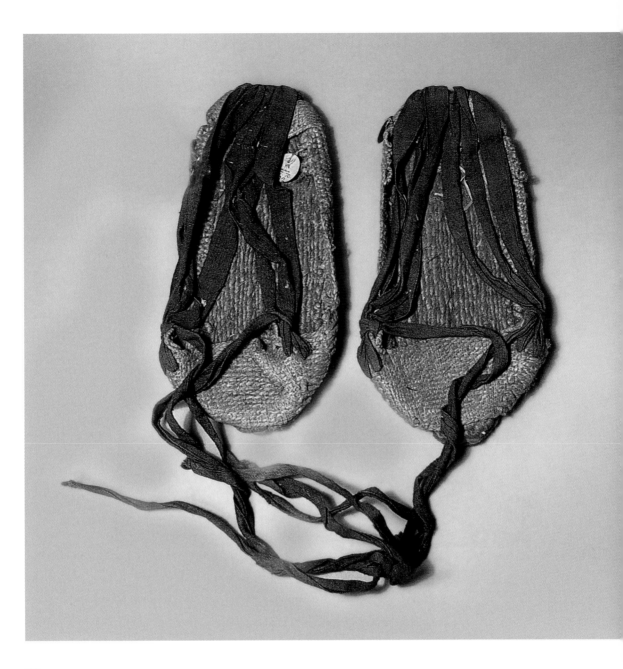

86
Pair of sandals belonging to A. Tinne

87
Scarf
Region: Maghreb (North-African Coast)
Description: scarf, woven of coloured silk.

420

88
Scarf
Region: Maghreb (North-African Coast)
Description: scarf, woven of coloured silk.

89
Photo of Alexine Tinne's house at Tripoli

90
Photo, representing a group of Touareg leaders at Tripoli

Catalogue
Alexine Tinne collection

List of objects, collected by Alexine Tinne before and during the Bahr el-Ghazal expedition (Jan. 1863-December 1864).

References are made to similar items, collected by other contemporary Sudan-travellers.
A catalogue-number of the Tinne-collection refers to items in other collections by a subdivision (for instance: 2a, 2b and 28c, 28d, 28e, 28f, 28g).

Details, as acquisition date, dimensions, accession numbers, reference literature and the museum where the item is registered, are mentioned in the additional list of data here below.

1 Pipe
World Museum Liverpool, National Museums Liverpool
Inventory number: WML 30.8.66.3
Acquisition: donated by J.A. Tinne, 1866
Material: wood, metal and clay
Dimensions: L. 59 x W. 8 x 5,1 cm.
Ref. lit.:
Lejean, 1862, Ill. Coll. Castelbolognesi 'Bahr el-Ghazal' (fig.6), Heuglin, von, 1865: 5 ('Bongo'), Schweinfurth, 1875 tab.v, 30, tab. x, 1 ('Bongo'), Ratzel, 1885, 1: 513 (no attribution), Bassani, 1979, nr.185 ('Bongo').
1A Detail
2 String with pegs
World Museum Liverpool, National Museums Liverpool
Inventory number: WML 30.8.66.7
Acquisition: donated by J.A. Tinne, 1866

Material: wood, leather, fibre
Dimensions: L. 17,5 cm.
Ref. lit.:
Petherick, 1869, I: 249 ('Djour'), Schweinfurth 1875 tab. xiv, 17 (Azande ['Niam Niam']).
2A Necklet
Museo di Storia Naturale, Venice
Collection Miani, Inv. nr. 6902 (registered as: 'before 1860, Bari'), Museo di Storia Naturale, Venice
Material: wood, animal hide, iron and fibre
Dimensions: L. 76 cm.
2B Necklet
Collection Petherick, Inv.nr. 1884.75.3 (registered as: 'collected 1856-'58, Bongo'), Pitt Rivers Museum, Oxford
Materials: wood, animal bone, animal hide
Dimensions: L. 30 cm.

3 Head ornament
World Museum Liverpool, National Museums Liverpool
Inventory number: WML 30.8.66.9
Acquisition: donated by J.A. Tinne, 1866
Material: leather (skin) and hair
Dimensions: Diam. 33,5 x 3,3 x 2,5 cm.
Ethnic group: Shilluk
Description: Headdress of skin and hair from neck of lion [?]
Ref. lit.:
Ratzel, 1885, I: 491, 492 ('Shilluk-head-dress').

4A+B Harp
World Museum Liverpool, National Museums Liverpool
Inventory number: WML 30.8.66.12 (vanished)
Acquisition: donated by J.A. Tinne, 1866
Material: wood, bark, bone and leather
Dimensions: Old records indicate in 2 pieces a) body and b) neck – measurements incomplete
a) L. 48,2 x 19 cm.
b) L. 41 cm.
Ref. lit.:
Inner-Afrika, 1863: Illustration, 'Ethnographische Gegenstände' (Azande ['Njamjam'], Heuglin, von, 1869: 216 (Azande ['Niamaniam']), Schweinfurth, 1874 I: 445, II: 26, Schweinfurth, 1875: Tab. XIV, nr. 6 (Azande ['Niam-Niam']), Ratzel, 1885, I: 534 (Azande ['Njam-Njam']), Castelli, 1984: 82 ('Azande'), De Dampierre, 1991: 81-87 ('Azande').

5 Canister
World Museum Liverpool, National Museums Liverpool
Inventory number: WML 30.8.66.13
Acquisition: donated by J.A. Tinne, 1866
Material: leather (skin) and fibre
Dimensions: H. 24 x 13 cm.
Ref. lit.:

Schweinfurth 1875 tab. XIII, nr. 21 (Azande ['Niam-Niam'], representing an identical object on a tripod base).

6 Basket
World Museum Liverpool, National Museums Liverpool
Inventory number: WML 30.8.66.19
Acquisition: donated by J.A. Tinne, 1866
Material: fibre
Dimensions: H. 11 x 16,5 cm.
Ref. lit.:
Schweinfurth 1875 tab. XIII, nr. 22 (Azande ['Niam Niam']).

7 Bowl
World Museum Liverpool, National Museums Liverpool
Inventory number: WML 30.8.66.20
Acquisition: donated by J.A. Tinne, 1866
Material: earth
Dimensions: H. 16,5 x 16 x 9 cm.
Ref. lit. :
Lejean, 1862, ill. Coll. Castelbolognesi 'Bahr el-Ghazal' (nr. 17: 'bournua, cruche en terre noire…'), Schweinfurth 1875 tab.v, nr. 2 ('Bongo').

8 Bed or bench
World Museum Liverpool, National Museums Liverpool
Inventory number: WML 30.8.66.21
Acquisition: donated by J.A. Tinne, 1866
Material: wood (bamboo) and fibre
Dimensions: L. 115,5 x W. 49,1 x 23,5 cm.
Ref. lit.:
Schweinfurth (1875, tab. XVII, nr.18) presents a rather identical bed or bench with concave-shaped feet as 'Monbuttu' (also in: Ratzel, 1885, I: 542); Schweinfurth (1874, II: 26) presents a somewhat identical shaped bed or bench on prolonged feet, describing it as 'the ordinary bench in the interior of every Niam-Niam hut', named 'Kittipallah' (Schweinfurth 1875, tab. XI, nr. 7).

8A Detail

9 Bell
World Museum Liverpool, National Museums Liverpool
Inventory number: WML 30.8.66.22
Acquisition: donated by J.A. Tinne, 1866
Material: iron
Dimensions: H. 9,7 x W. 7 x 5 cm.
Ref. lit.:
Schweinfurth, 1874, II: 29, Schweinfurth, 1875, Tab. XIV, 8 (Azande ['Niam-Niam']), Junker, 1889, I: 382 ('Azande', 'Makrakà'), Thomas, 1923/24: 13 ('Azande').

9A Bell
Museo di Storia Naturale, Venice
Collection Miani, inv. nr. 7339 (registered as: 'before 1860, Azande'), Museo di Storia Naturale, Venice
Material: iron
Dimensions: L. 29,3 (with cord) x W. 9,6 cm.

9B Bell
Collection Petherick, inv. nr. 1884.108.6 (registered as: 'collected in 1858, Nuer'), Pitt Rivers Museum, Oxford
Material: iron, animal hide, bead, glass
Dimensions: H. 29, 3 (with cord) x W. 9,6 cm.

10 Spoon
World Museum Liverpool, National Museums Liverpool
Inventory number: WML 30.8.66.24
Acquisition: donated by J.A. Tinne, 1866
Material: bone (horn?)
Dimensions: L. 23,1 x W. 6,5 cm.
Ref. lit.:
Schweinfurth 1875 tab. IV, 10, 11 ('Bongo'), Castelli, 1984: 86 ('Azande').

10A Spoon
Collection Antinori, Inv. nr. 49524, Museo Archeologico Nazionale dell'Umbria, Perugia
Material: ivory

Dimensions: L. 15 x 6 cm.
Ref. lit.:
Castelli, 1984: 86 ('Azande').

11 Tobacco cake
World Museum Liverpool, National Museums Liverpool
Inventory number: WML 30.8.66.28
Acquisition: donated by J.A. Tinne, 1866
Material: tobacco
Dimensions: L. 40,3 x W. 9,4 x 6 cm.
Ref. lit.:
Schweinfurth, 1874, I: 269 (with description of 'Bongo tobacco-cakes'), Schweinfurth, 1875, tab. X, nr.2 ('Mittu'; referring to a differently shaped tobacco-cake): 'the tobacco, which so frequently circulates in commerce as a substitute for money among all negro-tribes of the Upper-Nile territory…'
Cf. WML 7.7.70.68 and WML 7.7.70.69 (vanished): two blocks of rhomboidal form.

12 Rope
World Museum Liverpool, National Museums Liverpool
Inventory number: WML 30.8.66.31
Acquisition: donated by J.A. Tinne, 1866
Material: plant fibre and wood
Dimensions: L. 43 x 3,7 cm.

12A Rope
Museo Archeologico Nazionale dell'Umbria, Perugia
Collection Antinori, inv. nr. 49549, Museo Archeologico Nazionale dell'Umbria, Perugia
Material: fibre
Dimensions: L. 200 cm.
Ref. lit.:
Castelli, 1984, nr. 85 ('Denka').

13 Basket
World Museum Liverpool, National Museums Liverpool
Inventory number: WML 7.7.70.1
Acquisition: donated by J.A. Tinne, 1870

Material: fibre, cane
Dimensions: H. 5 x Diam. 21,6 cm.

14 **Basket and cover**
World Museum Liverpool, National Museums Liverpool
Inventory number: WML 7.7.70.2
Acquisition: donated by J.A. Tinne, 1870
Material: fibre, cane
Dimensions: H. 26,5 x Diam. 24 cm.

15 **Cover**
World Museum Liverpool, National Museums Liverpool
Inventory number: WML 7.7.70.3
Acquisition: donated by J.A. Tinne, 1870
Material: fibre, cane
Dimensions: H. 15,5 x Diam. 21 cm.

16 **Basket**
World Museum Liverpool, National Museums Liverpool
Inventory number: WML 7.7.70.5
Acquisition: donated by J.A. Tinne, 1870
Material: fibre, cane
Dimensions: H. 27 x Diam. 15 cm.

17 **Tray**
World Museum Liverpool, National Museums Liverpool
Inventory number: WML 7.7.70.6
Acquisition: donated by J.A. Tinne, 1870
Material: fibre, cane
Dimensions: H. 1,8 x Diam. 18,5 cm.

18 **Cover**
World Museum Liverpool, National Museums Liverpool
Inventory number: WML 7.7.70.7
Acquisition: donated by J.A. Tinne, 1870
Material: fibre, cane and parchment
Dimensions: H. 15,5 x Diam. 22 cm.
Ref. lit.:
Thomas, 1923/24: 33 ('North-East Sudan').

19 **Cover**
World Museum Liverpool, National Museums Liverpool

Inventory number: WML 7.7.70.8
Acquisition: donated by J.A. Tinne, 1870
Material: fibre, cane
Dimensions: H. 13,5 x Diam. 30,8 cm.

20 **Cushion case**
World Museum Liverpool, National Museums Liverpool
Inventory number: WML 7.7.70.10
Acquisition: donated by J.A. Tinne, 1870
Material: fibre, cane
Dimensions: L. 65 x Diam. 24,7 cm.

21 **Pair of baskets**
World Museum Liverpool, National Museums Liverpool
Inventory number: WML 7.7.70.11a, b
Acquisition: donated by J.A. Tinne, 1870
Material: fibre, cane
Dimensions (a): L. 21,8 x Diam. 12,7 cm.
Dimensions (b): L. 22 x Diam. 14 cm.

22 **Basket**
World Museum Liverpool, National Museums Liverpool
Inventory number: WML 7.7.70.12
Acquisition: donated by J.A. Tinne, 1870
Material: fibre, cane
Dimensions: L. 17,8 x Diam. 13 cm.

23 **Cup**
World Museum Liverpool, National Museums Liverpool
Inventory number: WML 7.7.70.15
Acquisition: donated by J.A. Tinne, 1870
Material: fibre, cane
Dimensions: H. 14,7 x Diam. 14,6 cm.
Ref. lit.:
Hartmann, 1863, Illustration in Appendix (incl. dish cover similar to Catalogue nr. 18), Hartmann 1884: 87 ('Fundj').

24 **Animal figure**
World Museum Liverpool, National Museums Liverpool
Inventory number: WML 7.7.70.17

Acquisition: donated by J.A. Tinne,
1870
Material: wood
Dimensions: H. 4 x L. 13,2 x Diam.
4 cm.

24A **Animal figure**
*Museo Archeologico Nazionale
dell'Umbria, Perugia*
Collection Piaggia, Inv. nr. 49543,
Museo Archeologico Nazionale
dell'Umbria, Perugia
Material: wood
Dimensions: H. 12 x L. 28 cm.
Ref. lit.:
Castelli, 1984: fig. 90 ('Bahr el-
Ghazal').

25 **Tub**
*World Museum Liverpool, National
Museums Liverpool*
Inventory number: WML 7.7.70.18
Acquisition: donated by J.A. Tinne,
1870
Material: wood
Dimensions: H. 27 x Diam. 40,5 cm.
*Presumably a gift to Alexine Tinne in
November 1863, having an Azande
origin.*
Ref. lit.:
Heuglin, von, 1869: 224, where is
referred to a 'neatly elaborated wooden
tub', given by a 'Niam-Niam depute'.

25A **Detail**

26 **Pounding-dish**
*World Museum Liverpool, National
Museums Liverpool*
Inventory number: WML 7.7.70.19
Acquisition: donated by J.A. Tinne,
1870
Material: wood, fibre
Dimensions: H. 14,4 x L. 11,9 x Diam.
31,8 cm.
Ref. lit.:
Schweinfurth, 1875, tab. XIII, nr.28
(Azande ['Niam Niam'] with pounder).

27 **Harp**
*World Museum Liverpool, National
Museums Liverpool*
Inventory number: WML 7.7.70.24

Acquisition: donated by J.A. Tinne,
1870
Material: wood, fibre
Dimensions: H. 61 x Diam. 23 x
W. 18 cm.
Ref. lit.:
Schweinfurth, 1874: 413, Schweinfurth,
1875, tab. IX: 4 ('Mittu').

27A **Harp**
Collection Petherick, Inv. nr. AF2691
(registered as: 'Bongo'), The British
Museum
Material: leather, wood, gut, horn
Dimensions: H. 49,5 x Diam. 22,9 cm.

28 **Harp**
*World Museum Liverpool, National
Museums Liverpool*
Inventory number: WML 7.7.70.25
Acquisition: donated by J.A. Tinne,
1870
Material: wood, leather, fibre
Dimensions: L. 73 (Diam.) x W. 31 cm.
Ethnic group: Azande
Ref. lit.:
Inner-Afrika, 1863: Illustration ,
Ethnographische Gegenstände'
(Azande ['Njamjam'], Heuglin, von,
1869: 216 (Azande ['Niamaniam']),
Schweinfurth, 1874 I: 445, II: 26,
Schweinfurth, 1875: Tab. XIV, nr. 6
(Azande ['Niam-Niam']), Ratzel, 1885,
I: 534 (Azande ['Njam-Njam']),
Castelli, 1984: 82 ('Azande'), De
Dampierre, 1991: 81-87 ('Azande').

28A **Detail**

28B **Harp**
Collection Petherick, PRM 1884.113-10
(registered as: 'Zande' [?]), Pitt Rivers
Museum, Oxford
Material: wood, leather, fibre
Dimensions: L. 53 (Diam.) x W. 28,2
cm.
Ref. lit.:
Ratzel, I: 534 (Azande ['Njam-Njam']),
De Dampierre, 1991: 73-75 ('Azande'),
Entry: Sparks, 2005, http://southern-
sudan.prm.ox.ac.uk ('Azande').

28C **Detail**

28D **Harp**
Collection Antinori, nr. 49687
(registered as: 'Zande'), Museo
Archeologico Nazionale dell'Umbria,
Perugia
Material: wood, leather, fibre
Dimensions: L. 60 x 19 cm.
Ref. lit.:
Castelli, 1984: 82 ('Azande'),
De Dampierre, 1991: 80 ('Azande').

28E **Detail**

28F **Harp**
*Museo Archeologico Nazionale
dell'Umbria, Perugia*
Collection Antinori, nr. 49688
(registered as: 'Zande'), Museo
Archeologico Nazionale dell'Umbria,
Perugia
Material: wood, leather, fibre
Dimensions: L. 55 x 14 cm.
Ref. lit. :
Castelli, 1984: 82 ('Azande'),
De Dampierre, 1991: 80 ('Azande').

28G **Detail**

29 **Adze**
*World Museum Liverpool, National
Museums Liverpool*
Inventory number: WML 7.7.70.35
Acquisition: donated by J.A. Tinne,
1870
Material: wood, iron
Dimensions: L. 27 x W. 15 x 3,5 cm.
Ethnic group: Jur
Ref. lit.:
Petherick, 1869, I: 249 ('Djour') and/or
Dōr, Cf. Heuglin, von, 1865: 5. ('Djur'
and 'Dōr') ['They make smaller and
larger benches, which are hacked out of
a wood-block by means of a small adze
with a traverse-blade.'].

29A **Adze**
Collection Petherick, inv. nr.1884.33.19
(registered as: 'Southern Sudan?'),
Pitt Rivers Museum, Oxford
Material: iron, wood, fibre, animal
hide
Dimensions: L. 27 x L. 20,7 (blade) cm.

30 **Bowl**
*World Museum Liverpool, National
Museums Liverpool*
Inventory number: WML 7.7.70.43
Acquisition: donated by J.A. Tinne,
1870
Material: clay, broken and repaired
Dimensions: H. 12,5 x Diam. 11,8 cm.
Ethnic group: Bongo (Dōr)
Ref. lit.:
Schweinfurth 1875 tab. v, 3 ('Bongo').

31 **Lid**
*World Museum Liverpool, National
Museums Liverpool*
Inventory number: WML 7.7.70.51
Acquisition: donated by J.A. Tinne,
1870
Material: fibre, cane
Dimensions: Diam. 30,8 x 4 cm.
Ethnic group: Kababish, Bisharin.

31A **Top of lid**
*World Museum Liverpool, National
Museums Liverpool.*

32 **Hat**
*World Museum Liverpool, National
Museums Liverpool*
Inventory number: WML 7.7.70.72
Acquisition: donated by J.A. Tinne,
1870
Material: resin, seeds and leather
Dimensions: H. 17 x Diam. 21 cm
Ethnic group: Dinka
Ref. lit.:
Schweinfurth, 1875, Plate I, nr. 2
('Dinka'; garnished with feathers).

33 **Girdle**
*World Museum Liverpool, National
Museums Liverpool*
Inventory number: WML 7.7.70.74
Acquisition: donated by J.A. Tinne,
1870
Material: fibre, leather and shells
Dimensions: L. 81 x Diam. 26 cm.
Ethnic group: Bisharin [?].

34 **Girdle**
*World Museum Liverpool, National
Museums Liverpool*
Inventory number: WML 7.7.70.75

Acquisition: donated by J.A. Tinne,
1870
Material: fibre, leather, shells, mother-
of-pearl
Dimensions: L. 81 x Diam. 26cm
Ethnic group: Bisharin [?]

35 **Ornament**
*World Museum Liverpool, National
Museums Liverpool*
Inventory number: WML 7.7.70.76
Acquisition: donated by J.A. Tinne,
1870
Material: canework
Dimensions: Diam. 22,8 x 1 cm.
Ethnic group: Bari [?]
Ref. lit.:
Ratzel, 1885, I: 492 ('Bari').

36 **Necklace**
*World Museum Liverpool, National
Museums Liverpool*
Inventory number: WML 7.7.70.86
Acquisition: donated by J.A. Tinne,
1870
Material: fibre and seeds
Dimensions: L. 42 cm.
Ethnic group: Shilluk (Shuli, Bari?)
Ref. lit.:
Ratzel, 1885, I: 490, 491 ('Shilluk'),
494 ('Shuli').

37 **Necklace**
*World Museum Liverpool, National
Museums Liverpool*
Inventory number: WML 7.7.70.87
Acquisition: donated by J.A. Tinne,
1870
Material: fibre, seeds and glass
Dimensions: L. 34 cm.
Ethnic group: Nilotic people.

38 **Necklace**
*World Museum Liverpool, National
Museums Liverpool*
Inventory number: WML 7.7.70.90
Acquisition: donated by J.A. Tinne,
1870
Material: fibre, roundels of shell
Dimensions: L. 28,7 cm.
Ethnic group: Shilluk, Bari [?]
Ref. lit.:

Ratzel, 1885, I: 490 ('Shilluk').

39 **Necklace**
*World Museum Liverpool, National
Museums Liverpool*
Inventory number: WML 7.7.70.94
Acquisition: donated by J.A. Tinne, 1870
Material: fibre, seeds and glass
Dimensions: L. 32,2 cm.
Ethnic group: Nilotic people [?]

40 **Arrows**
*World Museum Liverpool, National
Museums Liverpool*
Selection out of nrs.: 7.7.70.95-106
Acquisition: donated by J.A. Tinne, 1870
Material: wood, reed (cane), iron
Dimensions: Lengths varying between:
85-95 cm.
Ethnic group: Jur, Dinka [?]
Ref. lit.:
Schweinfurth, 1875: Tab. I, nr. 7
('Denka'), Schweinfurth, 1874: 205,
Schweinfurth, 1878, illustr. on page 67
('Djur').

41 **Club**
*World Museum Liverpool, National
Museums Liverpool*
Inventory number: 7.7.70.107
Acquisition: donated by J.A. Tinne, 1870
Material: wood
Dimensions: L. 91,2 x 6,8 x 6,3 cm.
Ethnic group: Dinka.

41A **Club**
Collection Binder, inv. 639E
('Agar'=Denka cf. Santandrea, 1964:
22), The 'ASTRA' National Museum
Complex, Sibiu, Romania
Material: wood
Dimensions: L: 107 cm.

42 **Club**
*World Museum Liverpool, National
Museums Liverpool*
Inventory number: 7.7.70.110
Acquisition: donated by J.A. Tinne, 1870
Material: wood, fibre
Dimensions: L. 73 x Diam. 3,8 cm.
Ethnic group: Bari
*This club has presumably been collected
by A. Tinne on her White Nile journey*

where she ascended the river up to
Gondokoro nearing the Bari-regions.

42A **Club**
Museum für Völkerkunde, Vienna
Collection Knoblecher, inv. nr.
119027 (registered as: 'Upper-Nile
regions'), Museum für Völkerkunde,
Vienna
Material: wood
Dimensions: L. 68 cm.

43 **Club**
World Museum Liverpool, National
Museums Liverpool
Inventory number: 7.7.70.111
Acquisition: donated by J.A. Tinne,
1870
Material: wood
Dimensions: L. 84 x Diam. 3,5 cm.
Ethnic group: Bari [?]
This club has presumably been collected
by A. Tinne on her White Nile journey
where she ascended the river up to
Gondokoro.

44.1 **Cover**
World Museum Liverpool, National
Museums Liverpool
Inventory number: 27.9.70.32a
Acquisition: donated by J.A. Tinne,
1870
Material: cane, fibre
Dimensions: H. 4,5 x Diam. 21,5 cm.
Ethnic group: Kababish, Bisharin.

44.2 **Tray**
World Museum Liverpool, National
Museums Liverpool
Inventory number: 27.9.70.32b
Acquisition: donated by J.A. Tinne,
1870
Material: cane, fibre
Dimensions: H. 7 x Diam. 27,5 cm.
Ethnic group: Kababish, Bisharin.

45 **Tray or cover**
World Museum Liverpool, National
Museums Liverpool
Inventory number: 27.9.70.33
Acquisition: donated by J.A. Tinne,
1870
Material: cane, fibre

Dimensions: H. 5 x Diam. 30 cm.
Ethnic group: Kababish, Bisharin.

46 **Basket**
World Museum Liverpool, National
Museums Liverpool
Inventory number: 27.9.70.34
Acquisition: donated by J.A. Tinne,
1870
Material: grass, fibre, leather, shell
Dimensions: H. 6,5 x Diam. 19,6 cm.
Ethnic group: Kababish, Bisharin.

47 **Girdle**
World Museum Liverpool, National
Museums Liverpool
Inventory number: 27.9.70.45
Acquisition: donated by J.A. Tinne,
1870
Material: leaf (palm), seeds, cord
(coconut fibre)
Dimensions: L. 143 x 3 cm.
Ethnic group: Kababish, Bisharin.

48.1 **Girdle**
World Museum Liverpool, National
Museums Liverpool
Inventory number: 27.9.70.46
Acquisition: donated by J.A. Tinne,
1870
Material: leaf (palm), seeds, cord
(coconut fibre)
Dimensions: L. 143 x 3 cm.
Ethnic group: Kababish, Bisharin.

48.2 **Girdle**
World Museum Liverpool, National
Museums Liverpool
Inventory number: 27.9.70.46
Acquisition: donated by J.A. Tinne,
1870
Material: leaf (palm), seeds, cord
(coconut fibre)
Dimensions: L. 143 x 3 cm.
Ethnic group: Kababish, Bisharin.

48.3 **Girdle**
Inv.nr. Af,+.852, British Museum.
Acquisition: donated by J.A. Tinne
to the Liverpool Public Museum,
1870, and registered as nr. 27.9.70.45,
being part of an ensemble of three
girdles

Donated by Sir Augustus Wollaston
Franks to The British Museum in 1878.
Description: Girdle made of leaf
(palm), seeds, cord (coconut fibre)
Ethnic group: Kababish, Bisharin
Dimensions: L. 78,7 cm.

49 Throwing knife
*World Museum Liverpool, National
Museums Liverpool*
Inventory number: 27.9.70.61
Acquisition: donated by J.A. Tinne,
1870
Material: iron, fibre
Dimensions: L. 43,5 x W. 28,8 cm.
Ethnic group: Azande, Jur
Ref. lit.:
Lejean, 1862, Ill. Collection Castel-
bolognesi 'Bahr el-Ghazal' (fig. 13),
Inner-Afrika, 1863: Illustration
'Ethnographische Gegenstände'
(Azande ['Niamniam']), Heuglin, von,
1863, nr. 14 (Azande ['Niamniam']),
Hartmann, 1863, illustration in
Appendix (Jur, Azande ['Niam-
Niam']), Heuglin, von, 1869: 214
(Azande ['Niamniam'], Petherick,
1869, I: 281 (Azande ['Neam Neam']),
Schweinfurth, 1874: II, 10 (Azande
['Niam-niam']), Schweinfurth 1875
tab. XII ill. 1-15 (Azande [Niam-niam']),
Thomas, 1923/24: 182/83 ('Azande'),
Bassani, 1979: 148 ('Azande'), Castelli,
1984: 79 ('Azande'). Schmidt, Wester-
dijk, 2006: 50 ('Azande', ref. RMV
2669-2410, ex-collection
J.M. Schuver)
Cf. Collection Von Heuglin, nr.58.

49A Detail
49B Throwing knife
Collection Petherick, PRM 1884.25.1
(registered as: 'collected in 1858,
Zande?')
Material: iron, fibre
Dimensions: L. 45,4 x W. 27,3 (central
blade) cm.
49C Throwing knife
*Museo Archeologico Nazionale
dell'Umbria, Perugia*

Collection Antinori, inv.nr. 49473
(registered as: 'Azande'), Museo
Archeologico Nazionale dell'Umbria,
Perugia
Material: iron, fibre
Dimensions: L. 42,5 x W. 39 cm.

50 Dagger
*World Museum Liverpool, National
Museums Liverpool*
Inventory number: 27.9.70.65
Acquisition: donated by J.A. Tinne,
1870
Material: iron, wood, wire (iron)
Dimensions: L. 28,2 x W. 9,2 cm.
Ethnic group: Azande
Ref. lit.:
Inner-Afrika, 1863: Illustration ,
Ethnographische Gegenstände', nr.3,
Heuglin, von, 1869: 215, Petherick,
1869, I: 281 (Neam Neam'), Ratzel,
1885, I: 532 (Azande [Niam-Niam']
and 'Tuareg').

50A Detail
50B Pair of daggers
Museum für Völkerkunde, Vienna
Collection Natterer, inv. nrs. 00463,
00464, Museum für Völkerkunde,
Vienna
Material: iron, wood, wire (iron)
Dimensions: L. 29, 5 and L. 29 cm.

51 Dagger
Inv. nr.: BM Af,+.855
Acquisition: donated by J.A. Tinne to
the Liverpool Public Museum, 1866,
and registered as nr. 30.8.66.1
Donated by Sir Augustus Wollaston
Franks to The British Museum in
1878.
Description: Dagger made of iron,
wood, wire (iron)
Ethnic group: Azande
Dimensions: L. 28,5 cm.

52 Bench
*World Museum Liverpool, National
Museums Liverpool*
Inventory number: 2.2.71.1
Acquisition: donated by J.A. Tinne, 1871
Material: wood

Dimensions: L. 44 x W. 27 x 20.5 cm.
Ethnic group: Bongo (Dōr)
Ref. lit.:
Lejean, 1862: Ill. Coll. Castelbolognesi
'Bahr el-Ghazal' (fig.1), Schweinfurth,
1874: 283 ('Bongo'), Schweinfurth 1875
tab. IV, 2 ('Bongo').

52A Underside of bench
*World Museum Liverpool, National
Museums Liverpool.*

52B Bench
Collection Binder, inv. nr. 030E
(registered as 'Bari'), The 'ASTRA'
National Museum Complex, Sibiu,
Romania
Material: wood
Dimensions: L. 39 x H. 21 cm.

52C Bench
*Museo Archeologico Nazionale
dell'Umbria, Perugia*
Collection Piaggia, inv. nr. 49680
(registered as 'Bongo'), Museo
Nazionale Archeologico dell'Umbria
Material: wood
Dimensions: L. 39 x H. 23 cm.

52D Bench
Museo di Storia Naturale, Venice
Collection Miani, Inv.nr. 7250 (regis-
tered as: 'before 1860, Bongo'), Museo
di Storia Naturale, Venice
Material: wood
Dimensions: L. 51 x W. 29,2 x H. 27,6
cm.

52E Bench
Collection Petherick, Inv.nr: Af. 2721
(registered as: 'Shillook'), The British
Museum
Acquisition date: 1860-1869
Material: wood
Dimensions: H. 13 x W. 14 x L. 26 cm.

53 Bench
*World Museum Liverpool, National
Museums Liverpool*
Inventory number: 2.2.71.2
Acquisition: donated by J.A. Tinne,
1871

Material: wood
Dimensions: H. 19 x Diam. 25,5 cm.
Ethnic group: Bongo (Dōr)
Ref. lit.:
Schweinfurth, 1875, tab. IV, 3 ('Bongo').

54 Ornament
Inv.nr. BM Af,+.853, the British
Museum
Acquisition: donated by J.A. Tinne to
the Liverpool Public Museum, 1870 and
registered as nr. 7.7.70.84
Donated by Sir Augustus Wollaston
Franks to The British Museum in 1878.
Description: Ornament made of iron
beads and red leather
Ethnic group: Jur [?]
Dimensions: L. 58,4 cm.

55 Belt or necklace
Inv.nr. BM Af,+.854, the British
Museum
Acquisition: donated by J.A. Tinne to
the Liverpool Public Museum, 1870 and
registered as nr. 27.9.70.53
Donated by Sir Augustus Wollaston
Franks to The British Museum in 1878.
Description: Belt or necklace made of
beads (shell), fibre (cord)
Ethnic group: Shilluk [?]
Dimensions: L. 83,8 cm.

55A Belt or necklace
*The 'ASTRA' National Museum Complex,
Sibiu, Romania*
Collection Binder, Inv.nr. 086E
(registered as: 'Shilluk'), The 'ASTRA'
National Museum Complex, Sibiu,
Romania
Material: shells, fibre (cord)
Dimensions: L. 184 cm.

55B Belt or necklace
Collection Petherick, Inv.nr: Af.
96.94.6, The British Museum
Acquisition date: 1894
Ethnic group: Shilluk [?]
Material: fibre cord, discs of white shell
Dimensions: L. 33 cm.

Catalogue
Von Heuglin collection

List of objects, collected by Heuglin during the Bahr el-Ghazal expedition (Jan. 1863-December 1864), in the Linden-Museum Stuttgart.

References are made to similar items, collected by other contemporary Sudan-travellers.
A catalogue-number of the Heuglin-collection refers to items in other collections by a subdivision (for instance: 57b, 57c, 57d and 65a, 65b, 65c).

Details, as acquisition date, dimensions, accession numbers, reference literature and the museum where the item is registered, are mentioned in the additional list of data here below.

56 Quiver
Inventory number: F 55241a
Material: leather, glass-pearls (black)
Dimensions: L. 52,5 cm.
Ethnic group: people of Dar Fertit [Kresh?]
Ref. lit.:
Heuglin, von, 1869: 177.

56.1-6 Arrows
Selection out of nrs. F 55241 c1-c79
Material: iron, (bamboo) cane, fibre
Dimensions: Lengths varying between: 36-42 cm.
Ethnic group: people of Dar Fertit [Kresh?]
Ref. lit.:
Heuglin, von, 1869: 177.

57 Sickle-bladed knife
Inventory number: F 55242
Material: iron, copper and wood
Dimensions: L. 50 cm.
Ethnic group: Azande, Mangbetu

Ref. Lit.:
Inner-Afrika, 1863: Illustration, Ethnographische Gegenstände' (Azande ['Njanjam'], Heuglin, 1869: 214 (Azande ['Niamaniam']), Petherick, 1869, I: 281 (Azande ['Neam Neam']), Schweinfurth, 1874, II: 107 (Mangbetu ['Monbuttoo']); '*The Azande are stated to possess knives with blades, like sickles. These blades they receive from the Mangbetu*' (ibidem: 9). Schweinfurth, 1875: tab.18 nr.8 (Mangbetu ['Monbuttu'], Thomas, 1923/24: 181/182 ('Mangbetu'), Bassani, 1979: 148 ('Azande'), Castelli, 1984: 78 ('Azande').

57A Detail

57B Sickle-bladed knife
Museo Archeologico Nazionale dell'Umbria, Perugia
Collection Antinori, Inv.nr. 49469 (registered as: 'Mangbetu, Zande'),

Museo Archeologico Nazionale
dell'Umbria, Perugia
Material: wood, copper, iron
Dimensions: L. 43 cm.

57c Sickle-bladed knife
*The 'ASTRA' National Museum Complex,
Sibiu, Romania*
Collection Binder, inv.nr. 12E (registered as: 'Mombutta – Blow Weapon in
the Land of the Djur'), The 'ASTRA'
National Museum Complex, Sibiu,
Romania
Material: iron, wood
Dimensions: L. 48 cm.

57d Sickle-bladed knife
Museo di Storia Naturale, Venice
Collection Miani, Inv. nr. 7396
(registered as: 'before 1860, Azande'),
Museo di Storia Naturale, Venice
Material: iron, wood
Dimensions: L. 45,7 x 25 cm.

58 Throwing weapon
Inventory number: F 55243
Material: iron, plant fibre
Dimensions: L. 44,5 x W. 29 cm.
Ethnic group: Azande, Jur
Ref. lit.:
Lejean, 1862, Ill. Collection Castelbolognesi 'Bahr el-Ghazal' (fig. 13),
Inner-Afrika, 1863: Illustration ,
Ethnographische Gegenstände'
(Azande ['Niamniam']), Heuglin, von,
1863, nr. 14 (Azande ['Niamniam']),
Hartmann, 1863, illustration in
Appendix (Jur, Azande ['NiamNiam']), Heuglin, von, 1869: 214
(Azande ['Niamniam'], Petherick,
1869, 1: 281 (Azande ['Neam Neam']),
Schweinfurth, 1874: 11, 10 (Azande
['Niam Niam']), Schweinfurth 1875 tab.
XII ill. 1-15 (Azande ['Niam Niam']),
Thomas, 1923/24: 182/83 ('Azande'),
Bassani, 1979: 148 ('Azande'), Castelli,
1984: 79 ('Azande'), Schmidt,
Westerdijk, 2006: 50 ('Azande', ref.
RMV 2669-2410, ex-collection
J.M. Schuver).

58A Detail F 55243
58B Throwing weapon
*The 'ASTRA' National Museum Complex,
Sibiu, Romania*
Collection Binder, inv.nr. 728E
(registered as 'Jur'), The 'ASTRA'
National Museum Complex, Sibiu,
Romania
Material: iron, fibre
Dimensions: L. 24 cm. x W. 28 cm.

58C Detail
58D Throwing weapon
Museo di Storia Naturale, Venice
Collection Miani, Inv. nr. 7395
(registered as: 'before 1860, Azande'),
Museo di Storia Naturale, Venice
Material: iron, fibre
Dimensions: 46,5 x W. 33,8 cm.

59 Spoon
Inventory number: F 55248
Material: horn
Dimensions: L. 25 cm. (without strap)
Ethnic group: Bongo (Dōr)
Ref. lit.:
Schweinfurth 1875 tab. IV, 10, 11
('Bongo').

60 Spoon
Inventory number: F 55249
Material: horn
Dimensions: L. 22 cm. (without cord)
Ethnic group: Bongo (Dōr)
Ref. lit.:
Schweinfurth 1875 tab. IV, 10, 11
('Bongo').

61 Spoon
Inventory number: F 55250
Material: horn
Dimensions: L. 23 cm. (without cord)
Ethnic group: Jur, Bongo (Dōr)
Ref. lit.:
Schweinfurth 1875 tab. IV, 10, 11
('Bongo'), Castelli, 1984: 86 ('Azande').

62 Spoon
Inventory number: F 55251
Material: iron, plant fibre
Dimensions: L. 23 cm. (without ribbon)
Ethnic group: Jur.

63 **Knife**
Inventory number: F 55253
Material: iron
Dimension: L. 81 cm.
Ethnic group: Bongo (Dōr).

64 **Spear**
Inventory number: F 55254
Material: iron
Dimension: L. 56 cm.
Ethnic group: Bongo (Dōr).

65 **'Spear points'**
Inventory numbers: F 55255, F 55256
Material: iron
Dimensions: L. 38,5 cm. and 31,5 cm.
Ethnic group: Bongo (Dōr)
Ref. lit.:
Heuglin, von, 1863: illustrated on map
('Bongo'), Wood, 1870, I: 449 ('Djour'),
Bassani, 1979: 150-151 ('Bongo'),
Castelli, 1984: 48-49 ('Bongo').

65A+B **'Spear points'**
*Museo Archeologico Nazionale
dell'Umbria, Perugia*
Collection Piaggia, inv.nrs. 49527-
49528 (registered as: 'Bongo'), Museo
Archeologico Nazionale dell'Umbria,
Perugia
Material: iron
Dimensions: L. 36,5 x 5 cm. and L. 28,5
x 4,5 cm.

65C **'Spear point'**
Collection Petherick, Inv.nr. 1884.63.28
(registered as: 'collected in 1858,
Bongo?'), Pitt Rivers Museum, Oxford
Materials: iron
Dimensions: L. 23,7 x W. 3,36 cm.

66 **Spear point**
Inventory number: F 55257
Material: iron
Dimensions: L. 32 cm.
Ethnic group: Bongo (Dōr).

67 **'Spear point'**
Inventory number: F 55259
Material: iron
Dimension: L. 56 cm.
Ethnic group: Bongo (Dōr)
Ref. lit.:
Heuglin, von, 1863: illustrated on map

('Bongo'), Bassani, 1979: 150-151
('Bongo'), Castelli, 1984: 48-49
('Bongo').

67A **'Spear point'**
Collection Petherick, Inv.nr. 1884.99.2
(registered as: 'collected in 1858,
Bongo?'), Pitt Rivers Museum, Oxford
Material: iron
Dimensions: L. 60,8 x W. 14,6 cm.

67B **'Spear point'**
*Museo Archeologico Nazionale
dell'Umbria, Perugia*
Collection Piaggia, inv. nr. 49500
(registered as: 'Bongo, Mittu'), Museo
Archeologico Nazionale dell'Umbria,
Perugia
Material: iron
Dimensions: L. 59 x 7 cm.

68 **Tobacco pipe**
Inventory number: F 55260
Material: clay and wood
Dimensions: L. 89 cm. (a: 46 cm.
b: 43 cm.)
Ethnic group: Bongo (Dōr).

68A-C **Tobacco pipe (detail)**
68D **Tobacco pipe**
Museum für Völkerkunde, Vienna
Collection Natterer, inv. nr. 2706.4466
(registered as: 'Bongo'), Museum für
Völkerkunde, Vienna
Material: wood, clay
Dimensions: L. 54 cm.

69 **Bowstring**
Inventory number: F 55261
Material: cane, wood and plant-fibre
Dimension: L. 101 cm.
Ethnic group: people of Dar Fertit
[Kresh?].

70 **Waistband, girdle**
Inventory number: F 55262
Material: plant fibres, reptile skin
Dimension: L. 62 cm.
Ethnic group: people of Nyambara
region [Bari?].

71 **Waistband, girdle**
Inventory number: F 55263
Material: grass, kauri-shells, glass-
pearls

Dimension: L. 107 cm.
Ethnic group: people of Nyambara region [Bari?].

72 **Apron**
Inventory number: F 55264
Material: plant-fibre, kauri-shells, glass-pearls
Dimension: L. 23 x 8,5 cm.
Ethnic group: people of Nyambara-region [Bari?].
Ref. lit.:
Castelli, 1984: 60 refers to an object with a rather similar decoration in the Collection Antinori nr. 49444, Museo Archeologico Nazionale dell'Umbria, Perugia (registered as 'Nyambara, Madi, Cir').

72A **Apron**
Collection Miani, Inv. nr. 7000 (registered as: 'before 1860, Dinka, Bor, Chir'), Museo di Storia Naturale, Venice
Material: leather hide, glass-pearls, fibre
Dimensions: L. 70 x 16 cm.

73 **Waistband, girdle**
Inventory number: F 55270
Material: grass and plant-fibre
Dimension: L. 84,5 cm.
Ethnic group: Bongo (Dōr).

74 **Waistband, girdle**
Inventory number: F 55271
Material: plant-fibre, leather (a.o. reptile)
Dimension: L. 71,5 cm.
Ethnic group: people of Dar Fertit [Kresh?].

75 **Necklace**
Inventory number: F 55272
Material: plant-fibre, glass-pearls, kauri-shells
Dimension: L. 49,5 cm.
Ethnic group: Jur.

76 **Necklace**
Inventory number: F 55273
Material: plant-fibre and glass-pearls
Dimension: L. 40 cm.
Ethnic group: Jur.

77 **Collar**
Inventory number: F 55274
Material: plant-stems, copper, leather, kauri-shells
Dimension: L. 44,5 cm.
Ethnic group: Jur.

78 **'Spear point'**
Inventory number: F 55284
Material: iron
Dimensions: L. 58 cm.
Ethnic group: Bongo (Dōr)
Ref. lit.:
Heuglin, von, 1863: illustrated on map ('Bongo'), Bassani, 1979: 150-151 ('Bongo'), Castelli, 1984: 48-49 ('Bongo').

79 **Hairpin**
Inventory number: F 55289
Material: ivory
Dimension: L. 34,5 cm.
Ethnic group: Bisharin.

80 **Hairpin**
Inventory number: F 55290
Material: ivory
Dimension: L. 29 cm.
Ethnic group: Bisharin
The list of the 1865-exhibition at Württemberg refers to two ivory hairpins (nr. 38) as having a Bisharin provenance. These two pins Von Heuglin could have acquired with Alexine Tinne on their way in September 1864 through the Nubian desert to Suakim.

80A **Detail**

80B **Hairpin**
Museo Archeologico Nazionale dell'Umbria, Perugia
Collection Antinori, inventory number: 49675 (registered as: 'Zande, Mangbetu'), Museo Archeologico Nazionale dell'Umbria, Perugia
Material: ivory
Dimension: L. 29 cm.
Ethnic group: Azande
This Azande-hairpin shows similar characteristics with the previous number with a Bisharin provenance.

Ref. lit.:
Castelli, 1984: 72 ('Azande').

81 Bow
Inventory number: F 55342
Material: wood, leather
Dimension: L. 88,5 cm.
Ethnic group: people of Dar Fertit
[Kresh?].

82 Illustration
Illustration 'Ethnographische Gegen-stände aus den Negerländern westlich
vom Bahr el Abiad', in: *Inner-Afrika*
(Frontispiece), Gotha, 1863.

83 Illustration
Illustration 'Armes, Parures, Ustensils
divers des Noirs, sur les Rives du
Bahr-el-Gazal', in: Lejean, G. (III),
1862, Ill. 'D'après les dessins de M.
[Castel]Bolognesi'.

The Tinne collection.
Appendix

84 Projectile, Weapon
World Museum Liverpool, National Museums Liverpool
Inventory number: WML 27.9.70.62
Acquisition: donated by J.A. Tinne, 1870
Material: iron, leather
Dimensions: L. 80 x 22 cm.
Ethnic group: Touaregs
Ref. lit.:
Denham, Clapperton, *Narrative of Travels and Discoveries in Northern and Central Africa, in the Years 1822, 1823, and 1824...* Paris, 1826 (Atlas, Planche XII)
Hartmann, 1863, Illustrations ('Qulbê-dah')
Duveyrier, 1864, Planche XXV, fig. 5 'Changuermanguer').

85 Pair of sandals belonging to A. Tinne
World Museum Liverpool, National Museums of Liverpool
Inventory number: WML 7.7.70.82
Acquisition: donated by J.A. Tinne, 1870
Date: This pair has been retrieved in Tripoli in 1869/1870
Dimensions: L. 21 cm.

86 Pair of sandals belonging to A. Tinne
World Museum Liverpool, National Museums of Liverpool
Inventory number: WML 7.7.70.81
Acquisition: donated by J.A. Tinne, 1870
Date: This pair has been retrieved in Tripoli in 1869/1870
Dimensions: L. 21 cm.

87 Scarf
World Museum Liverpool, National Museums Liverpool
Inventory number: WML 2003.21.3
Acquisition: donation A. Tinne, 2003
Material: silk

Dimensions: 132,5 x 90 cm.
Region: Maghreb (North-African Coast).

88 **Scarf**
World Museum Liverpool, National Museums Liverpool
Inventory number: WML 2003.21.4
Acquisition: donation A. Tinne, 2003
Material: silk
Dimensions: 141 x 95 cm.
Region: Maghreb (North-African Coast).

89 **Photo of Alexine Tinne's house at Tripoli** (see: p. 187)
Tinne Family Archive
On the heavily damaged glass-positive, vague contours of a house with arches are discernible (with reverse side covered).
Dimensions: 9 x 12 cm.
Date: 1870
Digital image from Ambrotype.

90 **Photo representing a group of Touareg leaders at Tripoli** (see: p. 187)
Tinne Family Archive
On the heavily damaged glass-positive, vague contours of a group of four men are discernible (with reverse side covered).
Dimensions: 9 x 12 cm.
Date: 1870
Digital image from Ambrotype.

Bibliography

1. Archival Sources

National Archives, The Hague (NA)
NA 2.21.008.01 (nrs. 217-249)

Royal Library, The Hague (KB)
KB CEN79D40

Tinne Family Archive, England
(T.F.A.)
Includes: Letters by Margaret Tinne-Sandbach to her children in Liverpool, sent during her stay with John in Alexandria and Cairo between 11 January and 24 February 1865. Notebook containing the diary of John A. Tinne, kept during his visit to Alexine Tinne in Cairo.

Archive Von Heuglin, Linden-museum, Stuttgart.

Collection Archives, Liverpool World Museum, Liverpool. Donations J.A. Tinne, 1866-1870.

2. List of primary literature used

Anon., 'Nouvelles de l'expédition allemande dans l'Afrique Central, du Soudan Égyptien et du Haut Fleuve-Blanc', in: *Nouvelles Annales des Voyages*, 1862, tome IV: 120-123.

Antinori, O., 'Viaggi di O. Antinori e C. Piaggia nell'Africa Centrale nord, con carta e profili del socio Orazio Antinori', in: *Bollettino della Società Geografica Italiana*, Anno 1° – Fasciculo 1°, August 1868 : 91-165.

Aucapitaine, H., 'Les Yem-Yem, tribu anthropophage de l'Afrique Centrale', in: *Nouvelles Annales des Voyages*, tome IV, 1857: 58-66.

Baker, S., *The Albert Nyanza, Great Basin of the Nile*, London and Philadelphia, 1866.

Bary, E de, *Le dernier Rapport d'un Européen sur Ghât et les Touareg de L'Aïr : Journal de Voyage*, Paris, 1898.

Bisson, R. du, *Les Femmes et les Eunuches et les Guerriers du Soudan*, Paris, 1868.

Bollettino della Società Geografica Italiana, first year, first vol., 1868.

Bono, A. de, *Recenti Scoperti sul Fiume Bianco*, Alexandria, 1862.

Brehm, A. E., *Reiseskizzen aus Nord-Ost-Afrika…*, Jena, 1855.

Browne, W. G., *Travels in Africa, Egypt and Syria 1792 to 1798*, London, 1799.

Brun-Rollet, A., *Le Nil Blanc et le Soudan*, Paris, 1855.

Dandolo, E., *Viaggio in Egitto, nel Sudan, in Siria ed in Palestina*, Milan, 1854.

D'Escayrac de Lauture, P. H. S., *Le Désert et le Soudan. Études sur l'Afrique au Nord de l'Équateur…*, Paris, 1853.
– –, *Memoire sur le Soudan…*, Paris, 1855-1856.

Didier, Ch., *500 Lieues sur le Nil*, Paris, 1858.

Duveyrier, H., *Les Touaregs du Nord*, Paris, 1864.
– –, 'L'Afrique nécrologique', in: *Bulletin de la Société de Géographie*, 1874: 561-644.

Eyth, M. von, *Im Strom unserer Zeit*, Stuttgart, Leipzig and Heidelberg, 1909 (2006).

Gentz, W., 'Alexandrine Tinne', in: *Die Gartenlaube*, no. 27 (1869): 601-602.

Hartmann, R., *Reise des Freiherrn Adalbert von Barnim durch Nord-Ost-Afrika in den Jahren 1859 und 1860*, Berlin, 1863.

Heuglin, Th. von, *Tagebuch einer Reise von Chartum nach Abyssinien, mit besonderer Rücksicht auf Zoologie und Geographie unternommen in den Jahren 1852 bis 1853*, Gotha, 1857.
– –, *Reise in das Gebiet des Weissen Nil und seiner Zuflüssen in den Jahren 1862-1864*, Leipzig and Heidelberg, 1869.
– –, 'Nachrichten über neueste Reisen in den Nil-Ländern', in: *Petermann's Mittheilungen*, 1863: 105-107.
– –, 'Die Tinne'sche Expedition im Westlichen Nil-Quellgebiet 1863 un 1864. Aus dem Tagebuch von Th. von Heuglin', *Ergänzungsheft nr. 15 zu Petermann's Geographische Mittheilungen*, 1865. [PM, 1865]

Inner-Afrika Nach dem Stande der Geographischen Kenntniss in den Jahren 1861 bis 1863, Gotha, 1863.

Junker, W., *Reisen in Afrika*, 3 vols, Vienna, 1889.

Keane, E. H., *Ethnology of Egyptian Sudán*, London, 1884.

Kotschy, Th. and J. Peyritsch, *Plantae Tinneanae sive descriptio plantarum in expeditione Tinneana ad flumen Bahr El-Ghazal eiusque affluentias…*, Vienna, 1867.

Krapf, L., *Travels, Researches, and Missionary Labours…*, London, 1860.

Lane, E. W., *An Account of the Manners and Customs of the Modern Egyptians*, London, 1860 (5th ed.).

Lejean, G., 'La queue des Nyams-Nyams', in: *Le Tour du Monde*, 1861, 1e semestre: 187-188.
– –, 'Le Bahr El Gazal', in: *Nouvelles Annales des Voyages*, 1862, sixième série, vol. 1: 257-268.

– –, 'Nouvelles de l'expédition allemande dans l'Afrique Central, du Soudan Égyptien et du Haut Fleuve-Blanc', in: *Nouvelles Annales des Voyages*, 1862, sixième série, vol. IV: 120-123.

– –, 'Voyage au Fleuve des Gazelles (Nil Blanc) par M.A. Bolognesi 1856-'57 – Texte (traduit de l'Italien) et dessins inédits, in: *Le Tour du Monde*, V (1862), no. 129 (June): 385-397.

– –, 'Observations sur les pays et les peuples à l'ouest du lac No et du fleuve Blanc', *Nouvelles Annales des Voyages*, 1865, neuvième série, vol. I: 5-24.

– –, *Voyage aux deux Nils: Nubie, Kordofan, Soudan Occidental, exécuté de 1860 a 1864 par Ordre de l'Empereur*, Paris, 1865.

Maltzan, H. Freiherr von, *Reise in den Regentschaften Tunis und Tripolis*, Leipzig, 1870.

Malte-Brun, V. A. (ed.), 'L'Exploration des Dames Tinné dans la Région a l'Ouest du Fleuve Blanc, 1863-1864', *Nouvelles Annales des Voyages*, 1865, neuvième série: 129-148.

Melly, G., *Lettres d'Egypte et de Nubie*, London, 1852.

– –, *Khartoum and the Blue Nile and White Niles*, 2 vols, 1851 (1852).

Morlang, F., *Missione in Africa Centrale, Diario 1855-1863*, Bologna: Nigrizia, 1973.

Munzinger, W., 'Die deutsche Expedition in Ost-Afrika, 1861 und 1862', Ergänzungsheft Nr. 13 of *Petermann's Mittheilungen*, 1864.

Nachtigal, G., 'Relation de la mort de Mademoiselle Alexina Tinné et voyage au Tibesti (lettre à M. Henry Duvey-rier), in: *Bulletin de la Société de Géographie*, 1870: 89-106.

Nachtigal, G., *Sahara und Sudan*, 3 vols, Berlin, 1879-1881.

Nouvelles Annales des Voyages, 1862, sixième série.

[*Petermann's Mittheilungen*] *Mittheilungen aus Justus Perthes' Geographischer Anstalt über Wichtige Neue Erforschungen auf dem Gesammt-gebiete der Geographie von Dr. A. Petermann*, Gotha, 1862-1868. [*PM*]

Petherick, J., *Egypt, The Soudan and Central Africa*, London, 1861.

Petherick, Mr. and Mrs. [John], *Travels in Central Africa*, 2 vols, London, 1869.

Proceedings of the Royal Geographical Society, Session 1863-64, vols VII and VIII.

Rohlfs, G., *Von Tripolis nach Alexandrien*, Bremen, 1871.

– –, *Quer durch Afrika*, 2 vols, Leipzig, 1874/75.

Schweinfurth, G., *Im Herzen von Afrika*, Leipzig, 1874.

– –, *The Heart of Africa*, 2 vols, New York, 1874.

– –, *Artes Africanae*, Leipzig and London, 1875.

Speke, J. H., *Journal of the Discovery of the Source of the Nile*, 1863.

Taylor, B., *Journey into Central Africa*, New York, 1854.

Tinne, J. A., *Geographical Notes of Exhibitions in Central Africa by Three Dutch Ladies*, Liverpool, 1864.

Trémaux, P., *Voyages Au Soudan Oriental…*, Paris, n.d.

Waller, H., *The Last Journals of David Livingstone in Central Africa…*, London, 1874.

3. List of secondary literature used

Ali, M., *The British, The Slave Trade and Slavery in the Sudan 1820-1881*, Khartoum, 1972.

Almagía, R., 'Il contributo degli italiani alla esplorazione del bacino del Nilo', in: *Estratto da L'Universo, Rivista bimestrale dell'Isituto Geografico Militare*, 1957: nr. 6; 1958: nrs. 1/2.

Bacmeister, W., 'Theodor Heuglin, Forschungsreisender 1824-1876', in: Haering, H., *Schwäbische Lebensbilder* (v), Stuttgart, 1950: 395-423,.

Bassani, E., *Carlo Piaggia, nella Terra dei Niam-Niam*, Lucca, 1978.
– –, *Carlo Piaggia e L'Africa, Mostra fotografica – Catalogo*, Lucca, 1979.

Bassnett, S., 'Travel writing and gender', in: P. Hulme and T. Youngs (eds) *The Cambridge Companion to Travel Writing* (Cambridge) 2002: 225-242.

Baxter, P. T. W. and Butt, A., *The Azande, and Related Peoples of the Anglo-Egyptian Sudan and Belgian Congo*, East Central Africa Part ix, London, 1953.

Binder, K., *Reisen und Erlebnisse eines Siebenburger Sachsen*, Hermannstadt, 1930.

Blanton, C., *Travel Writing, The Self and the World*, New York and London, 1995.

Blunt, A., *Travel, Gender, and Imperialism. Mary Kingsley and West Africa*, New York and London, 1994.

British Museum, *Handbook to the Ethnographical Collections* (2nd ed.), London, 1925.

Bunzl, M., and Glenn Penny, H. (eds), *Worldly Provincialism. German Anthropology in the Age of Empire*, Ann Arbor, 2003.

Castelli, E., 'Origine des Collections Ethnographiques Soudanaises dans les Musées Français (1800-1878)', in: *Journal des Africanistes*, 1984, nr. 54, 1: 97-114.
– –(ed.), *Orazio Antinori in Africa Centrale, 1859-1861 – Materiali e Documenti Inediti*, Perugia, 1984.

Castelli, E., 'Antoine Brun Rollet in Africa: una collezione etnografica ritrovata', in: *Africa*, 1987, vol. 42, no 1: 107-149.

Eggink, C., *De Merkwaardige Reizen van Henriette en Alexandrine Tinne*, Amsterdam, 1960 (The Hague, 1976).

Evans-Pritchard, E. E., 'Sources, with Particular Reference to the Southern Sudan', *Cahiers d'Études Africaines*, 1971, 11/1: 129-79.
– –, 'Zande Cannibalism', in: *The Position of Women in Primitive Societies and other Essays in Social Anthropology* (London) 1965.

Eyth, M. von, *Im Strom unserer Zeit*, Stuttgart, Leipzig, Heidelberg, 1909.

Gladstone, P., *Travels of Alexine. Alexine Tinne 1835-1869*, London, 1970.

Gray, R., *A History of the Southern Sudan 1839-1889*, Oxford, 1961.

Hall, R., *Lovers on the Nile: An Idyll of African Exploration*, London, 1980.

Hartmann, R., *Die Nilländer*, Leipzig and Prag, 1884.

Hill, R., *A Biographical Dictionary of the Sudan*, 2nd ed., London, 1967.
– –, *Egypt in the Sudan 1820-1881*, London, 1959.

Holt, P. M., *The Mahdist State in the Sudan 1881-1898*, Oxford, 1958.

Ibrahim, H. A. and Ogot, B. A., 'The Sudan in the nineteenth century', in: J. E. A. Ajayi, *Africa in the Nineteenth Century until the 1880s*, Paris, 1989: 356-375.

Imanse, H., *'Something nobler was my motive'. Juan Maria Schuver and his African collection*, Digital publication of the National Museum of Ethnology, Leiden, 2002.

James, W., Baumann, G. and Johnson, D. (eds), *Juan Maria Schuver's Travels in North East Africa 1880-1883*, London, 1996.

Johnson, D. H., 'Recruitment and entrapment in private slave armies: the structure of the *zara'ib* in the Southern Sudan', in: E. Savage (ed.), *The Human Commodity, Perspectives on the Trans-Saharan Slave Trade*, London, 1992: 162-73.
– –, 'The structure of a legacy: military slavery in northeast Africa', *Ethnohistory*, 36/1, 1989: 72-88.

Kainbacher, P. (ed.), *Tegethoff und Heuglin's Reise in Nordost-Afrika*, Baden bei Wien, 2005.
– – (ed.), *Franz Binder's Reise im Orient und Afrika*, Baden bei Wien, 2006.

Kan, C. M., *Ontdekkingsreizen in Afrika*, n.p., 1870.

Lane, P. and Johnson, D. H., 'The archaeology and history of slavery in South Sudan in the nineteenth century', in A. Peacock (ed.), *The Frontiers of the Ottoman World, Proceedings of the British Academy 156*, Oxford, 2009: 509-37.

Mills, S., *Discourses of Difference. An Analysis of Women's Travel Writing and Colonialism*, New York, 1991.

Pellegrinetti, G. A., *Le Memorie di Carlo Piaggia*, Florence, 1941.

Posthumus, N. W., *Freule Tinne, de Nederlandsche Reizigster door Afrika*, Amsterdam, 1874.

Ratzel, F., *Völkerkunde*, 3 vols, Leipzig, 1885-89.

Rose, G., *Feminism and Geography: The Limits of Geographical Knowledge*, Oxford, 1993.

Rushton, P., *Mrs. Tinne's Wardrobe…*, Liverpool, 2006.

Santandrea, S., *A Tribal History of the Western Bahr El Ghazal*, Verona, 1964.

Santi, P. and Hill, R. (eds), *The Europeans in The Sudan*, 1980, Oxford.

Schildkrout, E. and Keim, C. A., *The Scramble for Art in Central Africa*, Cambridge, 1998.

Schmidt, A. and Westerdijk, P., *The Cutting Edge. West Central African 19th Century Throwing Knifes in the National Museum of Ethnology Leiden*, Leiden, 2006.

Schmidt, R., 'Theodor von Heuglin', in: *Deutschlands Koloniale Helden und Pioniere der Jultur im schwarzen Kontinent*, I, Braunschweig, 1896: 199-269.

Stocking, G., *Victorian Anthropology*, London, 1987.

Sutherland, W., *Alexandrine Tinne...*, Amsterdam, 1935.

Thomas E. S., 'Catalogue of the Ethnographical Museum of the Royal Geographical Society of Egypt', in: *Bulletin de la Société Royale de Géographie d'Egypte*, tome XII, 1923-1924: 1-75, 159-185; tome XII, 1924: 5-71.

Toniolo, E. and Hill, R. (eds), *The Opening of the Nile Basin*, London, 1974 (1975).

Tothill, B. H., 'An Expedition in Central Africa by three Dutch ladies, extracted and translated from "Plantae Tinneanae"', in: *Sudan Notes and Records*, 1947, vol. XXVIII: 25-49.

Udal, J. O., *The Nile in Darkness: Conquest and Exploration 1504-1862*, Norwich, 1998.

Wells, W., *The Heroine of the White Nile; or, What a Woman Did and Dared. A Sketch of the Remarkable Travels and Experiences of Miss Alexandrine Tinné*, New York, 1871.

Willink, R. J., *Stages in Civilisation. Dutch Museums in Quest of West Central African Collections*, Leiden, 2007.
– –, 'Van Schuver uit Equatoria', in: *Erfgoedverhalen...*, The Hague, 2007: 68-73.
– –, 'La Mission Congolaise et les collections 'Azande' de l'Ordre des Croisiers', in: *Clairlieu* (69th year), 2011: 79-95.

Wood, J. G., *The Uncivilized Races of Men, of All Countries of the World*, 2 vols., Hartford, 1870.

Zaghi, C., *La Via del Nilo*, Naples, 1971.

Zurcher, M., 'Mademoiselle Tinne 1861-1869 – Texte et Dessins inédits', in: *Le Tour du Monde*, 1871, nr. 566, XXII: 289-304.

Index

Abdallah, attendant of Alexine Tinne,
158, 170, 180, 183, 316 (illustrations
19, 20 and 21)

Ablaing, Baron Daniël d', Dutch
explorer, 62, 89, 90, 93, 101-110, 121,
124-138, 143, 152, 155-157, 242

Abyssinia, 27, 54, 55, 59, 61, 62, 67, 72,
76, 78, 89, 103, 111, 217, 225, 304,

Ali Amuri, Khartoum trader, 100, 113,
114, 118, 123, 125, 129, 153, 154, 288

Anna, maid to Henriette Tinne-van
Capellen, 29, 91, 126, 128, 131-134, 137,
138, 144-146, 148, 158, 159, 214, 235,
236, 241-243

Antinori, Marchese Orazio d', Italian
explorer and naturalist, 11, 266-275
- as collector of ethnographic
items, 319, 320

Apostolic Vicariate of Central Africa,
231

Arnaud, Joseph-Pons d', French
engineer and explorer, 27, 229, 263,
296

Austria-Hungary, and Catholic
Mission to Africa, 54, 76, 80, 214, 215,
231, 284

Azande, Sudanic ethnic group,
- 'cannibalism', 87, 88, 287, 313, 327
- place in 19th century ethnographic science, 86-88, 311-316, 327
- tales about 'tailed people', 87, 88,
272, 273, 287, 297
- ultimate destination of expedition, 71, 75, 76, 82, 83, 86-89

Bahr el-Abiad *see* White Nile

Bahr el-Ghazal (*also* Gazelle-river),
- as destination of the Tinne-
Heuglin expedition, 68, 76, 78,
79, 81-83, 85, 86
- as place and region of international geographic interest,
29-31
- descriptions of diseases in the
region of, 133, 225, 226
- the mapping out of routes to, and
region of, 75-79, 83, 98-100,
266-268, 296

Bahr el-Zeraf, 97, 140

Baker, Samuel (and Florence), explorer,
later Governor-General, 67, 119, 120,
193, 198, 216, 222, 234, 287, 290, 293

Barth, Heinrich, German explorer, 53,
111

Bari, Sudanic ethnic group, 70, 78, 215,
229, 270, 306, 315, 317, 322

Barthélémy, Delphin, French Khartoum trader, 270, 285

Berber (town), 63, 147, 152, 156, 157-159,
161, 217, 240, 241, 243, 305, 317

Bastian, Adolf, German scientist and
explorer, 192, 314, 315

Binder, Franz, Transsylvanian trader,
101, 214, 230, 294
- as collector of ethnographic
items, 308, 320, 321

Biselli, *maghrabi* Bahr el-Ghazal trader,
77, 84, 109, 110, 112-114, 128-136, 138,
143, 153, 154, 224, 267, 289, 290, 305

Photo credits

Courtesy: World Museum Liverpool, National Museums Liverpool
Cat. nrs.: 1, 1A, 2, 3, 4A, 4b, 5, 6, 7, 8, 8A, 9, 10, 11, 12, 13, 14, 15, 16, 17, 18, 19,
20, 21, 22, 23, 24, 25, 25A, 26, 27, 27A, 28, 28A, 29, 30, 31, 31A, 32, 33, 34, 35, 36,
37, 38, 39, 40, 41, 42, 43, 44.1, 44.2, 45, 46, 47, 48.1, 48.2, 49, 49A, 50, 50A,
52, 52A, 53, 84, 85, 86, 87, 88

Courtesy: Pitt Rivers Museum, University of Oxford
Cat. nrs.: 2B, 9B, 28B, 28C, 29A, 49B, 65C, 67A

Courtesy: Museo di Storia Naturale, Venice
Cat. nrs.: 2A, 9A, 52D, 57D, 72A

Courtesy: Museo Archeologico Nazionale dell'Umbria, Perugia
Cat. nrs.: 10A, 12A, 24A, 28D, 28E, 28F, 29G, 49C, 52C, 57B, 65A, 65B, 67B, 80B

Courtesy: The 'ASTRA' National Museum Complex, Sibiu, Romania
Cat. nrs.: 41A, 52B, 55A, 55B, 57C, 58B, 58C

Courtesy: Museum für Völkerkunde, Vienna
Cat. nrs.: 42A, 50B, 68D

Copyrights: The Trustees of The British Museum, London
Cat. nrs.: 48.3, 51, 52E, 54, 55

Courtesy: Linden-Museum Stuttgart
Cat. nrs.: 56, 56.1-6, 57, 57A, 58, 58A, 59, 60, 61, 62, 63, 64, 65, 66, 67, 68,
68A, 68B, 68C, 69, 70, 71, 72, 73, 74, 75, 76, 77, 78, 79, 80, 80A, 81